Federal Jurisdiction
in Australia

Cowen and Zines's

Federal Jurisdiction in Australia

Third edition

Leslie Zines

THE FEDERATION PRESS
2002

Published in Sydney by
    The Federation Press
        PO Box 45, Annandale, NSW, 2038.
        71 John St, Leichhardt, NSW, 2040.
        Ph (02) 9552 2200. Fax (02) 9552 1681.
        E-mail: info@federationpress.com.au
        Website: http://www.federationpress.com.au

First edition 1959
Second edition 1978
Third edition 2002

National Library of Australia
Cataloguing-in-Publication entry
    Cowen, Zelman, Sir
    Cowen and Zines's federal jurisdiction in Australia

    3rd ed
    Includes index
    ISBN 1 86287 432 8

    1. Australia. High Court. 2. Jurisdiction – Australia. 3. Judicial power – Australia. 4.
    Courts – Australia. I. Zines, Leslie. II. Title.

347.94022

Typeset by The Federation Press, Leichhardt, NSW.
    Printed by Ligare Pty Ltd, Riverwood, NSW.

Preface

I am very grateful to Judith Wilson, who prepared the manuscript of this book in its many versions, for her care, ability and professional pride. Her great experience in preparing manuscripts for publication was invaluable. Thanks are also due to Zoe Guest, a law student at the Australian National University, who, as my research assistant, checked references to citations, quotations and statutes. I acknowledge the strong support I have received from Professor Peter Cane, head of the Law Program in the Research School of Social Sciences at the ANU, and Chris Treadwell, the Administrator of that Program.

Leslie Zines
August 2002

Contents

Introduction

The first edition of this work, published in 1959, had a single author, Zelman Cowen. He deplored the amount of original jurisdiction conferred on the High Court by the Constitution and by Commonwealth legislation. The High Court was given general appellate jurisdiction in all State and federal matters, and it was therefore argued that there was little sense in loading that Court, in s 75 of the Constitution, with original jurisdiction in respect of such matters as those concerning treaties or consuls or between residents of different States, which could satisfactorily be determined by State courts. Much of this had come about from unthinking copying of the United States Constitution, where different conditions had prevailed. Additional grants of jurisdiction under legislation, pursuant to s 76(ii) of the Constitution, in relation to such matters as taxation and intellectual property, made the situation worse.

In that edition the view was expressed that, so far as the Constitution allowed, a rational and integrated national judicial system could best be achieved by relying on State courts to exercise State and federal jurisdiction at first instance and at the first appeal stage, with the High Court as final court of appeal in all State and federal matters. It was recognised, however, that there was much to be said for the High Court's original jurisdiction in constitutional matters and in suits between Governments, and that Parliament might want a federal court in some specialised areas. The main impediment to achieving this scheme was the entrenched original jurisdiction vested in the High Court by s 75 of the Constitution. It was argued that the Court had a duty to exercise that jurisdiction when it was invoked, whether or not another court was available.

The second edition, with Sir Zelman Cowen and Leslie Zines as authors, was published nearly two decades later, in 1978. With the creation of the Federal Court in 1977, nearly all the statutory original jurisdiction of the High Court under s 76(ii) was removed. It was transferred to the Federal Court or State courts or both. In some cases original jurisdiction was vested in the State Supreme Courts and appellate jurisdiction in the Federal Court.

For about a decade before the Federal Court came into existence there had been numerous proposals to create a Commonwealth Superior Court with jurisdiction over the whole range of matters in ss 75 and 76 of the Constitution. Others warned that that would give rise to jurisdictional arguments and "split proceedings" requiring litigants to go to two courts to have different aspects of their litigation determined. They argued that that could be best avoided by using the State courts.

The creation of the Family Court and the Federal Court seemed to be a compromise. The Attorney-General, Mr Ellicott, emphatically rejected the earlier attempts to establish a general federal court which, he said, would weaken the status of, and the quality of work in, the State courts. The Federal Court, he said, would be a court for special matters which for policy or historical reasons should be dealt with by a federal court. As things turned out, however, the second edition appeared at the start of what was to develop as a new era for the Australian judicial system.

The work of the Federal Court gradually, but consistently, expanded as a result of legislation and judicial decision. A problem arose where there were federal and non-federal claims in the same proceedings. This difficulty was alleviated somewhat when the High Court interpreted the concept of "matter" in Chapter III of the Constitution to include non-federal claims that were based substantially on the same facts and transactions as the federal claims.[1] While this approach assisted litigants in the federal courts, fear was expressed that the State courts would be deprived of much of their important jurisdiction. As a result, various proposals were put forward to create a single national system involving all Australian Governments. The Advisory Judicial Committee of the Constitutional Commission and the Commission itself rejected the view expressed decades earlier by Sir Owen Dixon that the courts should not be seen as pertaining to any particular governments in our federal system, but should be independent organs which derived their existence from the Constitution. The Commission said that there should be one Parliament and Government politically responsible for the establishment, maintenance, organisation and jurisdiction of, and appointments to, any court. Involving all Governments in the operation of a single judicial institution would, they declared, "fetter boldness and innovation and foster conservatism and inertia".[2]

The result of the various proposals, and the recommendations of the Australian Constitutional Convention and the Constitutional Commission, was the cross-vesting scheme, which worked well for almost 12 years. Under the scheme the Commonwealth, States and the Northern Territory vested the jurisdiction of their superior courts (with some exceptions) in all other Australian superior courts, other than the High Court. There was also provision for transferring cases from one court to a more appropriate court. The scheme was judged to be a great success in achieving the avoidance of many of the intricate technical issues of federal jurisdiction that have little or no social purpose. In 1999, however, the High Court held a vital part of the scheme invalid, namely the vesting of State jurisdiction in federal courts with the legislative consent of the Commonwealth.[3] Many jurisdictional difficulties therefore once again made their appearance to bedevil the court system. That development, among others, has made it appropriate to publish a new updated edition of this book.

---

1   *Fencott v Muller* (1983) 152 CLR 570.

2   *Final Report of the Constitutional Commission*, 1988, vol 1, pp 365-369.

3   *Re Wakim; ex parte McNally* (1999) 198 CLR 511.

In 1997 the gradual increase in the jurisdiction of the Federal Court (which, from 1983, included most of the jurisdiction in s 75(v) to issue constitutional writs) culminated in legislation conferring on it nearly all the jurisdiction in s 76(i) and (ii), that is, matters arising under the Constitution or involving its interpretation, and those arising under any laws made by the Parliament (except for criminal matters). What we now have is a fully fledged dual system of federal and State courts. The Federal Court is no longer a specialist court as envisaged at its creation, but is substantially a general federal court with nearly all those heads of federal jurisdiction that are most commonly invoked.

The pressure that was on the High Court as a result of its constitutionally entrenched original jurisdiction has been lessened as a result of the general power of remitter given to it by s 44 of the *Judiciary Act* 1903 in 1977, extended in 1983. This power is freely exercised. While there is no decision to that effect, the Court has clearly taken the view (contrary to that expressed in the earlier editions of this book) that it is not duty bound to exercise its jurisdiction in s 75 of the Constitution, where there is power to remit to another court.

The system has undergone great change over the past quarter of a century. In contemplating the heads of federal jurisdiction the questions for consideration now relate less to the effect on the work of the High Court (although that is still a relevant factor) and more to the relationship between federal and State courts generally. The court system is likely to remain a dual one and its operation would be greatly improved by a constitutional alteration to restore the cross-vesting scheme. So far as s 75(iii) and (v) are concerned, however, their importance goes beyond these considerations. Those provisions ensure that there is a constitutionally entrenched jurisdiction to determine matters in which it is claimed that the Commonwealth or its officers have acted beyond their powers.

Some of the problems noted in the last edition have since been resolved. Decisions which restricted the use by State courts exercising federal jurisdiction of registrars and like officers have been overruled.[4] The same principle was applied to federal courts, subject to the judges having sufficient control of the officers' determinations, as required by Chapter III of the Constitution.[5]

The problem of the relationship between imperial jurisdiction under the *Colonial Courts of Admiralty Act* 1890 and federal jurisdiction referable to s 76(iii) of the Constitution — Admiralty and maritime jurisdiction — has been largely resolved by the enactment of the *Admiralty Act* 1988. While it is doubtful whether the attempt in that Act to repeal the Imperial Act, in so far as it applies to a State court, is valid, it is clear that only federal jurisdiction is operative with respect to any matter covered by the Commonwealth Act.

---

4   *Commonwealth v Hospital Contribution Fund of Australia* (1982) 150 CLR 49.

5   *Harris v Caladine* (1991) 172 CLR 84.

The problems associated with jurisdiction in the Territories are as difficult as ever. While the Court has affirmed earlier decisions that s 72 of the Constitution does not apply to Territorial courts, it is divided on whether a Territorial court can exercise federal jurisdiction and, if so, whether a law made by the legislature of a self-governing Territory arises under a Commonwealth Act creating the legislature and conferring its power. Similar problems occur in respect of common law matters in the Territories. There continue to be difficulties when a Commonwealth law, operating throughout Australia and beyond, gives jurisdiction to Territorial courts without limiting the jurisdiction to matters or parties that have a sufficient nexus with the Territory.

As was the case with previous editions, this work does not examine the law that is applicable in the exercise of federal jurisdiction except where it is closely connected with discussion concerning the meaning of the head of jurisdiction. The separation of judicial power arising from Chapter III is dealt with only briefly and in so far as it concerns the powers of courts rather than administrative bodies. No examination has been made of substantive or procedural rights that may flow from Chapter III.

The new writing in this edition is the work of Leslie Zines.

Table of Cases

Chapter 1

Original Jurisdiction of the High Court

If it be suggested that the volume of business that will flow from the new head of jurisdiction established by this decision is in itself not likely to be very heavy, it is pertinent to say that it is true of the Court's business also that many a mickle makes a muckle.[1]

The Constitutional Scheme

The influence of American precedents on Australian constitution making was considerable.[2] In no area, probably, was that influence stronger than on the judicature chapter of the Constitution. At the preliminary Federal Conference, at Melbourne in 1890, Alfred Deakin expressed the opinion that the American distribution of federal jurisdiction fitted Australian needs.[3] At the Sydney Convention in 1891 the task of drafting the judicature provisions of the federal bill was assigned to a committee under the chairmanship of Inglis Clark, who was an ardent admirer of the United States Constitution. Although there were some important departures from the American model in this committee's proposals, they largely consisted of quotations from the American Constitution.[4] Further changes were made in the course of the meetings of the Convention of 1897-1898, but it remained true that in the Constitution as finally enacted "the organisation of the federal courts and, for the most part, their jurisdiction followed American precedent".[5]

The copying of the American judicature provisions was not slavish and, for present purposes, it suffices to draw attention to two major departures from the American model. In the first place, the High Court of Australia was designed as a *general* court of appeal, from State courts exercising *State* as well as *federal* jurisdiction, and from inferior federal courts.[6] In this respect, its functions were very different from those of the Supreme Court of the

---

1   Per Frankfurter J in *Williams v Austrian* 331 US 642 at 681 (1947).
2   For a general study see Hunt, *American Precedents in Australian Federation*, 1930.
3   Debates, Melbourne, 1890, p 89.
4   Hunt, op cit p 188.
5   Hunt, op cit p 199.
6   Commonwealth of Australia Constitution, s 73.

United States, whose appellate functions were much more narrowly confined.[7] This points to a very marked difference of attitude on the part of the founding fathers in the two federations. In the United States, there was a strong suspicion of the new central authority and it was not seriously argued that general appellate functions should be vested in the Supreme Court of the United States. In Australia, a desire for the establishment of a general court of appeal from State courts had been expressed as early as 1849. In 1870 the Victorian Government appointed a Royal Commission to consider and report on the expediency of establishing a general court of appeal for the Australian colonies, and this commission reported in favour of the project.[8] Even the most ardent admirers of the American judicial structure, Inglis Clark included, supported the establishment of a general court of appeal for the new Commonwealth of Australia. This difference of attitude was very clearly stated in the first great commentary on the Commonwealth Constitution in 1900:

> In Australia, as in Canada, the appellate jurisdiction is not one of those jealously guarded State rights which make anything more intimate than a federal union impossible. We are accustomed to a common court of appeal in the shape of the Privy Council: we are so assured of the independence and integrity of the Bench that the advantages of having one uniform Australian tribunal of final resort outweigh all feelings of localism, and the federal tribunal has been entrusted (subject to the rights reserved with respect to the Privy Council) with the final decision of all cases, whether federal or purely local in their nature.[9]

This trust in the new High Court was matched by a willingness to accept State courts as repositories of federal jurisdiction. In the United States Constitution no provision was made for conferring federal jurisdiction on State courts, and the judicial power of the United States was vested in the Supreme Court of the United States and in such inferior *federal* courts as the Congress might from time to time create.[10] The Australian Constitution inferentially authorised the establishment of inferior federal courts *and* also the investment of State courts with federal jurisdiction.[11]

Having regard to these differences in the two constitutional schemes, it might have been thought that there was little need for an extensive *original* jurisdiction for the High Court. But the Commonwealth Constitution both grants and authorises the grant of an extensive original jurisdiction to the High

---

7   United States Constitution, Art III, s 2.

8   "The decisions of the various Supreme Courts of the colonies upon purely colonial affairs would thereby be brought into harmony and uniformity of law be thus encouraged, to the great advantage of commerce." Parliamentary Papers (Victoria) 1870, vol 2, p 711.

9   Quick and Garran, *The Annotated Constitution of the Australian Commonwealth*, 1901, p 725.

10   Article III, s 1.

11   Sections 71, 77(iii).

Court.[12] It is much broader than the original jurisdiction conferred on the Supreme Court of the United States,[13] which is "narrowly confined and strictly construed".[14] Several matters which in the United States Constitution are assigned to federal jurisdiction, but lie within the original jurisdiction of *inferior* federal courts, are by the Australian Constitution assigned to the original jurisdiction of the High Court.

This matter does not appear to have been elaborately discussed in the Australian Constitutional Conventions. No doubt the difference may be explained in this way. The theory which underlay the assignment of particular matters to federal jurisdiction was that for varying reasons it was thought desirable to have such matters decided by *national* rather than *State* courts. In the American system, a hierarchy of distinctively national or federal courts was envisaged, and this object could be achieved by assigning original juris-diction for the most part to inferior federal courts, leaving only very special cases to the original jurisdiction of the Supreme Court of the United States. The Australian constitutional system provided for the establishment of inferior federal courts and for the investment of State courts with federal jurisdiction, but the intendment was that the State courts should be used, and this was what was done. This meant that, apart from particular federal courts with specialised functions, the only established national court was the High Court. If subject-matters of federal jurisdiction were to be assigned as a matter of original jurisdiction to a *national* court, the High Court was therefore the inevitable repository.

This reasoning is intelligible, but it is doubtful whether it carries much conviction. It assumes the desirability or the necessity of referring the various matters of federal jurisdiction to a national court. In view of the differences in the two Constitutions, and particularly in view of the general appellate juris-diction conferred on the High Court and of the grant of federal jurisdiction to State courts – both of which were very significant departures from the American model – it might have been thought that there was very much less call for the allocation of original jurisdiction to a national court in Australia. Moreover, the Australian Federal Conventions do not appear to have subjected the particular subject-matters of original jurisdiction assigned to the American federal courts to very close scrutiny in considering their suitability for allocation to the original jurisdiction of the High Court. It will be argued that many of these did not warrant assignment to original federal jurisdiction in Australia.

The result is that the Commonwealth Constitution placed a considerable burden on the High Court. Not only is it invested with important constitutional functions and with a general appellate jurisdiction, but it has been loaded with

---

12   Sections 75, 76.

13   Article III, s 2.

14   Freund, "The Supreme Court of the United States" (1950) 29 Canadian BR 1080 at 1083.

an original jurisdiction which, if it were invoked to the full, would impose an intolerable burden on the court. Sir Owen Dixon said that that stood in the way of "the efficient, speedy and orderly administration of the law".[15] With the growth of Australia's population and the diversification of the country's activities the burden imposed upon the High Court in respect of its original and appellate jurisdiction became very great. In 1978 the Australian Constitutional Convention recommended a considerable reduction of the Court's original jurisdiction by amendment of s 75 of the Constitution.[16] In 1988 the Constitutional Commission recommended some reduction and modification of that jurisdiction. More significantly it proposed that Parliament be empowered to limit or exclude a part of the jurisdiction to the extent that it was conferred on another federal court, or on State and Territorial courts.[17] In practice, the work of the Court has been more efficiently dealt with as a result of the ample power given to the Court in 1976 and 1983 by s 44 of the *Judiciary Act* 1903 to remit any matters, including nearly all matters within s 75 of the Constitution, to another court.[18] Similarly in 1984 almost all the appellate jurisdiction of the Court was made dependent on the grant by it of special leave.[19]

The Extent of the Court's Jurisdiction

The original jurisdiction of the High Court is dealt with in ss 75 and 76 of the Constitution, which provide:

> 75. In all matters –
> (i)   Arising under any treaty:
> (ii) Affecting consuls or other representatives of other countries:
> (iii) In which the Commonwealth, or a person suing or being sued on behalf of the Commonwealth, is a party:
> (iv) Between States, or between residents of different States, or between a State and a resident of another State:
> (v)   In which a writ of Mandamus or prohibition or an injunction is sought against an officer of the Commonwealth:
> the High Court shall have original jurisdiction.

> 76. The Parliament may make laws conferring original jurisdiction on the High Court in any matter –
> (i) Arising under this Constitution, or involving its interpretation:
> (ii) Arising under any laws made by the Parliament:

---

15 Then Mr Dixon KC, in Royal Commission on the Constitution, Minutes of Evidence, 1927, p 785.

16 *Proceedings of the Australian Constitutional Convention*, 1978, Perth, p 204.

17 *Final Report of the Constitutional Commission*, 1988, vol 1, pp 373-374.

18 Page 136 below.

19 Sections 35, 35AA of the *Judiciary Act*.

(iii)   Of Admiralty and maritime jurisdiction:
(iv)   Relating to the same subject-matter claimed under the laws of different States.

It will be seen that s 75 conferred original jurisdiction on the High Court by direct operation of the Constitution, while s 76 authorised the Commonwealth Parliament to confer additional original jurisdiction on the Court. These sections have to be read together with s 77, which authorises the Parliament, with respect to any of the matters mentioned in ss 75 and 76, to make laws (i) defining the jurisdiction of any federal court other than the High Court; (ii) defining the extent to which the jurisdiction of any federal court shall be exclusive of that which belongs to or is invested in the courts of the States; and (iii) investing any court of a State with federal jurisdiction. Under this section, jurisdiction in matters which constitute the actual or potential original jurisdiction of the High Court may be vested in State courts exercising federal jurisdiction or in inferior federal courts. Section 77(i) and (iii) contemplate the possibility of *concurrent* original jurisdiction in State and federal courts *and* in the High Court. Under s 77(ii), reading the words "any federal court" as including the High Court,[20] there is power to make the jurisdiction of the High Court *exclusive* of that of State courts in respect of any matter in which it either has, or is invested under s 76 with, original jurisdiction. It is interesting to note that the matters in respect of which jurisdiction may be conferred on State courts or inferior federal courts are all matters within the description of the actual or potential *original* jurisdiction of the High Court. This raises the interesting question whether it is possible under s 77(i) and (iii) to vest inferior federal courts and State courts with *appellate* jurisdiction in respect of these matters.[21]

The Commonwealth Parliament has never fully exercised its power under s 76 to invest the High Court with original jurisdiction. By the *Judiciary Act*, s 30, the High Court was invested with original jurisdiction in all matters arising under the Constitution or involving its interpretation, and in trials of indictable offences against the laws of the Commonwealth. The *Judiciary Act* 1914 invested the Court with jurisdiction in all matters of Admiralty *or* maritime jurisdiction, but this was repealed by the *Judiciary Act* 1939. There has never been any *general* investment of original jurisdiction in any matter arising under any laws made by the Parliament[22] for the obvious reason that this would have imposed an intolerable burden on the Court.

The High Court until the 1970s had a great deal of original jurisdiction in respect of matters arising under a variety of particular statutes related to taxation, patents, trade marks, income tax, gift duty, estate duty, enemy

---

20   *Pirrie v McFarlane* (1925) 36 CLR 170 at 176.
21   See *Ah Yick v Lehmert* (1905) 2 CLR 593 at 604; see also *Collins v Charles Marshall Pty Ltd* (1955) 92 CLR 529. See pp 129ff below.
22   *R v Bevan; ex parte Elias* (1942) 66 CLR 452 at 465 per Starke J.

property and other subjects. It was divested of this jurisdiction after the establishment of the Federal Court of Australia in 1976.[23] One exception is the Court's jurisdiction as a Court of Disputed Returns under the *Commonwealth Electoral Act* 1918. Under s 30(c) of the *Judiciary Act* the Commonwealth has original jurisdiction in "trials of indictable offences against the laws of the Commonwealth". As mentioned below, it may be that jurisdiction is included in s 75(iii), namely, matters "in which the Commonwealth ... is a party".

There is some doubt as to whether the Parliament may delegate its powers under ss 76 and 77 of the Constitution. This matter will be dealt with in relation to the investing of State courts with federal jurisdiction.[24] Assuming, however, that an Act can validly authorise the making of legislation conferring jurisdiction on courts, the High Court will require the clearest possible language before holding that that was the intention of Parliament.

In *Willocks v Anderson*,[25] the High Court held invalid, as not being authorised by the Act under which they were made, regulations purporting to confer jurisdiction on the High Court to determine disputes relating to the election of members of a statutory board. The judgment of six members of the Court expressed their concern that the Court's ability to carry out its chief functions as constitutional interpreter and final court of appeal should not be impaired by the grant of additional original jurisdiction. They said:

> Under the Constitution this Court is entrusted with the most important of judicial functions. To confer additional original jurisdiction upon it may well impair its ability to discharge its major functions with despatch. The question whether in any particular circumstances, original jurisdiction should be conferred on this Court is of such great significance as to warrant the careful attention of the Parliament. Even if the power to do so may be validly delegated to the Governor-General it is not a matter to be left to the initiative of the Executive except after that attention has been given to the question by the Parliament. If after such consideration the Parliament for reasons sufficiently compelling in a particular case should decide to delegate the power, its intention to do so should be expressly and clearly stated. It cannot be held that the Parliament intended that the time of this Court should be taken up in hearing in its original jurisdiction appeals against elections to commodity boards, such as the Australian Apple and Pear Board, without a clear and unmistakable expression of such an intention. General words should not readily be construed as expressing the necessary intention.[26]

The jurisdiction conferred by the *Judiciary Act*, s 30(c), in trials of indictable offences against the laws of the Commonwealth raises some

---

23   *Jurisdiction of Courts (Miscellaneous Amendments) Act* 1979.
24   Chapter 5 below.
25   (1971) 124 CLR 293.
26   Ibid at 299, 300. This case was examined and applied in *DJL v Central Authority* (2000) 201 CLR 226.

interesting points which were discussed in *R v Kidman*.[27] That was an indictment for conspiracy to defraud the Commonwealth. Both Griffith CJ and Isaacs J indicated that the jurisdiction of the High Court in respect of indictable offences against the laws of the Commonwealth might derive from s 75(iii) of the Constitution – matters in which the Commonwealth, or a person suing or being sued on behalf of the Commonwealth, is a party. Isaacs J was of opinion that s 75(iii) covered all justiciable issues both in civil and criminal actions and that it therefore included matters in which the King in right of the Commonwealth complained of some breach of public law to which a penal consequence was attached.

It has been suggested that the phrase "suing and being sued" in s 75(iii), if it is applicable also to "the Commonwealth", is inapt to describe a prosecution for a crime.[28] While that could be so in respect of ordinary legislation, the principle that the Constitution should be given a broad and liberal construction might be a countervailing factor in supporting the views of Griffith CJ and Isaacs J. In fact an indictable offence has not been tried in the High Court for many years and no doubt such a matter, if commenced in the High Court, would ordinarily be remitted to another court under s 44 of the *Judiciary Act*, which is discussed below.

In *Kidman*, Isaacs J expressed the view that s 75(iii) also extended to some matters involving an offence at common law, rather than under an Act of the Commonwealth.[29]

To the extent that s 75(iii) covers jurisdiction in trials of indictable offences against the laws of the Commonwealth, s 30(c) of the *Judiciary Act* is unnecessary, since under s 75 the High Court possesses original jurisdiction without need for further parliamentary action. In *R v Kidman*, Griffith CJ also drew attention to the difficulties involved in basing s 30(c) of the *Judiciary Act* upon the power conferred by s 76(ii) of the Constitution – matters arising under any laws made by the Parliament. He observed that the *Judiciary Act* provision was concerned with offences against the laws of the Common-wealth, and that there was no warrant for treating laws of the *Commonwealth* (*Judiciary Act*, s 30) and laws made by the Parliament (Constitution, s 76(ii)) as necessarily synonymous.[30]

This view assumes that a rule of common law can be described as a "law of the Commonwealth" within the meaning of *Judiciary Act*, s 30.[31] In recent times, however, the High Court has in a number of cases declared that there is

---

27   (1915) 20 CLR 425.

28   Lane, *Lane's Commentary on the Australian Constitution*, 2nd edn, 1997, p 562 n10.

29   (1915) 20 CLR 425 at 444.

30   "Having regard to the sense in which the term 'the laws of the Commonwealth' is used in the Constitution, eg in ss 61 and 120, and the term 'any law of the Commonwealth' in s 80, I think it is impossible to contend successfully that they can be treated as synonymous. The only result would be that the enactment (ie in the *Judiciary Act*, s 30) was unnecessary" (at 439).

31   Wynes, *Legislative, Executive and Judicial Powers in Australia*, 5th edn, 1976, pp 58-60.

an Australian common law as distinct from a common law of the several States and Territories.[32] It seems to follow that it would be incorrect to describe a common law rule or principle as a "law of the Commonwealth" except in a geographical sense, which is obviously not intended.[33] Clearly, however, it can be argued that federal jurisdiction should extend to common law crimes in so far as they have the object of protecting the Crown in the right of the Commonwealth or its institutions.

It has already been said that the Constitution contemplates the vesting of *exclusive* and *concurrent* original jurisdiction in the High Court. Under s 77(ii) Parliament may make laws defining the extent to which the jurisdiction of a federal court shall be exclusive of that of a State court. Parliament may make the jurisdiction of the High Court exclusive of that of inferior federal courts by appropriate exercise of its powers under s 77(i) in defining the jurisdiction of inferior federal courts. By s 38 of the *Judiciary Act*, Parliament exercised its powers under s 77(ii) to prescribe five matters in which the jurisdiction of the High Court should be exclusive of the jurisdiction of the several courts of the States. They were (a) matters arising directly under any treaty; (b) suits between States, or between persons suing or being sued on behalf of different States, or between a State and a person suing or being sued on behalf of a State; (c) suits by the Commonwealth, or any person suing on behalf of the Commonwealth, against a State or any person being sued on behalf of a State; (d) suits by a State or any person suing on behalf of a State, against the Commonwealth, or any person being sued on behalf of the Commonwealth; (e) matters in which a writ of mandamus or prohibition is sought against an officer of the Commonwealth or a federal court. In respect of the matters with which it dealt, s 38 of the *Judiciary Act* made the jurisdiction of the High Court exclusive of that of *all* State courts.[34] The section is subject to the power of the High Court, under s 44 of the *Judiciary Act*, to remit a matter to a State court and to some limited judicial review jurisdiction conferred on State Supreme Courts relating to criminal matters, under s 39B.

Between 1907 and 1976 s 38A of the *Judiciary Act* provided that in matters (other than trials of indictable offences) involving any question however arising as to the limits inter se of the constitutional powers of the Commonwealth and those of any State or States, or as to the limits inter se of the constitutional powers of any two or more States, the jurisdiction of the High Court shall be exclusive of the jurisdiction of the Supreme Courts; so that the Supreme Court of a State shall not have jurisdiction to entertain or

---

32 For example, *Lange v Australian Broadcasting Corporation* (1997) 189 CLR 520; *Lipohar v R* (1999) 200 CLR 485; *John Pfeiffer Pty Ltd v Rogerson* (2000) 203 CLR 503.

33 Zines, *The Common Law in Australia: Its Nature and Constitutional Significance*, Centre for International and Public Law, ANU, Paper no 13, 1999.

34 It should be noted also that the *Judiciary Act*, s 57, specifically provides that claims by a State against the Commonwealth in contract or in tort may be brought in the High Court and s 59 makes similar provision in case of suits between States.

determine any such matter, either as a court of first instance or as a court of appeal from an inferior court. Section 40A provided machinery for the removal of such inter se questions when they arose in the Supreme Court of a State. It was declared that it was the duty of the court to proceed no further in the cause which was automatically removed to the High Court. Section 41 provided that when a cause was removed into the High Court the Court should proceed as if the cause had been originally commenced there.

Sections 38A and 40A were originally enacted in 1907. They were designed to give effect to a legislative policy that inter se questions should be finally determined in Australia by the High Court and that no appeal should lie to the Privy Council except on the certificate of the High Court. This policy had been expressed in s 74 of the Constitution, which provides that on an inter se question no appeal shall be permitted from the High Court to the Privy Council unless the High Court grants a certificate authorising such an appeal. This embodied the compromise on appeals to the Privy Council which was reached between the Australian delegation and the United Kingdom Government in 1900.[35] An attempt was made to circumvent s 74 by taking an appeal from the Supreme Court of a State direct to the Privy Council without going to the High Court at all.[36] To cover this gap in the scheme it was thought necessary to prevent inter se questions from being decided by State Supreme Courts and this was done by enacting ss 38A and 40A of the *Judiciary Act*.

Sections 38A, 40A and 41 were held valid in *Pirrie v McFarlane*[37] to the extent that they related to inter se questions as between the Commonwealth and the States. The Parliament had, under s 76(i) of the Constitution, vested the High Court with jurisdiction in any matter arising under the Constitution or involving its interpretation (s 30(c) of the *Judiciary Act*) and under s 77(ii) it had power to define the extent to which the jurisdiction of any federal court should be exclusive of State courts.

Sections 38A and 40A were repealed by the *Judiciary Amendment Act* 1976. It was clear by then that the condition in s 39(2)(a) of the *Judiciary Act*, prohibiting appeals to the Privy Council from any State court exercising federal jurisdiction, was valid. It was considered therefore that ss 38A and 40A were no longer necessary for achieving the object of preventing appeals to the Privy Council in relation to inter se questions. It follows that the jurisdiction of the High Court to deal with these matters is now concurrent with State Supreme Courts as well as with other courts. Appeals to the Privy Council from State Supreme Courts were terminated by the *Australia Act* 1986 (Cth), s 11. The *Australia Act* 1986 (UK), s 11, is in the same terms.

---

35   For an account of the negotiations and matters in dispute, see Garran, *Cambridge History of the British Empire* (1933) vol vii, pp 451-452 and La Nauze, *The Making of the Australian Constitution*, 1972, pp 248-269.

36   See *Webb v Outtrim* [1907] AC 81; *Baxter v Commissioner of Taxation (NSW)* (1907) 4 CLR 1087; *Pirrie v McFarlane* (1925) 36 CLR 170 at 177, 195-196.

37   (1925) 36 CLR 170.

Section 40 of the *Judiciary Act* provides for the removal of a cause or a part of a cause from a federal, Territory or State court into the High Court. Where the cause is one arising under the Constitution or involving its interpretation, the High Court may order its removal into the High Court on the application of a party on such terms as the Court thinks fit. It is further provided that an order of removal shall be made as of course on the application by the Attorney-General of the Commonwealth, of a State, of the Australian Capital Territory, or of the Northern Territory (s 40(1)).

In the case of other causes pending in a federal or Territory court or in a State court exercising federal jurisdiction, the cause may be removed into the High Court by order of that Court upon application of a party or of the Commonwealth Attorney-General (s 40(2)). As the causes that may be so removed include those with respect to which the High Court has not otherwise been invested with jurisdiction (for example, a matter arising under a law made by Parliament), s 40(3) confers jurisdiction to hear and determine the cause that is removed "to the extent that jurisdiction is not otherwise conferred on the High Court". In the case of an order for removal under s 40(2), that is non-constitutional matters, the High Court is prohibited from making an order unless all parties consent to it or the Court is satisfied that it is appropriate to make the order having regard to all the circumstances, including the interests of the parties and the public interest (s 40(4)).

Before 1976, power to remove causes into the High Court under s 40 of the *Judiciary Act* was confined to the removal from State courts of matters arising under the Constitution or involving its interpretation. There was no power to order removal from federal or Territorial courts. As is the case at present in relation to constitutional questions, it was provided that the order should be made as of course on the application of the Attorney-General of the Commonwealth or of a State.

The special standing of a Commonwealth or State Attorney-General was referred to by Isaacs J in *Ex parte Walsh and Johnson; In re Yates*:

> If a party applies, he must show sufficient cause, and must submit to terms if the Court thinks fit. But an Attorney-General – of the Commonwealth, if he thinks Commonwealth interests involved, or of a State, if he thinks State interests involved – may obtain the order as of course. Parliament recognising that, if the Commonwealth or a State desires the removal, that is in itself sufficient guarantee of materiality in the first instance.[38]

The validity of s 40, in the form in which it was then, was upheld by the High Court in that case. To understand the argument, it is necessary to refer to s 39 of the *Judiciary Act*. Section 39(1), which is an exercise of Commonwealth legislative power under s 77(ii) of the Constitution, declared that the jurisdiction of the High Court, so far as it was not already exclusive of the

---

38   (1925) 37 CLR 36 at 73.

jurisdiction of any State court under ss 38 and 38A of the *Judiciary Act*, should be exclusive of the jurisdiction of the several courts of the States except as provided in this section. Section 39(2), which is an exercise of power under s 77(iii), then invested State courts with federal jurisdiction in all matters in which the High Court has original jurisdiction or may have original jurisdiction conferred upon it, except as provided in ss 38 and 38A, and subject to conditions which are set out in paras (a) to (d) of the subsection. Under paras (a) to (c) appeals from State courts exercising federal jurisdiction were specially regulated, and s 39(2)(d) prescribed the constitution of State courts of summary jurisdiction when exercising federal jurisdiction. (Section 39 is in similar form today except that s 38A has been repealed as well as the condition in para (b) of s 39(2), which provided for an appeal to the High Court from a State court where an appeal lay to the State Supreme Court.)[39]

The nub of the section is s 39(2)(a) which was designed to ensure that appeals from State courts exercising federal jurisdiction should not bypass the High Court. This section, like s 38A, was part of a legislative scheme designed to shut out appeals to the Privy Council. The validity of this elaborate legislative scheme, so far as it purported to regulate these appeals, was considered and upheld in decisions of the High Court.[40] The enactment of s 39 meant that State courts were deprived of *State* jurisdiction in respect of certain matters and invested with *federal* jurisdiction in respect of those very matters. It also meant that in certain matters the High Court and the courts of the States exercised concurrent original federal jurisdiction. For example, the section deprived State courts of their pre-existing *State* jurisdiction in matters between residents of different States and then invested them with federal jurisdiction in these matters. The High Court and the State courts have concurrent original federal jurisdiction in these matters.[41]

In *Ex parte Walsh and Johnson*,[42] the High Court pointed out that jurisdiction in matters arising under the Constitution or involving its interpretation had been taken away from State courts as a matter of State jurisdiction by s 39(1) and invested in State courts as a matter of federal jurisdiction by s 39(2). The power to invest State courts with federal jurisdiction under s 77(iii) authorised the imposition of conditions on the exercise of such jurisdiction. Starke J said:

> The *Judiciary Act*, s 40, simply provides for the removal from the State Courts in certain cases of any cause or part of a cause arising under the Constitution or involving its interpretation. But as the jurisdiction exercised by the State Courts is, as we have seen, Federal jurisdiction, the provisions of ss 76 and 77 of the Constitution contain ample authority, in my opinion, for the Parliament to withdraw any matter from that jurisdiction, and

---

39   *Judiciary Amendment Act* 1976.
40   See pp 217ff below.
41   See pp 89-90 below.
42   (1925) 37 CLR 36.

remove it into the High Court or any other Federal Court, and to provide for its remission again, as in s 42, to the State Courts. I entertain no doubt of the validity of the provisions of s 40 of the *Judiciary Act*.[43]

As has been mentioned, s 40 now goes beyond constitutional matters and permits removal from a State court of any cause involving the exercise of federal jurisdiction by that court or of any cause pending in a federal or Territorial court.

So far as removal from State courts is concerned, the reasoning in *Ex parte Walsh and Johnson* regarding the validity of s 40 in its old form may not be fully applicable to the present section. When s 40 was confined to matters arising under the Constitution or involving its interpretation, it was clear that the State court could be exercising only federal jurisdiction because any State jurisdiction had been excluded by s 39(1) and federal jurisdiction conferred by s 39(2). However, in respect of matters within s 76 of the Constitution, where original jurisdiction has not been conferred on the High Court by the Parliament, s 39(1) could not, of course, operate. But under s 39(2) federal jurisdiction was conferred on State courts in all matters enumerated in ss 75 and 76 and is authorised by s 77(iii) of the Constitution. It was suggested in a number of cases that in certain matters State courts could exercise both federal and State jurisdiction with different requirements as to the composition of courts of summary jurisdiction and with different rights of appeal depending on whether the case was tried in State or federal jurisdiction.[44]

If this were the case the operation of s 40(2) in respect of, for example, a matter arising under a Commonwealth law would depend on whether the State court was, in respect of the particular matter, exercising federal jurisdiction or State jurisdiction. If it were State jurisdiction s 40(2) would not operate, nor could it constitutionally do so. The High Court has held, however, that where a State court can possibly exercise State or federal jurisdiction in respect of the same matter, s 109 of the Constitution operates to deprive the State court of its State jurisdiction.[45] This will be discussed later.[46] When the cause is removed into the High Court, s 40(3) confers on the High Court jurisdiction to hear and determine the matter if the High Court does not otherwise have jurisdiction, that is when it is not a matter coming within s 75 of the Constitution, s 30 of the *Judiciary Act* or within any other law conferring jurisdiction on the High Court.

There would seem no doubt as to the constitutional validity of s 40 in so far as it deals with the removal of causes from federal or Territory courts. Clearly, if the cause is pending in a federal court, it must be a matter within

---

43 Ibid at 129.

44 See, for example, *Booth v Shelmerdine* [1924] VLR 276; p 90 below.

45 *Moorgate Tobacco Co Ltd v Philip Morris Ltd* (1980) 145 CLR 457 at 471, 479ff; *Felton v Mulligan* (1971) 124 CLR 367 at 412-413.

46 See pp 235ff below.

federal jurisdiction. So far as Territorial courts are concerned, this will be dealt with later.[47]

It will be seen from the foregoing account that the High Court possesses a substantial original jurisdiction, part of which is exclusive and part concurrent. The constitutional power to make jurisdiction exclusive under s 77(ii) is a power to make it exclusive of State courts, and s 77(i), which confers power to define the jurisdiction of federal courts other than the High Court, authorises Parliament to define the extent to which the original jurisdiction of the High Court should be exclusive of that of other federal courts.

The original jurisdiction of the Supreme Court of the United States is much more narrowly confined. Article III, s 2, provides:

> The judicial power shall extend to all Cases, in Law and Equity, arising under this Constitution, the Laws of the United States, and Treaties made, or which shall be made, under their Authority; to all Cases affecting Ambassadors, other public Ministers and Consuls; to all Cases of admiralty and maritime Jurisdiction; to controversies to which the United States shall be a Party; to Controversies between two or more States; between a State and Citizens of another State; between Citizens of different States; between Citizens of the same State claiming lands under Grants of different States, and between a State, or the Citizens thereof, and foreign States, Citizens or Subjects.
>
> In all Cases affecting Ambassadors, other public Ministers and Consuls, and those in which a State shall be a Party, the Supreme Court shall have original jurisdiction. In all the other Cases before mentioned, the Supreme Court shall have appellate jurisdiction both as to Law and Fact, with such Exceptions, and under such Regulations as the Congress shall make.

Article III, s 2, has to be read subject to the Eleventh Amendment, ratified in 1795, which provides that "the Judicial power of the United States shall not be construed to extend to any suit in law or equity, commenced or prosecuted against one of the United States by Citizens of another State, or by Citizens or Subjects of any Foreign State". This amendment was adopted following the decision in *Chisholm v Georgia*[48] where it was held that there was jurisdiction to try a case which a citizen of one State might bring against another State notwithstanding the refusal of consent by the defendant State to the assumption of jurisdiction. It is now the law that in these circumstances a State may only be sued with its consent, although it may freely bring an action as plaintiff. A proposal to include a provision comparable to the Eleventh Amendment in the Judicature Chapter of the Commonwealth Constitution was made at the Constitutional Convention of 1897.[49] The clause provided that "nothing in this Constitution shall be construed to authorise any suit in law or equity against

---

47 See Chapter 4.
48 2 Dall 419 (1793).
49 Debates, 1897, pp 989-990.

the Commonwealth or any person sued on behalf of the Commonwealth, or against a State or any person sued on behalf of a State by any individual person or corporation, except by the consent of the Commonwealth, or of the State, as the case might be", but it was unceremoniously struck out.[50]

The original jurisdiction of the Supreme Court of the United States is specifically conferred by the Constitution, so that there is no power in Congress to restrict it. The same is true of the original jurisdiction conferred by s 75 of the Commonwealth Constitution. On the other hand, there is no American counterpart to s 76 of the Australian Constitution authorising parliamentary extension of the original jurisdiction of the High Court, and the Supreme Court ruled early in *Marbury v Madison*[51] that Congress has no such power. Article III, s 2, in prescribing the original jurisdiction of the Supreme Court, has not been read as conferring a necessarily exclusive original jurisdiction, and it is now well settled that Congress may provide that matters within the original jurisdiction may be concurrently invested in inferior federal courts, and may reach the Supreme Court on appeal.[52] The *Judiciary Act* 1789 first delimited the exclusive and concurrent original jurisdiction of the Supreme Court. The present situation is that the Supreme Court possesses *exclusive original* jurisdiction in all controversies between two or more States and in all actions or proceedings against ambassadors or other public ministers of foreign states or their domestic servants which are not inconsistent with the law of nations.[53] The Court has *concurrent* original jurisdiction in all actions or proceedings brought by ambassadors or other public ministers of foreign states or to which consuls or vice-consuls of foreign states are parties, in all controversies between the United States and a State, and in all actions or proceedings by a State against the citizens of another State or against aliens. In general, it will be seen that the existing and potential original jurisdiction of the High Court of Australia is considerably larger than that of the Supreme Court of the United States. Only in respect of the jurisdiction against aliens is the American jurisdiction wider, for the Commonwealth Constitution does not in terms confer original jurisdiction on the High Court in suits between States and non-resident aliens. Under s 75(iii), in a case in which the Commonwealth is a party, the High Court has original jurisdiction, and it is possible that the other party may be an alien. Likewise, under one or other of the heads of jurisdiction in s 76, a case may arise in which a State and a non-resident alien will be parties.

---

50   Hunt, op cit p 196.

51   1 Cranch 137; 5 US 137 (1803).

52   See Wagner, "The Original and Exclusive Jurisdiction of the United States Supreme Court" (1952) 2 St Louis University LJ 111; Surridge, "Jurisdiction over Suits against Foreign Consuls in the United States" (1932) 80 U of Pennsylvania LR 972; note (1926) 39 Harvard LR 1084; Fallon, Meltzer and Shapiro, *Hart and Wechsler's The Federal Courts and the Federal System*, 4th edn, 1996, pp 294–347.

53   28 USC s 1251.

"Matters" : Advisory Opinions, Standing

It is to be noted that the original jurisdiction of the High Court under ss 75 and 76 arises only in respect of matters. In *In re Judiciary and Navigation Acts*,[54] it was held that s 88 of the *Judiciary Act* 1903 was invalid. This purported to give the High Court jurisdiction to "hear and determine" any question referred to it by the Governor-General as to the validity of any enactment of the Parliament of the Commonwealth. The Court construed the section as a grant of judicial power invalidly conferred because ss 75 and 76 of the Constitution defined the jurisdiction of the High Court by reference to "matters", which postulated the existence of a lis inter partes.

> We do not think that the word "matter" in s 76 means a legal proceeding, but rather the subject-matter for determination in a legal proceeding. In our opinion there can be no matter within the meaning of the section unless there is some immediate right, duty or liability to be established by the determination of the Court.[55]

The terms of the Constitution, on this reading, precluded the giving of advisory opinions. Article III, s 2, of the United States Constitution, which adopts the language of cases and controversies rather than of matters, has likewise been construed as forbidding the giving of advisory opinions by the Supreme Court of the United States.[56]

It has been questioned whether the power to give an advisory opinion might be more appropriately described as non-judicial and therefore the purported grant of such power would be invalid as a result of the doctrine in the *Boilermakers' Case*.[57] In the *Boilermakers' Case* itself, it was not necessary for either the Privy Council or the High Court to determine that question. The doctrine of the *Boilermakers' Case* was questioned by two judges of the High Court[58] and it has been argued that the Court should refuse to follow that case. If it were held that a federal court can be given non-judicial functions but that its judicial functions are restricted to the matters specified in Chapter III of the Constitution, the correctness of the classification of advisory opinions in *In re Judiciary and Navigation Acts* could become important. It was reaffirmed by Jacobs J[59] and by other judges in recent times.[60]

The rigour of this rule preventing the conferring on federal courts of power to give advisory opinions has been mitigated by the broad scope which

---

54   (1921) 29 CLR 257.

55   *In re Judiciary and Navigation Acts* (1921) 29 CLR 257 at 265.

56   See Small and Jayson (eds), *The Constitution of the United States of America: Analysis and Interpretation*, 1964, pp 616-617; *Hart and Wechsler*, op cit pp 92-98.

57   *Attorney-General (Cth) v The Queen; ex parte Boilermakers' Society of Australia* (1957) 95 CLR 529 at 541 (PC). See also (1956) 94 CLR 254 at 272-274 (HC).

58   *R v Joske* (1974) 130 CLR 87 at 90, 102.

59   *Commonwealth v Queensland* (1975) 134 CLR 298 at 327.

60   *Re Wakim* (1999) 198 CLR 511 at 541-542; *Gould v Brown* (1998) 193 CLR 346 at 421, 440.

the High Court has given to the declaratory judgment remedy in public law litigation. The Court has infrequently directed its attention to the justiciability of the particular issue – certainly less frequently than does the Supreme Court of the United States – and there are cases in which the High Court has entertained suits for declarations in circumstances where, as has been aptly said, "the prematurity and breadth of the challenge, and the abstract manner in which the legal issues were presented, make the suit resemble a proceeding for an advisory opinion".[61] It seems probable that the High Court has been influenced in these cases, which are exceptional, by the importance of the legislation challenged, the desirability of a speedy determination of its validity, and in some cases by the inconvenience attendant on delaying a decision until after the enactment had come into full operation. Such a case was *Attorney-General (Vic) v Commonwealth*,[62] where an application was made in the original jurisdiction of the High Court for a declaration that the *Pharmaceutical Benefits Act* 1944 was unconstitutional and void, on the ground that it was ultra vires the Commonwealth Parliament. The Act had not been proclaimed and it was unsuccessfully argued on the authority of *In re Judiciary and Navigation Acts* that there was no "matter" before the Court but merely an abstract question of law. It was pointed out that the Act would shortly be proclaimed, and that the necessary preliminary steps were being taken so that it could be brought into effective operation. It followed that the question would shortly arise whether the public in the various States was entitled to the benefits and subject to the obligations imposed by the Act. The cause of action was founded on the right of an individual in some instances, and in others of the public, or a section of the public, to restrain a public body clothed with statutory powers from exceeding those powers. On this view there was a "matter" for decision, and the Attorney-General had standing to sue on behalf of the public of the State of Victoria. There are other cases of this type.[63] Some judges have gone further and stated that a State may challenge the constitutional validity of Commonwealth Acts, even where no injury to the public is shown, on the ground that the nature of the Constitution is such that the Commonwealth and each State has a right to the observance of constitutional limits by the other.[64]

---

61 Foster, "The Declaratory Judgment in Australia and the United States" (1958) 1 Melbourne ULR 347 at 391. It was, however, noted in *Bass v Permanent Trustee* (1999) 198 CLR 334 at 356 that a declaration will not be made where the dispute is based on facts that are purely hypothetical.

62 (1945) 71 CLR 237, esp at 277-279.

63 See, for example, *Union Label Case* (1908) 6 CLR 469; *Commonwealth v Queensland* (1920) 29 CLR 1; *South Australia v Commonwealth* (1942) 65 CLR 373; *Australian National Airways Ltd v Commonwealth* (1945) 71 CLR 29; *Bank of New South Wales v Commonwealth* (1948) 76 CLR 1; *Australian Communist Party v Commonwealth* (1951) 83 CLR 1; see Foster, op cit 373ff; *Attorney-General (Vic) v Commonwealth* (1962) 107 CLR 529.

64 *Victoria v Commonwealth* (1975) 134 CLR 338 at 381 per Gibbs J, 401-402 per Mason J; *Attorney-General (Vic) v Commonwealth* (1981) 146 CLR 559 at 589.

As liberal as the Court has been in this regard, it held that there was no "matter" where the Commonwealth Attorney-General's claim was not concerned with the power or other interest of the Commonwealth. In *Re McBain; ex parte Australian Catholic Bishops Conference*,[65] an action was brought by the Attorney-General (Cth) at the relation of the Bishops Conference for certiorari to quash an order of the Federal Court, on the ground of error of law on the face of the record. The Attorney-General had not been a party to the proceedings in the Federal Court, where it was held that a State law was inconsistent with a federal law by virtue of s 109 of the Constitution and was, therefore, invalid. The parties to that case chose not to appeal. The High Court held by majority (Gleeson CJ, Gaudron, Gummow and Hayne JJ; contra: McHugh, Kirby and Callinan JJ) that the application by the Attorney-General did not constitute a "matter". It was accepted by all parties that the Federal Court judge had acted within his jurisdiction. The Attorney-General was not seeking to obtain relief in respect of any right or interest of the Commonwealth or its public. The matter was within the sphere of the State Attorney-General, whose function it is "to represent the interest of the public of that State in vindicating the laws of that State".[66] The State had accepted the decision as binding; yet the Commonwealth Attorney-General was seeking to have affirmed the operation of the State Act in the face of s 109.

Gaudron and Gummow JJ summed up the position by saying that "the Attorney-General, consistently with Chapter III, cannot have a roving commission to initiate litigation to disrupt settled outcomes in earlier cases, so as to rid the law reports of what are considered unsatisfactory decisions respecting constitutional law".[67]

McHugh J, with whom Callinan J agreed, considered that there was a "matter" because, among other things, any person could seek certiorari on the ground that the record of a court was defective. That issue is discussed below.[68] While Kirby J expressed doubts about the grant of a fiat by an Attorney-General in the Australian constitutional setting,[69] he held that the relator proceedings constituted a "matter" separate from the earlier proceedings even though it involved making submissions to uphold a State Act. It is suggested that the reasoning of the majority is convincing. The special powers of an Attorney-General in respect of constitutional issues are for the purpose of maintaining the powers and interests of the polity that the Attorney represents and its public.

In *Attorney-General (Cth); ex rel McKinlay v Commonwealth*,[70] the Commonwealth Attorney-General granted a fiat to permit a challenge to

---

65   (2002) 188 ALR 1.
66   Ibid at 20.
67   Ibid at 21.
68   Pages 19-20.
69   (2002) 188 ALR 1 at 54-55.
70   (1975) 135 CLR 1.

Commonwealth legislation. No question of standing was raised. Jacobs J in *Commonwealth v Queensland*[71] stated that the Commonwealth Attorney-General could seek a declaration as to the validity of a Commonwealth Act. If this is so, there is, as His Honour pointed out, scarcely any difference in substance between that procedure and the provisions of s 88 of the *Judiciary Act* that were invalidated. The difficulty with that view is that the other party to the suit would be the Commonwealth and there would be little guarantee that the suit would be an adversary one. Under the invalidated provisions, notice of the hearing was required to be given to the Attorney-General of each State, who was given a right to appear and to be represented at the hearing. Section 78A of the *Judiciary Act*, as amended in 1976, gives a right to the Attorneys-General of the Commonwealth and the States to intervene in proceedings relating to the Constitution and s 78B requires a court, including the High Court, in such matters not to proceed until the court is satisfied that notice has been given to the Attorneys-General. In the circumstances, therefore, if the Attorney-General of the Commonwealth may seek a declaration as to the validity of Commonwealth legislation, it may be, as Jacobs J suggested in *Attorney-General (NSW); ex rel McKellar v Commonwealth*,[72] that *In re Judiciary and Navigation Acts* does no more than affect the manner of bringing constitutional questions before the court.

In *Attorney-General (Cth) v T & G Mutual Life Society Ltd*,[73] it was held that the Attorney-General of the Commonwealth had standing to sue for a declaration that Commonwealth legislation prohibiting appeals to the Privy Council from the High Court was valid. In that case, however, there was an opposing party, namely, a defendant who was seeking special leave to appeal to the Privy Council from a judgment of the High Court. The standing of the Attorney-General was based on the view that the legislation was not only for the benefit of private persons but was enacted in the interest of the community.

The relationship of rules relating to standing to the meaning of "matter" and to the decision in *In re Judiciary and Navigation Acts* was the subject of discussion in *Croome v Tasmania*,[74] where there was a suit against Tasmania for a declaration that a State law prohibiting sexual intercourse between males was inconsistent with a Commonwealth Act. The State admitted that the plaintiff had standing because he had engaged in the proscribed conduct and proposed to continue doing so in the future. But it was argued that there was no "matter" within the meaning of Chapter III of the Constitution because the Government had not acted to enforce the law. The argument was rejected on the ground that it was a misunderstanding of *In re Judiciary and Navigation*

---

71   (1975) 134 CLR 298 at 326.
72   (1977) 139 CLR 527.
73   (1978) 144 CLR 161.
74   (1997) 191 CLR 119.

Acts. The judges had difficulty in severing the concepts of standing and matter. Gaudron, McHugh and Gummow JJ said:

> During the course of argument it became apparent that the attempted severance in this case between questions going to the standing of the plaintiffs and those directed to the constitutional requirement of the exercise of federal jurisdiction with respect to a 'matter' was conceptually awkward, if not impossible.[75]

They went on to say that where the issue is whether federal jurisdiction has been invoked with respect to a "matter", "questions of 'standing' are subsumed within that issue".

In *Truth About Motorways Pty Ltd v Macquarie Infrastructure Investment Management Ltd*,[76] the Court upheld the validity of provisions of the *Trade Practices Act* 1974 (Cth) giving standing to "a person" and to "any other person" to seek a declaration that specified provisions of the Act were infringed. The Court said that the provisions were designed to protect the public, and the standing provisions had the object of establishing the violation of statutory norms of conduct. The concept of matter did not require mutuality or reciprocity of right and liability between the parties. As the duties for determination were those owed to the public, Parliament could validly decide that the best way to enforce such public rights and corresponding duties was to give standing to any member of the public. As the Court pointed out, it is on this basis that a "stranger" is permitted to apply for a writ of prohibition against an officer or tribunal for acting in excess of power or jurisdiction.[77]

The basis of the rule in relation to prohibition is that it is regarded as for the public interest that tribunals be confined within their jurisdiction.[78] That view was upheld in *Re Refugee Tribunal; ex parte Aala*.[79] The Court, however, has a discretion to refuse the writ whether or not the applicant is a stranger.[80] McHugh and Callinan JJ have held that the same broad view of standing applies also to certiorari.[81] In so far as the writ of certiorari is sought on the ground of jurisdictional error, there is no reason why the rationale applicable to prohibition should not apply. Their Honours found, however, that the same rule of standing also applied to an application to quash a court order for non-jurisdictional error on the face of the record. It is difficult to see how the same considerations of public interest apply in that case. The cases and literature relied on by McHugh J all emphasise the public importance of

---

75   Ibid at 132.
76   (2000) 200 CLR 591.
77   Ibid at 627-628, 652-653.
78   *R v Federal Court of Australia; ex parte Western Australian National Football League* (1979) 143 CLR 190 at 204.
79   (2000) 204 CLR 82.
80   Ibid at 89, 105-106, 136-137.
81   *Re McBain; ex parte Australian Catholic Bishops Conference* (2002) 188 ALR 1 at 24, 75.

not allowing orders made beyond jurisdiction to go unchallenged.[82] He then went on to say that those statements "apply with equal force to *records* of curial proceedings, made within jurisdiction, but which on their face demonstrate an error of law".[83] It is not clear why that follows. It is suggested that the majority in the *Catholic Bishops Case* were correct in holding that, in those circumstances, there was no "matter" within Chapter III.

A tendency in other respects to confine the scope of the legislative restriction in *In re Judiciary and Navigation Acts* in respect of advisory opinions to abstract questions of law is reflected in recent decisions on the scope of the appellate jurisdiction of the High Court under s 73 of the Constitution. That section confers appellate jurisdiction from "all judgments, decrees, orders and sentences" of specified courts and tribunals. The High Court, in interpreting that expression, has adopted the same approach as that followed in respect of the meaning of "matter" in original jurisdiction. It has been held that there can be no appeal from an advisory opinion or abstract declaration, and *In re Judiciary and Navigation Acts* has been relied on to determine that issue.[84] In *Mellifont v Attorney-General (Qld)*,[85] the Court held that an appeal lay under s 73 from a decision of the Court of Criminal Appeal of Queensland brought by the Attorney-General where a person had been acquitted of a charge and the Appeal Court's decision did not affect the verdict.[86] The Court said that, although the reference and decision could not affect the rights of the parties, they "*arise out of* the proceedings and the indictment and are a statutory extension of those proceedings". As the questions related to the rulings of the judge and his interpretation of legal instruments in the context of the charge, the decision was with respect to a "matter". It "was not divorced from the ordinary administration of the law".[87] *In re Judiciary and Navigation Acts* was distinguished on the ground that in that case the opinion was academic and in response to an abstract question, unrelated to any actual controversy between parties.[88]

Nevertheless, the Court has taken a stricter stance in refusing to determine issues not based on facts established by evidence or agreed to by the parties. In *Bass v Permanent Trustee Co Ltd*,[89] the determination of such issues was

82 For example, *Worthington v Jeffries* (1875) LR 10 CP 379 at 382; *Re Federal Court of Australia; ex parte WA National Football League* (1979) 143 CLR 190 at 204; Wade, "Unlawful Administrative Action: Void or Voidable" (1967) 83 Law Quarterly R 499 at 503.
83 (2002) 188 ALR 1 at 24.
84 *Mellifont v Attorney-General (Qld)* (1991) 173 CLR 289 at 302-303.
85 Ibid.
86 The Court overruled *Saffron v The Queen* (1953) 88 CLR 523.
87 (1991) 173 CLR 289 at 305.
88 The Court also declared incorrect earlier decisions which held that there was no appeal from answers given to a special or stated case where those issues did not determine the parties' rights: Ibid at 304.
89 (1999) 198 CLR 334.

regarded as an advisory opinion even though it was to assist in the resolution of very complex litigation involving numerous parties.

The Heads of Jurisdiction

In a discussion of the various heads of federal jurisdiction under Art III, s 2, of the United States Constitution, the Supreme Court of the United States observed that "it is apparent upon the face of these clauses that in one class of cases the jurisdiction of the courts of the Union depends on the character of the cause, whatever may be the parties, and on the other on the character of the parties, whatever may be the subject of controversy".[90] The subject-matters of original jurisdiction of the High Court of Australia under ss 75 and 76 of the Constitution are similarly classified. Section 75(i) matters arising under any treaty, s 76(i) matters arising under this Constitution or involving its inter-pretation, s 76(ii) matters arising under any laws made by the Parliament, s 76(iii) matters of Admiralty and maritime jurisdiction and s 76(iv) matters relating to the same subject-matter claimed under the laws of different States are all concerned with "the character of the cause, whatever may be the parties". Section 75(ii) matters affecting consuls or other representatives of other countries; s 75(iii) matters in which the Commonwealth or a person suing or being sued on behalf of the Commonwealth is a party; s 75(iv) mat-ters between States or between a State and a resident of another State are matters depending "on the character of the parties whatever may be the con-troversy". Section 75(v) matters in which a writ of mandamus or prohibition or an injunction is sought against an officer of the Commonwealth, which as a matter of original jurisdiction has no counterpart in the United States Consti-tution, has traces of both elements, since it depends partly upon the character of the remedy sought and partly upon the character of the parties.[91]

It is clear that, in selecting the subject-matter of federal jurisdiction, the framers of the Commonwealth Constitution relied heavily on American precedent. The main departure was s 75(v), which forms "no part of Article III but [was] inspired by the provisions of the American *Judiciary Act* held invalid in *Marbury v Madison*".[92] This was more fully explained by Barton J in *Ah Yick v Lehmert*.[93] In *Marbury v Madison*,[94] the *Judiciary Act* provision which was held invalid authorised the Supreme Court in its original jurisdiction to issue a mandamus against a non-judicial officer of the United States. Since the Constitution did not specifically confer original jurisdiction

---

90   *United States v Texas* 143 US 621 (1892) per Harlan J.

91   See *Carter v Egg and Egg Pulp Marketing Board (Vic)* (1942) 66 CLR 557 at 579 per Latham CJ.

92   *Collins v Charles Marshall Pty Ltd* (1955) 92 CLR 529 at 544.

93   (1905) 2 CLR 593 at 609.

94   1 Cranch 137; 5 US 137 (1803).

on the Supreme Court to issue a mandamus in such a case, it was held that the purported congressional grant of power was ultra vires.[95] But even here the American influence was so strong that two leading lawyer members of the 1897-98 Convention, who subsequently became justices of the High Court, were led into error. For reasons which will appear later, this clause was under heavy attack by Mr Isaacs. In the course of the debate, Mr Higgins said: "The provision was in the Bill of 1891 and I thought it was taken from the American Constitution."[96] Mr Barton was equally ill-informed: "I fancy it is in some part of the American Constitution."[97] In this situation, when leading lawyer members of the Convention were so obviously vague and ill-informed about the purpose and origins of the clause, Mr Isaacs carried the day and the clause was struck out. Mr Barton, better briefed, came back a little later to explain the point of the clause by reference to *Marbury v Madison*. Mr Isaacs pressed his objections, but the clause was restored in its present form.[98]

Another clause which, it has been said, does not appear to have an American counterpart is s 76(iv) – matters relating to the same subject-matter claimed under the laws of different States. Mr Barton when questioned said it was in the American Constitution.[99] In his evidence before the Royal Commission on the Constitution in 1927, Mr Owen Dixon KC said of s 76(iv) that "so far, the meaning of this and the application of it has been elucidated by no one".[100] Another writer, confessing perplexity, suggested that under s 76(iv) the High Court might be invested with original jurisdiction in all matters "of interstate private international law".[101]

The Australian Constitutional Convention recommended its repeal.[102] The Advisory Committee to the Constitutional Commission recommended that it be preserved because it might be of use in resolving matters of conflict of laws, including statutes. The Constitutional Commission, somewhat unenthusiastically, said that that was a "possible interpretation" because the Court was required to give it "some meaning".[103]

---

95 "It is well known that there is a difference between our Constitution and that of the United States, because in the former, original jurisdiction is by s 75(v) given to the High Court in matters in which mandamus is sought against a non-judicial [quaere] officer of the Commonwealth. That case was not provided for in the United States Constitution, and hence the decision in *Marbury v Madison* that mandamus to a non-judicial officer was outside the powers of the Constitution, and that therefore the Act of Congress purporting to authorise the grant of such a mandamus was not valid." *Ah Yick v Lehmert* (1905) 2 CLR 593 at 609 per Barton J.

96 Debates, Melbourne, 1898, vol 1, p 321.

97 Ibid p 321.

98 Ibid vol 2, p 1875; La Nauze, op cit pp 233-234.

99 Debates, Melbourne, 1898, vol 1, p 321.

100 Royal Commission, Minutes of Evidence, p 786.

101 Wynes, "The Judicial Power of the Commonwealth" (1938) 12 ALJ 8 at 9.

102 Convention Proceedings, Perth, 1978, pp 204-205.

103 *Final Report of the Constitutional Commission*, 1988, vol 1, p 382.

The history of this paragraph was examined by Leslie Katz, who concluded that it was intended to be an extension of a head of jurisdiction in Art III, s 2, of the United States Constitution, namely, "Controversies ... between citizens of the same State claiming lands under grants of different States ...". Such controversies would usually arise when each State claimed the land as part of its territory. Inglis Clark had included in his draft constitution, in preparation for the 1891 Convention, an extended version of this jurisdictional subject. He referred to disputes about "land or other property" and "any right, franchise, or privilege so claimed". Charles Kingston considered Clark's draft and prepared one of his own in which he included a head of jurisdiction in language similar to s 76(iv) of the Constitution. Katz points out that it is likely Clark regarded the new version as equivalent to, or as an improvement on, his own, because the Judiciary Committee which recommended a clause like that in the Kingston draft had Kingston as a member and had been presided over by Clark, who drafted the report, which was, on this point, unanimous.[104]

All the early writers on the Constitution – Quick and Garran, Clark, Groom and Harrison Moore – regarded s 76(iv) as taken from, but more extensive than, the American provisions.[105]

In the light of all the matters presented by Katz, his conclusion is convincing that the Australian provision is intended to cover "all matters in which resolution of conflicting claims of interest in or in relation to land or waters depended upon the determination of the respective boundaries of States".[106] The fact is that this jurisdiction has not been conferred on the High Court or any federal court. It is, however, included within the scope of s 39(2) of the *Judiciary Act* investing State courts with federal jurisdiction. It seems never to have been invoked.

Treaties : Section 75(i)

Section 75(i) and (ii) very clearly reflect the influence of the American model. Article III, s 2, conferred federal jurisdiction in all cases arising under treaties made under the Constitution and laws of the United States and in all cases affecting ambassadors, other public ministers and consuls. The Supreme Court was given original jurisdiction in cases involving ambassadors, other public ministers and consuls. In the Commonwealth Constitution, the High Court was given original jurisdiction in all matters arising under any treaty and in matters affecting consuls or other representatives of other countries. Section 38 of the *Judiciary Act* added a complication by providing that in matters arising

---

104 Katz, "History of Section 76(iv) of the Commonwealth Constitution" (1991) 2 Public LR 228.

105 Ibid at 238-239.

106 Ibid at 239.

directly under any treaty, the jurisdiction of the High Court should be exclusive of that of the State courts. This means, in the absence of competent federal courts, that it is the exclusive forum for such cases in Australia. In matters arising, otherwise than *directly*, under a treaty, and in matters affecting consuls or other representatives of other countries, the *Judiciary Act*, s 39(1) and (2), operate to confer concurrent original jurisdiction on the High Court and State courts, which can exercise only federal jurisdiction in respect of such matters. From the time of the first *Judiciary Act*, in cases in which ambassadors and public ministers were *defendants*, the Supreme Court of the United States had exclusive original jurisdiction. When ambassadors and public ministers were plaintiffs and when consuls were parties, there was concurrent original jurisdiction in the Supreme Court and inferior federal courts. Since 1978 the Supreme Court has original but not exclusive jurisdiction in both classes of cases.[107]

In the *Federalist Papers*, Hamilton expounded the case for conferring original jurisdiction on the Supreme Court in respect of ambassadors, public ministers and consuls as follows:

> Public Ministers of every class are the immediate representatives of their sovereigns. All questions in which they are concerned are so directly connected with the public peace, that as well for the preservation of this, as out of respect to the sovereignties they represent, it is both expedient and proper that such questions should be submitted in the first instance to the highest judiciary of the nation. Though consuls have not in strictness a diplomatic character, yet as they are the public agents of the nations to which they belong, the same observations are in a great measure applicable to them.[108]

This touches the question of the proper forum in actions affecting ambassadors and public ministers. It does not touch the question of diplomatic immunity, that is, whether such persons may claim immunity from judicial process in any court. As the law stands, diplomatic immunity may be invoked to exclude the jurisdiction of the courts altogether where actions are brought against diplomatic representatives and their diplomatic families, and the decision on waiver of privilege rests with the sovereign and not with the diplomatic representative.[109] Moreover, consuls appear to bob along in the rear, drawn in by the magnetic influence of superior foreign representatives. It has been suggested that the rationale of the rule which attracts the original jurisdiction of the Supreme Court to cases affecting consuls is that they are appointed to, and received by, the Union and not by the States, which

---

107 28 USCA s 1251(b)(1).

108 *Federalist Papers*, no 81.

109 See Wagner, "The Original and Exclusive Jurisdiction of the United States Supreme Court" (1952) 2 St Louis LJ 111.

abandoned all their international law personality to the United States.[110] Here also, there are problems of consular immunities.[111]

Alexander Hamilton, of course, argued his case in the light of the conditions and circumstances which attended the making of the United States Constitution. It has already been pointed out that federal and State elements distrusted each other; that it was not considered possible or desirable to create an integrated judicial system in which the Supreme Court of the United States would exercise *general* appellate jurisdiction, or in which the State courts would discharge national (that is, federal) judicial functions. Since the foreign relations of the United States were the preserve of the national government, it followed that State courts had to be prevented from tampering with national foreign policies. So far as foreign diplomatic representatives were concerned this object was achieved by excluding the jurisdiction of the State courts.[112] It is a little surprising that the American founding fathers thought it necessary that certain cases affecting ambassadors and public ministers should be tried in the original jurisdiction of the Supreme Court, but were quite prepared to relegate cases arising under treaties to the original jurisdiction of inferior federal courts. It might have been thought, having regard to the importance of foreign relations, that it was at least as important to direct justiciable issues arising out of treaties into the original jurisdiction of the supreme federal court. In the Australian scheme, matters arising directly under treaties were assigned to the exclusive original jurisdiction of the High Court, but there was no provision for exclusive jurisdiction in the case of matters affecting consuls and other representatives of other States.

Having regard to the very different circumstances which attended the making of the Australian Constitution – specifically the difference in attitude to the jurisdiction of the High Court as a general court of appeal and to the investment of State courts with federal jurisdiction – it has to be asked whether the reasoning which led to the assignment of these matters to federal jurisdiction in the United States has any application to Australian circumstances. An explanation of the treaty jurisdiction was offered by Latham CJ in *R v Burgess*.[113] After considering the plan of the Constitution which, as interpreted, conferred power on the Executive to make treaties (s 61) and on the Legislature to implement them (s 51(xxix)), he said:

> Questions may arise under treaties with other countries, and accordingly the plan is completed by a provision in s 75 of the Constitution that the High Court shall have original jurisdiction in all matters arising under a

---

110 Ibid p 132.

111 See Beckett, "Consular Immunities" (1944) 21 British Year Book of International Law 34.

112 For a time from 1875 to 1911 the State courts were given concurrent jurisdiction in cases involving consuls. See Surridge, "Jurisdiction over Suits against Foreign Consuls in the United States" (1932) 80 U of Pennsylvania LR 972; *Hart and Wechsler*, op cit pp 335-336.

113 (1936) 55 CLR 608 at 643-644.

treaty. Thus in the provisions of the Constitution dealing with the three functions of government, executive, legislative and judicial, the same principle is found. O'Connor J said in 1908 that the powers of the Constitution "vest in the Commonwealth the power of controlling in every respect Australia's relations with the outside world".

This, with respect, is hindsight. The Australian founding fathers at no stage envisaged that s 61 of the Constitution would be the source of executive power to conclude treaties, for the very simple reason that they did not contemplate that the treaty-making function would pass out of imperial into colonial hands. The original form of the legislative power was "external affairs and treaties", and the words "and treaties" were struck out, since treaties were not a matter for colonial action.[114] When s 75(i) – matters arising under any treaty – was under discussion at the Melbourne meeting of the Convention in 1898, one member moved to have the clause struck out on the ground that "the court cannot decide upon a treaty, otherwise it might abrogate the Imperial law or polity upon the question at issue".[115] To this, an apparently satisfactory answer was given by Mr Symon of South Australia: "Some day hereafter it may be within the scope of the Commonwealth to deal with matters of this kind … It cannot do any harm to leave this provision in the clause."[116] It is fairly clear that the founding fathers were not very sure of what they were doing here. Mr Dixon in his evidence before the Royal Commission on the Constitution said:

> No one yet knows what is meant by the expression "matter arising under a treaty". The word "matter" refers to some claim the subject of litigation. It must, therefore, be a claim of legal right, privilege or immunity. Under a British system, the executive cannot, by making a treaty, regulate the rights of its subjects. A state of war may be ended or commenced, and the rights and duties of persons may be affected by the change from one State to another, but this results from the general law relating to peace and war, and not from the terms of the treaty. If a treaty is adopted by the legislature and its terms are converted into a statute, it is the statute and not the treaty which affects the rights and duties of the persons.[117]

The judicial power with respect to treaties has a more obvious meaning in the United States where a treaty may be self-executing under the terms of Art VI, s 2, so that on being made in proper form under Art II, s 2, it may become the law of the land without any necessity for congressional implementation.

---

114 Debates, Melbourne, 1898, vol 1, p 30.
115 Ibid p 320.
116 Ibid p 320.
117 Royal Commission, Minutes of Evidence, p 785.

This situation was quite clearly envisaged by the American founding fathers.[118] Australia, on the other hand, adopted the British distinction between treaty-*making* and treaty *implementation*. This distinction was stated in the Privy Council by Lord Atkin:

> Within the British Empire there is a well established rule that the making of a treaty is an executive act, while the performance of its obligations, if they entail alteration of the existing domestic law, requires legislative action. Unlike some other countries, the stipulations of a treaty duly ratified do not within the Empire, by virtue of the treaty alone, have the force of law.[119]

This being the case, the problem is to determine when a matter will arise under a treaty within the terms of s 75(i). An issue may arise whether legislation in purported implementation of a treaty is validly enacted under s 51(xxix), but that would appear to be a matter in which the High Court would have original jurisdiction under s 76(i) of the Constitution (*Judiciary Act*, s 30(a)) as a matter arising under the Constitution or involving its interpretation. If there is a question arising out of the legislative implementation of a treaty, which does not involve constitutional interpretation, the appropriate head of jurisdiction might be s 76(ii): matters arising under any laws made by the Parliament, but in this case there has been no general grant of original jurisdiction to the High Court. The question is how to formulate a justiciable issue which would arise squarely under the terms of s 75(i), and to give a meaning to the word "directly" in the case of matters arising directly under any treaty which are assigned to the exclusive original jurisdiction of the High Court by the *Judiciary Act*, s 38.

Most of the judicial observations and legal commentaries (including those of the authors in earlier editions of this book) have as their focus the problem of treaties needing legislative implementation. It has been argued, however, that to understand s 75(i) and s 38(a) of the *Judiciary Act* it would be better to concentrate on the few exceptions to the rule that treaties do not by their own force alter domestic rights and duties.[120] That argument is referred to below after examination of the case law.

An attempt was made in *Bluett v Fadden*[121] to interpret s 75(i) and the corresponding clause in s 38 of the *Judiciary Act*. In proceedings in the

---

118 See Sutherland, "Restricting the Treaty Power" (1952) 65 Harvard LR 1305 at 1315. One of the first great cases involving the self-executing operation of the US treaty power was *Ware v Hylton* 3 Dall 199 (1796).

119 *Attorney-General for Canada v Attorney-General for Ontario* [1937] AC 326 at 347; see also a statement of the same principle in *R v Burgess; ex parte Henry* (1936) 55 CLR 608 at 644 per Latham CJ; *Bradley v Commonwealth* (1973) 128 CLR 557; *Koowarta v Bjelke-Petersen* (1982) 153 CLR 168 at 193, 211-212; *Minister for Immigration and Ethnic Affairs v Teoh* (1995) 183 CLR 273 at 286-287, 315; see Chafee, "Amending the Constitution to Cripple Treaties" (1952) 12 Louisiana LR 345.

120 Leeming, "Federal Treaty Jurisdiction" (1999) 10 Public LR 173.

121 [1956] SR (NSW) 254. See also *Civil Aviation (Carriers' Liability) Act* 1959 (Cth), s 19.

Supreme Court of New South Wales, the plaintiffs challenged an order made by the Commonwealth Treasurer vesting certain shares in the Controller of Enemy Property under authority conferred by the *Trading with the Enemy Act* 1939 (Cth). The defendants argued that the shares were German enemy assets within the meaning of Art 6 of the Agreement on Reparation from Germany on the Establishment of an Inter-Allied Reparation Agency and on the Restitution of Monetary Gold, to which the Commonwealth of Australia was a party, and that the order in question was made pursuant to a regulation authorised by the Act for the purpose of giving effect to Art 6 of the Agreement. The defendants argued further that the suit involved a matter directly arising under a treaty, within s 38 of the *Judiciary Act*, with the consequence that it lay within the exclusive original jurisdiction of the High Court.

McLelland J adverted to the matters already discussed, and to the different legal situation with respect to treaties in the United States and Australia. He concluded, however, that s 75(i) covered the case where the decision involved the interpretation of a treaty.

> Section 75 must, I think, be taken to refer to cases where the decision of the case depends upon the interpretation of the treaty. In such cases, the matter in question arises under the treaty.
>
> It is, of course, primarily the legislation which has to be interpreted but, where the terms of the treaty have by legislation been made part of the law of the land, it is in a very real sense the treaty which is being interpreted. I may add that I find it difficult to ascertain any subject-matter falling within s 75, if s 75 does not refer to the type of case I have mentioned.[122]

The defendants were subsequently allowed to amend to plead that the dealings with the shares were for the fraudulent purpose of cloaking German enemy interests and thus saving them harmless from the effects of control measures regarding German enemy interests, and that they were German enemy assets within the meaning of Art 6 of the Agreement. McLelland J held that this raised a question of the interpretation of the treaty, and that the matter was one directly arising under a treaty, so that it fell within the *exclusive* original jurisdiction of the High Court.

Miles CJ in the Supreme Court of the Australian Capital Territory rejected the decision in *Bluett* in *R v Donyadideh*.[123] The case involved a prosecution under the *Crimes (Internationally Protected Persons) Act* 1976 (Cth), which implemented an international convention. It was argued that the Supreme Court of the ACT did not have jurisdiction because the matter came within s 75, including s 75(i), and that the Commonwealth's power to vest such jurisdiction extended only to federal courts and State courts by virtue of s 77 of the Constitution. That argument was rightly rejected on the ground that s 122 –

---

122 Ibid at 261.
123 (1993) 115 ACTR 1.

the Territories power – was sufficient for the purpose. (Territorial jurisdiction is examined in Chapter 4.) Miles CJ, however, held that the matter did not come within s 75(i). He denied that it was sufficient that the interpretation of a treaty was involved, pointing to the difference in wording between s 76(ii) – matters arising under any laws made by the Parliament – and s 76(i) – matters arising under this Constitution, *or involving its interpretation*.[124] The distinction had been stressed in a number of High Court cases.[125] It followed that s 76(ii) did not extend to a matter merely because it involved the interpretation of a federal Act. Miles CJ held that the same reasoning applied to s 75(i). What was necessary for a matter to "arise under a treaty" was that the right or duty in question should owe its existence to the treaty or depend upon it for its enforcement. He concluded that the source of liability in that case was to be found in the Act rather than the treaty. This left open the question as to what possible operation s 75(i) had.

The extent of s 75(i) was raised in the High Court in *Re East; ex parte Nguyen*,[126] but the Court found it unnecessary to decide whether *Bluett v Fadden* was correct. Kirby J, however, expressed the view that it was correct because, inter alia, of the need to give meaning to the provisions of the Constitution, the principle of giving a broad interpretation to constitutional terms and the unlikelihood, in view of the power of remittal, that any inconvenience to the High Court would result.

McLelland J's judgment in *Bluett* seems restricted to the case where the legislation refers to a provision of the treaty. It would not extend to a situation where the draftsman had spelled out the provisions of the treaty and without any specific reference to it. The treaty, then, would not be interpreted. It is difficult to see how the adoption of a shorthand technique of direct reference to the treaty can intelligibly affect the situation.

Professor Lane has suggested that, by analogy to the broad interpretation given to s 76(ii) (dealt with below in Chapter 3), a right or liability established by an Act which implements a treaty should be regarded as arising under the treaty.[127] If that were the case, the only matters within that category not covered by s 76(ii) would be those that arise under a State Act which implements a treaty, such as the *Sale of Goods (Vienna Convention) Act* 1989 (Vic). It may be that Kirby J in *East* embraced this view as he referred to a right or duty which "directly or indirectly draws upon the treaty as the source of the right or duty in controversy" (at 385).

As indicated above, Mr Mark Leeming has pointed to the exceptions to the rule against treaties affecting private rights and suggested they "provide

---

124 Emphasis added.

125 *R v Commonwealth Court of Conciliation and Arbitration; ex parte Barrett* (1945) 70 CLR 141 at 152, 153; *Felton v Mulligan* (1971) 124 CLR 367 at 387, 408-409.

126 (1998) 196 CLR 354.

127 Lane, *Lane's Commentary on the Australian Constitution*, 2nd edn, 1997, pp 556-557.

content to the conferral of jurisdiction by s 75(i), refuting the contention that it is void of content".[128] He referred to a treaty that changes status, such as one recognising a foreign government, which gives rise to rights and immunity from suit, and a peace treaty which changes the status of former enemy aliens enabling them to sue without licence of the Crown.[129] He further suggested that in certain circumstances a justiciable controversy might depend on the location of international land or water boundaries determined by treaty. As Owen Dixon said in his evidence, however,[130] these results are a product of "the general law". A state of peace, alteration to boundaries or recognition of a foreign government can result from other forms of executive action, not involving a treaty. For example, while the war with Japan was terminated by treaty,[131] that with Germany was accomplished by a declaration of peace of the Governor-General.[132] On the view propounded a matter relating to the latter would not come within s 75(i), while one concerning the former would. Similarly, boundaries can be altered by non-treaty prerogative action.

Nevertheless, it may still be possible to argue that in the above circumstances a state of affairs brought about by treaty may give rise to a matter "arising under" that treaty. At the same time it seems rather unlikely that a head of jurisdiction constitutionally entrenched would be intended to have such limited use. The better approach might be, as McLelland J impliedly did, to give the phrase "arising under" an operation different from that in s 76(ii) because of the place of treaties in our legal system as compared with statutes. In any case, it will be seen later that the interpretation of "arising under" in s 76 is such that it is difficult to envisage a case where the interpretation of a federal Act is involved which does not "arise under" that Act, even though the Court insisted that there was a distinction.[133]

The Constitutional Commission had difficulty understanding the meaning of s 75(i) but, on the advice of its Advisory Committee on the Australian Judicial System, recommended that it be extended to matters involving the interpretation of a treaty. It agreed that the latter was a suitable subject of federal jurisdiction and agreed to the retention of the present subject as a head of federal jurisdiction (but not as entrenched High Court jurisdiction) because of "the possibility of a matter arising under a treaty in a manner that is beyond our present conception".[134] Up to the present the jurisdiction has served no practical purpose. The situation is made more confusing by s 38(a), which should be repealed, as the Australian Law Reform Commission has

---

128 Leeming, "Federal Treaty Jurisdiction" (1999) 10 Public LR 173 at 175.

129 Starke (1974) 48 ALJ 368.

130 Page 26 above.

131 See *Treaty of Peace (Japan) Act* 1952 (Cth). The Treaty is a schedule.

132 *Gazette*, no 49, 9 July 1951, p 1737.

133 *Felton v Mulligan* (1971) 124 CLR 367; p 68 below.

134 *Final Report of the Constitutional Commission*, 1988, p 380.

recommended.[135] Since 1984 the Court under s 44(2) of the *Judiciary Act* is empowered to remit to another court its jurisdiction under s 38(a).

It is to be noted that McLelland J's decision in *Bluett v Fadden* denied jurisdiction to the Supreme Court of New South Wales, and that he allowed the defendants (though penalised in costs) to amend specifically to raise a jurisdictional plea. If the High Court differed from McLelland J's interpretation of s 75(i) and s 38 of the *Judiciary Act*, it would on the particular facts of *Bluett v Fadden* still retain jurisdiction under s 75(iii), as the Commonwealth was a defendant. In these circumstances, it is to be noted, the State Supreme Court would have concurrent jurisdiction. But if it had not been possible to discover another head of original jurisdiction for the High Court, and if that Court had dissented from McLelland J's reading of s 75(i) and s 38 of the *Judiciary Act*, the High Court would have been obliged to dismiss the suit for want of jurisdiction. The case would then, perforce, have come up a *third* time for the *first* trial on the merits. This seems to demonstrate pretty clearly the case for the most careful scrutiny of the original and especially the exclusive original jurisdiction of the High Court.

Consuls etc : Section 75(ii)

Section 75(ii) is not a perfect transcription from the American Constitution. Ambassadors and public ministers disappear in the Australian text, and consuls, who are at the bottom of the American hierarchy, are at the head in the Australian clause. As Quick and Garran pointed out in 1901, there was good reason for this variation, as the diplomatic relations of Australia were conducted by the United Kingdom Government. More than 20 years later, three justices of the High Court found it "difficult to imagine an Ambassador to Australia".[136] At the date of federation, Australia's independent external relations were conceived as primarily commercial in character. The difference in the form of the Australian clause raises a question of interpretation. If consuls were deliberately put at the head of the list, and ambassadors and public ministers deliberately omitted, is it proper, even in the changed circumstances of today, to read the words "other representatives of other countries" as including ambassadors, ministers and other distinctively diplomatic representatives? It might fairly be argued that in these circumstances it would not be proper to read the words "other representatives of other countries" as including superior diplomatic representatives. Should the problem arise, however, it is likely that the Court would read those words as including "all persons officially accredited to the Commonwealth by foreign governments".[137] This was the meaning suggested by Quick and Garran, who never,

---

135 *Report on the Judicial Power of the Commonwealth*, 2001, p 183.
136 *Commonwealth v New South Wales* (1923) 32 CLR 200 at 208 per Isaacs, Rich and Starke JJ.
137 Quick and Garran, op cit p 772.

of course, envisaged that such representatives would include ambassadors and ministers.

The Australian Constitutional Convention, the Advisory Committee to the Constitutional Commission and the Constitutional Commission recommended that the paragraph be altered to read "Affecting ambassadors, high commissioners, consuls or other representatives of other countries". If it is the international status of the parties that makes it a suitable subject of federal jurisdiction it should be extended to representatives of international bodies and supra-national groups, such as the European Union, which are not "countries".

There are other problems of interpretation. The Australian clause followed American precedent in copying the word "*affecting*" consuls. When does a matter *affect* a consul? This has occasioned some difficulty in the United States.[138] Is the jurisdiction of the High Court attracted by a matter in which a consul is affected in his or her *private* capacity? Quick and Garran pointed to this uncertainty and expressed the opinion that the clause applied only to consuls and other representatives in their official capacities.[139] These difficulties and obscurities were mentioned by Mr Dixon in his evidence before the Royal Commission in 1927.

> When does a matter affect a consul? He may be prosecuted in the police court for failing to register his dog; he may be sued for money borrowed. He may, and often does, conduct an independent business as well as exercise the office of consul. Do all proceedings arising out of the business affect him so that in all his legal relations he is the subject of federal jurisdiction? If he is an employer, and the party to an industrial dispute, and is summoned to a compulsory conference in the Arbitration Court, does this raise a question under s 75(ii)?[140]

Quick and Garran's view that a matter arises under s 75(ii) only when a consul is acting in his official capacity has the clear merit of restricting the jurisdiction, but the matter is still unresolved. It is unfortunate that the founding fathers, who had sufficient perspicacity to see that the American model was in some respects inapplicable to Australian conditions in 1900, did not apparently see these other difficulties and obscurities in the clause. This seems to be another case of transcribing blindly. It may be, as stated in earlier editions, that they should have asked a question put by Mr Dixon: "Why should a State court be any the less fit to entertain litigation affecting ... [a consul] ... than it was when it was a court of a colony?"[141] So far as the High Court is concerned

---

138 Small and Jayson (eds), *The Constitution of the United States of America*, 1964, p 645.

139 Op cit p 772. See also Lumb and Moens, *Constitution of the Commonwealth of Australia Annotated*, 5th edn, 1995, p 394. Contra Lane, *Lane's Commentary on the Australian Constitution*, 2nd edn, 1997, p 558.

140 Minutes of Evidence, p 785.

141 Ibid.

there is no justification for burdening it with this jurisdiction. As the Court now exercises the wide power of remittal under s 44 of the *Judiciary Act* it would no doubt require an unusual case for it to hear and determine a matter under s 75(ii).

Commonwealth or States as Parties : Section 75(iii), (iv)

Section 75(iii) and (iv) deal with matters in which the Commonwealth or States are parties. Section 75(iv) also provides for jurisdiction in matters between residents of different States. In this particular case, except for the substitution of the word "residents" for "citizens", and for the investment of original jurisdiction in the High Court instead of in an inferior federal court, the Australian founding fathers once again transcribed the American diversity jurisdiction provisions without any inquiry as to their applicability to Australian conditions or needs. The diversity clause will be considered in detail at a later stage.[142]

Section 75(iii) confers original jurisdiction on the High Court in matters in which the Commonwealth, or a party suing or being sued on behalf of the Commonwealth, is a party. Section 75(iv), excluding the diversity clause, confers jurisdiction in matters between States or between a State and a resident of another State. Sections 38, 57 and 59 of the *Judiciary Act* make special provision with respect to States. Section 56(1) of the *Judiciary Act* provides that a person making a claim against the Commonwealth, whether in contract or tort, may in respect of the claim bring a suit against the Commonwealth in the High Court, the Supreme Court of a State or Territory in which the claim arose or any court of competent jurisdiction of the State or Territory where the claim arose. "Court of competent jurisdiction" includes any court exercising jurisdiction in the capital city of a State or the principal or only city or town of a Territory which would be competent to hear the suit if the Commonwealth were and had at any time been a resident in that city or town.

Section 58 makes provision for suits against a State, whether in contract or tort, in matters within federal jurisdiction, but requires the claim to be brought in the High Court (if it has original jurisdiction) or in the Supreme Court of the State. Until 1960 a person suing the Commonwealth was also compelled to choose the Supreme Court of a State as an alternative to the High Court. While s 56 was amended to provide as a forum a wider range of State courts, no similar amendment has been made to s 58 where, for example, there is a suit between a State and a resident of another State. It is difficult to see why this distinction has been made.

Article III, s 2, of the United States Constitution declared that controversies to which the United States was a party were matters of federal jurisdiction. It also included controversies between two or more States, and

---

142 See Chapter 2.

between a State and a citizen of another State, as matters of federal jurisdiction, and declared further that all cases of federal jurisdiction in which a State was a party should fall within the original jurisdiction of the Supreme Court of the United States. It is interesting to note that in this respect suits involving the *United States* and *States* as parties were differently treated. The principle on which controversies involving the United States as a party were assigned to federal jurisdiction was stated by Story in terms of the proposition that a sovereign must have the power to sue in his own courts, and that, unless such a power were given, the enforcement of the rights of the national government would be at the mercy of the States. This "would prostrate the Union at the feet of the States. It would compel the national government to become a supplicant for justice before the judicature of those who were by other parts of the Constitution placed in subordination to it".[143] This has very little relevance to Australian conditions, as was shown by the willingness of the Commonwealth Parliament to submit most cases involving the Commonwealth as a party to the concurrent jurisdiction of State courts. No doubt the explanation for its inclusion in the Australian Constitution was the disposition to copy the American heads of federal jurisdiction without overmuch thought. Perhaps here there was some general feeling that it was appropriate that cases involving the Commonwealth as a party should properly find their way into the original jurisdiction of the one constitutionally entrenched national tribunal.

The assignment to the original jurisdiction of the Supreme Court of the United States of cases in which a State is a party was justified by Hamilton on the basis that "in cases in which a State might happen to be a party, it would ill suit its dignity to be turned over to an inferior tribunal".[144] The dignity of the United States was, apparently, less easily outraged. As the plan of original jurisdiction was elaborated, the Supreme Court was given *exclusive* original jurisdiction in suits between States, while this original jurisdiction was made *concurrent* in the case of suits between the United States and a State and in actions and proceedings by a State against the citizens of another State or against aliens. The Eleventh Amendment foreclosed a suit by a citizen of another State or an alien against a State.

In Australia, the case of suits between States appears to be one in which there is good sense in the grant of original jurisdiction to the High Court. The position of the States in the Australian constitutional framework is such that it seems most appropriate to have justiciable disputes between them tried in the High Court. Similar considerations apply to suits between the Commonwealth and a State. In all these cases, as we have seen, the jurisdiction of the High Court was made exclusive. On the other hand, it is doubtful whether in suits between a State and a resident of another State there was any particular justification for conferring original jurisdiction. Here the considerations of

---

143 *Commentaries*, s 1674.
144 *Federalist Papers*, no 81.

policy were substantially the same as those involved in the grant of diversity jurisdiction – the fear of partiality or bias on the part of a State court. The arguments against the grant of original jurisdiction in diversity matters in Australia[145] apply equally in this case.

Since 1984 the High Court has had power, under s 44(2) of the *Judiciary Act*, to remit to other courts suits between States and between the Commonwealth and a State. Section 44(2A) enables remittal to the Federal Court of matters in which the Commonwealth or a person suing or being sued on behalf of the Commonwealth is a party. The validity of these provisions is discussed later.[146]

The terms of s 75(iii) were rather different from those of Art III, s 2. In the first place, in the United States Constitution federal jurisdiction was conferred in controversies "to which the United States shall be a party". In the Australian clause, the High Court's original jurisdiction extended to matters in which the Commonwealth *or a person suing or being sued on behalf of the Commonwealth* is a party. The italicised words indicate that it was part of the constitutional plan that the Commonwealth should be liable to suit, and s 78 of the Constitution specifically authorised the making of laws conferring rights to proceed against the Commonwealth or a State in respect of matters within the limits of the judicial power. As Dixon J said in *Bank of New South Wales v Commonwealth (Bank Nationalisation Case)*:[147] "The purpose of s 75(iii) obviously was to ensure that the political organisation called into existence under the name of the Commonwealth and armed with enumerated powers and authorities, limited by definition, fell in every way within a jurisdiction in which it could be impleaded and which it could invoke." He went on to observe that this clause should be read together with s 75(v), conferring jurisdiction in matters in which mandamus or prohibition or an injunction is sought against an officer of the Commonwealth, "which, it is apparent, was written into the instrument to make it constitutionally certain that there would be a jurisdiction capable of restraining officers of the Commonwealth from exceeding Federal power".[148]

In *Commonwealth v New South Wales*,[149] there was a strong expression of opinion by the majority that s 75(iii) itself imposed a substantive liability in tort on the Commonwealth. In that case, the Commonwealth brought an action in the original jurisdiction of the High Court claiming damages in respect of a collision between ships belonging to the plaintiff Commonwealth and the defendant State. The majority in the High Court overruled the defendant State's objection to the jurisdiction, and expressed the opinion that s 75(iii)

---

145 See pp 85-88 below.
146 Pages 83-84 below.
147 (1948) 76 CLR 1 at 363.
148 Ibid at 363. See also per Starke J at 321.
149 (1923) 32 CLR 200.

enabled the Commonwealth to sue a State in tort without need for legislation under s 78, which, in their view, applied to s 76 but not to s 75 of the Constitution. It was said that s 75 of the Constitution, which bound Commonwealth and States alike, imposed tortious liability on the Crown in right of the Commonwealth or a State. The majority thought that the word "matters" in s 75 included actions in tort and, on the reasoning of the Privy Council in *Farnell v Bowman*,[150] it was said that the provision of jurisdiction to entertain such actions also imposed substantive liability in tort on the Crown. Higgins J dissented, arguing that s 75(iii) conferred jurisdiction only, and that the source of substantive tortious liability must be found elsewhere. If the view of the majority were correct, it would apply equally to cases arising under s 75(iv), as was pointed out by Evatt J in *New South Wales v Bardolph*,[151] which was an action in the original jurisdiction of the High Court between a resident of South Australia and the State of New South Wales.

The reasoning of the majority in *Commonwealth v New South Wales* was sharply criticised by Mr Dixon in his evidence before the Royal Commission[152] and this criticism was adopted in the Report of the Commission.[153] On the other hand, it was approved by Evatt J on a number of occasions in the High Court.[154] There was, however, considerable judicial criticism of the reasoning in the High Court, notably by Dixon J. He pointed to some of the difficulties in *Musgrave v Commonwealth*[155] and in *Werrin v Commonwealth*[156] he elaborated this criticism:

> If it were not for the views expressed in the joint judgment [in *Commonwealth v New South Wales*] I should have felt little or no hesitation in saying that the Federal Parliament had complete authority over all ordinary causes of action against the Commonwealth and over the remedies for enforcing them. I should have thought that the right of the subject to recover from the Crown in right of the Commonwealth, whether in contract or in tort, is the creation of the law which the Federal Parliament controls. No doubt when a jurisdiction is conferred like that given by s 75(iii) and (iv) the source whence the substantive law is to be derived for determining the duties of the governments presents difficulties. But I should not have thought that s 75 itself could be the source of the substantive liability.

---

150 (1887) 12 App Cas 643.

151 (1934) 52 CLR 455. See also *Daly v Victoria* (1920) 28 CLR 395 at 400.

152 Page 785.

153 Pages 102-103. See, however, Moore, "Suits Between States Within the British Empire" (1925) 7 Journal of Comparative Law 155 at 161.

154 *New South Wales v Commonwealth (No 1)* (1932) 46 CLR 155 at 210-211, 215; *New South Wales v Bardolph* (1934) 52 CLR 455 at 458-459; *Heinemann v Commonwealth* (1935) 54 CLR 126 at 129; *Musgrave v Commonwealth* (1937) 57 CLR 514.

155 (1937) 57 CLR 514 at 546.

156 (1938) 59 CLR 150 at 167.

Werrin v Commonwealth exposed a peculiar difficulty arising from the majority reasoning in *Commonwealth v New South Wales. Werrin's Case* involved a money claim against the Commonwealth and raised the question whether the Commonwealth Parliament might legislatively extinguish a cause of action against the Commonwealth. In *Musgrave v Commonwealth*, Dixon J had observed that if the reasoning in *Commonwealth v New South Wales* were correct, so that tort liability was imposed on the Commonwealth by force of the Constitution itself, this liability could not, presumably, be impaired or controlled by legislation. In *Werrin's Case*, he again adverted to this difficulty, but said that this consequence was probably not intended by the majority in *Commonwealth v New South Wales*. In any event, Dixon J said that he was "not prepared to interpret the joint judgment as deciding that s 75 provides a source of substantive liability so that no Act of the Commonwealth Parliament can extinguish a cause of action which has accrued against the Commonwealth".[157]

In *Werrin*, Dixon J said that, in relation to the question of the actionable liability of the Crown, the distinction between substance and procedure had never been steadily maintained. One way of accounting for the absence of Crown liability for tort was the principle that the Crown could not be sued without its consent and no fiat could be granted for a petition of right for tort. The case of *Farnell v Bowman* held that the grant of a general remedy against the Crown made torts committed on its behalf actionable. This assumed that the Crown's substantive responsibility existed in law but was a duty of imperfect obligation. On that basis one could treat the obligation as having been made perfect by the creation of a jurisdiction in s 75.

After *Werrin* many judges attributed the liability of the Commonwealth to s 56 of the *Judiciary Act*.[158] Others regarded the liability as based on a combination of ss 56 and 64 or on s 64 alone.[159] Section 64 provides, in part, that in a suit to which the Commonwealth is a party the rights of the parties shall as nearly as possible be the same as in a suit between subject and subject.

In *Commonwealth v Mewett*,[160] a majority of the High Court (Brennan CJ, Gaudron, Gummow and Kirby JJ) followed the view expressed by Dixon J and held that the liability of the Commonwealth in tort was created by the common law. Gummow and Kirby JJ (with whom Brennan CJ and Gaudron J agreed on this point) said that the creation of the jurisdiction in s 75(iii) denied the Commonwealth any executive immunity from suit in respect of that common law action. Section 56 of the *Judiciary Act* recognises rather than creates

---

157 Ibid at 168.

158 *Washington v Commonwealth* (1939) 39 SR (NSW) 133 at 140, 142; *James v Commonwealth* (1939) 62 CLR 339; *Suehle v Commonwealth* (1967) 116 CLR 353.

159 *Maguire v Simpson* (1977) 139 CLR 362; *Commonwealth v Evans Deakin Industries Ltd* (1986) 161 CLR 254.

160 (1997) 191 CLR 471.

Commonwealth liability. This approach leaves the Commonwealth Parliament free to legislate to abolish, reduce or increase Commonwealth liability as illustrated by s 64 of the *Judiciary Act*.

It is to be noted that s 75(iii) confers jurisdiction in a matter in which a person suing or being sued on behalf of the Commonwealth is a party. These words do not appear in Art III, s 2, of the United States Constitution, which simply includes within the scope of federal jurisdiction cases to which the United States is a party. It was early settled that this head of federal jurisdiction did not, of itself, authorise suit against the United States without the consent of Congress expressed in a general or special enactment.[161] The harshness of this rule was mitigated by the rule that a servant or agent of the United States Government was personally liable and could not defend simply on a plea of authorisation or direction by the executive government. As Dixon J noted in the *Bank Nationalisation Case*,[162] this gave rise to a readiness to admit proceedings against officers or agencies of the United States in respect of claims in which they had little or no personal interest, and in which the United States was the party really affected. There was a disposition in the cases to determine the question whether the United States was a party to a case by reference to the actual party on the record, even though it might be clear that the named party (for example, the Postmaster-General) was not, and the United States was, the substantial party in interest to the actual controversy. As Higgins J observed in *R v Murray and Cormie*,[163] "it was no doubt because of these decisions that in s 75(iii) of the Constitution the words were added 'or a person suing or being sued on behalf of the Commonwealth'". This ensured that the scope of the jurisdiction was wide enough to cover cases in which the Commonwealth was a named party and also those in which officers and agencies of the Government were suing or being sued in their official or governmental capacities.[164] As the course of American authority evolved, considerable difficulty was experienced, and it was not found possible to maintain the test based simply on the party disclosed on the face of the record. It was found necessary to draw a distinction between cases in which a suit was brought against officials in respect of acts for which they were personally responsible – where the action would lie against the official only – and cases in which suit was brought against an official "in respect of acts ... in which it is sought to affect the interests of the United States by suing him in his official capacity".[165] In the latter situation it was held that the action was, in effect,

---

161 See Wright, *Law of Federal Courts*, 5th edn, 1994, p 128. See also *Bank of New South Wales v Commonwealth* (1948) 76 CLR 1 at 364 et seq per Dixon J.

162 (1948) 76 CLR 1 at 364.

163 (1916) 22 CLR 437 at 468.

164 *Bank Nationalisation Case* (1948) 76 CLR 1 at 367 per Dixon J.

165 Ibid at 365.

against the United States and could not be brought without congressional consent.[166]

The meaning of the words "person suing or being sued on behalf of the Commonwealth" fell to be considered by the High Court in the *Bank Nationalisation Case*. The problem arose out of provisions which authorised the acquisition of the assets of private trading banks by the Treasurer of the Commonwealth. The assets so acquired were vested in the Commonwealth Bank, which was an incorporated body. Liability to pay compensation for assets so acquired was imposed on the Commonwealth Bank. Failing agreement, the quantum of compensation was to be determined *exclusively* by a Court of Claims established under s 71 of the Constitution and invested with jurisdiction as a superior court of record under s 77. The object was to shut out the original jurisdiction of the High Court. It was clearly not possible to do this if the case fell within s 75(iii), as the original jurisdiction of the High Court under s 75 was constitutionally guaranteed. The question then was whether the Commonwealth Bank was a person being sued on behalf of the Commonwealth.

The problem was posed by Dixon J in these terms:

> Does the third paragraph of s 75 intend to give a jurisdiction confined to matters in which the Crown ... is itself a party, whether suing or sued in the name of the King *or by the Attorney-General or some other officer or nominal party authorised for the purpose as a matter of procedure*[167] or, on the other hand, does the paragraph intend to place within the jurisdiction of the High Court all matters in which a claim of right is made by or against any part of the central government of the country in its executive department including the corporate and other agencies by which it is administered?[168]

Four members of the Court – Rich, Starke, Dixon and Williams JJ – had no doubt that the latter alternative was to be preferred. The question then arose whether the Commonwealth Bank was an agency or instrumentality of the Commonwealth so as to bring it within the definition of a person being sued on behalf of the Commonwealth and these four judges had little difficulty in holding, after examination of its structure and functions, that the Commonwealth Bank was such an agency or instrumentality. As Starke J put it, this was "manifest"[169] from a study of the provisions of the relevant Acts. Latham CJ and McTiernan J dissented. The Chief Justice said that in order to

---

166 "This extreme view [ie, that the United States was only a party where it was named on the record] has been modified in more recent decisions; and it may be accepted that the same result has been achieved by judicial decisions as in s 75(iii) of our Constitution by express words", per Higgins J in *R v Murray and Cormie* (1916) 22 CLR 437 at 468. See Wright, op cit pp 130-131.

167 Italics supplied.

168 *Bank Nationalisation Case* (1948) 76 CLR 1 at 358.

169 Ibid at 322.

determine whether a case fell within the terms of s 75(iii) it was necessary to find out who was actually being sued and then to ask whether that person was being sued on behalf of the Commonwealth. If it were the Attorney-General or a minister or a nominal defendant, the answer would be easy. Here, however, the defendant was the Bank and any allegation with respect to any alleged liability of the Commonwealth was irrelevant. "Accordingly, in my opinion, in such an action the corporation which was the defendant (the Commonwealth Bank) would be shown by the record not to be a person being sued on behalf of the Commonwealth, and the action would not come within the provisions of s 75(iii)."[170] Latham CJ went on to examine the structure of the Bank to determine whether it might be properly described as a department of the Commonwealth Government.

The approach of the majority in the *Bank Nationalisation Case* was followed in *Inglis v Commonwealth Trading Bank of Australia*,[171] where the Court held (Barwick CJ, Kitto and Windeyer JJ; Owen J dissenting) that a suit against the Commonwealth Trading Bank was a matter within s 75(iii) of the Constitution. Kitto J (with whom the other two majority judges agreed) regarded the conclusion of the majority in the *Bank Nationalisation Case* as based on the following statement by Dixon J: "[T]he purpose of providing a jurisdiction which might be invoked by or against the Commonwealth could not, in modern times, be adequately attained and secured against colourable evasion, unless it was expressed so as to cover the enforcement of actionable rights and liabilities of officers and agencies in their official and governmental capacity, when in substance they formed part of or represented the Commonwealth".[172] Dixon and Starke JJ, in arguing for a broad interpretation of the scope of the jurisdiction conferred by s 75(iii), took the view that an authority did not have to be within the shield of the Crown in the strict sense to attract the jurisdiction. Rich and Williams JJ were prepared to hold that in regard to the activities involved in that case the bank was an agent of the Crown in the strict sense. This aspect was not discussed in the *Inglis Case*. It is suggested, however, that if the purpose of the jurisdiction is taken to be that stated in the passage from Dixon J's judgment, set out above, the principles relating to whether a body is within the shield of the Crown cannot be conclusive. As His Honour pointed out, the question whether a statutory instrumentality should be given the privileges and immunities of the Crown is one for Parliament to determine.[173] But if one of the purposes of s 75(iii) is to secure jurisdiction "against colourable evasion" parliamentary intention cannot be the test.

170　(1948) 76 CLR 1 at 226.
171　(1969) 119 CLR 334.
172　Ibid at 367.
173　76 CLR 1 at 359.

Therefore, the fact that a corporation or other body does not enjoy the immunity of the Commonwealth does not answer the question whether it is "the Commonwealth or a person suing or being sued on behalf of the Commonwealth". In *Maguire v Simpson*,[174] Jacobs J said that, for the reasons given by Dixon J, s 75(iii) should be given a broad interpretation. It followed that merely because a body came within the description in s 75(iii) did not mean it was entitled to the Commonwealth's privileges and immunities derived from the prerogative. That statement was followed later by McHugh and Gummow JJ when they said that there was a lack of identity between the bodies included in the words of s 75(iii) and those entitled to the benefit of the implied constitutional doctrine illustrated by *Commonwealth v Cigamatic Pty Ltd*[175] under which the Commonwealth is not bound by State legislation in certain circumstances.[176]

Section 75(iv) refers to matters between States, or between residents of different States, or between a State and a resident of another State. What bearing have the cases defining the subject of s 75(iii) on the meaning of "States" or "State" in s 75(iv)? In the cases holding that a body is within s 75(iii), there have been differences of opinion whether it is "the Commonwealth" or "a person suing or being sued" on its behalf. In *Inglis*, for example, Barwick CJ placed the bank in the former category,[177] while Kitto J regarded it as in the latter.[178] In *Maguire v Simpson*, Barwick CJ changed his mind, but Mason J agreed with his earlier view.[179] For the purpose of s 75(iii) it is not important to determine the particular category to which a body, included within s 75(iii), belongs. However, the issue becomes important in arguing or deciding whether a body is a "State" within the meaning of s 75(iv). That provision refers only to "State" or "States" and not to persons suing or being sued on their behalf. Section 38(b) of the *Judiciary Act*, on the other hand, makes exclusive to the High Court (subject now to the power of remitter in s 44): "suits between States or between persons suing or being sued on behalf of different States or between a State or a person suing or being sued on behalf of another State".[180]

---

174 (1977) 139 CLR 362 at 406.

175 (1962) 108 CLR 372.

176 *Re Residential Tenancies Tribunal (NSW); ex parte Defence Housing Authority* (1997) 190 CLR 410 at 458, 464-465. See also *State Bank of New South Wales v Commonwealth Savings Bank of Australia* (1986) 161 CLR 639 at 648-649.

177 (1969) 119 CLR 334 at 336.

178 Ibid at 342.

179 (1977) 139 CLR 362 at 398.

180 Paragraphs (c) and (d), referring to suits between the Commonwealth and a State, use the same phrase. These paragraphs are in any case supported by s 75(iii) because the other party comes within the wording of s 75(iii), but the issue is relevant, as a matter of statutory interpretation, to the question whether the High Court has exclusive jurisdiction in the matter.

In *Crouch v Commissioner of Railways (Qld)*,[181] it was held that a suit between a resident of Western Australia and the Commissioner of Railways of Queensland was a matter within s 75(iv). The Commissioner, a corporation sole, was created by statute. It was argued that the matter was, at best, a suit against a person who was being sued on behalf of the State, while the High Court's jurisdiction required the defendant to be the State itself. The distinction between the wording of s 75(iii) and (iv) was used to support the argument.

In upholding its jurisdiction the High Court seemed to regard the concept of "State" in s 75(iv) as having a breadth that was the same as, or similar to, the more extended wording of s 75(iii). That view was justified on two grounds. First, it was pointed out that para (iii) refers to the Commonwealth as a "party". As explained earlier, the equivalent American provision does not have the extended phrase. There was a tendency to determine whether the United States was a party by reference to the party named. That was largely motivated by avoidance of the immunity from suit of the United States. The phrase in s 75(iii), the Court said, was intended to ensure that "the Commonwealth" included its instrumentalities and agents.[182] But, they pointed out, in s 75(iv) the word "party" is not used;[183] therefore, there was no inhibition on giving the paragraph a broad interpretation which referred to the substance of the controversy rather than the mere form of the legal proceedings. Elsewhere in the Constitution "State" had been given a similarly wide interpretation. (For example, in *Sydney Municipal Council v Commonwealth*,[184] it was held that a municipal rate was a tax imposed by the State for the purposes of s 114 of the Constitution, which prevents a State from taxing Commonwealth property.)

The second ground for rejecting s 75(iii) as a reason for a restrictive interpretation of s 75(iv) was that the term "matter" in s 75 was one of substance and not to be determined merely by the form of the proceedings. If the party sued is an instrumentality through which the State Government discharges its functions, even though it is a separate corporation, the matter is "in substance" one involving the State.[185]

While there is general agreement that the words of s 75(iii) and (iv) should be given a broad interpretation so as to further their policy of preventing "colourable evasion" of jurisdiction by the Commonwealth or a State, the question of how one determines whether a separate entity is an instrumentality of government for the purpose of s 75 has not been clearly answered by the Court. In *State Bank of New South Wales v Commonwealth Savings Bank of Australia*,[186] the State bank was not under the direct control of the executive government. In holding that it was a "State" for purposes of

---

181 (1985) 159 CLR 22.
182 Ibid at 40-41.
183 Ibid at 42.
184 (1904) 1 CLR 208.
185 (1985) 159 CLR 22 at 33, 37-39.
186 (1986) 161 CLR 639.

s 75(iv) and that the suit came within s 38(d) of the *Judiciary Act* the Court relied on the accumulated effect of a number of factors, including the absence of corporators, the power of the Governor to appoint six of the seven directors (indicating a measure of control), the public character of its objectives, the guarantee of payments by the Government, the payment of profits into consolidated revenue, scrutiny by the auditor-general, and a (somewhat narrow) power to make by-laws.

The Court said[187] that the issue of executive control was "obviously an issue of central importance". The control over the bank (which was found sufficient) was largely indirect, being that which was reflected in the power of appointing members of the governing body. As the Commonwealth or a State might choose to conduct an activity or exercise a function by means of an independent statutory body, it is suggested that the degree of control by the executive government should not be regarded as an important factor provided other indicia of a "public body" exercising "public functions" are present.

There is no need for the High Court to be given original jurisdiction in all matters in which the Commonwealth is a party provided either the State courts or a federal court has the jurisdiction, and the High Court can exercise its appellate jurisdiction under s 73 of the Constitution. This policy was reflected in the recommendation of the Constitutional Commission that s 75(iii) remain within the original jurisdiction of the High Court, but empowering Parliament to limit or exclude the jurisdiction to the extent that it has been conferred on State and Territory courts or a federal court.[188]

Section 75(iii), together with s 75(v), provide a constitutional guarantee that there is a jurisdiction in which the Commonwealth and its officers are made accountable for observance of the law, including the Constitution. The High Court's jurisdiction in s 30(a) of the *Judiciary Act* in respect of matters arising under the Constitution or involving its interpretation is not entrenched in s 75, but derives from s 76(i) and, so, is left to the discretion of Parliament. As mentioned below, the State courts probably do not have any State jurisdiction in matters where the Commonwealth is a defendant, even apart from the operation of s 39 of the *Judiciary Act*.[189] So, s 75(iii) and (v) ensure that there is a jurisdiction to deal, among other things, with the constitutional validity of Commonwealth legislation and executive action.

Suits Between Governments

There can be little doubt about the propriety of the grant of original jurisdiction to the High Court in suits between governments. It is appropriate that justiciable disputes between governments should be submitted in the first

---

187 Ibid at 648.
188 *Final Report of the Constitutional Commission*, 1988, vol 1, p 374.
189 See p 47 below.

instance to the highest national tribunal and s 75(iii) and (iv) provide for such cases.

Suits between governments have provided the great body of case law in the original jurisdiction of the Supreme Court of the United States. It was established in *United States v Texas*[190] that the Supreme Court had original jurisdiction in suits between the United States and a State. The most spectacular modern instances of the jurisdiction authorised by *United States v Texas* were the famous *Tidelands Oil* disputes.[191] There have been many important cases involving suits between States. Such cases, as we have seen, lie within the exclusive jurisdiction of the Supreme Court. Boundary disputes were the first cases between States in which the Supreme Court exercised this jurisdiction. Latterly, other problems have loomed large, and the great development of irrigation, flood control and hydro electric power has given rise to many disputes over water rights. Other cases have arisen out of disputes over sewage disposal, claims to natural gas, double taxation, and so on. Suits between States are the most numerous class of suits heard by the Supreme Court in its original jurisdiction.[192] The first of the boundary cases was *Rhode Island v Massachusetts*.[193] There the Court asserted its power to decide a boundary dispute despite the refusal of the respondent State to enter an appearance. A further challenge to the jurisdiction, on the ground that the questions involved in boundary disputes were political and not justiciable, was unsuccessfully raised in *Virginia v West Virginia*.[194] Some doubts have been expressed, both judicially and extra-judicially, as to the effectiveness and utility of this jurisdiction. As Frankfurter J observed in *Texas v Florida*:[195]

> There are practical limits to the efficacy of the adjudicatory process in the adjustment of inter-state controversies. The limitations of litigation – its episodic character, its necessarily restricted scope of inquiry, its confined regard for considerations of policy, its dependence on the contingencies of a particular record, and other circumscribing factors – often denature and even mutilate the actualities of a problem and thereby render the litigious process unsuited for its solution.[196]

---

190   143 US 621 (1892).

191   *US v California* 332 US 19 (1947); *US v Louisiana* 339 US 699 (1950); *US v Texas* 339 US 707 (1950). See *Hart and Wechsler*, op cit p 306.

192   Wright, *Federal Courts*, 5th edn, 1994, p 808. For a list of all cases in original jurisdiction to 1959, see appendix to "The Original Jurisdiction of the United States Supreme Court" (1959) 11 Stanford LR 665. For cases between 1960 and 1993, see McKusick, "Discretionary Gatekeeping" (1993) Maine LR 185.

193   12 Pet 657 (1838).

194   11 Wall 39 (1871).

195   306 US 398 at 428 (1939).

196   See also *Pennsylvania v West Virginia* 262 US 553 (1923) per Brandeis J. See note in (1926) 39 Harvard LR 1084 at 1087: "The method of settling interstate disputes by original suit in the Supreme Court must be regarded as subordinate to the other method provided in the Constitution, that of compacts." See also Heady (1940) 26 Washington ULQ 61.

Nonetheless, Frankfurter J and other judges have pointed out that this juris-diction serves important ends in the working of American federalism.[197]

In Australia there have been many actions between Commonwealth and States, and between States.[198] In many of these, substantive constitutional ques-tions have been involved. Others, like *Commonwealth v New South Wales*,[199] involved a simple tort claim as between the parties. The only Australian case raising a boundary dispute was *South Australia v Victoria*.[200] The action was framed as a claim for possession of the land in dispute, for an injunction to restrain the defendants from further acts of trespass, and other similar remedies. The defendants raised an objection to jurisdiction on the ground that the matter was not justiciable before federation, that it was "undoubtedly political"[201] and that the proper authority to decide the dispute was the King in Council. It was argued further that the American authorities supporting the existence of original jurisdiction in boundary disputes were distinguishable.

The High Court stated that its jurisdiction was limited to the determination of *justiciable* disputes, and noted that the American and Australian situations, as at the date of federation, were not identical. At the date of federation in the United States there were existing boundary disputes between several States. Moreover, the American federation was a union of sovereign States whose boundary disagreements were analogous to disputes between independent nations, and subject to no clearly established binding law. When the United States Constitution was enacted provision was made as a matter of necessity for the settlement of these disputes by conferring jurisdiction on the Supreme Court in controversies between States. In Australia the situation was different, because the States were subject to the authority of imperial law. It was sug-gested that this might make for a difference in the character of the boundary disputes which could be decided by the courts in the two federations.[202] Nonetheless, the Commonwealth Constitution by s 75(iv) conferred original

---

197 *Texas v Florida* 306 US 398 at 428 (1939). See also Scott, "Judicial Settlement of Contro-versies Between States of the Union", passim; Caldwell, "The Settlement of Interstate Disputes" (1920) 14 AJIL 38 at 68; Heady, "Suits by States Within the Original Jurisdiction of the Supreme Court" (1940) 26 Washington ULQ 61; Barnes, "Suits Between States in the Supreme Court" (1954) 7 Vanderbilt LR 494.

198 See Moore, "The Federation and Suits Between Governments" (1935) 17 Journal of Comparative Law (3rd series) 163; Campbell, "Suits Between the Governments of a Federation" (1971) 6 Sydney LR 309.

199 (1923) 32 CLR 200.

200 (1911) 12 CLR 667.

201 Ibid at 672.

202 "When, in the framing of the United States Constitution, the power to adjudicate in 'contro-versies between the States' was conferred on the Supreme Court of the United States, it was clearly intended to vest in that tribunal all the power of settlement and adjudication which up to then had been exercised by the Confederation, that is to say, the power to determine matters not justiciable as well as matters justiciable ... The Australian Constitution, on the other hand, limits the power of settling disputes between States in boundary disputes, as in other cases, to those in which the matters in controversy can be determined by the application of recognised legal principles." Ibid at 708-709 per O'Connor J.

jurisdiction in plain terms in matters between States. It followed that boundary disputes fell within the scope of the clause provided that they were, as here, capable of being determined on recognised legal principles. The test of justiciability in disputes between States was propounded by Griffith CJ:

> In my opinion a matter between States, in order to be justiciable, must be such that a controversy of like nature could arise between individual persons, and must be such that it can be determined upon principles of law. This definition includes all controversies relating to the ownership of property or arising out of contracts.[203]

It was held that the claim in this case satisfied the test of justiciability.

Having regard to the point of distinction between the original jurisdiction of the Supreme Court of the United States and the High Court which was made in this case, it should be noted that the Supreme Court has, on a number of occasions, shown reluctance to assume jurisdiction in suits between States. It has refused leave to file an original complaint on the ground that the State has failed to allege sufficient injury, that the controversy is not justiciable, that it is premature, and so forth.[204] The Supreme Court has also been faced with the problem of deciding whether a State is a real party in interest in such an action. Jurisdiction has been denied in suits which, on their face, appear to be suits between States, but which are brought by a State on behalf of individual citizens.[205] The assumption of jurisdiction in such cases would defeat the object of the Eleventh Amendment, which forbids suits by citizens of one State against another State. The principle upon which jurisdiction will be assumed or declined has been stated as being that the State has the right as parens patriae to protect its citizens in respect of its quasi-sovereign interests and to invoke the original jurisdiction of the Supreme Court for that purpose; but it does not have standing as parens patriae to represent a citizen for the purpose of enforcing his individual claims in contract, tort or under statute.[206] This problem is of no significance in Australia, as an individual resident of a State may freely bring an action against another State in the original jurisdiction of the High Court under s 75(iv). The Eleventh Amendment has no Australian counterpart.

Writs and Remedies Against Public Officers: Section 75(iii) and (v)

Section 75(v): matters in which a writ of mandamus or prohibition or an injunction is sought against an officer of the Commonwealth was, as we have seen, written into the Commonwealth Constitution because it was not in the

---

203 Ibid at 675.
204 See Barnes (1954) 7 Vanderbilt LR at 508 et seq.
205 See *New Hampshire v Louisiana* 108 US 74 (1883). Compare *South Dakota v North Carolina* 192 US 286 (1904). See also *North Dakota v Minnesota* 263 US 365 (1923). *Pennsylvania v New Jersey* 426 US 660 (1976).
206 See Moore, *Commentary on the US Judicial Code*, 1949, pp 624-625.

United States Constitution; and the power of the Supreme Court of the United States to issue mandamus in its original jurisdiction against a non-judicial officer of the United States had been expressly denied in *Marbury v Madison*.[207] It appears to have been accepted that a State court exercising State[208] jurisdiction could not issue a mandamus against an officer of the Commonwealth. In *Ex parte Goldring*,[209] it was held by the Supreme Court of New South Wales that in the exercise of its State jurisdiction it had no power to grant an application to make absolute a rule nisi for mandamus against the Commonwealth Collector of Customs. The Court relied on American authority, and the principle was stated by Stephen ACJ: "We cannot compel a federal officer to discharge a duty which he owes to the Federal Government … He owes no duty to the State Government."[210] The proposition goes beyond the single case of mandamus, and the accepted view is that in its State jurisdiction a State court could not entertain a suit against the Commonwealth, or grant prohibition against an officer of the Commonwealth.[211]

Some reference has already been made to the history of this clause in the Federal Conventions.[212] Its most redoubtable opponent was Mr Isaacs, who argued[213] first that it was unnecessary because s 75(iii) provided all necessary power, and second that the mention of the particular remedies named in s 75(v) might raise the implication that the High Court had no jurisdiction with respect to other remedies not mentioned, such as habeas corpus and certiorari. At one stage Mr Isaacs carried the day and the clause was deleted, but when his lawyer colleagues, particularly Mr Barton, had come back with some better understanding of the clause, it was reinstated.[214]

Traditionally a writ of mandamus would not issue against the Crown or a person acting on its behalf. Quick and Garran relied on this for showing that s 75(iii) and 75(v) did not cover the same ground.[215] Isaacs J also made the distinction where he contrasted the duty of an officer under the law with his or her duty as representing the state, which is then supposed to be itself performing the duty by the officer's agency.[216] Mandamus was available only in the former case. This distinction has been given far less significance in recent

---

207 See p 14 above.

208 Clearly if a State court were invested with *federal* jurisdiction under s 77(iii) in respect of the matters covered by s 75(v), the situation would be different.

209 (1903) 3 SR(NSW) 260.

210 Ibid at 262. See also Harrison Moore, *Commonwealth of Australia*, 2nd edn, 1910, pp 212-213; Bailey, "The Federal Jurisdiction of State Courts" (1940) 2 Res Judicatae 109 at 111.

211 Bailey, op cit p 111.

212 See pp 21-22 above.

213 Convention Debates, Melbourne, 1898, pp 1879, 1882.

214 See p 22 above.

215 Op cit p 779.

216 *R v Murray and Cormie; ex parte Commonwealth* (1916) 22 CLR 437 at 456.

times. It was rejected by the House of Lords in *M v Home Office*.[217] Lord Woolf declared the distinction to be artificial because mandamus was always brought against Ministers in their official capacity.

The High Court has not given a definitive pronouncement on this issue; but a number of judges have stated that the writs of mandamus and prohibition in s 75(v) are not properly called "prerogative writs". In *Re Refugee Review Tribunal; ex parte Aala*,[218] Gaudron and Gummow JJ said that the term "prerogative writs" was used in England because they were conceived as being intimately connected with the rights of the Crown and to prevent encroachment upon the prerogative. In Chapter III of the Constitution, however, the Crown is not an element in the judicature. What the writs enforce is fidelity required by s 5 of the *Constitution Act*, which declares the supremacy of the Constitution and federal laws made under it. They said that the shorthand expression "constitutional writs" was preferable to "prerogative writs". Kirby J agreed.[219] This approach strengthens the view that if there was otherwise any validity in the distinction between duty to the public and duty to the Crown for mandamus purposes it is inapplicable to mandamus under s 75(v). It has always been accepted that mandamus could issue to an officer of the Commonwealth in respect of a breach of the Constitution whatever the nature of the officer's duty to the Crown or public.[220]

There is a considerable overlap between s 75(iii) and (v) because of the broad interpretation that has been given to the former head of jurisdiction. "At least to a large extent the jurisdiction conferred by [s 75(v)] is also comprehended by [s 75(iii)]."[221] Some judges have queried whether all of the content of s 75(v) might be included in s 75(iii).[222] In *Re Refugee Review Tribunal; ex parte Aala*,[223] Gaudron and Gummow JJ said that s 75(v) "may not add to the jurisdiction conferred by s 75(iii)" and suggested that the former provision was a safeguard against the possibility that s 75(iii) might be read down in the light of United States case law.

It is possible, however, that one group of "officers of the Commonwealth" within the meaning of s 75(v) may not come within the scope of s 75(iii), namely, judges of federal courts. It is arguable that they cannot be described as "the Commonwealth" or persons "being sued on behalf of the Commonwealth". Apart from that, however, it is likely that the overlap between the two heads of jurisdiction is very great. In those circumstances the Court's power to

---

217 [1994] 1 AC 377 at 416.

218 (2000) 204 CLR 82 at 92-93.

219 Ibid at 133-134.

220 For a full discussion of the general issue, see Aronson and Dyer, *Judicial Review of Administrative Action*, 2nd edn, 2000, pp 585-588.

221 *Deputy Commissioner of Taxation v Richard Walter Pty Ltd* (1995) 183 CLR 168 at 204.

222 Ibid at 179, 221, 231.

223 (2000) 204 CLR 82 at 92.

issue remedies is not limited to those referred to in s 75(v) or to the officers specified in that provision.

In *R v Registrar of Titles for Victoria; ex parte Commonwealth*,[224] Griffith CJ and Isaacs J held that the Court might in appropriate circumstances issue mandamus to the Registrar of Titles for Victoria to compel him to register a lease of land to the Commonwealth by a Victorian municipality. As the majority of the Court held in that case that there was no such duty on the Registrar, they did not deal with the jurisdictional question.

In *Collett v Loane*,[225] the Court ordered the issue of a mandamus to a State stipendiary magistrate in relation to an application for registration as a conscientious objector under the *National Service Act*. It would appear that the jurisdiction of the Court was based on s 75(iii) as the Minister for Labour and National Service was made a respondent.

In *R v Murray and Cormie; ex parte Commonwealth*, an application was made in the original jurisdiction of the High Court for prohibition directed to a judge of a State court. It was held by Isaacs, Higgins, Gavan Duffy and Rich JJ, with Griffith CJ and Barton J dissenting, that jurisdiction was not attracted under s 75(v) because a State judge exercising federal jurisdiction was not an "officer of the Commonwealth" for the purpose of that provision. It was then argued that the Court had jurisdiction under s 75(iii). Although in the circumstances it was held that the Court did not have jurisdiction under that provision, a majority of the Court – Griffith CJ, Barton, Isaacs and Powers JJ – held that where the Commonwealth was a real party in interest the Court had jurisdiction by virtue of s 75(iii).

It was agreed that jurisdiction under s 75(iii) was not attracted merely because the King was a party on the face of the record. The essential feature in the view of the majority was that the Commonwealth should be an applicant for the writ. The reason it was held that the Court had no jurisdiction in the circumstances to issue the writ was that the Commonwealth had on the facts no substantial interest in the subject-matter relating to the excess of juris-diction. Isaacs J considered that although the Commonwealth was a "party" there was no "matter", while Higgins, Gavan Duffy and Rich JJ held that the Commonwealth was not a party. It now seems clear that, if the Common-wealth is a real party in interest, the Court has jurisdiction to issue prerogative writs on the Commonwealth's application under s 75(iii).

Not only has the High Court jurisdiction to grant the named remedies in pursuance of jurisdiction granted outside the provisions of s 75(v), it also has original jurisdiction to issue other writs in appropriate circumstances.[226] The *Judiciary Act*, s 33, confers specific power on the High Court to make orders or direct the issue of writs of mandamus and habeas corpus (inter alia) and

---

224 (1915) 20 CLR 379.

225 (1966) 117 CLR 94.

226 PHL, "High Court's Jurisdiction to Issue Writs" (1967) 41 ALJ 130.

s 33(2) declares that the section shall not be taken to limit by implication the power of the High Court to make any order or direct the issue of any writ. It is clear that the power to issue mandamus conferred by this section is not a general one, but is controlled by the Constitution.[227] The section also assumes that the High Court may grant writs of habeas corpus, and this has been affirmed by the Court.[228] As in the case of mandamus, s 33 cannot be read as conferring an unconfined and general power on the High Court to grant habeas corpus, but the power must be read as operating in aid of one or other of the heads of jurisdiction conferred on the High Court by the Constitution, or by Parliament pursuant to the authority of the Constitution. As Starke J said in *Jerger v Pearce*:[229] "It must not be taken for granted that this Court has a general power to direct the issue of writs of habeas corpus under s 33 of the *Judiciary Act*, but I apprehend that the Court has jurisdiction to exercise this power in aid of its appellate or original jurisdiction." There are cases of applications for habeas corpus in matters arising under the Constitution or involving its interpretation (Constitution, s 76(i), and *Judiciary Act*, s 30(a))[230] and in matters between residents of different States (Constitution, s 75(iv)).[231]

It has been regarded as surprising that injunctions are coupled with mandamus and prohibition in s 75(v). Quick and Garran observe: "The necessity for the mention of injunctions here is not quite apparent. An injunction is on a different footing altogether from mandamus and prohibition: it is an ordinary remedy in private suits between party and party. It was probably added because of the analogy which exists, in effect, between a mandamus and an injunction."[232] It has, however, been pointed out by Gummow and Kirby JJ[233] that the authority given in s 75(v) to issue injunctive relief against officers of the Commonwealth, including Ministers, settled an issue which was regarded as uncertain in the United Kingdom until the decision in *M v Home Office*.[234]

In *Abebe v Commonwealth*,[235] Gaudron J drew attention to the fact that mandamus and prohibition under s 75(v) are available only to correct jurisdictional errors. She pointed out, however, that s 75(v) extended to applications for an injunction, and added:

227 See *R v Governor of South Australia* (1907) 4 CLR 1497. See also *Ex parte Australian Timber Workers' Union; Veneer Co Ltd* (1937) 37 SR (NSW) 52.
228 See *Jerger v Pearce* (1920) 28 CLR 588; *Ex parte Walsh and Johnson; in re Yates* (1925) 37 CLR 36; *Ex parte Williams* (1934) 51 CLR 545; *R v Carter; ex parte Kisch* (1934) 52 CLR 221; *R v Bevan; ex parte Elias* (1942) 66 CLR 452; *Re Officer in Charge of Cells, ACT Supreme Court; ex parte Eastman* (1994) 123 ALR 478.
229 (1920) 28 CLR 588 at 590; *Ex parte Williams* (1934) 51 CLR 545 at 548, 551, 552; *R v Bevan; ex parte Elias* (1942) 66 CLR 452.
230 See cases cited in n 228.
231 *R v Langdon* (1953) 88 CLR 158; *R v Macdonald* (1953) 88 CLR 197. See Cowen, "Diversity Jurisdiction: The Australian Experience" (1955) 7 Res Judicatae 1 at 5.
232 Op cit p 783.
233 *Commonwealth v Mewett* (1997) 191 CLR 471 at 548.
234 [1994] 1 AC 377.
235 (1999) 197 CLR 510 at 551-552.

Given the potential for administrative decisions to impact on existing rights and interests, and, also, on important and valuable statutory rights ... it may well be that an injunction will lie to prevent an officer of the Commonwealth from giving effect to an administrative decision based on error, even if that error is not jurisdictional error.[236]

Certiorari

The most glaring omission from s 75(v) is certiorari. It has been said that the omission has resulted in the High Court liberally granting prohibition where certiorari would be an appropriate remedy. It has extended the scope of prohibition beyond its generally accepted limits elsewhere;[237] but the Court has rejected the argument that s 75(v) impliedly confers jurisdiction to grant certiorari even though it would not otherwise possess original jurisdiction to do so.[238]

As in the case of other writs and remedies, the Court can issue certiorari where it is ancillary to some other head of jurisdiction. As Windeyer J said: "It is at least questionable whether certiorari to quash proceedings of an inferior tribunal can issue from this Court as a substantive remedy *not ancillary to some proceeding otherwise within the original jurisdiction of the Court.*"[239]

While certiorari is not among the writs expressly referred to or described in s 33 of the *Judiciary Act*, it would seem to be authorised by s 32, which empowers and requires the Court to grant any remedies that a party is entitled to, so that, so far as possible, all matters in controversy may be completely and finally determined.[240] This provision operates only where the Court otherwise has jurisdiction.

---

236 See also *Re Minister for Immigration and Multicultural Affairs; ex parte Durairajasingham* (2000) 168 ALR 407 at 415 per McHugh J; *Re Minister for Immigration and Multicultural Affairs; ex parte Miah* (2001) 179 ALR 238 at 291 [211] per Kirby J. In the case of a tribunal, as distinct from a lower court, it seems that any error of law may be treated as jurisdictional error in the absence of a contrary legislative indication: *Minister for Immigration and Multicultural Affairs v Yusuf* (2001) 180 ALR 1 at 22; *Craig v South Australia* (1995) 184 CLR 163 at 179.

237 See Anderson, "The Application of Privative Clauses to Proceedings of Commonwealth Tribunals" (1956) 3 U of Queensland LJ 34 at 34-35: "So long as the decision of the tribunals the validity of which is questioned has a continuing effect on the rights and duties of the persons affected – as of course is usually the case – the High Court regards prohibition as an appropriate remedy for invalidity, even after the decision has been made, and even where enforcement of the rights and duties created by the decision lies with some other tribunal or court, so that the tribunal in question might well be regarded as functus officio. Prohibition lies not only to the tribunal which made the invalid decision but also to prohibit any party to the proceedings before it from taking steps to enforce the decision. As a result of this liberality with prohibition, certiorari is rarely applied for in the High Court. No doubt this development is at least in part due to the fact that s 75(v) gives a constitutional guarantee of prohibition – to what extent, I propose to consider – but not of certiorari."

238 *R v Bowen; ex parte Federated Clerks Union* (1984) 154 CLR 207 at 211. See also *R v Gray; ex parte Marsh* (1985) 157 CLR 351 at 387.

239 *R v District Court; ex parte White* (1966) 116 CLR 644 at 655. Italics supplied.

240 *Re McBain; ex parte Australian Catholic Bishops Conference* (2002) 188 ALR 1 at 22, 68.

In *Re Mcbain; ex parte Australian Catholic Bishops Conference*,[241] an application for certiorari in the case of an alleged matter arising under the Constitution was dismissed, but not on the ground that the writ could not be granted under that head of jurisdiction. Three judges expressly held that certiorari was available (McHugh, Kirby and Callinan JJ), but dismissed the application on discretionary grounds. The other four held that there was no "matter" (Gleeson CJ, Gaudron, Gummow and Hayne JJ). There was much discussion of the circumstances in which a writ of certiorari for error on the face of the record could issue, but that did not deny the power of the Court to grant the writ on proper grounds and in appropriate circumstances as ancillary to any matter in which the Court had original jurisdiction.[242]

The Court has issued certiorari when the only head of jurisdiction called on was s 75(v). In *Pitfield v Franki*,[243] there was an application for prohibition and certiorari in relation to an award of the Conciliation and Arbitration Commission. The issue was whether the employees of fire fighting authorities came within a provision of the Act relating to the registration of industrial organisations. There was no discussion of the source of jurisdiction. The Court simply said that the appropriate order was a writ of certiorari to bring up the registration order so that it may be quashed. Mason J later attempted to explain that decision by suggesting that the Court was of the view that the Registrar's authority to register an association was necessarily confined, by limitations derived from s 51(xxxv) of the Constitution (the conciliation and arbitration power), to register only an association that "in truth (as distinct from opinion)" came within the statutory provision. He added that "this circumstance [which relies on jurisdiction derived from s 76(i) of the Constitution], possibly taken in conjunction with a bona fide claim for prohibition, gave the Court jurisdiction, despite the absence of any reference to certiorari in s 75(v) of the Constitution".[244] The latter part of this statement proved fruitful.

The question whether the Court can issue certiorari has arisen in those cases where s 75(v) was thought to be the only source of jurisdiction and where (a) the impugned order is beyond jurisdiction, (b) prohibition prevents it being enforced, but (c) only certiorari can result in the quashing of the order. In *R v Cook; ex parte Twigg*,[245] an application was made for prohibition and certiorari directed to the Family Court in respect of a conviction of a solicitor for contempt of court. It was held that the conviction was erroneous and should be quashed by certiorari. Barwick CJ gave as a possible explanation of *Pitfield v Franki* that the Court had jurisdiction under s 75(v) because the prohibition was sought in good faith. The Court then had power under s 31 of

---

241 Ibid.

242 Per Gaudron and Gummow JJ at 16.

243 (1970) 123 CLR 448.

244 *R v Marshall; ex parte Federated Clerks Union of Australia* (1975) 132 CLR 595 at 609.

245 (1980) 147 CLR 15.

the *Judiciary Act* to grant the more appropriate remedy. He also referred to the possible constitutional ground of jurisdiction mentioned by Mason J in *Marshall*. Gibbs J followed *Pitfield* but said that did not preclude the Court from examining its correctness in the future. Stephen J was of the same view. Although Mason and Wilson JJ thought that the applicant should have sought relief from the Full Court of the Family Court, they followed Gibbs J. The only discussion in any depth of the certiorari issue was by Aickin J.

Aickin J[246] pointed to the fact that the issue of prohibition in the circumstances of the case was an unsatisfactory solution. It would prevent enforcement of the conviction but would leave it standing even though made without jurisdiction or justification. Only certiorari could quash it, and he held it should be granted. Aickin J gave as "the narrowest basis" for the writ in that case that, first, it was one where prohibition could properly issue. The application was made "not merely colourably but in good faith". Secondly, the writ of prohibition would be inadequate. Certiorari in those circumstances could be used as an adjunct to prohibition so as to make the order "fully effective". He regarded it as a merely procedural question whether the order for prohibition should be made as well as an order for certiorari, and concluded that it would be illogical to make both orders. He left open the question whether certiorari might be granted where prohibition was held not to be available.

In *Philip Morris Inc v Adam P Brown Male Fashions Pty Ltd*,[247] Barwick CJ described *Pitfield* as a case where the Court had jurisdiction to grant prohibition, and "the writ of certiorari was a convenient, indeed a more convenient, mode of exercising the jurisdiction". Later cases followed that view.[248] The Court has also granted both mandamus and certiorari in a number of cases.[249] Professor Lane points out that, despite early reservations expressed in the judgments,[250] the Court has more recently granted certiorari as ancillary relief with mandamus "without much anxiety".[251] In *Re Refugee Review Tribunal; ex parte Aala*,[252] Gaudron and Gummow JJ said that in the circumstances of that case the power to issue certiorari against an officer of the Commonwealth arose from the principle that "the conferral of jurisdiction to issue writs of prohibition and mandamus implies ancillary or incidental authority to the effective exercise of that jurisdiction". They added that the matter could also attract the exercise of power conferred by s 31 of the *Judiciary Act* to make judgments and orders necessary for the doing of complete justice in any matter.

---

246 Ibid at 31-32.
247 (1981) 148 CLR 457 at 477.
248 See, for example, *Re Ross-Jones; ex parte Green* (1984) 156 CLR 185.
249 Lane, *Lane's Commentary on the Australian Constitution*, 2nd edn, pp 587-588.
250 For example, *Re Australian Bank Employees' Union; ex parte Citicorp Australia Ltd* (1981) 167 CLR 513 at 521.
251 Lane, op cit p 588.
252 (2000) 204 CLR 82 at 90-91.

When certiorari has been sought with prohibition, it seems that the Court has not confined its power to issue certiorari to the "narrowest basis" suggested by Aickin J, namely, where prohibition could properly issue. In *R v Cook; ex parte Twigg*,[253] Gibbs J (with whose reasons Stephen, Mason and Wilson JJ agreed), in holding that certiorari should issue, said it was sufficient that the claim for prohibition was not "unarguable", but found no reason to express a view as to its correctness. Whether certiorari can issue depends on whether the High Court has jurisdiction. That normally depends on whether a claim answers any of the descriptions in s 75 or s 76(i). In the case of s 75(v), Gibbs J said it was sufficient that there is a bona fide (or perhaps "arguable") claim for the writ, not that the claim should be successful.[254]

The doubt that has in the past existed in respect of certiorari has arisen because the High Court lacks jurisdiction in respect of all matters arising under federal law (s 76(ii)). It would be open to Parliament to confer that jurisdiction, which would enable the Court to grant certiorari in appropriate circumstances. It seems, however, that in respect of federal officers, tribunals and statutory bodies, s 75(iii) might be a sufficient basis of jurisdiction, whether or not s 75(v) is available.[255] It is, however, too early to say that s 75(v) is unnecessary, and there is some doubt whether federal judges and courts could be regarded as being sued "on behalf of the Commonwealth".

It has been argued by Mr Lee Aitken[256] that if certiorari is the only available remedy it cannot be said that the Commonwealth or other person within s 75(iii) is "properly sued at all". He said "the question of relief is integral to the suit. One cannot sue in any accepted sense of the word for a remedy or relief which is unavailable". This suggests that there is no matter to which the issue of certiorari relief is ancillary. The matter, however, usually concerns a suit by an applicant to prevent what he or she argues is an ultra vires order or direction, made by a person referred to in s 75(iii), from being applied. It is difficult to see why that is not a matter within s 75(iii) and why the Court cannot, under s 32 of the *Judiciary Act*, grant an appropriate remedy, including certiorari. In the case of s 75(v), of course, the named remedies are at the heart of the matter.

The naming of the remedies in s 75(v) raises a problem mentioned by Mr Dixon in his evidence before the Royal Commission. He said that it was by no means clear how much of the common law governing the character and nature of these remedies, the procedure by which they are administered, the occasions upon which they may be granted, is stereotyped and made immutable by this provision.[257] Common law limitations regarding certiorari were raised by Deane J.

---

253 (1980) 147 CLR 15 at 26.
254 The question of "bona fides" or "arguability" is discussed later, pp 147-148 below.
255 See pp 47-48 above.
256 (1986) 16 Federal LR 370 at 376-377.
257 Minutes of Evidence, p 786.

The Federal Court and the Family Court is each a "superior court of record" under their respective constitutive Acts. It has been accepted for a long time in Australia that a writ of prohibition can issue against such a court in respect of an order in excess of jurisdiction. In *R v Ross-Jones; ex parte Green*,[258] a writ of certiorari was issued to the Family Court when an application had been made for prohibition and certiorari. That decision was questioned by Deane J in *R v Gray; ex parte Marsh*.[259] He did not deny that s 75(v) was available as a source of jurisdiction, and that in a proper case certiorari could issue. But he said that the substantive law, which included the common law, prevented the issue of certiorari to a superior court. Section 75(v), being merely a conferral of jurisdiction, did not affect that position. Deane J said that the scope of certiorari was different from prohibition. It notionally removed the record of the lower court into the High Court and it extended to errors of law on the face of the record that were committed within jurisdiction. Prohibition was available against a superior court because it was confined to excesses of jurisdiction.

Ultimately, Deane J recognised that earlier cases ran contrary to his view and, in any case, he did not have to decide the issue. He added, however, that if he were constrained to follow earlier decisions they should be regarded as going no further than making certiorari available for excess of jurisdiction. Dawson J expressed doubts similar to those of Deane J, and Mason J thought there was a question whether certiorari could issue for error of law on the face of the record.[260]

There has been criticism of the Court in respect of the issue of certiorari in s 75(v) cases. It might be said that in many of them the grant of certiorari to quash seems to go beyond what is merely incidental to an application for prohibition. If, for example, s 75(v) had extended to all remedies for judicial review, the appropriate action on some occasions might have been simply to apply for certiorari. Indeed, in some of the cases, such as *R v Cook; ex parte Twigg*, certiorari was granted and not prohibition. This makes the application for prohibition look contrived (even though that is not a sufficient reason to regard it as not bona fide, provided there is a "proper" case for prohibition).[261]

It is suggested that the High Court should continue to follow those cases where certiorari has been granted in respect of a matter coming within s 75(v). While cognisance must be taken of the technical differences between the remedies because of the specification of the three remedies, the heads of jurisdiction in Chapter III should be interpreted bearing in mind their place in a constitution and with regard to their purpose. The purpose divined by Dixon J

---

258 (1984) 156 CLR 185.
259 (1985) 157 CLR 351 at 388.
260 Ibid at 377 (Mason J), 397 (Dawson J).
261 Aitken, "The High Court's Power to Grant Certiorari. The Unsolved Question" (1986) 16 Federal LR 370.

in the *Bank Nationalisation Case* has been accepted for 50 years and is a likely one. There, Dixon J said that the purpose of s 75(v) was to make it "constitutionally certain that there would be a jurisdiction capable of restraining officers of the Commonwealth from exceeding Federal power".[262] The mischief is excess of power or jurisdiction. In those circumstances, a liberal interpretation of what remedies are ancillary and appropriate for determining matters within s 75(v) is as appropriate as the broad interpretation given to the words of s 75(iii). Both are designed (in part in the case of s 75(iii)) to subject the Commonwealth, its agencies and officers to the Constitution and to laws prescribing power, authority and jurisdiction. Such a consideration, however, also supports the view that while the issue of a writ of certiorari should be regarded, in appropriate circumstances, as ancillary to prohibition or mandamus, it should be limited to the ground of excess of jurisdiction.

The question whether certiorari can be granted under other heads of jurisdiction to quash a decision of a superior court for error on the face of the record remains unresolved. If it were so available it could have extraordinary results. This can be illustrated by the *Catholic Bishops Case*,[263] where the bishops, in their own right and at the relation of the Attorney-General of the Commonwealth, applied for certiorari to quash a decision of the Federal Court. The Court had held that a Victorian Act which prohibited the provision of in vitro fertilisation treatment to women who were not living with a husband or de facto husband was inconsistent with the *Sex Discrimination Act* 1984 (Cth) and was therefore inoperative by virtue of s 109 of the Constitution. The parties to the proceedings, which included the State, did not appeal. Neither the Bishops Conference nor the Commonwealth Attorney-General was a party.

While the majority of the Court dismissed the application because there was not a "matter",[264] the effect of this ground of certiorari on the operation of the judicial system can best be judged by examining the effect of the other judgments which upheld its availability. While dismissing the application on discretionary grounds, McHugh, Kirby and Callinan JJ held that certiorari was available to quash the order of the Federal Court, validly made within its jurisdiction, for an error of law which appeared on its face, at the suit of persons who were not parties to the Federal Court proceedings.

It is difficult to see how this fits with the notion that the essence of judicial power is the settling of disputes about rights and duties and the "quelling" of controversy. It seems also to cut across the structure of Chapter III of the Constitution, which, in s 77, provides for the conferring of jurisdiction to determine matters in ss 75 and 76, and, in s 73, makes provision

---

262 *Bank of New South Wales v Commonwealth* (1948) 76 CLR 1 at 363.
263 *Re McBain; ex parte Australian Catholic Bishops Conference* (2002) 188 ALR 1.
264 Page 17 above.

for appeals from those courts. The Constitution's method of providing for the correction of non-jurisdictional error is therefore by way of appeal, while s 75(v) ensures review for excess of, or refusal to exercise, jurisdiction. The view of Hayne J that this ground of review is anomalous and should not be extended has much to commend it.[265] The structure of the judicial system prescribed in Chapter III supports that view.

Assumption of Jurisdiction

In a number of cases where the High Court has assumed jurisdiction involving applications to issue writs to a State court, it has not always been clear what is the basis of the High Court's jurisdiction. *Collett v Loane*[266] was an application for mandamus directed to a State stipendiary magistrate who declined jurisdiction in relation to an application for registration as a conscientious objector under the *National Service Act*. The Minister for Labour and National Service was a respondent to the proceedings. The High Court granted the mandamus. The only basis for jurisdiction could be that the Minister was a party and was the Commonwealth or a person being sued on behalf of the Commonwealth within the meaning of s 75(iii), but jurisdiction was not discussed. In *R v District Court of Queensland Northern District; ex parte Thompson*,[267] application was made to the High Court for certiorari directed to the State Court in relation to an exemption from service under the *National Service Act* 1951 (Cth). The Minister for Labour and National Service and the Commonwealth were made respondents. The writ was refused. Barwick CJ, Kitto and Taylor JJ expressly refrained from determining the question of jurisdiction, preferring to decide on the merits that the writ be refused. McTiernan J, however, held that the Court had jurisdiction under s 75(iii) because the Minister had a right to be represented in the original proceedings under the *National Service Regulations* and was also given a right of appeal.[268] In *R v District Court; ex parte White*,[269] motions for prohibition against the District Court, the Minister for Labour and National Service and the Commonwealth prohibiting them from proceeding further upon an order of the District Court in relation to a similar matter under the *National Service Act*, and for certiorari to remove the record of proceedings of the District Court into the High Court, were refused. Barwick CJ considered that there was "a serious question" as to the Court's jurisdiction to grant certiorari and as to whether the Court in that case should grant prohibition.[270] Menzies J said that he was not satisfied that

---

265 (2002) 188 ALR 1 at 68-71.
266 (1966) 117 CLR 94.
267 (1968) 118 CLR 488.
268 Ibid at 495; Lane (1969) 43 ALJ 21.
269 (1966) 116 CLR 644.
270 Ibid at 648.

there was jurisdiction and Taylor J found it unnecessary to decide the question.[271] Windeyer J considered that both the Minister and the Commonwealth were proper parties interested in maintaining the order of the Court.[272] If in these cases the matters came within s 75(iii), it is clear, as Leslie Katz has said, that a generous interpretation has been given to the word "party" in s 75(iii).[273] In each case the respondents, other than the Court against which the writ was sought, were what Professor Lane has called "secondary respondents".[274]

It is suggested that the tendency disclosed by these cases of rushing into the merits before considering jurisdiction is, as has been stated, "a most unsatisfactory way of proceeding".[275] The alacrity with which the Court in these cases determined the issue despite the expression of doubts (often unexplained) regarding jurisdiction is strangely inconsistent with the expression of view from time to time by the judges that an increase in the Court's jurisdiction impairs its ability to discharge its major role as constitutional interpreter and final court of appeal.[276]

Remedies and Substantive Rights

Section 75(v), like s 75(iii) and (iv), on its face appears to confer a jurisdiction. As mentioned above, it was held in *Commonwealth v Mewett*[277] that s 75(iii) did not create any Commonwealth liability in tort, which arose under the common law. There are judicial statements that s 75(v) should be given a similar interpretation. It is clear that this was the intendment of the authors of the clause. At the Melbourne meeting of the Convention of 1898 the proposal to restore the clause was under heavy attack. Mr Kingston asserted that it would give the High Court power to interfere with the executive "to the very great detriment of constitutional government".[278] Mr Symon, with Mr Barton's support, energetically denied this: "The provision does not confer, and is not intended to confer – and I am sure Mr Barton will agree with me in this – any right whatever to interfere in such cases. It merely gives a jurisdiction."[279] Mr Barton agreed. Mr Symon reiterated the point: "It

---

271 Ibid at 652.

272 Ibid at 655.

273 (1975-77) 5 U of Tasmania LR 188.

274 Lane, op cit p 561 n5. In respect of *White's Case* Mr Katz pointed out that on any view it should have been held that the Court had jurisdiction under s 75(v) as prohibition was sought, inter alia, against the Minister as the applicant's opposing litigant before the Tribunal, so he was one of the primary respondents: ibid.

275 Katz, op cit p 193.

276 For example, *Willcocks v Anderson* (1971) 124 CLR 293.

277 (1997) 191 CLR 471.

278 Debates, Melbourne, 1898, p 1877.

279 Ibid.

does not give any right to get mandamus or prohibition … it merely gives a jurisdiction in certain applications … It is not provided that the right shall exist to get the mandamus or prohibition."[280] And when Sir John Forrest asked: "It means nothing then?"[281] he was given the answer that it meant that the jurisdiction was given to a federal court. On this basis, Quick and Garran appeared perfectly justified in making the statement that the clause did not confer any right of action against officers of the Commonwealth. The High Court had been given jurisdiction only; and the Court had to determine in each case whether, according to principles of law, an action lay.[282]

It is clear that while Parliament cannot deprive the High Court of the jurisdiction in s 75(v) it can alter the substantive law that the Court must apply in the course of exercising that jurisdiction. To do so would "merely alter the substantive law in a way which produced the consequence that, while the jurisdiction and the right to invoke it were unaffected, the particular ground for the grant of injunctive or other relief was removed".[283] That is, of course, subject to any constitutional limitations. As stated above, s 75(iii) and (v) together entrench a jurisdiction to grant relief against a purported exercise of invalid federal legislation or executive action.[284] One such limitation is that it would be contrary to Chapter III and the separation of judicial power to preclude a court from determining the relevant facts and law in relation to any matter when exercising federal jurisdiction.[285] However, the distinction between an Act purporting to direct courts as to "the manner and outcome of the exercise of their jurisdiction"[286] and one which alters the substantive or procedural law to be applied by the Court is not always clear. The principle is that Parliament cannot prevent the Court when exercising jurisdiction under s 75(v) from determining whether an allegedly invalid action by an officer of the Commonwealth is in fact invalid. That must be contrasted, for example, with a provision that renders statutory limitations on the officer's authority directory rather than mandatory.[287]

Contrary to the views expressed here (and to the tenor of the decision in *Mewett*) there are occasional judicial suggestions that s 75(v) may be a source

---

280 Ibid pp 1877, 1878.

281 Ibid p 1878.

282 Op cit p 784.

283 *Deputy Commissioner of Taxation v Richard Walter Pty Ltd* (1995) 183 CLR 168 at 207 per Deane and Gaudron JJ. See also at 178 per Mason CJ; *Re Refugee Review Tribunal; ex parte Aala* (2000) 204 CLR 82 at 139 per Hayne J; *Ince Bros and Cambridge Manufacturing Co Pty Ltd v Federated Clothing and Allied Trades Union* (1924) 34 CLR 457 at 464.

284 *Richard Walter* (1995) 183 CLR 168 at 204-205.

285 Ibid at 184-185 per Mason CJ.

286 *Chu Kheng Lim v Minister for Immigration* (1992) 176 CLR 1 at 37.

287 *Richard Walter* (1995) 183 CLR 168 at 185 per Mason CJ; *Project Blue Sky Inc v Australian Broadcasting Authority* (1998) 194 CLR 355.

of substantive rights which Parliament cannot impair. There is no decision to that effect, and such an opinion is difficult to reconcile with the principle that an officer's power or jurisdiction is determined by statute or, alternatively, by common law, which is, of course, amenable to change by statute. The possible contrary view is usually associated with matters relating to privative clauses, which are discussed below.[288] In *Construction, Forestry, Mining and Energy Union v Australian Industrial Relations Commission*,[289] it was held that the right of an applicant for prohibition to compel an officer to observe the limits of that officer's power arose under s 75(v) and not under the Act. The Court added that the officer's corresponding duty also derived from s 75(v). It is by no means clear what follows from those statements; but they do not detract from the power of Parliament to determine the limits of power or jurisdiction of officers of the Commonwealth. The determination of the right of the applicant and the corresponding duty of the officer must be governed by the extent of jurisdiction or power conferred by the Act.[290]

There is a question, as Dixon indicated in his evidence to the Royal Commission,[291] as to the extent to which Parliament can alter the rules associated with the remedies in s 75(v). It would seem that purported changes that would make them less effective to serve the purpose of granting relief to persons affected by invalid exercises of power would not be valid. This is supported by statements which query whether s 75(iii) may include all, or nearly all, of the jurisdiction in s 75(v). That view appears to assume that the remedies referred to in the latter paragraph are entrenched in s 75(iii). While it is unlikely that all the specific common law and equitable rules associated with mandamus, prohibition and the injunction are unalterable, the object of s 75(v) would require that the court be empowered to grant remedies that at least achieve the same substantive result. This is consistent with the principle that no procedural change can have the effect of preventing a court, within the limits of its jurisdiction, from giving effect to substantive rights.[292]

Officers with Commonwealth and State Powers

It remains to consider the case where an officer of the Commonwealth is authorised by Commonwealth legislation to perform functions conferred on the officer by State law. The issue arises whether s 75(v) of the Constitution or s 38(e) of the *Judiciary Act* is applicable when the officer is exercising those functions. It could be argued that in those circumstances he or she is acting as a State officer.

---

288 Pages 62-65.

289 (2001) 178 ALR 61 at 71.

290 See Gageler, "The High Court on Constitutional Law: The 2001 Term", a paper delivered to a constitutional conference, University of New South Wales, 15 February 2002.

291 Above p 54.

292 *Chu Kheng Lim v Minister for Immigration* (1992) 176 CLR 1 at 68.

In *Australian Iron and Steel Ltd v Dobb*,[293] the Court was concerned with the power of a Local Coal Authority which was invested with powers under Commonwealth and State legislation. The Authority made an order purporting to act under its State power. Application for a writ of prohibition was made to the Supreme Court of the State, which held the order to be within power. An appeal to the High Court was dismissed for the same reason. The Court avoided the question whether s 38(e) of the *Judiciary Act* operated to deprive the Supreme Court of jurisdiction. As indicated above, the provision makes exclusive to the High Court matters where a writ of mandamus or prohibition is sought against an officer of the Commonwealth. Fullagar and Taylor JJ dissented on the substantive issue. Fullagar J said[294] that as the foundation of the jurisdiction claimed by the Authority must be found in State law "I do not think that any question arises under s 38(e) of the *Judiciary Act* of the Commonwealth". Dixon CJ, on the other hand, said:[295] "True it is that Mr Dobb appears to claim only State power. But is he any the less a federal officer for that? It may be said that in truth he is a federal officer claiming to exercise a single power deriving so far as may be from State and federal sources." He found it unnecessary to pursue that question.

Similarly, in *R v Lydon; ex parte Cessnock Collieries Ltd*,[296] the Court held that a Local Coal Authority had power under State legislation to make an order and, so, a writ of prohibition was denied. A unanimous judgment of the Court said:

> In the view we take of the present case no constitutional difficulty arises nor does any occasion exist for pronouncing on the application of this Court's jurisdiction to send prohibition to a Commonwealth officer on whom State power as well as federal power is conferred when he acts outside all his powers.[297]

The Court eventually dealt with the issue in *Re Cram; ex parte NSW Colliery Proprietors' Association Ltd*,[298] where it was again concerned with joint Commonwealth-State bodies in the coal industry. The Coal Industry Tribunal and authorities appointed by it were empowered by the Commonwealth Act to determine, inter alia, interstate industrial disputes and industrial disputes within the State. The State Act was in substantially the same terms. It was held that the persons who constituted the Tribunal and the authority were officers of the Commonwealth within s 75(v) of the Constitution even when they exercised powers conferred by the State Act.

---

293 (1958) 98 CLR 586.
294 Ibid at 602.
295 Ibid at 596.
296 (1960) 103 CLR 15.
297 Ibid at 21.
298 (1987) 163 CLR 117.

The Court accepted, as had been previously held,[299] that the joint operation of the Acts created a single tribunal and not separate Commonwealth and State tribunals. It said that the State functions were exercisable by the Tribunal and authorities because of an implied legislative authorisation by the Commonwealth. The unanimous joint judgment of the Court declared:[300]

> Given then that the authorities derive their existence from the Commonwealth Act, although not exclusively so, and that the Commonwealth Act either confers or authorises the conferral on the authorities of all or any of their powers and functions, the persons constituting the authorities are necessarily officers of the Commonwealth and remain so in respect of the exercise of all their powers unless, perhaps, the Commonwealth Act evinces an intention that, in the exercise of powers derived from the State Act, the authorities function in some different capacity.[301]

Another way of looking at the issue is suggested by the passages quoted above from *Dobb* and *Lydon*. If one concludes that there is a single authority with powers derived from both Commonwealth and State legislation the issue in respect of prohibition is whether the authority has acted beyond the total power given to it. For example, although the authority might have purported to act under Commonwealth-conferred powers, but travelled beyond them, the order it made might in fact be justified by State-conferred power. In those circumstances prohibition could not issue.[302]

Privative Clauses

Questions have arisen touching the validity and effect of privative clauses which purport to deny power to the High Court to grant the remedies enumerated in s 75(v). An example was s 60 of the *Conciliation and Arbitration Act* 1904, which declared that an award of the Commonwealth Conciliation and Arbitration Commission shall be final and conclusive and shall not be challenged, appealed against, reviewed, quashed or called in question in any court and shall not be subject to prohibition, mandamus or injunction in any court on any account. A nearly identical provision is now

---

299 *Re Duncan; ex parte Australian Iron and Steel Pty Ltd* (1983) 158 CLR 535.

300 (1987) 163 CLR 117 at 128.

301 See, generally, Saunders, "Administrative Law and Relations Between Governments: Australia and Europe Compared" (2000) 28 Federal LR 263.

302 The extent to which the Commonwealth can authorise its officers and authorities to exercise State powers is at present doubtful: *Re Wakim; ex parte McNally* (1999) 198 CLR 511; *R v Hughes* (2000) 202 CLR 535. In *Hughes* the Court indicated that a Commonwealth Act can permit federal officers to perform functions under State law. Where, however, the State law places an obligation on the officer it may be necessary for the Commonwealth to have a substantive power with respect to the subject-matter of the obligation. The Court raised the possibility that ss 61 and 51(xxxi) – the executive and incidental powers – might be sufficient to authorise the imposition of the State obligation; but the judgment said that that "remains open to some debate" (at 555).

contained in s 150 of the *Workplace Relations Act* 1996 (Cth). A recent example is s 474 of the *Migration Act* 1958, enacted in 2001. There are similar clauses in other Acts which give expression to a policy that the bodies to which they apply shall have conclusive authority to determine all questions arising in the exercise of their functions, including the extent of their own jurisdiction. On the surface these clauses seem like a direct contradiction of the provisions of s 75(v) and on that view would be invalid because Parliament has purported to deprive the Court of jurisdiction with which it is invested under the Constitution. The remedies referred to in s 75(v), however, will not be available where the circumstances are such that no occasion has arisen for the grant of any of the specified remedies. Clearly, a privative clause cannot foreclose the grant of remedies mentioned in s 75(v) where the body in question purports to exercise power which the Commonwealth Parliament cannot lawfully confer on it.[303] Outside those limits Parliament may make the jurisdiction of a statutory body as broad or as narrow as it likes. The only duty of the Court in exercising jurisdiction under s 75(v) would, in those circumstances, be to ensure that the body keeps within the limits laid down by Parliament. It is possible to argue that the presence of a privative clause indicates an intention by Parliament to give full jurisdiction to the body to determine conclusively all relevant facts and questions of law. It would follow that a privative clause would operate to prevent the issue of the remedies named except where the body is purporting to exercise authority that is beyond the constitutional power of the Commonwealth Parliament to confer.[304]

That is not the way privative clauses have been interpreted. Their operation is somewhat obscure and the High Court has adopted a restrictive view of their scope. There was an attempt by Dixon CJ to develop a coherent theory for their application. That theory is to interpret privative clauses as validating any action by the authority concerned, so far as it can validate it constitutionally, provided that it is a bona fide attempt to exercise its powers, that it relates to the subject-matter of the legislation and is reasonably capable of reference to the power given to the authority.[305]

This principle has in recent years received strong support.[306] McHugh J suggested that the *Hickman* principle (as it is called) was a reconciliation between the demands of s 75(v) and the statutory privative clause.[307] Dixon J does refer to the entrenchment of jurisdiction in s 75(v) in his judgment, but

---

303 *R v Portus; ex parte McNeil* (1961) 105 CLR 537 at 540-541.

304 This view was favoured by Anderson, op cit p 54, and Sawer in Else-Mitchell (ed), *Essays on the Australian Constitution*, 2nd edn, 1961, p 83.

305 *R v Hickman; ex parte Fox and Clinton* (1945) 70 CLR 598.

306 *R v Coldham; ex parte AWU* (1983) 153 CLR 415; *O'Toole v Charles David Pty Ltd* (1990) 171 CLR 232; *Deputy Commissioner of Taxation v Richard Walter Pty Ltd* (1995) 183 CLR 168; *Darling Casino Ltd v NSW Casino Authority* (1997) 191 CLR 602.

307 *Richard Walter* (1995) 183 CLR 168 at 240.

his reasoning is based on the apparent contradiction between granting only limited power to a body, on the one hand, while appearing, on the other, to confer unlimited power by providing that the decisions of the body shall not be subject to judicial review. He applied the principle he enunciated also to State privative clauses.[308] It was regarded as so applicable, recently, in *Darling Casino Ltd v NSW Casino Authority*.[309] In *Hickman*, Dixon J said that the principle applied both "under Commonwealth law, and in jurisdictions where there is a unitary constitution".[310]

Strictly speaking, therefore, the *Hickman* principle is a rule of construction which is not reliant on s 75(v). There would seem no reason, for example, why Parliament could not make it clear (subject to other constitutional restraints) that the *Hickman* interpretation was not to apply.[311] Nevertheless, some judges have suggested that s 75(v) affects the extent to which the *Hickman* principle can be applied to a privative clause. In *Darling Casino*, Gaudron and Gummow JJ accepted that a federal privative clause broadens the power of the decision-maker so that a writ under s 75 will not issue when the decision-maker operates in the area so expanded. But they suggested this cannot be so in the case of provisions that go to jurisdiction. In that case they say that the federal privative clause cannot have operation because of s 75(v). That is because mandamus and prohibition are remedies in cases of jurisdictional error and "the terms of s 75(v) would be defeated if a privative clause operated to protect against jurisdictional errors".[312]

This approach seems to confuse two issues, namely, construing the privative clause in its context, and the operation of s 75(v). The *Hickman* principle is concerned with the first issue. If the result is to broaden the power of the decision-maker, it may be that no writ of prohibition will issue under s 75(v). What might have been beyond jurisdiction without the clause is within jurisdiction. It is difficult to see, in relation to the purpose of s 75(v), why it is necessary to distinguish between jurisdictional and non-jurisdictional questions in respect of the *Hickman* principle.[313] No other judges have followed this dictum of Gaudron and Gummow JJ.[314] In *Project Blue Sky Inc v*

---

308 For example, *Coal Miners' Union v Amalgamated Collieries of WA* (1960) 104 CLR 437.

309 (1997) 191 CLR 602.

310 (1945) 70 CLR 598 at 614-615.

311 Compare *Deputy Commissioner of Taxation v Richard Walter Pty Ltd* (1995) 183 CLR 168 at 221, 223, 233.

312 (1997) 191 CLR 602 at 633; see also *Re Minister for Immigration and Multicultural Affairs; ex parte Miah* (2001) 179 ALR 238 at 261 per Gaudron J.

313 Zines, "Constitutional Aspects of Judicial Review of Administrative Action" (1998) 1 *Constitutional Law and Policy Review* 50.

314 For a full examination of privative clauses, see Aronson and Dyer, *Judicial Review of Administrative Action*, 2nd edn, 2000, ch 18. See also Kirk, "Administrative Justice and the Australian Constitution" in Creyke and McMillan (eds), *Administrative Justice – the Core and the Fringe*, 2000, p 78; Zines, op cit.

Australian Broadcasting Authority,[315] the Court seemed to indicate that Parliament could stipulate that breach of its rules will not invalidate an officer's decision. Aronson and Dyer say that taking up this suggestion should mean that s 75(v) jurisdiction would remain, "but it would have nothing on which to bite".[316] Constitutional limitations, however, would remain.

From time to time, however, the view is expressed that the *Hickman* principle is somehow constitutionally entrenched. The remarks of McHugh J, referred to above, are to that effect relying on s 75(v). Since then Gaudron J has also suggested that the principle might be required by the Constitution, although she did not specifically refer to s 75(v). She said that Parliament might legislate so that relief will be refused if an erroneous decision is made. She added a proviso that the decision does not exceed the authority conferred by the legislation and "it constitutes a bona fide attempt to exercise the powers in issue and relates to the subject-matter of the legislation".[317] It is difficult to understand, however, why power cannot be given to an administrator which exceeds, or in other ways alters, that which would be conferred by the *Hickman* principle. It can nevertheless be assumed that the *Hickman* principle is consistent with s 75 of the Constitution.[318]

Matters Concerning the Constitution and Commonwealth Law : Section 76(i), (ii).

The Australian Constitution departed from American precedent in specifying subject-matters in which original jurisdiction might be vested in the High Court by Act of the Commonwealth Parliament. In the United States, all the heads of original jurisdiction and of federal jurisdiction were defined by the Constitution itself. The decision to separate those matters in which original jurisdiction was vested by the Constitution from those in which it might be conferred by Parliament was taken in the Australian Constitution Bill of 1891. Although the form of the provision was somewhat changed in 1897-98, the principle was preserved,[319] and the intendment is clear enough. As Quick and Garran put it: "[T]he cases mentioned in [s 76] are cases in which the Convention did not think it absolutely essential, at the outset, that the High Court should have original jurisdiction; but in which, on the other hand, such jurisdiction was appropriate and might prove to be highly desirable."[320] Of the four subject-matters of jurisdiction in s 76, the first three had counterparts in

---

315 (1998) 194 CLR 355.

316 Op cit p 689.

317 *Re Minister for Immigration and Multicultural Affairs; ex parte Miah* (2001) 179 ALR 238 at 261.

318 Gageler, "The Legitimate Scope of Judicial Review" (2001) 21 Australian Bar Review 279 at 288-290.

319 See Quick and Garran, op cit pp 789-790.

320 Op cit p 790.

Art III, s 2, of the United States Constitution, while the fourth – matters relating to the same subject-matter claimed under the laws of different States – was of uncertain meaning and was probably intended as an expanded version of the US head of jurisdiction relating to claims of land under grants of different States.[321]

It is not at all surprising that the jurisdiction in matters arising under any laws made by the Parliament was consigned to s 76. To have set this clause in s 75 would have imposed an intolerable burden on the High Court. The case of Admiralty and maritime jurisdiction raised special and difficult problems for many years; this will be considered in more detail in the next section. It is rather more surprising, having regard to the matters which were included in s 75, that the jurisdiction in matters arising under the Constitution or involving its interpretation was assigned to s 76 rather than s 75. Although it is by no means necessary for the effective administration of justice that all consti-tutional cases should be tried in the original jurisdiction of the High Court, it is manifestly convenient that there should be machinery for the prompt disposal of important constitutional questions by bringing them immediately before the High Court.[322] In 1903, by s 30(a) of the *Judiciary Act*, Parliament exercised its power under s 76 to invest the High Court with original juris-diction in matters arising under the Constitution or involving its interpretation, and special provision was made for dealing with certain constitutional cases by ss 38A, 40 and 40A of the *Judiciary Act*.[323]

Section 76(i) and (ii) differ somewhat in their terms. The scope of s 76(ii) fell to be considered by the High Court in *Collins v Charles Marshall Pty Ltd*.[324] The Court was considering the validity of s 31 of the *Conciliation and Arbitration Act* 1904, which purported to confer on the Commonwealth Arbitration Court an appellate jurisdiction:

> (a) in proceedings arising under the *Arbitration Act* or involving the interpretation of the Act;
> (b) in proceedings arising under an order or award or involving the interpretation of an order or award.

On the assumption that the Commonwealth Arbitration Court was a federal court within s 71 of the Constitution, this was a purported exercise of power under s 77(i) authorising the Commonwealth Parliament with respect to the matters enumerated in ss 75 and 76 to make laws defining the jurisdiction of any federal court other than the High Court. It was clear that the only possible source of power was s 76(ii), but the High Court demonstrated that s 31 of the *Arbitration Act* could not be supported by reference to that head of power.

---

321 See p 22-23 above.

322 See Dixon, Minutes of Evidence, p 784.

323 See pp 8-10 above. Sections 38A and 40A were repealed by the *Judiciary Act Amendment Act* 1976.

324 (1955) 92 CLR 529.

[A]n order or award of a Conciliation Commissioner or of the Court of Conciliation and Arbitration is not a law of the Commonwealth: *Ex parte McLean* (1930) 43 CLR 472 at pp 479 and 484. Where is to be found the legislative authority for conferring jurisdiction in matters arising under an order or award, as distinguished from under the Act? Where is the legislative authority for conferring jurisdiction in matters which do not arise under the Act but which do involve the interpretation of the Act or of an order or of an award? It cannot be found in the operation of s 76(ii) – matters arising under any laws made by the Parliament – upon s 77(i) – defining the jurisdiction of any Federal Court with respect (inter alia) to such matters.[325]

It follows, as was pointed out by Latham CJ in *R v Commonwealth Court of Conciliation and Arbitration; ex parte Barrett*,[326] that there is a distinction between a matter "arising under" the Commonwealth law and one involving the interpretation of such a law:

> This variation of language supports the view that, in order to bring a matter within s 76(ii) … the inquiry to be made is not whether the determination of the matter involves the interpretation of a Federal law. The relevant inquiry is whether the matter arises under the law. Thus one is compelled to the conclusion that a matter may properly be said to arise under a Federal law if the right or duty in question in the matter owes its existence to Federal law or depends on Federal law for its enforcement, whether or not the determination of the controversy involves the interpretation (or validity) of the law. In either of these cases, the matter arises under the Federal law. If a right claimed is conferred by or under a Federal statute, the claim arises under the statute … The construction of a Federal law, and perhaps a question of the validity of such a law, may be involved in such a matter. But it is not necessary that this should be the case in order that the matter may arise under the law.

This statement seems to refer to the claim being made by the plaintiff or applicant. A similar emphasis was given by the Court in *Collins v Charles Marshall Pty Ltd* where their Honours said:

> Clearly enough a matter or proceeding may involve the interpretation of the Act or of an order or of an award, although the proceeding does not arise under the Act … and it may be said that almost always it will be so where the Act order or award is relevant only to some matter of defence to a proceeding based on some cause of action or ground which is prima facie independent of the Act order or award.[327]

---

325 Ibid at 540 per Dixon CJ, McTiernan, Williams, Webb, Fullagar and Kitto JJ. The Court demonstrated that the legislation under review went beyond the scope of s 76(ii) in other respects: at 540-542.

326 (1945) 70 CLR 141 at 154.

327 (1955) 92 CLR 529 at 540.

It was held, however, in *Felton v Mulligan*[328] that, if a defence or answer is based on a Commonwealth law and is an issue for decision, the matter arises under that Commonwealth law. If the High Court were to be granted general jurisdiction over matters falling within s 76(ii) the decision in *Felton v Mulligan* would give rise to difficulties as it would be necessary to know when proceedings were instituted whether the Court had jurisdiction. However, as Walsh J remarked, that difficulty in relation to the jurisdiction of the High Court "is perhaps of theoretical rather than of practical significance".[329] In any case, it is a difficulty always present in relation to jurisdiction under s 76(i) where a question "involving the interpretation of the Constitution" can arise at any stage in the course of proceedings. As a practical matter, the issue is of more importance in relation to the jurisdiction of the Federal Court and the Family Court, to the question whether a State court is exercising State or federal jurisdiction, and in the exercise by the High Court of its power to remove a cause under s 40 of the *Judiciary Act*.

The decision in *Felton v Mulligan* has increased the difficulty of determining the distinction between a matter arising under a law made by Parliament and one that does not so arise but involves the interpretation of such a law. This difficulty is well illustrated by *Felton v Mulligan* itself. The plaintiff sought a declaration that, under a deed which provided for payment of periodical maintenance to her by her husband, she was entitled to have those payments continue by the deceased husband's executors. The executors contended that the deed was void on the ground of public policy in that it attempted to oust the jurisdiction of the court to make orders for maintenance. The Supreme Court of New South Wales upheld the contention, and the question of whether the court was exercising federal or State jurisdiction was relevant to the issue of whether the wife could appeal to the Privy Council. If it was federal jurisdiction, an appeal was prevented under s 39(2)(a) of the *Judiciary Act*.

While all the judges recognised that, in determining the question raised by the defence of public policy, regard needed to be had to the *Matrimonial Causes Act* 1959 (Cth), which provided for the making of maintenance orders, their Honours differed as to whether the Commonwealth Act was, in the words of Windeyer J, "lurking in the background" or standing "on the threshold".[330]

The meaning of "arising under" was taken a stage further in *LNC Industries Ltd v BMW (Australia) Ltd*.[331] The plaintiff sued on a contract with the defendant under which, it was alleged, the defendant held rights to import goods under customs legislation on trust for the plaintiff. The defendant succeeded in the Supreme Court on the ground that the contract was subject to

328 (1971) 124 CLR 367.
329 Ibid at 403.
330 Ibid at 391.
331 (1983) 151 CLR 575.

unfulfilled conditions. The High Court held that the matter arose under federal law and therefore there could be no appeal to the Privy Council. Although the claim was for specific performance or damages for breach of contract (being a cause of action and remedies under general law), it was also in respect of property, or of a right, created by federal law and, therefore, was a "matter arising under" that law. In that case, neither the interpretation nor application of the Commonwealth legislation seemed to be in dispute, but the Court held that in substance "the very subject of the issue between the parties is an entitlement under the Regulations".[332]

This increase in the area of federal jurisdiction by judicial decision was part of a long tradition, going back to the early days of the Court, of inter-preting the Constitution and legislation so as to further statutory attempts to prevent appeals to the Privy Council and the bypassing of the High Court. With the enactment of the *Australia Acts* 1986 (UK and Cth) that was no longer an issue. The tendency of the Court to favour expansion of the content of federal jurisdiction continued, however, as new social issues and policy choices arose.[333]

Parliament has made only limited use of its power under s 76(ii) to confer original jurisdiction in the High Court,[334] and this is an area in which restraint is obviously to be commended. Section 76(i) is wider in purview, and there has been a full grant of original jurisdiction to the High Court. The clause is not free from obscurities and difficulties, and it becomes necessary first to determine when a matter falls within the scope of the clause. A general answer was given in *James v South Australia*:

> Matters arising under the Constitution or involving its interpretation are those in which the right, title, privilege or immunity is claimed under that instrument, or matters which present necessarily and directly and not incidentally an issue upon its interpretation.[335]

It will be seen that this definition leaves an area of uncertainty and dispute. In the light of the decision of the majority in *Felton v Mulligan*, how-ever, there would seem to be very few matters involving the interpretation of the Constitution that do not arise under the Constitution. Dr Wynes pointed out that, as a result of that decision, "it is difficult to imagine a case in which mere interpretation of a federal Act is involved and which does not arise thereunder".[336]

---

332 Ibid at 582.
333 See Chapter 3 below. Zines, "Federal, Associated and Accrued Jurisdiction" in Opeskin and Wheeler (eds), *The Australian Federal Judicial System*, 2000, p 265.
334 See pp 5-6 above.
335 (1927) 40 CLR 1 at 40 per Gavan Duffy, Rich and Starke JJ.
336 Wynes, op cit, 5th edn, 1976, p 479.

Barwick CJ, who was among the majority in *Felton v Mulligan*, did state that, for the purposes of s 76(ii), it was not enough that a law made by the Parliament must be construed in the course of the decision of the case:

> There must be a matter arising under a law of the Parliament. The contrast between the language of s 76(i) and 76(ii) is relevant in this connection. The point at which interpretation of the federal statute, prima facie an apparently incidental consideration, may give rise to a matter arising under the statute is not readily expressed in universally valid terms. But the distinction between the two situations must be maintained.[337]

In the light of this passage and the actual decision in *Felton v Mulligan*, it would appear that, contrary to the statement in *James v South Australia* that is referred to above, s 76(i) might include matters in which the issue of constitutional interpretation is raised as an "incidental consideration".

In *Hopper v Egg and Egg Pulp Marketing Board*,[338] it was unsuccessfully argued that a charge imposed by the Board under Victorian legislation imposed an excise contrary to s 90 of the Constitution. A challenge was directed to the original jurisdiction of the High Court, but the majority held that the question raised was a matter within s 76(i). Starke J sharply dissented. The two views may be contrasted. Latham CJ, one of the majority, put it this way:

> The fact that the constitutional objection has failed does not deprive the court of jurisdiction if the facts relied on were bona fide raised and were such as to raise the question ... Although the claim based on the Constitution has failed, I cannot discern a satisfactory reason for saying that it was not a bona fide claim so based.[339]

Starke J, on the other hand, said:

> In my opinion an allegation of some contravention of the Constitution which on its face is not such a contravention does not attract or found the original jurisdiction conferred upon this court in matters involving the interpretation of the Constitution. The allegations in the present case are merely colourable: they do not raise any real question involving the interpretation of the Constitution and are in truth fictitious ... [cases cited] ... do not, I think, conflict with this view; the questions in those cases were real and not merely pleading allegations as in the present case. The jurisdiction of the court does not rest on the consent of the parties but upon the existence of some matter founding the jurisdiction of the court ... I think this case should be dismissed for want of jurisdiction in this court.[340]

In general, it appears that the Court has construed its jurisdiction under this head rather generously, and has at times found a basis for the Court's

---

337 (1971) 124 CLR 367 at 374.
338 (1939) 61 CLR 665.
339 Ibid at 673-674.
340 Ibid at 677.

jurisdiction where counsel was apparently unable to detect a problem of constitutional interpretation.[341]

On occasion the Court has emphasised that the constitutional point on which jurisdiction was based was raised bona fide,[342] but on the cases it would seem that a constitutional issue would have to be extremely far fetched or remote before the court would treat it as having been raised mala fide with the object of attracting jurisdiction. The issue of what is meant by a "bona fide" or "genuine" claim is dealt with below in connection with federal courts in Chapter 3. Authority to deal with non-federal claims that are regarded as "inseverable" from federal claims has become known as "accrued jurisdiction". Over the past two decades there has been a considerable expansion of decisional law on the issue. Nearly all the cases are concerned with the jurisdiction of the Federal Court and, to a lesser extent, the Family Court and are also discussed below in Chapter 3.

Admiralty and Maritime Matters : Section 76(iii)

In *In re Judiciary and Navigation Acts*,[343] the High Court reviewed the provisions of ss 75, 76 and 77 of the Constitution and said:

> This express statement of the matters in respect of which and the courts by which the judicial power of the Commonwealth may be exercised is, we think, clearly intended as a delimitation of the whole of the original jurisdiction which may be exercised under the judicial power of the Commonwealth, and as a necessary exclusion of any other exercise of original jurisdiction.

This was in the course of a decision that s 88 of the *Judiciary Act*, which purported to confer jurisdiction on the High Court to give an advisory opinion on the validity of an enactment of the Commonwealth Parliament, was unconstitutional. The passage suggests that ss 75 and 76 mark out the limits of the original federal jurisdiction of the High Court. It is clear, however, that so far as Admiralty jurisdiction is concerned, the source of the original jurisdiction of the High Court, was, for many years, the *Colonial Courts of Admiralty Act* 1890, an enactment of the United Kingdom Parliament, and not Chapter III of the Constitution. This was the case from 1939 until 1988. In *Huddart Parker v Ship Mill Hill*,[344] it was argued that because the Admiralty jurisdiction of the High Court derived from the *Colonial Courts of Admiralty Act* and not from

---

341 See *R v Bevan; ex parte Elias and Gordon* (1942) 66 CLR 452 at 465 per Starke J: "Consideration has led me to the conclusion that the matter before us involves the interpretation of the Constitution, which founds the original jurisdiction of this Court, though we heard no argument to that effect from counsel."

342 *Troy v Wigglesworth* (1919) 26 CLR 305 at 311; *Hopper v Egg and Egg Pulp Marketing Board* (1939) 61 CLR 665 at 673-674; *Re Cook; ex parte Twigg* (1980) 147 CLR 15.

343 (1921) 29 CLR 257 at 265 per Knox CJ, Gavan Duffy, Powers, Rich and Starke JJ.

344 (1950) 81 CLR 502.

the Constitution, it was not federal jurisdiction and that therefore s 79 of the *Judiciary Act*, prescribing a choice of law rule for the High Court sitting in its original jurisdiction, did not apply to the particular case of original Admiralty jurisdiction. The Court acknowledged that its Admiralty jurisdiction depended exclusively upon the Act of 1890, but held nevertheless that s 79 of the *Judiciary Act* applied.

Although it was clear that the High Court exercised original jurisdiction in Admiralty under the *Colonial Courts of Admiralty Act* exclusively, this was not always the case. Section 76(iii) of the Constitution authorised the Parliament to invest the High Court with original jurisdiction in matters of Admiralty and maritime jurisdiction. These words were copied directly from Art III, s 2, of the United States Constitution, where the jurisdiction was made *federal* but was not assigned to the original jurisdiction of the Supreme Court of the United States. The historical reasons for conferring federal jurisdiction in Admiralty and maritime cases in the United States are reasonably clear. Admiralty was a separate corpus of law which before the American War of Independence had been administered by British Vice-Admiralty Courts rather than by the ordinary colonial courts, so that general Admiralty jurisdiction covered an area in which the State courts and their predecessors had little experience. Moreover:

> Since one of the objectives of the Philadelphia Convention was the pro-
> motion of commerce through removal of obstacles occasioned by the
> diverse local rules of the States, it was only logical that it should contribute
> to the development of a uniform body of maritime law by establishing a
> system of federal courts and granting to these tribunals jurisdiction over
> Admiralty and maritime cases.[345]

The principal commerce of the period was maritime, and it was in this jurisdiction that disputes with foreigners were most likely to arise.

There is a further important point which bears on the scope of Admiralty and maritime jurisdiction in the United States. The struggle between the com-
mon law courts and the Admiralty Courts had resulted in the curtailment of Admiralty jurisdiction in England. There was, even at the date of constitution making, a much broader conception of the scope of Admiralty jurisdiction in the United States. It was early ruled by the federal courts that the extent of Admiralty and maritime jurisdiction was not to be determined by English law, but by principles of maritime law "as respected by maritime courts of all nations and adopted by most, if not by all of them, on the continent of Europe", and this broader definition was approved by the Supreme Court before 1850 in judgments which asserted that the constitutional grant of the jurisdiction was not to be controlled or limited by English rules of Admiralty law.[346]

---

345 *The Constitution of the United States of America*, op cit p 646.

346 *Waring v Clarke* 5 How 441 (1847); *New Jersey Steam Navigation Co v Merchants Bank* 6 How 344 (1848). See *The Constitution of the United States of America*, op cit pp 647, 653; *Owners of "Shin Kobe Maru" v Empire Shipping Co Ltd* (1994) 181 CLR 404 at 423-424.

English Admiralty jurisdiction, on the other hand, bore the marks of the struggle between the courts, and by 1840 was very narrowly confined. The jurisdiction of the English Courts of Admiralty was extended by statute in that year, and by subsequent legislation. Admiralty jurisdiction was a field in which uniformity and the preservation of Imperial control were regarded as important, and in the colonies the jurisdiction was conferred by Imperial statute on Vice-Admiralty Courts, and special Imperial Acts were passed from time to time extending their jurisdiction. In 1890 the *Colonial Courts of Admiralty Act* conferred Admiralty jurisdiction on courts in British possessions, while preserving a substantial measure of Imperial control. "Underlying the Act is the assumption that the matter is essentially of Imperial concern, and that such limited power of local regulation as might for convenience be conceded should be subject to the jealous control of the Imperial authorities."[347] The Act by s 2 vested Admiralty jurisdiction in every court of law in a British possession for the time being declared in pursuance of the Act to be a Court of Admiralty or which, if no such declaration was in force in the possession, had therein original unlimited jurisdiction, which was defined by s 15 as civil jurisdiction unlimited as to the value of the subject-matter at issue or as to the amount that could be claimed or recovered.

The jurisdiction conferred was that of the Admiralty jurisdiction of the High Court in England. It was provided that colonial laws might declare any court of unlimited civil jurisdiction to be a Colonial Court of Admiralty. Special provision was made for New South Wales and Victoria (among other named British possessions), where the Act came into operation, not in 1891, but by Orders-in-Council in 1911. Two important decisions of the Privy Council limited the jurisdiction of Colonial Courts of Admiralty. In *The Camosun*,[348] it was ruled that the Admiralty jurisdiction vested in colonial courts was that of the Admiralty Court in England before its incorporation in the English High Court by the *Judicature Acts* of 1873 and 1875, so that it was not possible to raise an equitable defence in a Colonial Court of Admiralty even in those British possessions which had adopted the *Judicature Acts* system. In *The Yuri Maru; the Woron*,[349] it was further held that the jurisdiction conferred by the Act was fixed as of 1890, so that subsequent statutory extensions of the Admiralty jurisdiction of the High Court in England did not extend the jurisdiction of Colonial Courts of Admiralty in British possessions.

---

347 McGrath, "Admiralty Jurisdiction and the Statute of Westminster" (1932) 6 ALJ 160 at 162.

348 [1909] AC 597.

349 [1927] AC 906. See *F Kanematsu and Co Ltd v Ship "Shahzada"* (1956) 96 CLR 477 at 482-483: "The Admiralty jurisdiction of the High Court, exercisable by virtue of the provisions of the *Colonial Courts of Admiralty Act* 1890, is no more extensive than that which was exercisable in the admiralty jurisdiction of the High Court in England 'as it existed at the time wh░░ the Act was passed'." It was held by Taylor J that the Court had no jurisdiction in that case.

In this area there is reason to doubt whether the Australian founding fathers knew what they were doing when s 76(iii) was written into the Constitution. In view of the Imperial interest in these matters, it is perhaps surprising that this clause was not more carefully scrutinised by the Imperial law officers when the Constitution Bill was submitted to the United Kingdom Parliament, and it is certainly not clear why it was felt that there was any need for a further grant of jurisdiction under the Constitution. No doubt the influence of American precedent was very strong, but it is very uncertain whether the founding fathers were aware of the fact that Admiralty and maritime jurisdiction had a significantly wider scope and meaning in the United States – one which differed, as we have seen, from the English jurisdiction. Quick and Garran saw some of the difficulties:

> Under this Constitution, however, the Parliament has power, independently of the *Colonial Courts of Admiralty Act*, to confer Admiralty and maritime jurisdiction on the High Court; and it seems clear that the limitations imposed by that Act on the jurisdiction of "Colonial Courts of Admiralty" within the meaning of that Act … cannot be read into the plenary powers conferred by this section.[350]

In 1914 the Commonwealth Parliament enacted two new provisions into the *Judiciary Act*.[351] Section 30(b) of the *Judiciary Act* was a purported exercise of power under s 76(iii) of the Constitution and conferred original jurisdiction on the High Court in all matters of Admiralty or maritime jurisdiction. It is to be noted that the jurisdiction was conferred in this disjunctive form, while s 76(iii) refers to Admiralty and maritime jurisdiction. Section 30A was an exercise of power under the *Colonial Courts of Admiralty Act* and declared the High Court to be a Colonial Court of Admiralty "within the meaning of the Imperial Act known as the *Colonial Courts of Admiralty Act*". This raised two questions. First, did s 30A, by declaring the High Court to be a Colonial Court of Admiralty, deprive the Supreme Courts of the States of their Admiralty jurisdiction under *the Colonial Courts of Admiralty Act*? Second, what was the relationship between Admiralty or maritime jurisdiction conferred by s 30(b) and the Admiralty jurisdiction of the High Court under the *Colonial Courts of Admiralty Act*?

The answers to these questions were not clear. Taking first the problem of s 30A, it was argued unsuccessfully in *John Sharp and Sons Ltd v Ship Katherine Mackall*[352] that the Commonwealth was not a British possession for the purposes of the *Colonial Courts of Admiralty Act*, that the States were British possessions for this purpose, and that the jurisdiction of the High Court in Admiralty matters depended on s 76(iii) and not on the Act of 1890. It was

---

350 Op cit p 800.
351 Act no 11 of 1914.
352 (1924) 34 CLR 420.

held in the High Court, on the authority of the *Imperial Interpretation Act* 1889, that the Commonwealth was a British possession for the purposes of the *Colonial Courts of Admiralty Act*. On this point the case was approved by the High Court in *McIlwraith McEacharn Ltd v Shell Co of Australia Ltd.*[353] It followed that, if s 30A was otherwise validly enacted, the declaration operated to deprive the State Supreme Courts of their Admiralty jurisdiction under the *Colonial Courts of Admiralty Act*. But whether s 30A was otherwise valid was not clear. In *John Sharp and Sons Ltd v Ship Katherine Mackall*, Isaacs J was of opinion that it was not valid because, as a reserved Bill, it had not satisfied the terms of s 60 of the Constitution, since the Royal assent had been notified outside the two-year period.[354] This view did not command the assent of the whole Court,[355] but it left the Admiralty jurisdiction of State Supreme Courts uncertain and attention was drawn to this by members of the High Court in later cases.[356] The matter was finally resolved by the enactment of the *Judiciary Act* 1939, which repealed s 30A.

The Attorney-General for the Commonwealth, introducing the Bill, said that there was some doubt, having regard to s 60 of the Constitution, whether s 30A had been validly enacted. If the section was valid, it probably deprived State Supreme Courts of Admiralty jurisdiction under the *Colonial Courts of Admiralty Act*. In view of these uncertainties, it was thought desirable to repeal the section to ensure that State Supreme Courts, as well as the High Court, were Colonial Courts of Admiralty, since there would no longer be any declaration in force, and State Supreme Courts were courts of unlimited civil jurisdiction.[357]

There remained the problem of the relationship between "Admiralty and maritime jurisdiction" under s 76(iii) and Admiralty jurisdiction under the *Colonial Courts of Admiralty Act*. In *John Sharp and Sons Ltd v Ship Katherine Mackall*,[358] Isaacs J drew attention to the very wide scope which had been attributed to this jurisdiction in the United States. He said that it was not conceivable that the framers of the Australian Constitution intended to follow American doctrine on such a subject of common Imperial concern in direct opposition to established English precedent. On the other hand it was not to be

---

353 (1945) 70 CLR 175 at 202-206.
354 (1924) 34 CLR 420 at 429-430. Section 60 provides: "A proposed law reserved for the Queen's pleasure shall not have any force unless and until within two years from the day on which it was presented to the Governor-General for the Queen's assent the Governor-General makes known, by speech or message to each of the Houses of Parliament, or by Proclamation, that it has received the Queen's assent."
355 See per Starke J (1924) 34 CLR 420 at 433. Knox CJ and Gavan Duffy J did not find it necessary to deal with the point.
356 See *McArthur v Williams* (1936) 55 CLR 324; *Union Steamship Co of New Zealand Ltd v The Caradale* (1937) 56 CLR 277; *Nagrint v Ship "Regis"* (1939) 61 CLR 688.
357 Debates (H of R), vol 161, p 162.
358 (1924) 34 CLR 420.

supposed that the scope of the jurisdiction under s 76(iii) was merely the stereotyped English common law jurisdiction. For the purposes of the case, it was not necessary to define the scope of the jurisdiction but Isaacs J observed:

> [I]f it became necessary to determine this case upon s 76(iii) of the Constitution and s 30(b) of the *Judiciary Act* there are some very difficult questions to answer … [W]ere the decision of this case dependent on the provision in s 76(iii) of the Constitution with the statutory exercise of the power, there would be a field of inquiry by no means clear.[359]

It was now clear that original jurisdiction under the *Colonial Courts of Admiralty Act* was vested in the High Court. It was also held that the Supreme Courts of the several States also had jurisdiction under that Act.[360]

The Commonwealth Parliament in 1939 also repealed s 30(b) of the *Judiciary Act* and since then the High Court has not been invested with jurisdiction under s 76(iii).

Since 1988 jurisdiction in Admiralty has been governed by the *Admiralty Act* 1988 (Cth). This Act repeals the *Colonial Courts of Admiralty Act* 1890 in so far as it was part of the law of the Commonwealth or an external Territory. It does not confer any jurisdiction on the High Court. Jurisdiction in respect of actions in personam is vested in all State and Territory courts, subject to conditions (s 9). Jurisdiction in respect of actions in rem is confined to the Federal Court, the Supreme Courts of the States and Territories (s 10) and other courts that the Governor-General may declare (s 11). The jurisdiction of the latter courts extends to a matter of admiralty and maritime jurisdiction, not otherwise within its jurisdiction, that is "associated" with a matter in which the jurisdiction of the court under the Act is invoked (s 12). To ensure that the Act does not go beyond constitutional power, it is provided that it does not confer or invest jurisdiction that is not of a kind mentioned in s 76(ii) – arising under any laws made by the Parliament – or s 76(iii) – Admiralty and maritime jurisdiction (s 13). The issue of "associated jurisdiction" is dealt with in Chapter 3 below.

In *Owners of the Ship "Shin Kobe Maru" v Empire Shipping Co Inc*,[361] the High Court generally followed United States decisions in holding that the term "maritime" in s 76(iii) extended jurisdiction beyond Admiralty jurisdiction as it existed in 1901. Despite Isaacs J's view that this paragraph was based on "established English precedent",[362] the Court said that ordinary

359 34 CLR 420 at 428.
360 *McIlwraith McEacharn Ltd v Shell Co of Australia Ltd* (1945) 70 CLR 175 at 204 per Dixon J: "The High Court as well as the Supreme Courts of the States are courts of unlimited civil jurisdiction within this definition. No doubt it is also true of the Supreme Courts of the Territories." *Lewmarine Pty Ltd v The Ship "Kaptayanni"* [1974] VR 465; *Union Steamship Co of New Zealand Ltd v Ferguson* (1969) 119 CLR 191.
361 (1994) 181 CLR 404.
362 *John Sharp and Sons Ltd v The Katherine MacKall* (1924) 34 CLR 420 at 428.

principles of constitutional interpretation required a liberal construction. Accordingly, s 76(iii) covers matters of the kind generally accepted by maritime nations as falling within a special jurisdiction, sometimes called Admiralty and sometimes called maritime jurisdiction, concerned with the resolution of controversies relating to marine commerce and navigation.[363] It was held that claims specified in the Act (s 4) were of a kind generally accepted by maritime nations as falling within that special jurisdiction. For this purpose they examined the 1952 International Convention of Rules relating to the Arrest of Sea-Going Ships. The Court left open whether some American decisions were too narrow for purposes of s 76(iii). These were cases which had held that contracts on land for the construction or sale of ships did not come within the jurisdiction. The judges referred to criticism within the United States of those decisions.[364]

The present position is that the High Court has no original jurisdiction in Admiralty or maritime matters, except where they may arise in relation to the exercise of other heads of jurisdiction such as s 75(iii) or (iv). The jurisdiction conferred on the Federal Court is pursuant to power in s 77(i) – defining the jurisdiction of any federal court. The jurisdiction invested in State courts is by virtue of s 77(iii). This jurisdiction seems to override and take the place of any Admiralty and maritime jurisdiction in State courts that derived from s 39(2) of the *Judiciary Act*. The jurisdiction conferred on Territorial courts is derived either from s 76(iii) or s 122. That is a general issue discussed in Chapter 4 below.

Forum Non Conveniens : Remitter

It is clear law that Parliament cannot shut out the original jurisdiction of the High Court so far as it has been conferred by s 75 of the Constitution.[365] It is not altogether clear, however, whether the High Court may decline to exercise jurisdiction conferred on it directly by s 75, or by Parliament under s 76. It may be argued that jurisdiction is the grant of authority to adjudicate, and does not necessarily require a court to exercise that authority. But there are many judicial statements in England, Australia and the United States to the effect that a grant of jurisdiction carries with it a duty to exercise that jurisdiction.[366] The writ of mandamus lies to compel lower courts to exercise their jurisdiction. This assumes the existence of a duty. While mandamus does not lie to so compel the High Court, the absence of the remedy is no reason for

---

363 (1994) 181 CLR 404 at 424.

364 Ibid at 424-425.

365 *Bank of New South Wales v Commonwealth* (1948) 76 CLR 1 at 357.

366 Lindell, "Duty to Exercise Judicial Review" in Zines (ed) *Commentaries on the Australian Constitution*, 1977, ch 5; Lindell, "The Justiciability of Political Questions: Recent Developments" in Lee and Winterton (eds), *Australian Constitutional Perspectives*, 1992, ch 7, pp 218-239.

distinguishing superior and inferior courts so far as the question whether there is a duty is concerned.[367]

In the United States, Marshall CJ affirmed that a grant of jurisdiction implied a judicial duty to exercise it in *Cohens v Virginia*.[368] He said: "We have no more right to decline the exercise of jurisdiction which is given, than to usurp that which is not given." It has been made clear, however, that this duty is subject to exceptions. In *Massachusetts v Missouri*,[369] the Supreme Court refused to hear a suit brought by Massachusetts for taxes allegedly owed by a citizen of another State. The Court said[370] that using it to collect State taxes in this way would create a burden "which the grant of original juris-diction cannot be regarded as compelling this Court to assume, and which might seriously interfere with the discharge by this Court of its duty in deciding the cases and controversies appropriately brought before it".

That approach was followed in *Ohio v Wyandotte Chemical Corp.*[371] The Court affirmed the "time-honoured maxim of Anglo-American common law tradition that a court possessed of jurisdiction generally must exercise it";[372] but again it was said that discretion was needed when another court was available and the burden of exercising the original jurisdiction might seriously interfere with the Court's function as a court of review. In the United States, legal opinion is divided on whether the Court is correct in invoking the doctrine of forum non conveniens in these circumstances.[373]

There is little authority on the matter in Australia. In *Fausset v Carroll*,[374] which was a matter between residents of different States tried in the original jurisdiction of the High Court, the short cover note report states that, while the Court has jurisdiction in such cases, it is important to note that the practice of bringing actions in the High Court merely because the plaintiff resides in one State and the defendant in another is not encouraged. In *Fausset v Carroll*, where the issue was one of fact and the sum at stake small, Gavan Duffy J said that he had consulted his colleagues, and that in future plaintiffs would not be allowed costs in such actions. On other occasions the Court has indicated that it will make a special order for reduced costs where a plaintiff brings a diversity action in the High Court where the case "is one normally and more appropriately" brought in the Supreme Court of a State and the action in the

---

367   *Ah Yick v Lehmert* (1905) 2 CLR 593; *R v Commonwealth Court of Conciliation and Arbitration; ex parte Ozone Theatre (Aust) Ltd* (1949) 78 CLR 389 at 398.

368   6 Wheat 264 at 404 (1821).

369   308 US 1 (1939).

370   Ibid at 19.

371   401 US 493 (1971).

372   Ibid at 496-497.

373   *Hart and Wechsler's The Federal Courts and the Federal System*, 4th edn, 1996, pp 329-336; Shapiro, "Jurisdiction and Discretion" (1985) 60 New York ULR 543.

374   (1917) 15 WN (NSW) No 12 Cover Note (19 August 1917).

High Court has resulted in a material increase in costs,[375] or where an action was one which could have been brought in a district or county court.[376] This is a curious and rather backhand way of invoking the doctrine of forum non conveniens. The Court did not directly question its obligation to provide a forum, but effectively denied it by a general prospective declaration that it would refuse or reduce costs. It is easy to sympathise with the Court's impatience with this time-wasting and purposeless jurisdiction, but the Constitution specifically confers the jurisdiction without any prescription of the amount in issue. In the United States, original diversity jurisdiction is exercisable by federal district courts, and then only if the amount in issue is not less than $50,000. If a smaller sum is involved, the parties must seek relief in State courts. But if, as is the case in Australia, the Constitution confers this original jurisdiction on the High Court without any such limit, it is difficult to see what can justify the Court in ruling that the jurisdiction is available, but that a party may be deprived of costs simply because that party exercises his or her constitutional right to invoke it. However, as explained below, the conferral on the Court of a general power of remittal to other courts will insure that this situation will rarely arise, if at all, in the future.

In *R v Langdon*,[377] an application was made to the High Court in its original diversity jurisdiction for a writ of habeas corpus in child custody proceedings. The application had originally been made in the Sydney registry of the Court and was transferred to Melbourne. The plaintiff husband was a Victorian resident and the wife resided in Tasmania. Taylor J had some doubt whether such a case fell within the diversity jurisdiction but, on the assumption that it did, proceeded to consider what law should be applied. This he held to be Tasmanian law as set out in the *Guardianship and Custody of Infants Act* 1934. After examining the provisions of this Act, Taylor J said:

> The 'Court' in each case is defined by the Act to mean the Supreme Court of Tasmania, and the jurisdiction which is conferred by these sections is a special statutory jurisdiction with respect to infants. I very much doubt whether the jurisdiction conferred by (s 10) is exercisable by this Court in its original jurisdiction merely because the husband and wife are residents of different States and I have no doubt that the jurisdiction of this Court to

375 *Marlow v Tatlow* noted in (1965) 39 ALJ 140.

376 *Cadet v Stevens* noted in (1967) 40 ALJ 361; *Morrison v Thwaites* (1969) 43 ALJR 452. A similar approach was taken in relation to the appellate jurisdiction of the Court. *In Ritter v North Side Enterprises Pty Ltd* (1975) 132 CLR 301, an appeal was brought from a judge of the Queensland Supreme Court to the High Court against an order for specific performance of a covenant. The appeal was allowed but the Court expressed the opinion that, as the appeal was a minor matter, the appellant should have gone to the Full Court of the Supreme Court and Gibbs J (with whom Stephen and Murphy JJ agreed) said, at 305: "I would in future be inclined to entertain the view that appellants who bring appeals of this kind to this Court rather than to the Full Court of the Supreme Court ought to be visited with consequences in costs."

377 (1953) 88 CLR 158.

issue a prerogative writ should not be exercised on the husband's application unless it is open to the Court to refuse the application in the exercise of a discretion similar to that reposed in the Supreme Court. The writ, although grantable ex debito justitiae, does not issue as of course ... and it may be sufficient to say that the husband's application should be refused on the ground that it would be more appropriate for this and similar applications to be made to the Court to whom the appropriate special jurisdiction has been committed. But it is quite clear that it should be refused unless it is open to this Court to exercise such a discretion as that given by the statute to the Supreme Court.

The proposition that, where parties are residents of different States, this Court may exercise powers conferred upon particular courts for special purposes involves such far reaching consequences that I think the question, if and when it arises in an appropriate case, should be determined by the Full Court ... . It would, I think, be most inappropriate for this Court to make an order for custody and maintenance where there exist courts specially constituted for this purpose and which may, if and as occasion requires, review the matter from time to time.[378]

Leaving aside any question as to the propriety of the choice of Tasmanian law to govern the case, the judgment raises a variety of problems posed by the availability of original jurisdiction in the High Court in diversity cases. It is apparent that the Tasmanian draftsman did not consider the possibility of such original jurisdiction in drafting the *Guardianship and Custody of Infants Act*, and other State Acts which ascribe special jurisdiction to particular courts have likewise been drawn without regard to the original jurisdiction of the High Court. Taylor J, in the passages cited, appears to suggest that in such a case, where relief is not available as of right, the High Court may refuse to make an order on the ground that a State court is, in the circumstances, a more appropriate forum. If this is a correct reading of *R v Langdon* it lends support to the view that it is open to the High Court to refuse a remedy on the ground that it is forum non conveniens. It has been argued that this case is not merely one where the Court chose not to deal with a matter because the case was minor and the time of the High Court should not be taken up with such questions. Rather it might be seen as a case where the High Court was not able to provide an appropriate remedy. This argument suggests that a principle of the conflict of laws should be adopted, namely that English courts will not determine a claim if the machinery by way of remedies is so different as to make the right sought to be enforced a different right.[379]

So in *R v Langdon*, while the High Court could have granted a writ of habeas corpus, it was assumed it could not have done so subject to the conditions and limitations that were laid down in the Tasmanian Act with

---

378   Ibid at 161-163.
379   *Phrantzes v Argenti* [1960] 2 QB 19; Pryles and Hanks, *Federal Conflict of Laws*, 1974, p 136; Nygh, *Conflict of Laws in Australia*, 6th edn, 1995, pp 262-263.

respect to the jurisdiction of the State Supreme Court. It is clearly undesirable that the High Court adjudicate on a case governed by State law where that court is unable adequately to administer that law. It should be noted, however, that this argument is based largely on the administration of justice as between the parties. The doctrine of forum non conveniens in the conflict of laws is confined to those considerations.[380] The leading High Court case is *Voth v Manildra Flour Mills Pty Ltd*.[381] The Court stayed an action on the ground that New South Wales was "an inappropriate forum". The majority[382] reiterated the principle that there is an obligation on Australian courts to exercise the jurisdiction conferred on them, but they held it did not extend to cases where the forum is clearly inappropriate. They considered that the United States position was similar, but differed in so far as it took into account the selected forum's administrative problems, such as congested lists and lack of judicial resources. These were, they said, the kind of matters "to which our courts do not usually have regard".[383]

As indicated above,[384] the United States Supreme Court has refused to accept jurisdiction where it would constitute a "burden" on the Court and interfere with the discharge of its duties in deciding cases that are thought to be more important. Sir Garfield Barwick, before he became Chief Justice, considered that this American doctrine might apply in Australia, at any rate, where another federal court was available to deal with the matter.[385] It has also been pointed out[386] that the view that the High Court cannot refuse to exercise its jurisdiction gives an undue advantage to the plaintiff to choose the forum that suits him or her best. Under s 40 of the *Judiciary Act* a cause within federal jurisdiction may be removed from a State, federal or Territorial court into the High Court. So, in those situations, the defendant is given an opportunity of arguing that the forum chosen by the plaintiff is not the most appropriate. As a matter of policy it would seem desirable that the defendant have a similar opportunity when the plaintiff commences a suit in the High Court.

It remains to consider s 44 of the *Judiciary Act*, which provides:

> (1) Any matter other than a matter to which subsection (2) applies that is at any time pending in the High Court, whether originally commenced in the High Court or not, or any part of such a matter, may, upon the application of a party or of the High Court's own motion, be remitted by the High

---

380 *Re Kernot* [1965] Ch 217.

381 (1990) 171 CLR 538.

382 Ibid at 559.

383 Ibid at 561. See also *Re Jarman; ex parte Cook* (1997) 188 CLR 595 at 634 per Gummow J.

384 Page 78.

385 (1964) 1 Federal LR 1 at 10-15.

386 Howard, *Australian Federal Constitutional Law*, 2nd edn, 1972, p 196.

Court to any federal court, court of a State or court of a Territory that has jurisdiction with respect to the subject-matter and the parties, and, subject to any directions of the High Court, further proceedings in the matter or in that part of the matter, as the case may be, shall be as directed by the court to which it is remitted.

(2) Where a matter referred to in paragraph 38(a), (b), (c) or (d) is at any time pending in the High Court, the High Court may, upon the application of a party or of the High Court's own motion, remit the matter, or any part of the matter, to the Federal Court of Australia or any court of a State or Territory.

(2A) Where a matter in which the Commonwealth, or a person suing or being sued on behalf of the Commonwealth, is a party is at any time pending in the High Court, the High Court may, upon the application of a party or of the High Court's own motion, remit the matter, or any part of the matter, to the Federal Court of Australia.

(3) Where the High Court remits a matter, or any part of a matter, under subsection (2) or (2A) to a court:

(a) that court has jurisdiction in the matter, or in that part of the matter, as the case may be; and

(b) subject to any directions of the High Court, further proceedings in the matter, or in that part of the matter, as the case may be, shall be as directed by that court.

Subsection (1) was enacted in 1976. (Before that date a similar provision, s 45, enacted in 1903, authorised the Court to remit matters on the application of a party to any court of a State which had federal jurisdiction.) The remainder of s 44 was added in 1983. Subsection (2) enables the Court to remit most of its jurisdiction made exclusive by s 38 except para (e) of the provision, which comprises applications for writs of mandamus or prohibition against an officer of the Commonwealth or a federal court. Subsection (2)(a) is referable to s 75(iii) of the Constitution, and ensures that a matter can be re-mitted to the Federal Court (which otherwise had no jurisdiction to determine such a matter).

In 1997, by virtue of s 39B(1) of the *Judiciary Act*, the Federal Court, with some exceptions, was given the High Court's jurisdiction in s 75(v).[387] That provision enables the High Court to remit such matters to the Federal Court under s 44(1) because it has jurisdiction "with respect to the subject matter and the parties".[388]

---

387 The exceptions to the Federal Court's jurisdiction are where the remedies are sought against persons holding office under the *Workplace Relations Act* 1996, or the *Coal Industry Act* 1946, or against a judge of the Family Court.

388 As a result of amendments made to the *Migration Act* 1958 in 1992 the exercise of jurisdiction of the Federal Court in reviewing migration matters under s 39B(1) was restricted, as was the High Court's power to remit such matters to the Federal Court. These provisions were upheld in *Abebe v Commonwealth* (1997) 197 CLR 510. By virtue of the *Migration Legislation Amendment (Judicial Review) Act* 2001 an attempt has been made to restrict much further the power of review of both the High Court and the Federal Court.

In 1977 Barwick CJ said that the High Court had, as a result of the enactment of s 44 of the *Judiciary Act*, begun remitting accident cases arising in the Court's diversity jurisdiction to appropriate State courts for disposal.[389] The Court has since then made frequent use of this power. In 1983 Gibbs CJ said that the power given by s 44 was extensively used, with the result that little original jurisdiction was exercised by the Court.[390] In 1985 he welcomed the increased power of remitter given by the 1983 amendments.[391]

In the earlier editions of this work[392] it was argued that s 75 of the Constitution should be read as requiring the High Court to exercise its original jurisdiction. On that view it would follow that the High Court could not invoke the doctrine of forum non conveniens either under a statute or of its own volition,[393] where the only consideration was the work of the Court rather than matters relevant to the exercise of jurisdiction in accordance with principles applied in conflict of laws cases as illustrated by *Voth v Manildra Flour Mills Ltd*. As explained above, those principles, as applied in Australia, exclude consideration of the forum's "administrative problems".[394] Those principles, however, would seem to support, by analogy, *R v Langdon* discussed above where the problem was that the Court did not have the machinery and remedies to administer the law adequately, but some other court did.[395]

In the light of the extensive practice of the High Court in remitting matters within its original jurisdiction, and the "welcome" given by Chief Justices of the Court to increases in the remittal power, arguing against its validity in respect of s 75 matters is, no doubt, as effective as whistling in the wind. Indeed, it was said in the previous edition that there could be little doubt that, as a matter of policy, the doctrine of forum non conveniens is desirable in the public interest by ensuring that the High Court is able to deal properly with its important constitutional functions and as a national final appeal court. Certainly, after a quarter of a century of High Court practice in remitting matters to other courts, any cessation of it now could have a great damaging effect.

---

389 Barwick, "The State of the Australian Judicature" (1977) 51 ALJ 480 at 489.

390 Gibbs, "The High Court Today" (1983) 10 Sydney LR 1.

391 Gibbs, "The State of the Australian Judicature" (1985) 59 ALJ 522 at 533.

392 2nd edn, p 81.

393 It was also argued, however, that the same considerations did not apply to jurisdiction derived from s 76, such as s 30 of the *Judiciary Act*, because s 76 would permit Parliament to qualify the jurisdiction it confers.

394 That situation was deplored by Spigelman CJ in *James Hardie Industries Pty Ltd v Grigor* (1998) 45 NSWLR 20 at 40-41.

395 In *R v Langdon* itself it would have been preferable for the High Court to have regarded itself as subject to the statutory fetters imposed by State legislation on the Supreme Court. "Such a result would appear to reconcile as far as possible the constitutional right to bring suit in the original jurisdiction of the High Court with the obligation under s 79 of the *Judiciary Act* to apply State statute law": Cowen (1955) 7 Res Judicatae 1 at 27. That sort of issue was examined, in relation to the Federal Court, in *Australian Securities and Investment Commission v Edensor Nominees Pty Ltd* (2001) 204 CLR 559.

The work that can potentially get to the Court under, for example, s 75(iii), (iv) and (v) has grown greatly in the past 25 years.

Ideally, the best approach would be to change s 75 as recommended by the Constitutional Commission. The Commission proposed that Parliament be empowered to limit or exclude much of the High Court's original jurisdiction in s 75 to the extent that the jurisdiction was conferred on a federal court or on a court in each State and Territory.[396] It also recommended that there be an express provision (s 76A) enabling Parliament to authorise the High Court to remit to some other court matters in respect of which original jurisdiction is vested by the Constitution.[397]

In the absence of such constitutional reform, it seems likely that the wider concept of forum non conveniens will be accepted as a principle establishing the validity of s 44 of the *Judiciary Act*. There is perhaps an argument that, historically, the national role of the High Court as a final court of appeal and its function, as Deakin put it, "to protect the Constitution against assaults"[398] were seen as its major purposes. If practical circumstances, arising out of developments since federation, threaten them, s 44 of the *Judiciary Act* may be seen as reasonably incidental to their fulfilment and so authorised by s 51(xxxix) of the Constitution: "matters incidental to the execution of any power vested by this Constitution in ... the Federal Judicature ...".

---

396 Two exceptions were matters arising under the Constitution or involving its interpretation (which the Commission proposed should be in s 75) and matters between Governments.

397 *Final Report of the Constitutional Commission*, 1988, vol 1, pp 373-374.

398 Commonwealth Parliamentary Debates, vol 8 (1902) p 10967.

Chapter 2

Jurisdiction Between Residents of Different States

Reasons for Diversity Jurisdiction

In the course of the debates on the Judicature Chapter of the Commonwealth Constitution in the Federal Convention of 1897-98, references to the American Constitution came thick and fast. One member could not restrain his impatience:

> We have heard too much about the example of the United States all through the meetings of this Convention. If the Constitutions of the United States and Canada had been burned before the Convention met we should have done more practical work, and we should probably have evolved a Constitution quite as suitable, if not more suitable to the people we represent.[1]

It is interesting to note that these words were spoken by a South Australian delegate, by name Mr Solomon. We have already noted that there were some significant departures from the American model.[2] The High Court of Australia was designed as a general court of appeal, and federal jurisdiction might be vested in State courts. The method of appointment and removal of justices of the High Court followed British rather than American patterns,[3] and the provisions with respect to the appellate jurisdiction of the Privy Council obviously had no counterpart in the American Constitution.[4] In conferring federal jurisdiction, the Australian draftsmen omitted some matters which appeared in the American instrument and incorporated others which were novel.[5]

But there was heavy reliance on American precedent. This is certainly true in the case of diversity jurisdiction, which appears in the American Constitution, Art III, s 2: "The judicial power shall extend ... to Controversies ... between Citizens of different States." In the 1890 meeting at Melbourne, Alfred Deakin had drawn attention to the pattern of federal jurisdiction in the

---

1   Debates, Melbourne, 1898, p 303.
2   See pp 1-2 above.
3   See Constitution, ss 71, 72.
4   Sections 73, 74.
5   For example, s 75(v); see pp 21-22 above.

United States, including diversity jurisdiction, and said that this exactly fitted the needs of Australia.[6] At the 1891 Convention in Sydney, a committee on the judiciary was appointed under the chairmanship of Inglis Clark.[7] The committee reported in favour of a provision that "the Judicial power of the Union shall extend to disputes between residents of different States".[8] It is clear that Inglis Clark intended to reproduce the American diversity provision.[9] At the 1898 meeting in Melbourne, Barton moved to add the words of diversity jurisdiction – "or between residents of different States" – and this was adopted without discussion.[10] This was the history of the provision which appeared in s 75(iv) of the Commonwealth Constitution: "In all matters – (iv) between residents of different States ... the High Court shall have original jurisdiction."

It is appropriate to ask why this clause was incorporated into the Constitution apparently without expressed doubt or hesitation on the part of anyone. This in turn leads us to an enquiry into the origins and purpose of the American diversity clause. The classic statement is in the opinion of Marshall CJ in *Bank of the United States v Deveaux*:

> However true the fact may be, that the tribunals of the States will administer justice as impartially as those of the nation, to parties of every description, it is not less true that the constitution itself either entertains apprehensions on this subject, or views with such indulgence the possible fears and apprehensions of suitors, that it has established national tribunals for the decision of controversies ... between the citizens of different States.[11]

The traditional explanation of diversity jurisdiction emphasises the necessity for protection of out-of-State litigants against local prejudice in State courts. Whether this danger was real at the date of constitution-making in the United States is a matter of some doubt.[12] It has been argued that diversity jurisdiction

---

6   Debates, Melbourne, 1890, pp 89ff.

7   See Reynolds, "Inglis Clark and His Influence on Australian Federation" (1958) 32 ALJ 62; La Nauze, *Making of the Australian Constitution*, 1972, p 12.

8   Text printed in Hunt, *American Precedents in Australian Federation*, 1930, p 261.

9   See Inglis Clark, *Australian Constitutional Law*, 1901, p 164, speaking of American diversity jurisdiction as being conferred "in the same words as those by which the like jurisdiction is conferred upon the federal courts of the Commonwealth by the Constitution of the Commonwealth".

10   Debates, Melbourne, 1898, p 1885.

11   5 Cranch 61 at 87 (1809).

12   See Friendly, "The Historic Basis of Diversity Jurisdiction" (1928) 41 Harvard LR 483. His conclusion is that the diversity jurisdiction "had its origin in fears of local hostilities which had only a speculative existence in 1789, and are still less real today" (at 510). But see Yntema and Jaffin, "Preliminary Analysis of Concurrent Jurisdiction" (1930-31) 79 University of Pennsylvania LR 869; Frank, "Historical Bases of the Federal Judicial System" (1948) 13 Law and Contemporary Problems 3; Fallon, Meltzer and Shapiro, *Hart and Wechsler's The Federal Courts and the Federal System*, 4th edn, 1996, pp 1522-1524, 1572-1577; Wright, *Law of Federal Courts*, 5th edn, 1994, pp 141-152.

stemmed rather from fears of State legislatures than of State courts; it was felt that the new federal courts would provide more adequate protection for the interests of creditors and commercial enterprise.[13]

If there is some doubt about the original justification of diversity jurisdiction in the United States, the doubt about the Australian clause is much stronger. Quick and Garran, driven no doubt to find some explanation for the enactment of the provision, followed the classic American statement.[14] But it is perfectly clear that there was no fear of partiality or bias on the part of State tribunals in 1900; nor was there any felt necessity for protection of out-of-State commerce against legislative depredation enforced by State courts. The inappropriateness of carrying over the American provision into the Australian Constitution was the subject of judicial comment in the High Court in *Australasian Temperance and General Mutual Life Assurance Society Ltd v Howe*,[15] where it was held by a majority that a corporation was not a resident for the purposes of diversity jurisdiction. Higgins J (who had been a member of the Constitutional Convention which had adopted the clause) said:

> We might think that the jurisdiction given in matters "between residents of different States" is a piece of pedantic imitation of the Constitution of the United States, and absurd in the circumstances of Australia, with its State Courts of high character and impartiality.[16]

Starke J likewise observed that the fear of bias on the part of State tribunals was "little grounded in point of fact in Australia".[17] Mr Dixon stated in evidence before the Royal Commission on the Constitution in 1927 that there was no better reason for transcribing diversity jurisdiction into the Australian Constitution than the desire to imitate an American model.[18] Even if it could plausibly be argued that there might be bias in State courts against out-of-State litigants, the general appellate jurisdiction of the High Court might have been thought to provide an adequate safeguard – lacking in this respect in the United States where there was no single general appellate jurisdiction – without recourse to a special diversity jurisdiction.[19] At lowest it can be put as an

---

13   See esp Friendly, op cit; Frank, op cit.

14   *The Annotated Constitution of the Commonwealth*, 1901, p 776.

15   (1922) 31 CLR 290.

16   Ibid at 330.

17   Ibid at 339.

18   "We can see no better reason for this provision in the Australian Constitution than the desire to imitate an American model. The courts of no State were ever, so far as we are aware, accused of partiality towards their own citizens, nor does there seem any reason for suspecting them of it". Royal Commission on the Constitution, Minutes of Evidence, p 785.

19   Moore, *The Commonwealth of Australia*, 2nd edn, 1910, p 492: "Cases between residents of different States are of so common occurrence, and are so much in the ordinary experience of the courts that there seems no particular reason for giving the High Court original jurisdiction over them, or even for making them matters of federal jurisdiction at all, especially as the appellate jurisdiction of the High Court and the King-in-Council offers a sufficient protection."

oddity that the framers, who were on occasion prepared to jettison American precedents where they were thought to be inapplicable to Australian conditions and needs, let this particular provision slip in without proper analysis or consideration.

A further reason for conferring this jurisdiction on the High Court has been suggested. In *Howe's Case*, Starke J[20] pointed to the fact that at the time of federation the service of process and the enforcement of judgments beyond the limits of a State were somewhat technical proceedings and he considered that s 75(iv) was, in part, designed to cure those defects, by conferring jurisdiction on a court, the process and judgments of which ran throughout the Commonwealth. This was the reason given for this head of jurisdiction by Inglis Clark who, as has been mentioned above, in 1891 had been chairman of the Judiciary Committee which had recommended its inclusion in the Constitution.[21] Similarly, Quick and Groom, writing in 1904, were able to say:

> The reason which influenced the framers of the American Constitution to federalise inter-State litigation never existed to any extent in Australia. ... Considerations of convenience, facilitation of legal proceedings and the avoidance of circuity of procedure, were the main justification of the inclusion of this sub-section in the new Constitution.[22]

Having regard to the power conferred on the Commonwealth by s 51(xxiv) to make laws with respect to "The service and execution throughout the Commonwealth of the civil and criminal process and the judgments of the courts of the States", that rationalisation is not convincing. The *Service and Execution of Process Act* 1901, enacted in pursuance of that power, provided for a nation-wide system for the service of process and the execution of judgments, and State laws also had provisions for service out of the jurisdiction. A more streamlined procedure is provided by the *Service and Execution of Process Act* 1992. It has been said that original suit in the High Court is nevertheless simpler.[23] It is suggested, however, that such advantage as remains from this point of view in suing in the High Court rather than in a State court is not sufficient to justify this head of jurisdiction.

Diversity Jurisdiction in State Courts

Taken a step further, the story becomes stranger. The classical justification for the existence of diversity jurisdiction in the United States puts it upon the basis of possible bias in State courts. An out-of-State party could opt to have his or her case tried in the federal court. But failing the exercise of such an option, the case might be tried in a *State* court in the exercise of the normal

---

20   (1922) 31 CLR 290 at 339, 340.

21   Inglis Clark, *Studies in Australian Constitutional Law*, 2nd edn, 1904, pp 157-158.

22   Quick and Groom, *The Judicial Power of the Commonwealth*, 1904, pp 112-113.

23   Pryles and Hanks, op cit p 115.

State jurisdiction. Diversity jurisdiction therefore assumes a choice between the two jurisdictions. More than that, it was only in certain cases that a party was entitled to bring a diversity suit in a federal court. The first congressional enactment with respect to diversity jurisdiction provided that the federal circuit courts should have concurrent jurisdiction with the State courts in civil suits at law or equity where the amount in dispute exceeded $500 in value.[24] The present minimum jurisdictional requirement in the federal district courts is $50,000.[25] Moreover, it has been held that federal courts will not grant probate of wills, nor administer deceased estates, nor grant divorces, nor interfere in other matters of intimate domestic relations, such as the custody of children.[26] This means that a litigant in a diversity case may opt for a federal court and federal jurisdiction only if the matter in issue is not one upon which the federal courts have declined to adjudicate. In any event, the litigant clearly has no right to invoke the original jurisdiction of the Supreme Court of the United States: he or she must go to a federal district court.

The Australian situation is different. For purposes of diversity jurisdiction, the only existing federal court is the High Court of Australia, which is invested with diversity jurisdiction in general terms by s 75(iv). It appears that a party may bring an action under s 75(iv) in the High Court without any restriction fixed by the amount in issue. *Fausset v Carroll*,[27] *Marlow v Tatlow*[28] and other cases, which have already been discussed,[29] suggested that a party invoking the diversity jurisdiction of the High Court might be penalised in costs, but it is doubtful whether this is good doctrine. It also appears that the American gloss on the subject-matter of diversity suits has not been carried over into Australian law. It appears to be the view of the High Court that child custody suits are within the diversity jurisdiction of the Court.[30]

What is peculiar in the Australian situation is that there is no *State* jurisdiction in diversity actions at all. This follows from s 39 of the *Judiciary Act*, the operation of which has already been described.[31] Apart from that legislation, a litigant's choice of forum in a diversity suit would be between the High Court and a State court exercising jurisdiction by authority of State law. But s 39(1) of the *Judiciary Act* operates to deprive State courts of all jurisdiction in matters in which the High Court has original jurisdiction, and

---

24   *Judiciary Act* 1789, s 25.

25   Title 28 USC, s 1332 (1988). See Ilsen and Sardell, "The Monetary Minimum in Federal Court Jurisdiction" (1954) 29 St John's LR 1.

26   Hart, "The Relations between State and Federal Law" (1954) 54 Columbia LR 489 at 509. See also Wright, *Federal Courts*, 5th edn, 1994, pp161-164.

27   (1917) 15 WN (NSW) No 12, Cover Note.

28   Noted in (1965) 39 ALJ 140.

29   See pp 78-79 above.

30   *R v Langdon* (1953) 88 CLR 158; *R v Macdonald* (1953) 88 CLR 197; *R v Oregan* (1957) 97 CLR 323 at 333.

31   See pp 10-11 above. See also pp 217ff below.

s 39(2) confers federal jurisdiction on State courts in respect of those matters, among others. In the context of diversity jurisdiction, this means that the *content* of the jurisdiction of State courts remains the same, but the *source* is different and the conditions and regulations imposed by s 39(2) are attached.

No doubt the draftsmen of the *Judiciary Act* had no special concern for diversity jurisdiction, which fell into the scheme along with the other subject-matters of original High Court jurisdiction under s 75, but the consequence is that diversity jurisdiction, whether exercised by the High Court or by any other tribunal, can only be an exercise of federal jurisdiction. There cannot be any State jurisdiction in such cases. So, for Australia, the classical raison d'être of diversity jurisdiction so far as it postulates a choice for litigants as between State and federal jurisdiction has no meaning. In Australia, the mere fact that a case has diversity elements inexorably makes it a matter of federal jurisdiction. The litigant's choice is between the High Court and a State court, both exercising federal jurisdiction.

As a practical matter, the exercise of federal jurisdiction by a State court in a diversity action may give rise to difficulties and inconveniences. As the famous Monsieur Jourdain is reported to have talked prose without knowing it, so too a State court may exercise federal jurisdiction without knowing it. It is possible, as Mr Dixon told the Royal Commission on the Constitution, at least in the case of a matter between residents of different States, that neither the court nor the parties may know of the facts which render the jurisdiction federal.[32] In *Sanderson and Co v Crawford*,[33] a Victorian plaintiff sued a New South Wales defendant for a small sum in a Victorian Court of Petty Sessions which was constituted by a police magistrate *and* two honorary justices. On appeal, the Supreme Court of Victoria held that the court had no jurisdiction. As Hood J put it:

> The Court of Petty Sessions has only jurisdiction over matters between residents in different States by virtue of the legislation I have referred to,[34] and must exercise that jurisdiction subject to the conditions imposed. One of those conditions is that such jurisdiction shall not be judicially exercised except by a police magistrate, so in this case the Court which sat had no power to hear the matter.[35]

Compare with this *Alba Petroleum Co of Australia Pty Ltd v Griffiths*,[36] in which one of the interstate parties was a company. Corporations, as we shall see, have been held not to be residents for the purpose of diversity jurisdiction. The Court pointed out that *Sanderson and Co v Crawford* concerned diversity jurisdiction and was not therefore applicable to the instant case, which fell

---

32 Minutes of Evidence, p 788.
33 [1915] VLR 568.
34 *Judiciary Act*, s 39.
35 [1915] VLR 568 at 579.
36 [1951] VLR 185.

outside that jurisdiction and was a simple exercise of State jurisdiction by an inferior State tribunal constituted in accordance with State law. The same issue has arisen in other cases.[37]

This is a very unsatisfactory situation. If a case happens to involve diversity, the decision of an inferior State court may be upset on the ground that it was improperly constituted. It is not, however, such a great problem today. Having regard to the changes brought about under the laws of the States and Territories since 1903 in respect of the qualifications of those who may be members of a court of summary jurisdiction, the concerns reflected in para (d) of s 39(2) are not now so relevant. It would be rare for such a court to comprise or include persons who were not legally qualified and admitted to practise in the State or Territorial Supreme Court and with a prescribed minimum period of experience.[38]

Problems can occur in respect of appeals. If a case is heard in a State court, and happens to involve diversity, an appeal can be taken by special leave to the High Court;[39] if, on the other hand, no diversity element is present, it cannot, unless it is a judgment of a State Supreme Court.[40] These issues can be resolved by amendment of the *Judiciary Act* repealing the investiture of federal jurisdiction in relation to diversity cases. This would leave the State court to exercise its State jurisdiction free of the conditions set out in s 39(2) of the *Judiciary Act*. Before 1986, the main effect of such a move would have been to enable appeals to the Privy Council from decisions of State courts in such cases. Appeals to the Privy Council in diversity suits could not be brought under s 39 because the jurisdiction of the State courts is federal and para (a) of s 39(2) forbids appeals to the Privy Council. That is no longer an issue, as a result of the abolition of Privy Council appeals under the *Australia Act* 1986. Under s 44 of the *Judiciary Act* the High Court would as a general rule remit most diversity matters that came before it (and that rely only on s 75(iv)) to the appropriate State court. If the State court had no federal jurisdiction in the matter there is doubt whether that could be done. For this purpose, however, there is no reason why a State court should have general federal jurisdiction in diversity matters. It would be sufficient if it had the jurisdiction as a consequence of the remittal.[41] It is suggested that the Act should be amended to exclude diversity suits from the federal jurisdiction of State courts except to that extent. From the point of view of the High Court, the best solution would be a constitutional amendment deleting from s 75(iv) all the words after "Between States". This was recommended in 1978 by the

---

37 See, for example, *City and Suburban Parcel Delivery (Bryce) Ltd v Gourlay Bros Ltd* [1932] St R Qd 213.

38 Australian Law Reform Commission, *The Judicial Power of the Commonwealth*, Report 92, 2001, pp 168-170, 173-174. The Commission recommended an amendment of para (d).

39 *Judiciary Act*, ss 35, 39(2)(c); Constitution, s 73.

40 Constitution, s 73; *Judiciary Act*, s 35.

41 Compare s 44(3) of the *Judiciary Act*.

Australian Constitutional Convention[42] and in 1988 by the Constitutional Commission.[43]

"Between" Residents: Distribution of Parties

The words of the American diversity clause are "controversies between citizens of different States". The Australian provision speaks of "matters ... between residents of different States". A question was raised in the High Court in *R v Langdon*[44] and *R v Macdonald*[45] as to whether habeas corpus applications in child custody proceedings were "matters" so as to attract the original diversity jurisdiction of the court. In *R v Macdonald*, counsel informed the Court that the parties had reached agreement and desired that an order be made, and Fullagar J, who had raised this jurisdictional point, made the order. In *R v Langdon*, Taylor J referred to *R v Macdonald* on this point, but refused to make an order on other grounds. It has been noted that federal courts in the United States decline to assume jurisdiction in such cases. In respect of custody, the reason given in early cases was that although such matters were originally determined in chancery proceedings, the Chancellor assumed jurisdiction not in a judicial capacity, but by virtue of the royal prerogative as parens patriae to which the States and not the United States succeeded.[46] Later cases and academic writings disputed that reasoning.[47] This exception to diversity jurisdiction, however, was confirmed by the Supreme Court of the United States broadly on the ground of precedent and congressional acceptance of it.[48] No such principle appears to have troubled the Australian law of federal jurisdiction.

It has been suggested that there is some uncertainty in the word "between" (residents). If a trust is created in favour of a number of persons, some living in one State and some in another, and a controversy arises as to the proportion in which they are entitled to share the trust property, it may be that this is a matter "among" but not "between" residents.[49] Again, it has been held that there is no diversity jurisdiction if there are residents of the same State on each side. In *Watson and Godfrey v Cameron*,[50] an action was instituted in the original diversity jurisdiction of the High Court. The plaintiffs were a

---

42   *Report of the Australian Constitutional Convention*, 1978, pp 204-205.

43   *Final Report of the Constitutional Commission*, 1988, vol 1, pp 381-382.

44   (1953) 88 CLR 158.

45   (1953) 88 CLR 197.

46   See *Fountain v Ravenal* (1855) 17 How 369. See also "Jurisdiction of the Federal Courts over Domestic Relations" (1948) 48 Columbia LR 154.

47   For example, *Spindel v Spindel* 283 F Supp 797 (1968).

48   *Ankenbrandt v Richards* 504 US 689 (1992). See *Hart and Wechsler*, op cit pp 1323-1333.

49   Mentioned by Dixon KC in evidence before the Royal Commission, p 786.

50   (1928) 40 CLR 446.

Victorian and a New South Wales resident and the defendant was a resident of New South Wales. It was held that there was no jurisdiction, since diversity was not shown. Where there was a resident of New South Wales on each side it was impossible to say that there was a matter between residents of different States. Isaacs J suggested that a contrary conclusion would lead to an alarming increase in the original jurisdiction of the High Court by resort to the device of adding an out-of-State party.[51] In *Union Steamship Co of New Zealand Ltd v Ferguson*,[52] the plaintiff commenced an action in the original jurisdiction of the High Court claiming damages for injuries received while working as a crew member of a ship owned by the defendant. The statement of claim alleged that the action was in the original jurisdiction of the Court on the ground that the parties were residents of different States. The plaintiff was a resident of South Australia and it was alleged that the defendant resided in Victoria. It had, however, been held some years earlier that a corporation could not be a resident within the meaning of s 75(iv).[53] This issue is discussed below. The plaintiff then made an application asking that the winchman of the ship, a resident of New South Wales, be added as a defendant. Windeyer J, however, said:

> [I]t was apparently thought that by making him an additional defendant, the action would be saved and could proceed with the defendant company still a party, although not a "resident". This was a mistaken view: cf *Watson and Godfrey v Cameron.*[54]

This statement of Windeyer J has been criticised on the ground that *Watson and Godfrey v Cameron*[55] had nothing to do with the issue. That case, it is said, merely held that if there were residents of the same State on both sides there was no diversity jurisdiction.[56] This aspect of *Ferguson*, however, conforms to the reasons of policy given by Isaacs J in *Watson and Godfrey v Cameron* that an interpretation of s 75(iv) should be avoided that would enable a plaintiff to resort to the Court, where he otherwise could not, by the device of adding an out-of-State party. Accepting that a suit against a corporation cannot come within the diversity jurisdiction, the danger that Isaacs J

---

51 Compare *Strawbridge v Curtis* 3 Cranch 267 (1806). It has been held by the Supreme Court, however, that that case was based on the construction of the statute and that for purposes of the Constitution it is enough that there is a claimant on each side from different States: *State Farm Fire and Casualty Co v Tashire* 386 US 523 (1967). See also Wright, op cit pp 157-158.

52 (1969) 119 CLR 191.

53 *Australasian Temperance and General Mutual Life Assurance Society Ltd v Howe* (1922) 31 CLR 290.

54 (1969) 119 CLR 191 at 196. It was held that the High Court nevertheless had jurisdiction under the *Colonial Courts of Admiralty Act*.

55 (1928) 40 CLR 446.

56 Pryles and Hanks, op cit p 127

saw of "an alarming increase" in the original jurisdiction of the High Court would certainly be present if the involvement of a corporation in the suit was regarded as not excluding the diversity jurisdiction where the other parties on either side of the suit otherwise conformed to the requirements of s 75(iv).

The view expressed by Windeyer J conforms to the decision of Dixon J in *Cox v Journeaux.*[57] In that case action was brought by a Queensland resident against natural persons resident in Victoria and two companies incorporated in Victoria. The order of Dixon J was that the suit should be dismissed as not being within s 75(iv) unless the plaintiff elected to proceed only against the defendants who were individuals. That case was followed by Gaudron J in *Rochford v Dayes.*[58] It has been suggested that, in the light of recent cases related to "accrued jurisdiction",[59] *Watson and Godfrey* and *Cox v Journeaux* may not be followed.[60] That issue is discussed below.

The onus of showing diversity is on the party seeking to establish jurisdiction. In *Dahms v Brandsch,*[61] there was a motion for judgment in the High Court in a foreclosure suit on an equitable mortgage by deposit of title deeds in Western Australia. The mortgagee was a resident of South Australia and the mortgagor's residence was unknown. It was stated that, when last heard of, his residence was in Victoria. Griffiths CJ dismissed the suit for lack of jurisdiction. The Court must be satisfied that the parties were residents of different States and here it was impossible to establish affirmatively that such was the case.

The Meaning of "Residents"

The most interesting problem in this area is the meaning to be assigned to "resident". This is a departure from the American phraseology which speaks of "citizens". In *Australasian Temperance and General Mutual Life Assurance Society Ltd v Howe,*[62] Higgins J dwelt on this difference. He observed that "citizen" was a republican word, not appropriate to subjects of a prince, and drew the conclusion (in the context of the question whether a corporation was a resident) that the difference of terminology produced a significant difference in result. In the report of Inglis Clark's Judiciary Committee of 1891, the word "resident" was used in this context, but Clark did not regard the change as possessing any significance.[63] In 1898 there had been a protracted debate on a

---

57   (1934) 52 CLR 282.

58   (1989) 84 ALR 405.

59   Discussed in Chapter 3, pp 137-147 below.

60   Lane, *Lane's Commentary on The Australian Constitution*, 2nd edn, 1997, pp 575-576.

61   (1911) 13 CLR 336. See also *Watson v Marshall and Cade* (1971) 124 CLR 621.

62   (1922) 31 CLR 290.

63   See p 86 above.

clause which finally emerged as s 117 of the Constitution, which provides that "a subject of the Queen, resident in any State, shall not be subject in any other State to any disability or discrimination which would not be equally applicable to him if he were a subject of the Queen resident in such other State". The earlier draft was in quite different form: "A State shall not make or enforce any law abridging any privilege or immunity of citizens of other States of the Commonwealth nor shall a State deny to any person within its jurisdiction the equal protection of the laws." In the course of the debate on this clause, a great deal of difficulty was found in the definition of citizenship[64] and this word finally disappeared from the clause. It may be that the form in which Barton subsequently introduced the diversity jurisdiction clause was influenced by this involved debate on citizenship, and that the substitution of residence here, as in s 117, was designed to avoid these difficulties. This may suggest that the distinctions later elaborated by Higgins J in *Howe* were not very convincing, but there is insufficient evidence on which a certain conclusion on the matter may be reached.

For natural persons, the American law is clear. Citizenship for purposes of diversity jurisdiction means domicile. In *Messick v Southern Pennsylvania Bus Co*,[65] it was said that:

"Citizenship" signifies the identification of a person with a State and a participation in its functions ... It implies a person possessing social and political rights and bearing social, political, and moral obligations to a particular state. Citizenship and domicile are substantially synonymous terms and, with respect to the jurisdiction of federal courts, domicile is the test of citizenship.

So far as diversity jurisdiction within the Australian framework of residence is concerned, it is equally clear that diversity of residence may be established without reference to domicile. This is supported by a group of cases involving suits between husband and wife. It was settled law for Australia that a wife took the domicile of her husband throughout the marriage, even though the parties were separated by court order. This was laid down in the Privy Council in *Attorney-General for Alberta v Cook*.[66] In *Renton v Renton*,[67] the Supreme Court of South Australia had to consider the validity of a summons issued

---

64 For an account, see Quick and Garran, op cit p 776.

65 59 F Supp 799 at 800 (1945). See also *Hart and Wechsler*, 4th edn, 1996, p 1524, where it is said that from the beginning the Court has steadily insisted that state citizenship for the purposes of the diversity jurisdiction is dependent upon two elements: first, United States citizenship; and second, domicile in the State, in the traditional sense of the conflict of laws.

66 [1926] AC 444. This rule was abolished by the *Domicile Acts* 1982 of the Commonwealth, the States and the Northern Territory. Previously it had been abolished in respect of recognition of marriage (*Marriage Act* 1961, s 5(4)(b)) and family law proceedings (*Family Law Act* 1975, s 4(3)(b)).

67 [1917] SALR 277. Reversed on other grounds by the High Court (1918) 25 CLR 291.

from a court of summary jurisdiction which was not properly constituted if it were exercising federal diversity jurisdiction. The summons was issued under the *Interstate Destitute Persons Relief Act* at the suit of a deserted wife. The Court concluded that there was diversity, as the wife was a resident of South Australia and the husband a resident of Queensland. It was specifically stated that the husband had never been domiciled in South Australia. It followed that the wife's South Australian residence depended on criteria other than those necessary to establish domicile. In *Coates v Coates,*[68] a similar case, a Victorian court held that diversity of residence had not been established, but it was implicit in the judgment that it was possible to establish such diversity as between husband and wife. Both these cases were decided before *Attorney-General for Alberta v Cook*, but the two decisions in *R v Langdon* and *R v Macdonald*, which were habeas corpus applications in child custody proceedings as between husband and wife, were decided without any apparent doubt that husband and wife might be proper parties in diversity suits.[69] So, too, in *Cohen v Cohen*[70] the High Court assumed jurisdiction in a money claim between spouses.

Apart from the cases of husband and wife, Higgins J in *Howe's Case*[71] contrasted the notions of domicile and residence on the footing that "residence is a mere question of fact; ... domicile is an idea of law". Residence appears as a requirement in various places in the Constitution. Section 34 requires as a qualification for membership in the House of Representatives three years' residence within the limits of the Commonwealth; s 100 deals with the rights of residents of a State to river waters for conservation or irrigation;[72] and s 117, as we have seen,[73] is concerned with discrimination against subjects of the Queen resident in one State, in other States. In *Howe's Case*, there were suggestions that residence does not necessarily have the same meaning in all these sections, and specifically that a decision that a corporation was not a resident for the purposes of diversity jurisdiction did not necessarily mean that it was not a resident within the terms of s 100.[74]

There has been little general discussion of the residence requirement for diversity jurisdiction. Quick and Garran considered that "it should be of a character to identify the resident to some extent with the corporate entity of

---

68 [1925] VLR 231.

69 See also *R v Oregan; ex parte Oregan* (1957) 97 CLR 323 at 332-333.

70 (1929) 42 CLR 91.

71 (1922) 31 CLR 290 at 329.

72 "The Commonwealth shall not, by any law or regulation of trade or commerce, abridge the right of a State or of the residents therein to the reasonable use of the waters of rivers for conservation or irrigation."

73 See pp 94-95 above.

74 (1922) 31 CLR 290 at 299.

the State".[75] This statement was approved by Isaacs J in *Howe's Case*.[76] After citing the passage, Isaacs J said:

> I would add … that the identification by reason of residence of the litigants with one State connotes his exclusion from similar identification by reason of residence with any other State. If I were to express it in a word, it is "status". Every Australian is, when all the facts are known, residentially identifiable pre-eminently with some one State and he is therefore a resident of that State and of that State alone, for the purposes of s 75(iv).

The judge stressed the *singleness* of residence and instanced the example of a man who had his family, home and chief place of business in Melbourne and had branch establishments in Adelaide and Perth in which he spent a week every month for the purposes of conducting the branch business. While in one sense he was resident in Adelaide and Perth, his status as a resident for the purposes of diversity jurisdiction was fixed in Victoria.

Such a notion of residence would seem to bring it very close to domicile, and it is to be noted that in the same case Higgins J expressly distinguished domicile as a matter of law from residence as a matter of fact. The view of Isaacs J was considered in *Coates v Coates*[77] by Irvine CJ of Victoria. The parties were husband and wife. The wife depended upon Victorian residence and the evidence of the husband's residence in New South Wales was very thin. Irvine CJ did not commit himself to full adoption of the views of Isaacs J in *Howe*, but indicated that residence involved "more than the mere fact of residing temporarily in that State for purposes of business or pleasure". In his evidence before the Royal Commission, Mr Dixon said: "Residence seems to be a strange criterion, moreover, to adopt. Some persons have no residence, and some have several."[78] This suggests some doubt as to the correctness of Isaacs J's insistence on the single and exclusive character of residence for diversity jurisdiction. However, Mr Dixon was not expressing a settled view of the meaning of residence, but was concerned to point out the ineptitude of the constitutional provision for diversity jurisdiction and the ambiguities and uncertainties in its language.

In *Watson v Marshall and Cade*,[79] the defendant was a resident of Victoria but there was some doubt and argument as to whether the plaintiff

---

75 "Residence in a State, for the purposes of [diversity jurisdiction] should … be interpreted as involving a suggestion of State membership and perhaps even of domicile … such residence as, if combined with British nationality, would constitute citizenship of the State in the general sense of the term. It is not meant by this that the residence should be such as is required by the laws of the particular State for the exercise of any particular franchise, but merely that it should be of such a character to identify the resident to some extent with the corporate entity of the State." Op cit p 776.

76 (1922) 31 CLR 290 at 307-308.

77 [1925] VLR 231 at 235.

78 Op cit p 785.

79 (1971) 124 CLR 621.

was a resident of New South Wales or of Victoria. Walsh J followed *Dahms v Brandsch*,[80] which held that the plaintiff was required to establish the facts that gave the court jurisdiction. In examining the facts, His Honour applied the reasoning of Isaacs J in *Howe's Case* that it was not permissible to treat the plaintiff as a resident, within the meaning of s 75(iv), of both States and that a choice had to be made.

The state of authority makes it clear that to establish residence for diversity purposes, proof of domicile is not required, at least in the case of persons whose domicile is governed by dependence. The cases show that a wife could sue a husband in the diversity jurisdiction, when her domicile was at law the same as her husband's, and presumably the same argument would apply to other persons of dependent domicile, such as infants. Apart from such cases, it may be suggested that the courts will continue to follow Isaacs J's view of the singleness of residence for the purpose of this jurisdiction, so that at any given time a person will be held to be resident in one State. Such residence would in most cases be in the State of domicile, although it seems likely that the strict requirements of domicile would not be invoked. For example, it would very probably be held that a person who had lived for a number of years in Victoria would be held to be resident in that State for the purposes of diversity jurisdiction, although under the technical rules relating to domicile, for want of sufficient proof of animus, he or she would be held to retain an English or other domicile of origin.[81] It would hardly be sensible to reject the strict requirements of domicile in suits between spouses and other dependent persons, and to insist upon them to establish residence in all other cases.

A further point was posed by Mr Dixon as to the time at which residence must attach. He asked whether a Victorian resident who was sued in the High Court by a New South Wales resident might defeat the action by instantly changing his residence to New South Wales.[82] This reveals another drafting uncertainty. Similar problems are encountered in other areas of the law, for example in divorce jurisdiction based on domicile. It seems to be established that the decisive date should be the institution of proceedings. This view has been adopted in a number of cases.[83] Thereafter jurisdiction should not be defeated by reason of a subsequent change of residence by a defendant.[84]

---

80   (1911) 13 CLR 336.

81   See *Winans v AG* [1904] AC 287; *Ramsay v Liverpool Royal Infirmary* [1930] AC 588.

82   Op cit p 786.

83   *R v Oregan; ex parte Oregan* (1957) 97 CLR 323 at 332-333; *Paretite v Bell* (1967) 116 CLR 528 at 529; *Dzihowski v Mazgay* noted (1967) 40 ALJ 361; *Watson v Marshall and Cade* (1971) 124 CLR 621 at 623.

84   Pryles and Hanks, op cit p 132 and Lane, op cit pp 573-574.

Corporations as Residents

Thus far the discussion of the meaning to be given to "resident" for the purposes of diversity jurisdiction has been directed to the case of natural persons. The question next arises as to the position of corporations. It is settled law in the United States that diversity jurisdiction may be invoked by or against a corporation, and suits involving corporations account for a very substantial part of diversity litigation.[85] This American doctrine was well settled at the date of the drafting and enactment of the Australian Constitution, and Quick and Garran in 1901 stated explicitly that "a corporation may clearly be a 'resident' within the meaning of this section".[86] In 1922, however, the High Court by a majority held in *Australasian Temperance and General Mutual Life Assurance Society Ltd v Howe*[87] that a corporation was not a resident for the purposes of diversity jurisdiction, and unanimously refused to reverse this decision when it was challenged some 12 years later in *Cox v Journeaux*.[88]

The American doctrine has a somewhat extraordinary history. The constitutional provision for diversity jurisdiction speaks of "citizens" of different States. In *Bank of United States v Deveaux*,[89] Marshall CJ stated that "that invisible, intangible and artificial being, that mere legal entity, a corporation aggregate, is certainly not a citizen; and consequently cannot sue or be sued in the courts of the United States, unless the rights of the members in this respect can be exercised in their corporate name". In this case it was held that the qualification rather than the general rule applied, and the bank was permitted to bring suit in the federal courts, on a showing that all of its members were citizens of one State and Deveaux was a citizen of another State.

Had this been the only class of case in which the diversity jurisdiction was open to a corporate party, it would have been of relatively little significance with the growth of corporations with shareholders in many States. It would then have been in comparatively rare cases that the requisite diversity could be shown. However, in *Louisville, Cincinnati and Charleston Railroad Co v Letson*,[90] the Supreme Court of the United States ruled: "[A] corporation created by and doing business in a particular State, is to be deemed at all

---

85 See Frankfurter, "Judicial Power of Federal and State Courts" (1928) 13 Cornell Law Quarterly 499 at 523: "An examination of ten recent volumes of the Federal Reporter shows that out of 3,618 full opinions, 959 or 27 per cent were written in cases arising solely out of diversity of citizenship. In 716 of these cases, or 80 per cent, a corporation was a party. Corporate litigation, then, is the key to diversity problems." See also McGovney, "A Supreme Court Fiction" (1943) 56 Harvard LR 853 at 1090, 1225; Wechsler, "Federal Jurisdiction and the Revision of the Judicial Code" (1948) 13 Law and Contemporary Problems 216 at 234-240.

86 Op cit p 777.

87 (1922) 31 CLR 290.

88 (1934) 52 CLR 282.

89 5 Cranch 61 at 86 (1809).

90 2 How 497 at 558 (1844).

intents and purposes as a person, although an artificial person, an inhabitant of the same State, for the purposes of its incorporation, capable of being treated as a citizen of that State, as much as a natural person". This gave rise to a conclusive and irrebuttable jurisdictional fiction that for purposes of establishing diversity all the shareholders were to be deemed citizens of the State of incorporation.[91] It was upon this decision, which has been subjected to trenchant criticism,[92] that the inclusion of corporations within the scope of diversity jurisdiction depended. The fiction did not purport to treat a corporation as a citizen; it achieved the same result by shutting out evidence that its members, for purposes of diversity jurisdiction involving the corporation, were citizens of States other than that of incorporation. The results were quite remarkable.

> The absurdity of the fiction is patent with respect to any large corporation whose shares are sold throughout the United States. The American Telephone and Telegraph Co had 630,902 shareholders of record, December 31, 1940, holding 18,686,794 shares. It is incorporated under the laws of New York. The Company's records show that it has some shareholders residing in every one of the forty-eight States. In taking jurisdiction of suits by or against this corporation, the judges of the lower federal courts are required by the Supreme Court to regard all shareholders as citizens of New York. The records of the corporation show that about one fourth of the shares are held in New York.
>
> Suppose, as is probably true, that one of the shareholders of this New York corporation is a Delaware corporation. In suits to which the Delaware corporation is a party all of its shareholders are regarded as citizens of Delaware to give it a fictitious Delaware citizenship, but in a suit to which the New York corporation is a party, this Delaware corporation is deemed to be a citizen of New York, or all of its shareholders are deemed to be citizens of New York.[93]

Bills were introduced from time to time to strike at the use of federal courts by corporations under shelter of this fiction and were strongly opposed by representatives of corporate interests.[94] In 1958 Congress amended s 1332

---

91 Small and Jayson (eds), *Constitution of the United States of America: Analysis and Interpretation*, 1964, pp 683-686.

92 It was called a "malignant decision" by Warren in his famous article, "New Light on the History of the Federal Judiciary Act of 1789" (1923) 37 Harvard LR 49 at 90. Warren observed further of the right of a foreign incorporated company to remove a case arising in a State in which it actually does business into a federal court that "no single factor has given rise to more friction and jealousy between State and Federal Courts or to more State legislation conflicting with and repugnant to Federal jurisdiction than has the doctrine of citizenship for corporations". See also Frankfurter, op cit p 523, McGovney, op cit esp p 1258. But see Green, "Corporations as Persons, Citizens and Possessors of Liberty" (1946) 94 University of Pennsylvania LR 202, esp at 217, 218, 227-228. See also *Hart and Wechsler*, op cit pp 1535-1537.

93 McGovney, op cit p 1097.

94 See McGovey, op cit p 1225 et seq.

of the United States Code by providing that, for this purpose, a corporation should be deemed a citizen of any State by which it has been incorporated and of the State where it has its principal place of business. This prevents corporations engaging in local business with a foreign charter from entering the federal courts on a showing of diversity; though it does not affect the position of a corporation doing business in a large number of States, except in the State in which it has its principal place of business. A further amendment in 1964 was designed to deal with the case where under a statute a plaintiff was empowered to sue directly a tortfeasor's insurance company. Under the amendment the insurance company is deemed to be a citizen of the State in which the insured was a citizen as well as of the State of its incorporation and of its principal business.

In Australia, this question has arisen in the context of corporate claims to invoke the original diversity jurisdiction of the High Court. In *Australasian Temperance and General Mutual Life Assurance Society Ltd v Howe*, the case for the plaintiff company was argued by Dixon KC, and there was no appearance for the defendant. The Court by a bare majority[95] held, however, that a corporation could not be a "resident" for the purposes of diversity jurisdiction under s 75(iv) of the Constitution.

The majority opinion of Knox CJ and Gavan Duffy J and the dissenting judgment of Isaacs J paid little attention to American authority. Consideration was directed primarily to matters of general principle and to a review of authorities, principally English, in which the question whether a corporation could be held to be a "resident" had been before the courts. Knox CJ and Gavan Duffy J took as a starting point the proposition that the ordinary connotation of "resident" was "living" and that this was the attribute of a natural person. The onus was therefore upon the party seeking to establish jurisdiction to show an affirmative legislative intent to vary the normal meaning of the word. The authorities gave no general assistance; those which ascribed residence to corporations did so under the compulsion of specific statutes. Furthermore, it did not follow that "resident" necessarily had the same meaning in every place in which it appeared in the Constitution; it might be (though no settled answer need be given) that a corporation was a resident for the purposes of s 100.[96] Isaacs J took precisely opposite ground. There was no justification for any presumption that residence could be ascribed only to natural persons; indeed the presumption operated the other way. The cases which ascribed residence to corporations were not to be treated as of such limited operation, but demonstrated that it was proper in the present context to treat a corporation as a resident. The original jurisdiction of the High Court in diversity cases conferred "a right as valuable to a corporation as an individual".[97] The general conclusion which Isaacs J reached was that a

---

95   Knox CJ, Higgins and Gavan Duffy JJ; Isaacs and Starke JJ dissenting.
96   Set out on p 96 n 72 above.
97   (1922) 31 CLR 290 at 307.

corporation might clearly and properly be a resident for the purposes of diversity jurisdiction. In the instant case the plaintiff company, on this reasoning, was a Victorian resident: it was incorporated in Victoria, and the head office and central management of its Australia-wide business was in that State. The defendant was a New South Wales resident and, upon this showing, Isaacs J held that the suit was properly brought in the original diversity jurisdiction of the High Court.

Higgins and Starke JJ looked more closely at the American diversity provision and its interpretation. Higgins J laid stress on the differences between the two diversity clauses; one spoke of "citizens", the other of "residents", and American decisions which were concerned with the status of corporations as citizens did not assist in the resolution of questions relating to residence. From this point he followed Knox CJ and Gavan Duffy J in regarding residence as presumptively attributable to natural persons only, and in treating the decisions ascribing residence to corporations as inapplicable to the case of diversity jurisdiction. Starke J, after referring to the "somewhat similar provision in the Constitution of the United States"[98] and to the views of Quick and Garran on the question of corporate standing under the diversity clause, found no apparent difficulty in holding that a corporation might be a "resident" for such purposes. He stated further that it had been the practice of the High Court to assume jurisdiction in cases involving corporations, although the point of jurisdiction had not been argued.[99]

In *Cox v Journeaux*,[100] action was brought in the High Court by a Queensland resident against, inter alios, two companies incorporated in and carrying on business in Victoria, and managed and controlled there. On an application by the companies for an order dismissing them from the action, the plaintiff argued that the decision in *Howe's Case* was wrong. Dixon J refused an application to refer this question to the Full High Court and, on application for leave to appeal, the Full Court (Gavan Duffy CJ, Starke, Evatt and McTiernan JJ) refused to reconsider *Howe's Case*.

A further attempt to have *Howe* overruled was made in *Crouch v Commissioner of Railways (Qld)*.[101] The Court unanimously refused to reconsider it. Gibbs CJ said he agreed with the view expressed by Higgins J in *Howe* that diversity jurisdiction was "a piece of pedantic imitation of the Constitution of the United States and absurd in the circumstances of Australia". No strong reason had been shown why the decision, which had stood for over 60 years, should be reopened. Later he added that the result was

---

98 Ibid at 339.

99 "Even this Court has entered judgments both in favour of and against corporations. True, the question of jurisdiction was not argued in connection with these judgments, and I refer to them, not as authorities, but in support of the statement that the received view was heretofore in favour of the jurisdiction of this Court." Ibid at 340.

100 (1934) 52 CLR 282.

101 (1985) 159 CLR 22.

a convenient one because it was difficult to see any good reason why the High Court should have original jurisdiction in cases of that kind.[102]

A joint judgment of the rest of the Court considered that the dissenting judgments of Isaacs and Starke JJ demonstrated that "the reasoning of the majority [in *Howe*] might be thought to be less than compelling",[103] but they came to the same conclusion as the Chief Justice.

It must therefore be taken as settled law for Australia that a corporation is not a resident for purposes of diversity jurisdiction. It is most unlikely that the decision in *Howe's Case* will be reversed. In this light, extended examination of the differing views expressed in the Court in *Howe's Case* would not be very profitable. It may be thought that on the level at which the argument was conducted, Isaacs J's dissent was very persuasive. There is a substantial body of English case law ascribing residence to corporations and the showing of the majority that these had no general application, and specifically no application to the case of diversity jurisdiction, does not carry conviction. The argument ad absurdum of Knox CJ and Gavan Duffy J that, if a corporation had standing to sue, it would follow that a corporation resident and conducting operations within a State would be entitled to invoke the diversity jurisdiction, while a corporation not so resident but conducting similar operations within the State would not,[104] carries no real conviction, because it applies equally to individuals whose right to invoke the diversity jurisdiction is beyond question. Again, it may be thought that the differences between the American and Australian diversity provisions which were emphasised by Higgins J would assist a conclusion that there is less difficulty in assigning residence than citizenship to a corporation, particularly in view of the substantial body of British authority on the point of residence of corporations which Isaacs J reviewed so convincingly.

Even if the dissenters had the better of the logic and the authority, it may nonetheless be suggested that the exclusion of corporations from the scope of diversity jurisdiction is to be welcomed. A distinguished American commentator, noting *Howe's Case*, observed:

> The Australian High Court, confronted with similar difficulties, avoided our pitfalls … The phrasing of the two Constitutions varies. But the real difference between our doctrines and the Australian decision is a difference of 100 years. The underlying assumption in Australia is that an Australian corporation no matter where registered, can obtain justice in every State court.[105]

Diversity jurisdiction has thrown a heavy burden on American federal courts, the greater part of which derives from cases involving corporate litigants. And

---

102 Ibid at 27.
103 Ibid at 34.
104 (1922) 31 CLR 290 at 300.
105 Frankfurter, op cit p 524.

there is a powerful argument that the reason for federal diversity jurisdiction in the United States has disappeared, if indeed it ever existed.

It has been argued (as Gibbs CJ observed in *Crouch*) that there never was any justification for writing a diversity jurisdiction clause into the Australian Constitution and that this was a piece of blind and unintelligent copying. It permitted a litigant to come into the High Court of Australia on a simple showing of diversity. Our Constitution placed a potentially great burden of original jurisdiction upon a court invested not only with special constitutional and other important federal functions, but also with a general appellate jurisdiction from State courts on matters of State law. In the United States original jurisdiction in diversity suits is vested not in the Supreme Court, but in district courts, and even there is restricted to suits involving specified minimum amounts, and is further restricted by judicial gloss as to the subject-matter of actions. That is not the case in Australia. As a result of the enactment in 1976 of the remittal power in s 44 of the *Judiciary Act*[106] and the view apparently accepted by the Court that it is not duty bound to exercise its jurisdiction under s 75 of the Constitution where remittal is available, the diversity jurisdiction is now no great burden on the Court. But the lack of con-vincing reason for this area of federal jurisdiction and the various difficulties referred to earlier provide a good reason for excluding corporations. If the result looks illogical it is not unreasonable to say that the less we have of a bad thing the better. It would be even better if the diversity jurisdiction was abolished.

Additional Parties as Accrued Jurisdiction

It has been suggested that in the light of the development of the principle of "accrued jurisdiction", which is discussed in Chapter 3,[107] *Watson and Godfrey* and *Cox v Journeaux* may not be followed today, at any rate in many circumstances. Without going into it here in any depth, the notion of "accrued jurisdiction" begins with the concept of "matter" in ss 75 and 76 of the Con-stitution. If the Court has, for example, jurisdiction under s 75(iii) because there is a claim against the Commonwealth, the jurisdiction extends to all other claims which are "inseparably connected" to the primary claim because they are all part of the same matter. A claim which on its own would not be within federal jurisdiction will be regarded as inseparable from one that is, if they both arise out of "common transactions and facts".[108]

In *McCauley v Hamilton Island Enterprises Pty Ltd*,[109] Mason J, in dealing with an action against a Commonwealth authority and two other

---

106 See pp 81-84 above.
107 Pages 137-147 below.
108 *Fencott v Muller* (1983) 152 CLR 570 at 610.
109 (1986) 69 ALR 270.

defendants, said that, as the Court had jurisdiction under s 75(iii) in respect of the claim against the Commonwealth authority, it had jurisdiction in relation to the other defendants because s 75(iii) conferred jurisdiction "in the whole matter in which a person being sued on behalf of the Commonwealth is a party, not merely jurisdiction vis-a-vis that person".[110]

This reasoning was relied on, in part, by the plaintiff in *Rochford v Dayes*,[111] a diversity jurisdiction case. It was argued that *Cox v Journeaux* had to yield to more recent authority related to accrued jurisdiction, including *McCauley*. The argument is that, if the Court has jurisdiction because the defendant is resident of a State different from that of the plaintiff, a corporation or a defendant from the plaintiff's State could be added as an additional defendant if the claims against them were based on substantially the same facts.

Gaudron J, sitting as a single judge, rejected this submission. She said that the reasoning was inapplicable because the issue raised in earlier diversity cases was whether the term "between" (residents of different States) meant simply that there must be a person on one side of the record that is resident in a State different from the person on the other side, or whether the term signified "the necessary and only permitted distribution of parties". She considered that authority supported the latter interpretation, while recognising that the reasoning in *Watson and Godfrey* was not compelling. She referred to *Crouch v Commissioner for Railways (Qld)*,[112] which had given a broad interpretation to the word "State" in another aspect of s 75(iv). In that case, however, the Court had also refused to overrule *Howe* and favoured a narrow interpretation of the diversity jurisdiction. For the reasons given there, the Court could take the same attitude against, in effect, overruling *Watson and Godfrey* and *Cox v Journeaux*. For the reasons given by Gibbs CJ in *Crouch*, and other reasons stated above, that would be the desirable course to follow.

---

110 Ibid at 272.
111 (1989) 84 ALR 405.
112 (1985) 159 CLR 22

Chapter 3

The Federal Courts

Neither from the point of view of juristic principle nor from that of the practical and efficient administration of justice can the division of the courts into State and federal be regarded as sound.[1]

The Supreme Court is the ultimate judicial exponent of federal rights; the lower federal courts are their vindicators ... It hardly seems open to doubt that a full system of independent federal courts plays a valuable part in furthering the rapid, widespread, yet uniform and accurate interpretation of federal law.[2]

The establishment of federal courts, other than the High Court of Australia, is contemplated by the Constitution. Section 71 authorises the vesting of the judicial power of the Commonwealth in such federal courts as the Parliament creates, s 77(i) empowers the Parliament, with respect to the matters enumerated in ss 75 and 76, to make laws defining the jurisdiction of any federal court other than the High Court, and s 77(ii) authorises the making of such laws defining the extent to which the jurisdiction of any federal court shall be exclusive of that which belongs to or is invested in the courts of States. The authority to create federal courts is implied;[3] nowhere in the Constitution is there any express power to establish them. In this respect, the Australian Constitution differs from the Constitution of the United States, which specifically authorises the constitution of tribunals inferior to the Supreme Court as one of the enumerated powers of Congress under Art 1, s 8. It is surprising that such an important power should have been left to implication in the Australian Constitution, although it has been suggested by the High Court that the Australian founding fathers, "who adopted so definitely the general pattern of Art III but in their variations and departures from its detailed provisions evidenced a discriminating appreciation of American experience",[4] may have thought it unnecessary to spell out a power to create federal courts in express terms.

---

1   Dixon, "The Law and the Constitution" (1935) 51 *Law Quarterly R* 590 at 606.
2   Mishkin, "The Federal 'Question' in the District Courts" (1953) 53 Columbia LR 157 at 170-171.
3   Quick and Garran, *The Annotated Constitution of the Australian Commonwealth*, 1901, p 726.
4   *R v Kirby; ex parte Boilermakers' Society of Australia* (1956) 94 CLR 254 at 268.

Federal Courts in the United States and Australia

The major departure from American precedent was the adoption of the "autochthonous expedient"[5] of conferring federal jurisdiction on State courts, and this has made for a significant difference in the judicial organisations of the two federations. In the United States, the decision to authorise the establishment of inferior federal courts was taken only after sharp debate in the Constitutional Convention. It was argued on the one side that "the State tribunals might and ought to be left in all cases to decide in the first instance, the right of appeal to the supreme national tribunal being sufficient to secure the national rights and uniformity of judgments; that it was making an unnecessary encroachment on the jurisdiction of the States, and creating unnecessary obstacles to their adoption of the new system", and to the contrary by Madison that "a government without a proper executive and judiciary would be the mere trunk of a body, without arms or legs to act or move". It was also argued that the establishment of a body of federal courts would be a burdensome expense. The original proposal to create a body of inferior federal courts by force of the Constitution itself was lost, but a compromise was finally reached which permitted the establishment of federal courts by Act of Congress.[6] The opponents of the federal courts did not even then wholly give up the fight; a resolution was introduced into the Senate in 1793 to amend the Constitution by authorising Congress to vest the judicial power of the United States in such of the State courts as it should deem fit.[7] This failed to carry, and the establishment of the federal courts was authorised without any alternative or complementary legislative authority to vest federal jurisdiction in State courts.

Congress took early action to constitute federal courts. The *Judiciary Act* 1789 established a system of federal courts throughout the country, which was divided into 13 districts, each with a federal district court. A second tier of federal courts was created by forming three circuits, each with two justices of the Supreme Court of the United States and one district judge within the circuit sitting twice a year in the various districts comprised within the circuit. The Supreme Court of the United States, with a Chief Justice and five associate justices, crowned the system.[8] Since 1789 the organisation of the federal court system has undergone some changes, but the United States has since that date possessed a self-contained structure of federal courts of original and appellate jurisdiction. The jurisdiction of the federal courts has grown and

---

5   Ibid.
6   See Prescott, *Drafting the Federal Constitution*, 1941; Fallon, Meltzer and Shapiro, *Hart and Wechsler's Federal Courts and the Federal System*, 4th edn, 1996, pp 8-9. See also *National Insurance Co v Tidewater Co* 337 US 582 at 647 (1949).
7   Frankfurter and Landis, *The Business of the Supreme Court*, 1927.
8   In 1863 the Supreme Court had its largest membership, ten. In 1869 the number became nine and it has since remained at that number.

the broad grant of jurisdiction to the district courts over federal questions by the *Judiciary Act* 1875 "in a very real sense revolutionized the nature of the federal judiciary"[9] by vastly increasing their jurisdiction. Congress has not only exercised its powers to create federal courts with what may be described as *general* federal jurisdiction; it has also from time to time created *specialised* federal courts, such as the United States Court of Appeals for the Federal Circuit, the United States Court of Federal Claims, the Court of International Trade and the United States Tax Court.[10]

The Australian story was quite different. Quick and Garran's prediction in 1900 that "it is probable that for some time there will be no necessity for the creation of any inferior federal courts, but that all the cases in which the original jurisdiction of the Commonwealth is invoked can be dealt with either by the High Court itself or by the Courts of the States"[11] proved substantially accurate. The Parliament made liberal use of the State courts as repositories of federal jurisdiction, and also until the 1970s made regrettably liberal use of the High Court as a court of original jurisdiction. Unlike the United States, the Commonwealth did not proceed to create a hierarchy of federal courts.

For many years the only federal courts were the Australian Industrial Court and the Federal Court of Bankruptcy. The Federal Court of Bankruptcy, which exercised jurisdiction only in New South Wales and Victoria, was created in 1930 by the insertion of s 18A into the *Bankruptcy Act* 1924 and continued in existence by s 21 of the *Bankruptcy Act* 1966. It was declared to be a superior court of record. In 1976 its jurisdiction was transferred to the Federal Court of Australia.[12] That Court and the Federal Magistrates Court now each have jurisdiction in bankruptcy and their jurisdiction is exclusive of all other courts, other than the High Court under s 75 of the Constitution.[13]

The *Commonwealth Electoral Act* 1918, s 354, constitutes a Court of Disputed Returns, but this is defined as the High Court.

The Commonwealth Industrial Court was created in 1956 by s 98 of the *Conciliation and Arbitration Act* 1904. Its name was changed to the Australian Industrial Court in 1973.[14] The Court, which was given original and appellate jurisdiction, was established together with the Australian Conciliation and Arbitration Commission.[15] The legislation was framed in light of the High Court's decision[16] (subsequently affirmed by the Privy Council[17]) in the

---

9   *Hart and Wechsler's The Federal Courts and the Federal System*, 4th edn, 1996, p 880.

10 Wright, *Law of Federal Courts*, 5th edn, 1994, pp 15-21.

11 Quick and Garran, op cit p 726.

12 *Bankruptcy Amendment Act* 1976.

13 *Bankruptcy Act* 1966, s 27.

14 No 138 of 1973, s 41.

15 No 44 of 1956.

16 *R v Kirby; ex parte Boilermakers' Society of Australia* (1956) 94 CLR 254.

17 *Attorney-General (Cth) v The Queen* [1957] AC 288.

Boilermakers' Case that the Commonwealth Court of Conciliation and Arbitration, which had been created on the assumption that it was a federal court constituted under the authority of ss 71 and 77(i) of the Constitution, was not such a court and was not competent to exercise the judicial power of the Commonwealth. In *Seamen's Union v Matthews*,[18] prohibition was sought against the Industrial Court on the ground that it was not validly constituted as a federal court. It was argued that a conglomerate mass of powers and functions had been conferred upon the Court, so that it could not lawfully exercise the judicial power of the Commonwealth within the rule of the *Boilermakers' Case*. The High Court unanimously rejected this argument. It pointed to the propriety of considering the history of the legislation, that it was passed after and in light of the High Court's decision in the *Boilermakers' Case*, that the legislative scheme of the *Conciliation and Arbitration Act* 1956 separated those powers of dealing with industrial matters falling within the main purpose of s 51(xxxv) of the Constitution from those conferred upon the Industrial Court, and that the Court had been constituted with due regard to s 72 of the Constitution so far as the tenure of the judges was concerned.

> When you look at the powers of the Commonwealth Industrial Court which, it is said, go beyond the judicial power of the Commonwealth it will be seen that they are of a kind which the legislature might well have thought appropriate to a judicial tribunal and are not manifestly of an industrial or arbitral character. We think that it is quite plain that in the light of the decision of the Court in *R v Kirby; ex parte Boilermakers' Society of Australia*, the legislature attempted to set up a new court for the judicial enforcement of the provisions of the Act and of the award and for the exercise of other judicial functions arising out of the *Conciliation and Arbitration Act*. On the assumption that provisions conferring authority upon the Court are found which do go outside Chapter III of the Constitution we think it is quite clear that the only result is that they must be severed as bad and that the Commonwealth Industrial Court is validly established and remains in possession of the judicial powers conferred on it by the Act.[19]

In 1976 the jurisdiction of the Australian Industrial Court was transferred to the Federal Court of Australia, which was provided with a separate Industrial Division, so as to preserve what the Attorney-General called the "special character of the industrial jurisdiction under the *Conciliation and Arbitration Act*".[20]

A Committee of Review of Australian Industrial Relations Law and Systems, known as the Hancock Committee, recommended in 1985 that there should be an Australian Labour Court, the judges of which would also hold

---

18 (1956) 96 CLR 529.

19 Ibid at 535.

20 Commonwealth Parliamentary Debates (H of R) 1976, p 2112.

commissions as members of the Australian Industrial Relations Commission. The purpose of this was to bring together the arbitral and judicial functions similar to the situation which existed before the *Boilermakers' Case*, but in a manner which, it was thought, would be consistent with that decision.[21]

That did not occur; but the *Industrial Relations Reform Act* 1993 established the Industrial Relations Court to which was transferred the industrial jurisdiction of the Federal Court. The judges of the new Court also held commissions as judges of the Federal Court. The Industrial Relations Court did not, as an effective institution, last long. The Act was extensively amended in 1996 and its name changed to the *Workplace Relations Act* 1996. The jurisdiction of the Industrial Relations Court was transferred back to the Federal Court from 25 May 1997. There was no reinstatement, however, of a separate Industrial Division.

The *Banking Act* 1947 made provision for the establishment of a Court of Claims, which was constituted as a federal court. It was given exclusive juris-diction to hear and determine claims and entitlements to compensation under the Act. In the *Bank Nationalisation Case*,[22] it was held that the grant of exclusive jurisdiction to the Court was unconstitutional and the Court was never in fact constituted.

The Family Court of Australia was created by the *Family Law Act* 1975. It is a superior court of record with wide jurisdiction in family law matters including divorce, nullity, guardianship and custody of children, maintenance and the declaration and alteration of property interests. It has both original and appellate jurisdiction (ss 28, 35). An amendment of the Act in 1988 created the office of Judicial Registrar to exercise powers delegated by the Court with respect to a range of matters. The Federal Court was also empowered to transfer certain proceedings within its jurisdiction to the Family Court.[23] The purpose was to give some variety of work to the Family Court judges. The validity of the provisions relating to the Judicial Registrars was upheld in *Harris v Caladine.*[24] That aspect is discussed in Chapter 5 below as it is con-nected to similar issues in relation to the functions of registrars of State courts exercising federal jurisdiction.[25] The Family Court also exercises jurisdiction under the *Marriage Act* 1961, the *Child Support (Registration and Collection) Act* 1988 and the *Child Support (Assessment) Act* 1989.

Much of the family law jurisdiction that the *Family Law Act* purported to confer was upheld as valid by a majority of the High Court in *Russell v Russell.*[26] In relation to matters involving maintenance and custody of children,

---

21 See Report of the Committee, 1985, pp 382-383.
22 (1948) 76 CLR 1; see p 39 above.
23 *Family Court of Australia (Additional Jurisdiction and Exercise of Powers) Act* 1988.
24 (1991) 172 CLR 84.
25 See pp 208-209 below.
26 (1976) 134 CLR 495.

the jurisdiction was held to be supported by the power with respect to marriage in s 51(xxi) of the Constitution by confining the operation of the provisions to proceedings by parties to a marriage. A provision relating to proceedings regarding "the property of a party to a marriage" was too broad for purposes of the marriage power because it comprehended any property whenever acquired. It was, however, read down by reference to the power with respect to "divorce and matrimonial causes" in s 51(xxii), and treated as conferring jurisdiction to grant ancillary relief in proceedings for divorce or annulment.

All the States other than Western Australia enacted legislation referring to the Commonwealth Parliament, under s 51(xxxvii) of the Constitution, power to make laws with respect to (a) the maintenance of children and payment of expenses in relation to children and child rearing and (b) the custody and guardianship of, and access to, children. The State Acts exclude children who are in the care or control of State authorities.[27] The *Family Law Amendment Act* 1987 expanded the jurisdiction of the Court to include the referred matters so that jurisdiction was not confined to the custody et cetera of children who were children of a marriage. There has been no referral of power relating to property disputes.

Provision is made for investing State Family Courts with federal jurisdiction to deal with matters under the Act in certain circumstances (s 41). The only State court that has been proclaimed for this purpose is the Family Court of Western Australia. The judges of that Court also hold commissions as judges of the Family Court.[28] Jurisdiction was also vested in the State and Territory Supreme Courts and, in the case of matrimonial causes not being proceedings for principal relief, in courts of summary jurisdiction of the States and Territories (s 39). However, the Governor-General is authorised by Proclamation to fix a date on which proceedings under the Act may not be instituted or transferred to those courts (ss 39(7) and 40(3)). The first day of June 1976 was fixed by Proclamation as the date on which proceedings were not to be instituted in the Supreme Courts of the States or Territories in relation to specified proceedings.[29] In relation to courts of summary jurisdiction, the only Proclamations made concern courts of summary jurisdiction in the metropolitan region of Perth.[30]

The Federal Court of Australia was created by the *Federal Court of Australia Act* 1976. It is a superior court of record and consists of a Chief Justice and such other judges as are appointed. The original jurisdiction of the Court is described in the *Federal Court of Australia Act* as being "such

---

27 *Commonwealth Powers (Family Law – Children) Act* 1986 (NSW), (Vic), 1990 (Qld), *Commonwealth Powers (Family Law) Act* 1986 (SA), 1987 (Tas).

28 French, "Federal Courts Created by Parliament" in Opeskin and Wheeler (eds), *The Australian Federal Judicial System*, 2000, p 142.

29 Australian Government Gazette, 27 May 1976.

30 The latest Proclamation is no GN45, 13 November 1996.

original jurisdiction as is vested in it by laws made by the Parliament, being jurisdiction in respect of matters arising under laws made by the Parliament".[31] The other Acts which actually invested the jurisdiction included the *Conciliation and Arbitration Act* 1904, ss 118A and 118B (which transferred the industrial jurisdiction of the Australian Industrial Court), the *Bankruptcy Act* 1966, s 28 (under which the Federal Court of Australia was substituted for the former *Federal Court of Bankruptcy* in exercising bankruptcy jurisdiction), and the *Federal Court of Australia (Consequential Provisions) Act* 1976, which transferred from the Australian Industrial Court to the Federal Court of Australia jurisdiction under other Acts including the *Trade Practices Act* 1974, the *Prices Justification Act* 1973, the *Financial Corporations Act* 1974 and the *Administrative Appeals Tribunal Act* 1975. The *Administrative Decisions (Judicial Review) Act* 1977 conferred jurisdiction on the Federal Court of Australia to review administrative decisions made or proposed to be made under any enactment of the Commonwealth, other than a decision of the Governor-General.

By 30 June 2000 the Federal Court reported that jurisdiction had been conferred on the Court by 149 Acts.[32] The major areas of jurisdiction, however, are trade practices, industrial relations, review of federal administrative action, admiralty, bankruptcy and native title.

In 1983 the Court was given jurisdiction to grant the remedies referred to in s 75(v) of the Constitution, except where relief is sought against judges of the Family Court and office-holders under industrial relations legislation. In 1987 jurisdiction in respect of taxation matters was made exclusive to the Court, and it acquired concurrent original jurisdiction under legislation relating to intellectual property. The *Admiralty Act* 1988 invested civil admiralty jurisdiction in the Court, concurrently with the Supreme Courts of the States and Territories. The *Corporations Act* 1989 gave jurisdiction in respect of civil proceedings under the *Corporations Law*. However, in so far as jurisdiction was derived from State Acts with federal statutory consent, it was held invalid.[33] As a result of the subsequent referral of corporation matters by the States to the Commonwealth, pursuant to s 51(xxxvii) of the Constitution, the Federal Court now has the jurisdiction previously denied to it.[34] The *Native Title Act* 1993 invested the Court with what French J has described as "major and resource intensive jurisdiction" in matters under that Act.[35]

---

31 Section 19.

32 Federal Court of Australia, Annual Report 1999-2000, Appendix 4. The list is set out in Australian Law Reform Commission, *The Judicial Power of the Commonwealth – A Review of the Judiciary Act 1903 and Related Legislation*, Discussion Paper no 64, December 2000, p 76.

33 *Re Wakim; ex parte McNally* (1999) 198 CLR 511. See pp 152-155 below.

34 *Corporations Act* 2001, Part 9.6A.

35 French, "Federal Courts created by Parliament" in Opeskin and Wheeler (eds), *The Australian Federal Judicial System*, 2000, p 154.

Legislation in 1997, however, changed the nature of the Federal Court from that originally envisaged by Mr Ellicott, the Attorney-General who had introduced the *Federal Court of Australia Bill* in 1976. Ellicott had condemned earlier attempts to establish a Commonwealth court of general federal jurisdiction, that is with all the jurisdiction included in ss 75 and 76 of the Constitution. He said that such a court would have resulted in the removal from State courts of the bulk of their federal jurisdiction and would have "greatly weakened the status of those courts and the quality of the work dealt with by them".[36] The rationale for creating the Federal Court was that it would relieve the High Court of much of its original jurisdiction and would provide a court that was more appropriate than the Industrial Court for determining matters that the Governments had determined, or would in the future determine, for policy or historical reasons, should be dealt with by a federal court.[37] It seems clear, therefore, that the Court was seen as one of specialised jurisdiction (though not narrowly specialised) dealing with matters of particular Commonwealth concern, which, it was thought, should be determined by a national court.

Legislation in 1997 resulted in the character of the Court moving towards that envisaged by the earlier proposals for a court of general federal juris-diction. Section 39B of the *Judiciary Act* (which conferred jurisdiction in relation to s 75(v) remedies) was amended by adding the following:

> (1A) The original jurisdiction of the Federal Court of Australia also includes jurisdiction in any matter:
> (a) in which the Commonwealth is seeking an injunction or a declaration; or
> (b) arising under the Constitution, or involving its interpretation; or
> (c) arising under any laws made by the Parliament.

The jurisdiction in para (a) derives from s 75(iii) of the Constitution, but does not encompass all the jurisdiction specified in that paragraph.[38] Paragraphs (b) and (c), on the other hand, comprise all the jurisdiction included in s 76(i) and (ii), respectively. In 1999, para (c) was qualified by adding "other than a matter in respect of which a criminal prosecution is instituted or any other criminal matter".[39]

The Federal Court has power, apart from s 39B(1A)(b), to determine a con-stitutional issue that is part of a matter arising under a federal law that is within its jurisdiction.[40] Paragraph (b) of s 39B(1A), however, is an inde-

---

36 Commonwealth Parliamentary Debates (H of R) 21 October 1976, p 2110, cited in French, op cit p 150.

37 Ibid p 2110; French, op cit pp 150-151.

38 Section 44(2A) of the *Judiciary Act* authorises the High Court to remit to the Federal Court any matters that come within s 75(iii).

39 *Law and Justice Legislation Amendment Act* 1999.

40 *Re Tooth and Co Ltd (No 2)* (1978) 34 FLR 112; *Grace Bros Pty Ltd v Magistrates of Local Courts of NSW* (1988) 84 ALR 492 at 496. These and other cases are discussed in Australian Law Reform Commission, Discussion Paper no 64, December 2000, pp 73-74.

pendent grant of jurisdiction and does not require the constitutional claim to be part of any other matter or to be associated with it. "Associated jurisdiction" is discussed later.[41]

The jurisdiction in para (c) – "arising under any laws made by the Parliament" – sits oddly with s 19 of the *Federal Court of Australia Act*, which clearly contemplates jurisdiction being conferred in respect of particular Acts. It is clear that the Federal Court can no longer be regarded as a specialised court. It possesses nearly all the important and most-used heads of federal jurisdiction, namely s 75(v) and s 76(i), (ii) and (iii). This leaves only s 75(i), treaties, s 75(ii), consuls, s 75(iii), Commonwealth as a party (except for jurisdiction in s 39B(1A)(a) and remittal by the High Court), s 75(iv), suits between States and diversity jurisdiction, and s 76(iv), claims under the laws of different States. Issues have arisen as to the relationship between specific statutes investing the Court with jurisdiction and the general jurisdiction in s 39B(1A)(c). In some cases the Federal Court has treated the latter provision as overriding specific limits on jurisdiction in individual Acts.[42] This type of legislation is distinguished from that which prohibits the Court from entering an area of jurisdiction. One example is s 485 of the *Migration Act* 1958, which expressly took away the Court's jurisdiction in respect of specified grounds of judicial review of administrative action.[43] The distinction between limits on jurisdiction which do not prevent the full operation of s 39B(1A)(c) and proscriptions that do is not, of course, always clear.[44]

The Federal Court of Australia is given appellate jurisdiction with some exceptions to determine appeals from:

(a) judgments of the Court constituted by a single judge;

(b) judgments of the Supreme Court of a Territory; and

(c) "in such cases as are provided by any other Act", appeals from judgments of a court of a State, other than a Full Court of the Supreme Court of a State, exercising federal jurisdiction (s 24);

(d) appeals from judgments of the Federal Magistrates Court exercising original jurisdiction under a law of the Commonwealth other than the *Family Law Act* 1975, the *Child Support (Assessment) Act*, 1989; the *Child Support (Registration and Assessment) Act* 1988; or regulations under those Acts.[45]

---

41 Pages 148-149 below.

42 *Transport Workers Union v Lee* (1998) 84 FCR 60; *Hooper v Kirella Pty Ltd* (1999) 167 ALR 358.

43 Campbell, "The Accrued Jurisdiction of the Federal Court in Administrative Law Matters" (1998) 17 Australian Bar Review 127 at 139.

44 For a general discussion, see Australian Law Reform Commission, op cit pp 79-82.

45 "Supreme Court of a Territory" in para (b) does not include the Northern Territory. Legislation is expected also to exclude the Australian Capital Territory; see Chapter 4.

With the creation of the Federal Court there was introduced the practice of vesting original jurisdiction, in some areas, in the Supreme Courts of the States and appellate jurisdiction in the Federal Court exclusive of State Supreme Courts. That was so under, for example, *Patents Act* 1952, s 114; *Income Tax Assessment Act* 1936, s 196; *Trade Marks Act* 1955, s 114; *Designs Act* 1906, s 401; and *Copyright Act* 1968, ss 131B, 248L. In 1987 the Federal Court was given exclusive original jurisdiction in taxation matters and concurrent original jurisdiction in matters of intellectual property;[46] but appellate jurisdiction exclusive of the State courts remains.[47]

The *Federal Magistrates Act* 1999, which came into operation on 23 December 1999, created the Federal Magistrates Court. The Act provides that the Court has such original jurisdiction as is vested in it by laws made by Parliament (s 10). Under the *Family Law Act* 1975, s 33B, the Family Court has power to transfer proceedings to the Magistrates Court having regard to specified criteria. In certain cases it is mandatory for the Family Court to transfer the proceedings (s 33C). The *Federal Court of Australia Act* 1976, s 32AB, gives power to that Court to transfer proceedings to the Magistrates Court. The discretion to transfer is exercisable subject to criteria stated in the Act and prescribed in any Rules of Court (sub-s (6)). Limited jurisdiction under the *Administrative Decisions (Judicial Review) Act* 1977 is conferred on the Magistrates Court, which is not dependent on Federal Court transfer. In addition, the Court has been given jurisdiction under the *Human Rights and Equal Opportunity Commission Act* 1986, the *Trade Practices Act* 1974 and, as mentioned above, the *Bankruptcy Act* 1966.

The Independence of Judges and the Separation of Judicial Power

The first paragraph of s 72 of the Constitution provides:

> The Justices of the High Court and of the other courts created by the Parliament –
> (i) Shall be appointed by the Governor-General in Council:
> (ii) Shall not be removed except by the Governor-General in Council, on an address from both Houses of the Parliament in the same session, praying for such removal on the ground of proved misbehaviour or incapacity:
> (iii) Shall receive such remuneration as the Parliament may fix; but the remuneration shall not be diminished during their continuance in office.

---

46   *Jurisdiction of Courts (Miscellaneous Amendments) Act* 1987. See *Patents Act* 1990, ss 154-158; *Trade Marks Act* 1995, ss 191-195.

47   See Opeskin, "Federal Jurisdiction in Australian Courts" (1995) 46 South Carolina LR 765 at 777-778; Australian Law Reform Commission, Discussion Paper no 64, December 2000, pp 213-215.

Until its amendment in 1977, this was all that s 72 contained. Article III, s 1, of the United States Constitution is differently phrased; it confers tenure during good behaviour on the judges of the Supreme Court and inferior federal courts. A constitutional requirement of tenure during good behaviour necessarily excludes an appointment of a federal judge for a term of years, but it was at least arguable that an appointment for a fixed term of years was not inconsistent with the rather different text of the first paragraph of s 72 of the Australian Constitution. In *Waterside Workers' Federation of Australia v JW Alexander Ltd*,[48] it was held, however, by a majority in the High Court that a court within the meaning of s 71 must be staffed by judges appointed for life, subject to the powers of removal set out in s 72. The matter for determination was the validity of the constitution of the Commonwealth Court of Conciliation and Arbitration, whose president was at that time appointed for a term of years. Dogmatic views were expressed on either side. Barton J, one of the majority judges, stated flatly that the argument that federal judges might be appointed for a term of years was "untenable"[49] and said that he did not think that the argument necessitated extended discussion. On the other side, Higgins J flatly stated that there was "not one word"[50] in the Constitution to justify a decision that a life tenure for federal judges was obligatory. Section 72 in providing that judges should not be removed except in stated circumstances meant only that a term of years could not otherwise be cut short by removal. In argument before the Privy Council in *Shell Co of Australia Ltd v Federal Commissioner of Taxation*,[51] an attack was made on the majority view in *Alexander's Case*, but the Board, without expressly deciding the point, stated that it was not prepared, as then advised, to dissent from the view that life tenure was required for federal judges. The ruling in *Alexander's Case* was followed by the High Court.[52]

In 1977, s 72 of the Constitution was amended following a referendum held in accordance with s 128. The following paragraphs were added:

> The appointment of a Justice of the High Court shall be for a term expiring upon his attaining the age of seventy years, and a person shall not be appointed as a Justice of the High Court if he has attained that age.

> The appointment of a Justice of a court created by the Parliament shall be for a term expiring upon his attaining the age that is, at the time of his appointment, the maximum age for Justices of that court and a person shall not be appointed as a Justice of such a court if he has attained the age that is for the time being the maximum age for Justices of that court.

48   (1918) 25 CLR 434.
49   Ibid at 457.
50   Ibid at 472.
51   [1931] AC 275 at 280 by Simon KC.
52   *Silk Bros Pty Ltd v State Electricity Commission* (1943) 67 CLR 1; *Peacock v Newtown etc Building Society* (1943) 67 CLR 25.

Subject to this section, the maximum age for Justices of any court created by the Parliament is seventy years.

The Parliament may make a law fixing an age that is less than seventy years as the maximum age for Justices of a court created by the Parliament and may at any time repeal or amend such a law, but any such repeal or amendment does not affect the term of office of a Justice under an appointment made before the repeal or amendment.

A Justice of the High Court or of a court created by the Parliament may resign his office by writing under his hand delivered to the Governor-General.

Nothing in the provisions added to this section by the *Constitution Alteration (Retirement of Judges)* 1977 affects the continuance of a person in office as a Justice of a court under an appointment made before the commencement of those provisions.

A reference in this section to the appointment of a Justice of the High Court or of a court created by the Parliament shall be read as including a reference to the appointment of a person who holds office as a Justice of the High Court or of a court created by the Parliament to another office of Justice of the same court having a different status or designation.

The result of the amendment is that any appointment to the High Court after the date of the amendment is for a term expiring when the judge attains 70 years of age. The position is the same for the appointment of a judge of any other federal court unless Parliament, before the appointment of that judge, fixes an age for retirement at less than 70 years.

The *Commonwealth Conciliation and Arbitration Act* was amended in 1926 to provide life tenure for the judges of the Conciliation and Arbitration Court.[53] The assumption in the Act of 1926 was that it was permissible to commingle functions which were primarily non-judicial with others that were judicial in a federal body assumed to be a court whose members satisfied the tenure requirements of s 72. In the *Boilermakers' Case*,[54] it was held that the Court of Conciliation and Arbitration, whose functions were construed as primarily arbitral, could not conjointly exercise judicial power. The Court stated the broad principle that the exercise of judicial power could not constitutionally be combined with the exercise of non-judicial power. This was stated by the High Court as follows:

> Chapter III does not allow the exercise of a jurisdiction which of its very nature belongs to the judicial power of the Commonwealth by a body established for purposes foreign to the judicial power, notwithstanding that it is organised as a court and in a manner which might otherwise satisfy ss 71 and 72, and Chapter III does not allow a combination with judicial

---

53 For the history of the legislation, see *R v Kirby; ex parte Boilermakers' Society of Australia* (1956) 94 CLR 254 at 284ff.

54 (1956) 94 CLR 254 (HC); [1957] AC 288 (PC).

power of functions which are not ancillary or incidental to its exercise but are foreign to it.[55]

The *Boilermakers' Case* imposes an important constitutional restraint on the grant of power to a federal court in so far as powers cannot validly be conferred upon it which go outside the conception of judicial power and what is incidental to it in the sense explained in that case and elsewhere.[56] The High Court in *Seamen's Union v Matthews*[57] indicated that while the Commonwealth Industrial Court was validly constituted as a federal court under ss 71 and 77(i), some of the powers conferred upon it might, within the rule of the *Boilermakers' Case,* be construed as non-judicial and therefore ultra vires, though severable. In *R v Spicer; ex parte Australian Builders' Labourers' Federation,*[58] the High Court unanimously held that s 140 of the *Conciliation and Arbitration Act* attempted to confer non-judicial power on the Commonwealth Industrial Court and, therefore, in accordance with the doctrine in the *Boilermakers' Case*, the section was held to be invalid. Section 140 purported to authorise the Industrial Court to disallow any rule of an industrial organisation on wide discretionary grounds, and had been copied from earlier versions of the *Conciliation and Arbitration Act*. When this power had been conferred on the former Commonwealth Conciliation and Arbitration Court, it had been held in *Consolidated Press Ltd v Australian Journalists' Association*[59] to be non-judicial, so that no appeal lay to the High Court under s 73(ii) of the Constitution. As Dixon CJ observed in *R v Spicer:*

> Section 140 was framed as one of the industrial powers of the Commonwealth Court of Conciliation and Arbitration to be exercised at the instance of the Court or a member of the organisation independently of any consideration which must govern a judicial determination within Chapter III, except that the Court should have assured itself that there was a compliance with one or other of the paragraphs (a), (b), (c) or (d) of sub-s (1) of s 140. In effect that is what was decided in *Consolidated Press Ltd v Australian Journalists' Association* and there is no sufficient reason for refusing to apply that decision.[60]

Again in *R v Spicer; ex parte Waterside Workers' Federation*[61] the High Court unanimously held that s 37 of the *Stevedoring Industry Act* 1954, which purported to confer appellate jurisdiction on the Commonwealth Industrial Court in respect of the cancellation or suspension of the registration of a waterside worker, was invalid for the same reason. In *R v Commonwealth*

55   (1956) 94 CLR 254 at 296. See also per Lord Simonds [1957] AC 288 at 318-319.
56   Zines, *The High Court and the Constitution*, 4th edn, 1997, chs 9 and 10.
57   (1956) 96 CLR 529.
58   (1957) 100 CLR 277.
59   (1947) 73 CLR 549.
60   (1957) 100 CLR 277 at 291.
61   (1957) 100 CLR 312.

Court of Conciliation and Arbitration; ex parte Ellis,[62] it had been held that a like power conferred on the Commonwealth Court of Conciliation and Arbitration by the *Stevedoring Industry Act* 1949 was, in effect, an authority to make an administrative review of an administrative decision, and that its re-enactment in like terms in 1956 as a grant of power to the Commonwealth Industrial Court must be read as an intention to confer a power to be governed by what might broadly be called administrative and industrial considerations, and therefore outside the permissible limits of the exercise of federal judicial power.

Section 140 was repealed and a new section inserted by s 24 of the *Conciliation and Arbitration Act* 1958, which empowered the Industrial Court to declare the rules of an organisation to be void on newly defined grounds. The new s 140(1) provided that a rule of an organisation "shall not", among other things, be contrary to the Act, the regulations or an award, or otherwise be contrary to law or impose on applicants for membership or members conditions, obligations or restrictions which, having regard to the objects of the Act and the purposes of the registration of organisations under the Act, are oppressive, unreasonable or unjust. A member of an organisation could apply to the Court for an order declaring that a rule contravened the section. Subsection (5) provided that, if the Court made an order declaring that a rule contravened the Act, the rule "shall be deemed to be void from the date of the order". The Court was further given power to adjourn proceedings for the purpose of giving the organisation an opportunity to alter its rules.

In *R v Commonwealth Industrial Court; ex parte Amalgamated Engineering Union, Australian Section,*[63] the Court unanimously held that the new s 140 conferred part of the judicial power of the Commonwealth on the Commonwealth Industrial Court, and was therefore valid.

The earlier provision had been declared invalid having regard to the total effect of a number of factors, including an earlier decision, the fact that the Court could act on its own motion, the use of the word "may" in conferring the power (which was said to be apt for a complete discretion based on industrial or administrative considerations), and the vagueness and generality of the criteria which seemed to refer to an industrial discretion rather than a legal standard.

The revamped section had deleted the provision allowing the Court to act on its own motion and the discretion given to the Court as to whether an order should be made. The Court was not given power "to disallow" a rule but merely to declare that it contravened the Act. However, the criteria was just as general, and sub-s (5) indicated that the Court's declaration operated only "in futurum" and therefore resembled a quasi-legislative order rather than a judicial one.

---

62   (1954) 90 CLR 55.

63   (1960) 103 CLR 368.

A majority of the judges (McTiernan, Fullagar, Taylor and Menzies JJ) considered that an infringement of s 140(1) resulted in invalidity from the time that the subsection operated. They regarded sub-s (5) as merely extending the operation of an order made under the section. Dixon CJ, Kitto and Windeyer JJ, however, were prepared to hold the provisions consistent with the exercise of judicial power even if a contravention of s 14(1) was not per se a cause of invalidity.

From the point of view of a government anxious to give a judicial body authority to deal with trade union rules, the differences between the old and new provisions were comparatively minor. From an analytical aspect the Court examined the cumulative effect of various factors without indicating that the absence or presence of any one of them was essential to the judgment. One could reply to each of the separate reasons given for holding that the old section conferred non-judicial power by pointing to courts that had traditionally exercised power in the form expressed; for example, a court acts on its own motion in dealing with a contempt of court and there are many areas in which courts have a discretion in making orders. The new provisions still left the Court a lot of discretion by virtue of the vagueness of the criteria and the fact that it could adjourn proceedings to enable an amendment of the rules.

Generally the High Court has in recent years been loathe to strike down powers given to federal courts on the grounds that they amount to an exertion of non-judicial power. Quite large discretions and very vague criteria have been held to come within the notion of the judicial power of the Common-wealth.[64] A discretion given to a judge to make an order if he or she considers it "just and equitable" or "proper" to do so has been upheld on many occasions as coming properly within the concept of the judicial power of the Commonwealth and therefore validly conferred on a federal court or a State court exercising federal jurisdiction.[65]

In *R v Joske; ex parte Australian Building Construction Employees and Builders Labourers Federation*,[66] a challenge was made to s 143 of the *Conciliation and Arbitration Act*. That provision enabled a person or organisation or the Registrar to apply to the Industrial Court directing the cancellation of the registration of an organisation on various grounds. The Court, however, was required to make the order directing the Registrar to cancel registration only if it did not consider that "having regard to the degree of gravity" of the matter, it would be unjust to do so. The High Court unanimously held that

---

64 *Cominos v Cominos* (1972) 127 CLR 588. See Zines, *The High Court and the Constitution*, 4th edn, 1997, pp 192-201.

65 *Lansell v Lansell* (1964) 110 CLR 353; *Sanders v Sanders* (1967) 116 CLR 366; *Peacock v Newtown, Marrickville and General Co-operative Building Society (No 4) Ltd* (1943) 67 CLR 25. Cf *Yanner v Minister for Aboriginal and Torres Strait Islander Affairs* (2001) 181 ALR 490 (FCA).

66 (1974) 130 CLR 87.

s 143 conferred judicial power on the Court. However, Barwick CJ questioned the whole doctrine of the *Boilermakers' Case.* He said:

> The principal conclusion of the *Boilermakers' Case* was unnecessary, in my opinion, for the effective working of the Australian Constitution or for the maintenance of the separation of the judicial power of the Commonwealth or for the protection of the independence of courts exercising that power. The decision leads to excessive subtlety and technicality in the operation of the Constitution without, in my opinion, any compensating benefit. But none the less, and notwithstanding the unprofitable inconveniences it entails, it may be proper that it should continue to be followed. On the other hand, it may be thought so unsuited to the working of the Constitution in the circumstances of the nation that there should now be a departure from some or all of its conclusions.[67]

Mason J also agreed that a "serious question" had arisen as to the course the High Court should adopt in relation to the *Boilermakers' Case.*[68] However, it was unnecessary for the Court to consider whether that case should be overruled.

As a result of these comments, an attempt to get the Court to depart from the *Boilermakers' Case* was made in *R v Joske; ex parte Shop Distributive and Allied Employees Association.*[69] That case involved, inter alia, ss 171C and 171D of the *Conciliation and Arbitration Act,* which empowered the Industrial Court to make orders in respect of the consequences of invalidity in the management or administration of an industrial organisation and to approve schemes for reconstitution of an organisation or part of an organisation which had ceased to exist or function effectively. The Court held that those provisions conferred judicial power and therefore found it unnecessary to consider the correctness of the *Boilermakers' Case.* Since then, however, the *Boilermakers'* principle has been unquestioned and has, from time to time, been referred to by judges with approval. For example, Deane J in *R v Tracey; ex parte Ryan*[70] relied on it to say: "The Executive Government cannot absorb or be amalgamated with the judicature by the conferral of non-ancillary executive functions upon the courts." All the judges in *Gould v Brown* regarded the principle as well settled.[71]

The Jurisdiction of Federal Courts

There is a further important limitation on the power to create federal courts and to define their jurisdiction. "The constitutional authority to create new

---

67   Ibid at 90.
68   Ibid at 102.
69   (1976) 135 CLR 194.
70   (1989) 166 CLR 518 at 580.
71   (1998) 193 CLR 346 at 400-401, 419, 440, 499-500.

federal courts is limited; the extent of the jurisdiction which Parliament may confer on any such court is determined solely by reference to the matters enumerated in ss 75 and 76."[72] This arises from the form of the power, s 77(i), which authorises the legislative definition of the jurisdiction of federal courts. The matters which may be the subject of such definition are those in ss 75 and 76, the matters of original or potential original jurisdiction of the High Court. Section 77(i) authorises the definition of jurisdiction with respect to all or any of these matters irrespective of any action by the Parliament under s 76 to invest the High Court with original jurisdiction. For example, if a matter falls within the description of s 76(ii), that is to say, arises under any law made by the Parliament, jurisdiction with respect to it may be conferred on an inferior federal court, even though there has been no grant of original jurisdiction to the High Court under s 76(ii).

Beyond the limits marked out by the matters in ss 75 and 76, it is not possible for the Commonwealth to confer jurisdiction on federal courts (putting aside matters relating to the Territories). A grant may therefore fail because it is not defined by reference to a "matter". In *Collins v Charles Marshall Pty Ltd*,[73] the High Court elaborately considered the validity of s 31 of the *Conciliation and Arbitration Act* 1904, which purported to confer jurisdiction on the Commonwealth Court of Conciliation and Arbitration[74] by providing that:

> (1) There shall be an appeal to the Court from a judgment or order of any other court
>   (a) in proceedings arising under this Act (including proceedings under s 59 of this Act or proceedings for an offence against this Act) or involving the interpretation of this Act; and
>   (b) in proceedings arising under an order or award or involving the interpretation of an order or award, and the Court shall have jurisdiction to hear and determine any such appeal.
> (2) Except as provided in the last preceding sub-section, there shall be no appeal from a judgment or order from which an appeal may be brought to the Court under that sub-section.

The section refers to "proceedings", not matters. On this point the Court observed:

> It is a distinction which s 31(1) fails to make and it may be that if pursued to its logical consequences this failure might prove in itself fatal. It is enough to quote the following passage from the joint judgment in *Re Judiciary and Navigation Acts*:[75] "It was suggested in argument that

---

72 *Collins v Charles Marshall Pty Ltd* (1955) 92 CLR 529 at 562 per Taylor J.

73 (1955) 92 CLR 529 at 537-538.

74 Counsel raised in argument the broader constitutional questions that were subsequently decided in the *Boilermakers' Case*, but the High Court disposed of the case without dealing with this question: (1955) 92 CLR 529 at 546-547.

75 (1921) 29 CLR 257.

'matter' meant no more than legal proceeding, and that Parliament might at its discretion create or invent a legal proceeding in which this Court might be called on to interpret the Constitution by a declaration at large. We do not accept this contention; we do not think that the word 'matter' in s 76 means a legal proceeding, but rather the subject-matter for determination in a legal proceeding. In our opinion there can be no matter within the meaning of the section unless there is some immediate right, duty or liability to be established by the determination of the Court. If the matter exists, the Legislature may no doubt prescribe the means by which the determination of the Court is to be obtained, and for that purpose may, we think, adopt any existing method of legal procedure or invent a new one."[76]

In *Philip Morris Inc v Adam P Brown Male Fashions Pty Ltd*,[77] the Court was concerned with s 86 of the *Trade Practices Act* 1974, which conferred on the Federal Court jurisdiction to hear and determine "actions, prosecutions and other proceedings under this Part". Mason J[78] held that it was a law which defined the jurisdiction of the Federal Court with respect to a matter mentioned in 76(ii) referable to s 77(i). This view was accepted by a majority of the Court (Mason, Murphy, Brennan and Deane JJ) in *Fencott v Muller*.[79]

In *Collins v Charles Marshall Pty Ltd*, apart from the non-correspondence between "matters" and "proceedings", s 31 was held bad – assuming, or in any event not passing on the question of, the validity of the constitution of the Arbitration Court under ss 71 and 77(i) – on the ground that the grant of jurisdiction was not referable to any of the heads of ss 75 and 76. The reasons were stated concisely by Taylor J:

> Unless they are matters which are mentioned in s 75 or s 76 there is no constitutional foundation for the provisions of s 31. The four categories specified by the last-mentioned section are: (1) proceedings under the Act; (2) proceedings involving the interpretation of the Act; (3) proceedings arising under an order or award; and (4) proceedings involving the inter-pretation of an order or award. Quite apart from the difficulties which arise from the use of the word "proceedings" it is clear that neither matters involving the interpretation of the Act nor matters involving the inter-pretation of an order or award, by virtue of that character alone, fall within the specification of matters contained in ss 75 and 76. Nor, I should think, do matters "arising under an order or award". Matters of these descriptions may on occasions, of course, present other features which may bring them within the purview of those sections as they would, for example, if they arose between residents of different States, or if any such matter should also involve the interpretation of the Constitution or if it arose under any laws made by Parliament, but the descriptions which have been selected by s 31 are quite inappropriate, in the main, to describe matters in respect of

---

76   (1955) 92 CLR 529 at 541-542.
77   (1981) 148 CLR 457.
78   Ibid at 507.
79   (1983) 152 CLR 570 at 602.

which the High Court is given original jurisdiction under s 75 or in respect of which it may be conferred upon it by s 76. This being so, they are not matters with respect to which Parliament may make laws either defining the jurisdiction of the Arbitration Court or defining the extent to which the jurisdiction of that court shall be exclusive of that which belongs to or is invested in the courts of the State.[80]

In such a case, the excess of jurisdiction is clear on the face of the definition itself, but the problem may arise in a less obvious form. A grant of jurisdiction may be made to a federal court over matters which on their face are within the legislative competence of the Parliament so as to be referable to s 76(ii). But it may be argued that the vice in the grant is that Parliament has been too sparing in the exercise of its powers and has made only a bare grant of jurisdiction without enacting a substantive law to which the exercise of jurisdiction is referable. In the United States, this problem has been discussed by reference to such an enactment as s 301(a) of the *Labor Management Relations Act* 1947, which provides that:

> [S]uits for violation of contracts between an employer and a labor organisation representing employees in an industry affecting commerce as defined in this Act or between any such labor organisations may be brought in any district court of the United States having jurisdiction of the parties without respect to the amount in controversy or without regard to the citizenship of the parties.

On what basis can such a grant of jurisdiction be supported? The argument against validity is that, absent diversity of citizenship, the judicial power of the United States attaches to a private party's case only if it arises under the Constitution of the United States, an Act of Congress or a treaty, and a case arises under an Act of Congress only if the Act itself supplies part of the basis of the party's claim. While the *Labor Management Relations Act* requires parties to bargain, it does not of itself give legal force to their agreement; that depends on State law and a suit for violation of such a contract does not arise under federal law. On this argument, s 301(a), as a bare grant of jurisdiction, is constitutionally defective.

To this two possible answers may be given. The first is that a substantive federal law to be applied in suits under s 301(a) may be spelled out of the section itself. The second is that the grant of jurisdiction may be supported by reference to a doctrine of protective jurisdiction.

> The power of the Congress to confer the federal judicial power ... should extend ... to all cases in which Congress has authority to make the rule to govern disposition of the controversy, but is content instead to let the States provide the rule so long as jurisdiction to enforce it has been vested in a federal court. Where, for example, Congress by the commerce power can

---

80   (1955) 92 CLR 529 at 556-557.

declare as federal law that contracts of a given kind are valid and enforceable, it must be free to take the lesser step of drawing suits upon such contracts to the district courts without displacement of the States as sources of the operative, substantial law. A grant of jurisdiction is, in short, one mode by which the Congress may assert its regulatory powers.[81]

It is clear under the commerce clause that Congress could have enacted a substantive law to which the exercise of jurisdiction under s 301(a) could have been referable and, so supported, the grant of jurisdiction would have been valid, and "it would be most regrettable if a federal constitution forbade the general government to exercise its regulatory powers in this forbearing, sanguine and initially perhaps experimental manner which turns to account the genius of a federal system. It would be regrettable for Congress to be forced instead to exert its authority to the full in order to employ it at all".[82]

In *Textile Workers' Union of America v Lincoln Mills of Alabama*,[83] an action for specific enforcement of an arbitration clause in a collective bargaining contract, the Supreme Court of the United States upheld the validity of s 301(a). Douglas J, speaking for five members of the court, discovered in the section a congressional direction to treat grievance arbitration agreements as enforceable and to apply federal law which the courts must fashion from the policy of the national labor laws. Burton and Harlan JJ concurred in the result, on the ground that the section was supportable as a grant of protective jurisdiction, but rejected the view that any obligation to apply federal law could be spelt out of s 301(a).

The concept of "protective jurisdiction" has been the subject of a considerable amount of literature in the United States.[84] The Supreme Court has, since the *Lincoln Mills Case*, avoided the issue in cases where it has been raised. In *Mesa v California*,[85] the Court referred to an argument based on protective jurisdiction as a view which would "unnecessarily present grave constitutional problems".[86]

---

81   Wechsler, "Federal Jurisdiction and the Revision of the Judicial Code" (1948) 13 Law and Contemporary Problems 216 at 224-225.

82   Bickel and Wellington, "Legislative Purpose and the Judicial Process: The Lincoln Mills Case" (1957) 71 Harvard LR 1 at 20-21.

83   353 US 448; 1 L Ed 2d 972 (1957). See *McCarroll v Los Angeles County District Council of Carpenters* 315 P 2d 322 (1957); (1957) 71 Harvard LR 1; Bunn, "Lincoln Mills and the Jurisdiction to Enforce Collective Bargaining Agreements" (1957) 43 Virginia LR 1247; Note, "Lincoln Mills: Labor Arbitration and Federal-State Relations" (1957) 57 Columbia LR 1123;

84   Wright, *Law of Federal Courts*, 5th edn, 1994, pp 121-124; *Hart and Wechsler's The Federal Courts and the Federal System*, 4th edn, pp 891-907; Goldberg-Ambrose, "The Protective Jurisdiction of the Federal Courts" (1983) 30 UCLA LR 542; Comment, "A Comprehensive Theory of Protective Jurisdiction: The Missing 'Ingredient' of 'Arising Under' Jurisdiction" (1993) 61 Fordham LR 1235.

85   489 US 121 (1989).

86   See also *Verlinden BV v Central Bank of Nigeria* 461 US 480 (1983).

The High Court of Australia has been concerned with broadly similar problems both in the contexts of the definition of federal jurisdiction under s 77(i) and the investment of State courts with federal jurisdiction under s 77(iii). In *R v Commonwealth Court of Conciliation and Arbitration; ex parte Barrett*,[87] there was a challenge to the validity of s 58E of the *Conciliation and Arbitration Act* 1904, which authorised the Court, on complaint by a member of an organisation, to make an order giving directions for the performance or observance of any of the rules of an organisation by any person who is under an obligation to perform or observe those rules. On the assumption that this was a grant of judicial power[88] it was argued that there was no support to be derived from s 76(ii) for this grant of jurisdiction – this being the only possible head to which the jurisdiction might be attributed – because the substantive rights and obligations arising under the rules of the organisation arose not under any law of the Parliament, but as a matter of State law. The High Court rejected this argument, and discovered in s 58E a body of substantive law to which the grant of jurisdiction was referable, so that it was supportable as a grant of jurisdiction under s 76(ii). Dixon J said:

> It appears to me, that, on the footing that s 58E includes judicial power, it must be taken to perform a double function, namely to deal with sub- stantive liabilities or substantive legal relations and to give jurisdiction with reference to them. It is not unusual to find that statutes impose liabilities, create obligations or otherwise affect substantive rights, although they are expressed only to give jurisdiction or authority, whether of a judicial or administrative kind.[89]

Dixon J observed that, under the general law, the rules of a voluntary association did not always confer enforceable rights on members. He referred to various Commonwealth Acts in which the High Court or the Supreme Courts of the States were given jurisdiction to make discretionary orders touching patents, trade marks and a wide variety of other matters. The legis- lature had preferred to arm the courts with a broad discretion, rather than to legislate specifically or to prescribe fixed rules of substantive law by reference to which the courts should be required to act in exercise of their jurisdiction.[90] It lay within parliamentary competence under s 51(xxxv) and (xxxix) to deal with the rules of organisations and, in appropriate circumstances, to prescribe the conditions of their enforcement. Parliament might have chosen to define the circumstances in which actions for the enforcement of rules might be brought; but it preferred to give the Court a discretionary power to intervene on the complaint of a member. "The grant of that discretionary power appears

---

87 (1945) 70 CLR 141.
88 *Jacka v Lewis* (1944) 68 CLR 455; see also *R v Commonwealth Court of Conciliation and Arbitration; ex parte Barrett* (1945) 70 CLR 141 at 164 per Dixon J.
89 (1945) 70 CLR 141 at 165-166.
90 Ibid at 167-169.

to me to involve an exercise of the legislative power under s 51, and, on the assumption that it is a judicial matter, either in whole or in part, an exercise of that power uno ictu with a use of the legislative power under s 77(i)".[91]

In *Fisher v Fisher*,[92] Mason and Deane JJ referred to the fact that s 79 of the *Family Law Act* 1975 authorised the making of Court orders altering interests in property belonging to parties to the marriage. While the provision did not give effect to antecedent rights, they said that, as in *Barrett*, the orders performed a dual function by creating and enforcing rights in one blow.

In *Precision Data Holdings Ltd v Wills*,[93] a unanimous Court referred approvingly to Dixon J's judgment in *Barrett*. The Court said:

> The Parliament can, if it chooses, legislate with respect to rights and obligations by vesting jurisdiction in courts to make orders creating those rights or imposing those liabilities. It is an expedient which is sometimes adopted when Parliament decides to confer upon a court or tribunal a discretionary authority to make orders which create rights or impose liabilities. This legislative technique and its consequences in terms of federal jurisdiction were discussed by Dixon J[94] ... [W]here a discretionary authority is conferred upon a court and the discretionary authority is to be exercised according to legal principle or by reference to an objective standard or test prescribed by the legislature and not by reference to policy considerations or other matters not specified by the legislature, it will be possible to conclude that the determination by the court *gives effect to rights and obligations for which the statute provides* and that the determination constitutes an exercise of judicial power.[95]

This conclusion does not depend on a doctrine of protective jurisdiction; it rests, like the reasoning of Douglas J in the *Lincoln Mills Case*, on the discovery within the text of the section conferring jurisdiction of a substantive rule of federal law, couched in discretionary terms, which the federal court is called on to apply. In *Hooper v Hooper*,[96] the High Court, this time in the context of the investment of State Supreme Courts with federal jurisdiction under s 77(iii), and in face of a similar argument, discovered a federal substantive law which the State courts, exercising federal jurisdiction, were required to apply. By the *Commonwealth Matrimonial Causes Act* 1945, s 10, jurisdiction in matrimonial causes, based on the residence of the petitioner, was conferred on State Supreme Courts invested with federal jurisdiction under s 77(iii). Section 11 of the Act was a choice of law rule directing the application of the lex domicilii. It was argued that as the Commonwealth

---

91 Ibid at 169.
92 (1986) 161 CLR 388.
93 (1991) 173 CLR 167 at 191.
94 In *Barrett's Case*.
95 Emphasis added. See also *Re McJannet; ex parte Minister for Employment, Training and Industrial Relations (Q)* (1995) 184 CLR 620 at 655-656.
96 (1955) 91 CLR 529.

Parliament had not exercised its powers under s 51(xxii) to enact a federal substantive law of matrimonial causes, s 10 was bad as a bare grant of jurisdiction not referable to s 76(ii), since the only applicable law was State law. The High Court had little difficulty in disposing of this argument. Section 10, read with s 11, gave a party *a federally created right* to have his or her case tried by the court according to the lex domicilii.

> What the Act does is to give the force of federal law to the State law. The relevant law is administered in a suit instituted under the Act not because it has the authority of a State, but because it is part of the law of the Commonwealth.[97]

Hooper v Hooper, as the High Court remarked, was an easier case than *R v Commonwealth Court of Conciliation and Arbitration; ex parte Barrett*, because the *Matrimonial Causes Act*, in s 11, provided an express choice of law rule. A more difficult question would have arisen had s 10 of the Act stood alone, unsupported by s 11. There is a possibility that the Court would have spelt out a grant of jurisdiction coupled with an implied direction to the Court to discover some federal choice of law rule, whether the lex fori or the lex domicilii. Whether the High Court would be prepared to support a grant of jurisdiction by reference to a doctrine of protective jurisdiction can only be a matter for conjecture. If a guess may be hazarded, it is very doubtful whether the Court would do so. Faced with arguments touching the validity of grants of federal jurisdiction, the Court has been concerned to discover a body of substantive law (even though framed in wide discretionary terms) which, on the face of the legislation, it is directed to apply.

It may be that in substance there will be little difference in the two approaches depending on how far the High Court is prepared to go in implying rules of substantive law. There would be no practical difference if the rule that is implied is an ambulatory provision incorporating State statutory or a common law rule. Assume, for example, a provision conferring on a federal court jurisdiction relating to contracts between interstate traders or exporters and their customers. Under the protective jurisdiction doctrine the grant of jurisdiction would be valid, as the transactions which provide the criterion for jurisdiction are within the legislative power of the Commonwealth, under s 51(i) of the Constitution, to control. Under the approach adopted in *R v Commonwealth Court of Conciliation and Arbitration; ex parte Barrett* and *Hooper v Hooper* it would be necessary to argue that the law of contract to be applied by the Court is derived from common law and State statutory law and that that law is incorporated by reference as federal law, that is, that there is to be implied a federal choice of law rule. (It is doubtful if it could be argued in these cases that s 79 of the *Judiciary Act*, which directs the application of State law by courts exercising federal jurisdiction, provides the rule of substance,

---

97   At 536.

namely a choice of law rule, as that section operates only if the court is antecedently exercising federal jurisdiction.)

It would, however, obviously be wise for the draftsmen to provide expressly for the application of the law of a particular State. If that is done, it would appear that an object similar to that of "protective jurisdiction" can be achieved. It is for this purpose, of course, necessary that the matter in respect of which jurisdiction is granted is one that can be controlled under Commonwealth law.

An example of a provision expressly providing for a federal choice of law rule is s 42(2) of the *Family Law Act* 1975, which provides:

> (2) Where it would be in accordance with the common law rules of private international law to apply the laws of any country or place (including a State or Territory), the court shall, subject to the *Marriage Act* 1961, apply the laws of that country or place.

The limits of the approach suggested above are illustrated by *Carter Bros v Renouf*.[98] Section 105 of the *Life Insurance Act* 1945 enabled a life insurance company to pay into Court any moneys payable by the company in respect of a policy for which, in the opinion of the company, no sufficient discharge could be obtained. Section 89 allowed payment into the Court where the company had received written notice of a trust or other specified interest in the policy. Dixon CJ[99] stated that those provisions operated as a discharge of the company's liability and a jurisdiction was by necessary implication given to the Court. His Honour regarded the jurisdiction as limited to determining a matter involving conflicting claims against the insurance company or which might affect its liability. All provisions of the Act relating to assignments, mortgages and trusts of policies dealt with them from the point of view of the company: "But, when once what was initially the company's problem has been solved, the rights and duties of the payee with respect to the policy moneys in his hands are not – or normally will not be – the concern of Commonwealth law."[100] As they fall for determination under State law, they are not capable of being determined by the High Court under s 76(ii).

Appellate Jurisdiction

It is settled law that the power to create federal courts and to define their jurisdiction pursuant to ss 71 and 77(i) authorises the creation of federal

---

98   (1962) 111 CLR 140.

99   Dixon CJ in that case delivered a judgment with the consent of the parties that had been prepared by Fullagar J, who died before he could deliver it.

100 (1962) 111 CLR 140 at 148. There could be a question whether, in the light of more recent cases, the State claim should be treated as part of the same "matter" as the federal claim and, therefore, within the Court's jurisdiction. See "Accrued Jurisdiction" at pp 137-147 below.

appellate courts. There can have been no doubt about *original* jurisdiction, but the authority to establish appellate courts was not so clear on the face of the Constitution. In the first place, the matters in ss 75 and 76, by reference to which the jurisdiction of federal courts may be defined, are all matters of original jurisdiction, actual or potential, of the High Court. This might have been found persuasive in fixing the character of the jurisdiction (as original or appellate) of any inferior federal courts created by the Parliament.[101] Moreover, as Taylor J observed in *Collins v Charles Marshall Pty Ltd*,[102] the organisation of appeals to the High Court under s 73 of the Constitution suggests an intention to restrict inferior federal courts to original jurisdiction. Section 73(ii) authorises appeals to the High Court from judgments, decrees, orders and sentences of any other federal court, or court exercising federal jurisdiction; or of the Supreme Court of any State or any other court of any State from which at the establishment of the Commonwealth an appeal lay to the Queen in Council. This grouping of the various courts from which an appeal lies to the High Court may suggest that the federal courts created by the Parliament should be courts of original jurisdiction, though the argument is not compelling.

The authorities, however, establish that it is within the power of Parliament to create federal appellate courts. This was the opinion of Quick and Garran[103] and it was affirmed in the broadest terms by the High Court in *Ah Yick v Lehmert*,[104] where it was held that, in investing State courts with federal jurisdiction under s 77(iii), s 39 of the *Judiciary Act* 1903 conferred jurisdiction on the courts of general sessions in Victoria to hear and determine an appeal from a conviction by a magistrate in respect of an offence against the *Immigration Restriction Act* 1901. Griffith CJ said:

> The term "federal jurisdiction" means authority to exercise the judicial power of the Commonwealth, and again that must be within limits prescribed. Then "federal jurisdiction" must include appellate jurisdiction as well as original jurisdiction. The whole scheme of the Constitution assumes that the judicial power includes both in the case of the High Court, and from the history of the Constitution and the practice in English-speaking countries, it must be taken for granted that the judicial power was known by the framers of the Constitution to include both, and that those framers intended that the judicial power might be exercised by courts of original jurisdiction or by courts of appellate jurisdiction ... Taking s 71

---

101 See *Cockle v Isaksen* (1957) 99 CLR 155 at 163, where the Court also draws attention to s 78, which provides that the Parliament may make laws conferring rights to proceed against the Commonwealth or a State in respect of matters within the limits of the judicial power.

102 (1955) 92 CLR 529 at 559.

103 Op cit p 802: "There may be established not only courts of original jurisdiction corresponding to the District Courts of the United States, but also courts of appellate as well as original jurisdiction, corresponding to the Circuit Courts of the United States."

104 (1905) 2 CLR 593.

into consideration, s 77(i) means that the Parliament may establish any court to be called a federal court, and may give it jurisdiction to exercise any judicial power of the Commonwealth, which the Parliament may think fit to confer upon it, either by way of appellate or original jurisdiction. Subsection (iii) must receive a precisely similar interpretation. Parliament may invest any court of a State with authority to exercise federal judicial power, again to the extent prescribed by the statute. There is nothing to restrict that judicial power to original jurisdiction any more than to appellate jurisdiction, and there is no reason why there should be a restriction. There can be no doubt that Parliament might think fit to invest one court exclusively with original jurisdiction, another with appellate jurisdiction, and another with both. There is nothing to limit that power.[105]

In this case, the Court was concerned with one paragraph of s 77, namely, para (iii), but the conclusion must be equally applicable to the whole section.[106] Though there have been doubts expressed as to the soundness of the reasoning which allows the grant of appellate jurisdiction to federal courts and State courts invested with federal jurisdiction, the High Court has refused to disturb the authority of *Ah Yick v Lehmert* and subsequent decisions[107] and has held that federal courts may exercise appellate jurisdiction.[108] The decisions are consistent with the principle that federal powers should be broadly interpreted.

In *Cockle v Isaksen*,[109] the High Court sustained the validity of s 113 of the *Conciliation and Arbitration Act*, which conferred appellate jurisdiction on the Commonwealth Industrial Court. That section provided (1) that the Court had jurisdiction to hear and determine an appeal from a judgment, decree, order or sentence of a State court (not being a Supreme Court) or a court of a Territory of the Commonwealth made, given or pronounced in a matter arising under this Act or under the *Public Service Arbitration Act* 1920; (2) that it was not necessary to obtain the leave either of the Industrial Court or the court appealed from in respect of appeals under sub-s (1); (3) that an appeal did not lie to the High Court from a judgment, decree, order or sentence from which an appeal might be brought to the court under sub-s (1); (4) that the jurisdiction of the Court under sub-s (1) was exclusive of the jurisdiction of a State court or court of a Territory to hear and determine an appeal from a judgment, decree, order or sentence from which an appeal might be brought to the Court under that subsection.

---

105 Ibid at 603-604.

106 *Cockle v Isaksen* (1957) 99 CLR 155.

107 *Collins v Charles Marshall Pty Ltd* (1955) 92 CLR 529 at 559 per Taylor J; *Cockle v Isaksen* (1957) 99 CLR 155.

108 See *New South Wales v Commonwealth* (1915) 20 CLR 54 at 90 per Isaacs J; *Commonwealth v Limerick Steamship Co Ltd and Kidman* (1924) 35 CLR 69 at 114 per Starke J; *Collins v Charles Marshall Pty Ltd* (1955) 92 CLR 529 at 557; *R v Spicer* (1957) 98 CLR 48; *Cockle v Isaksen* (1957) 99 CLR 155.

109 (1957) 99 CLR 155.

The policy of the section was to make the Industrial Court the exclusive court of appeal for the matters described.[110] So far as it purported to authorise appeals from State courts, it was an exercise of power under ss 71 and 77(i); so far as it purported to define the extent to which the jurisdiction of the Industrial Court should be exclusive of the jurisdiction of State courts, it was an exercise of power under s 77(ii). *Cockle v Isaksen* squarely raised the validity of s 113(3), which was held to be a legislative exception from the appellate jurisdiction of the High Court as defined in s 73. So far as it provided for appeals from Territorial courts it appeared to be an exercise of power under s 122 of the Constitution as interpreted in the cases, which are discussed in the following chapter.

Putting aside the thicket of problems which affect jurisdiction with respect to Territorial courts, it should be noted that there are qualifications upon the power to create federal appellate courts and to define their jurisdiction. In the first place, that jurisdiction is subject to the limits imposed by ss 75 and 76. In determining whether a grant of appellate jurisdiction to a federal court (or to a State court invested with federal jurisdiction) is validly made, the Court said that it is the matter arising on the *appeal* and not the matter arising in the *original proceedings* that must fall within the heads of ss 75 and 76. This was pointed out by the High Court in *Collins v Charles Marshall Pty Ltd*.

> If s 77(i) would suffice to empower the Parliament to confer appellate juris-diction over State courts in matters arising under a law made by the Parliament, it is the appeal and not the original proceeding that must answer the description. It may often be a distinction without a difference. But it need not always be so. In a "proceeding under the Act" in the primary court the whole matter so far as it rests on the Act may be confessed and reliance may be placed wholly on matter in avoidance which has nothing to do with the Act or an order or award and to that alone the appeal may be addressed. Yet it seems certain that the court, the jurisdiction of which is defined in terms of s 73(ii) [sic: should be s 76(ii)?] can receive jurisdiction only in respect of what, when that court becomes seised of it, is a matter arising under the law of the Parliament. The same distinction between the character of the original cause and of an appeal from the decision thereof sometimes arises in connection with s 76(i) and s 39(2) of the *Judiciary Act*. An ordinary proceeding in a court of petty sessions under State law may be decided without the intrusion of the federal Constitution or any other federal element. Thus there is no federal jurisdiction. On an appeal to general sessions or on an order nisi to review, an argument may be raised, for example, under one or other of ss 90, 92, 109, 117 or 118 of the Con-stitution. At once the appeal becomes one in federal jurisdiction with all the consequences under ss 39(2), 40, 79 and 80 of the *Judiciary Act*.[111]

---

110 *R v Spicer* (1957) 98 CLR 48.

111 (1955) 92 CLR 529 at 541.

These difficulties were briefly mentioned in the context of s 113 of the *Conciliation and Arbitration Act* in *R v Spicer*,[112] and in *Cockle v Isaksen* they were considered at length. The Court "with some misgiving"[113] concluded that the provision for appellate jurisdiction in s 113(1) could be sustained "as a law substantially with respect to matters arising under a federal law", namely the *Conciliation and Arbitration Act*, conferring jurisdiction in respect of such matters. It warned that there might still be an excess of power within s 113(1).

> At the same time it cannot be denied that the law is one going, or possibly going, beyond that category. The provision, however, is distributable and s 15A of the *Acts Interpretation Act* will operate to confine its operation to appeals which themselves come within s 77(i) of the Constitution. The central point is whether the section sufficiently manifests an intention to legislate with respect to a matter within s 76(ii) and, on the whole, we think that it does so, although owing to the form in which the sub-section is cast, it may include cases outside the required description.[114]

This view can create problems for federal courts in respect of appeals where the matter heard in original jurisdiction includes a claim under federal law and another claim which is non-federal but both are part of one in-severable "matter". Power to determine the non-federal claim is referred to as "accrued" jurisdiction and is discussed below.[115] For example, a matter that is within the original jurisdiction of a federal court, by virtue of s 76(ii) of the Constitution, might include a claim for breach of a trade mark under the *Trade Marks Act* 1995 and a common law claim for passing-off, based on substantially the same facts. If the only issue on appeal is the non-federal claim the view expressed in the above cases would mean that the federal court would not have jurisdiction to hear the appeal against the judgment of its own court. The same reasoning would apply in respect of an appeal to a federal court from a judgment of a State court exercising federal jurisdiction.

This approach, therefore, creates unnecessary complexity and is inconsistent with the otherwise liberal attitude taken by the Court in the "accrued" jurisdiction cases, where, as shown below, there has, for the most part, been an emphasis on practical solutions and, so far as possible, an avoidance of difficulty for litigants. The principle declared in *Collins v Charles Marshall Pty Ltd* and *Cockle v Isaksen* is unnecessary because it is not the only interpretation that can be given to s 77 and a broader interpretation is more consistent with the normal principles of constitutional interpretation. Section 77 is prefaced with the words "With respect to any of the matters mentioned in the last two sections [that is all the heads of jurisdiction in ss 75 and 76] the Parliament may make laws ...". In defining the appellate jurisdiction of a

112 (1957) 98 CLR 48 at 53.
113 (1957) 99 CLR 155 at 164.
114 Ibid at 165.
115 Pages 137-147.

federal court under s 77(i), appeals from judgments that decide matters referred to in ss 75 and 76 can reasonably be described as "with respect to" those matters. The phrase "with respect to" has from an early date been regarded in Australian constitutional law as one of broad connotation requiring "a relevance to or connection with the subject".[116] It is difficult to see why a conferral of appellate jurisdiction in respect of judgments determining the matters mentioned in ss 75 and 76 is not a law that has a close relevance or connection with those matters.

There are two further limitations on the power of the Commonwealth to create and to define the jurisdiction of federal appellate courts. The first is quite simple: judgments, decrees or orders of the High Court cannot be made subject to review by or appeal to any federal court. The Constitution envisages the High Court as the apex of the Australian judicial structure; an appeal from other federal courts lies to the High Court under s 73(ii), and under s 75(v) it may award mandamus, prohibition or injunction against officers of the Commonwealth, who, for this purpose, include judges of other federal courts.[117] The second qualification is that it is not possible to provide for appeals from State courts exercising State jurisdiction to a federal court other than the High Court. This arises by implication from the terms of the Constitution itself and as a matter of general federal implication. As the High Court in *Collins v Charles Marshall Pty Ltd* observed:

> The Commonwealth Constitution is unlike the Constitution of the United States in the manner in which the relation of Federal judicial power to State courts is dealt with specifically. Section 73(ii) is very specific in defining the jurisdiction of this Court to hear and determine appeals from State courts. Section 77(iii) gives a specific power to invest State courts with federal jurisdiction and s 77(ii) a specific power to define the extent of the jurisdiction of a Federal court which shall be exclusive of the jurisdiction belonging to the courts of the States. On the face of the provisions they amount to an express statement of the Federal legislative and judicial powers affecting State courts which, with the addition of the ancillary power contained in s 51(xxxix), one would take to be exhaustive. To construe the very general words of s 71 relating to the definition of their jurisdiction as containing a power to establish a further appellate control of State courts exercising State functions would seem to be opposed to the principles of interpretation, particularly those applying to a strictly federal instrument of government.[118]

---

116 *Grannall v Marrickville Margarine Pty Ltd* (1955) 93 CLR 55 at 77.

117 *Collins v Charles Marshall Pty Ltd* (1955) 92 CLR 529 at 538. This is so even though the federal court is declared to be a superior court of record: *R v Watson; ex parte Armstrong* (1976) 136 CLR 248 at 263, 267; *R v Gray; ex parte Marsh* (1985) 157 CLR 351 at 374, 392-394.

118 (1955) 92 CLR 529 at 543.

Taylor J said: "[T]o conclude otherwise would be to permit direct inter-ference with the exercise by the courts of the States of State judicial functions, and such a notion is, as I have already said, inconsistent with the maintenance of Federal and State judicial authority under the Federal system erected by the Constitution."[119] Though Australia has an integrated judicial structure in the sense that appeals lie from State courts on matters of State jurisdiction to the federal High Court; though State courts may be repositories of federal jurisdiction, so that an appeal from a State court exercising federal jurisdiction may be taken to a federal appellate court (as s 113 of the *Conciliation and Arbitration Act* contemplated and as s 422 of the *Workplace Relations Act* 1996 now provides), the courses of State jurisdiction and the jurisdiction of federal courts established pursuant to ss 71 and 77(i) run separately.[120]

It has been suggested that there is another limitation on the power to define federal appellate jurisdiction. Section 113 of the *Conciliation and Arbitration Act* excluded a judgment or order of the State Supreme Court from the ambit of the appellate jurisdiction of the Industrial Court. Kitto J considered that this exclusion was a matter of constitutional necessity and in *R v Spicer; ex parte Truth and Sportsman Ltd*[121] he said that "the exception in sub-s (i) of the judgment of a Supreme Court is attributable to the fact that the Constitution does not enable the Commonwealth Parliament to create any appellate tribunal over the Supreme Courts of the States".[122] Interestingly, Bills introduced to establish first a Commonwealth Superior Court, in 1968, and then a Superior Court of Australia in 1974, providing for broad federal jurisdiction, excluded judgments of the Supreme Courts of the States from the proposed appellate jurisdiction of those Courts.[123] In the case of the Federal Court of Australia, however, s 24 of the Act merely excludes from the appel-late jurisdiction that other Acts might confer on the Court, judgments of "a Full Court of the Supreme Court of a State". The *Patents Amendment Act* 1976 and the *Trade Marks Amendment Act* 1976, for example, invested the Federal Court of Australia with jurisdiction to hear appeals from orders of a single judge of a State Supreme Court.

Assuming that s 77(i) extends to appellate jurisdiction – and that is now established doctrine – any argument that a federal court cannot be invested with federal jurisdiction to hear an appeal from a judgment of a State Supreme Court exercising federal jurisdiction must rest on implication. It may be that such a view can be deduced from s 73 of the Constitution. That section gives the High Court jurisdiction "with such exceptions and subject to such

---

119 Ibid at 563.
120 *Re Wakim; ex parte McNally* (1999) 198 CLR 511.
121 (1957) 98 CLR 48.
122 Ibid at 61.
123 *Commonwealth Superior Court Bill* 1968, cl 20(1)(c); *Superior Court of Australia Bill* 1974, cl 21(1)(c).

regulations as the Parliament prescribes" to determine an appeal from a judgment or order of inter alia a federal court, a State court exercising federal jurisdiction and the Supreme Court of any State. The second last paragraph of s 73 provides:

> But no exception or regulation prescribed by the Parliament shall prevent the High Court from hearing and determining any appeal from the Supreme Court of a State in any matter in which at the establishment of the Commonwealth an appeal lies from such Supreme Court to the Queen in Council.

It has been held that a judgment of a judge of a Supreme Court exercising original jurisdiction is a judgment of the Supreme Court of a State for purposes of s 73.[124] It follows from s 73 that legislation cannot abolish appeals from a judgment of the Supreme Court in original jurisdiction to the High Court where an appeal lay in 1900 to the Privy Council.[125] The *Judiciary Act* provides for an appeal from the Supreme Court of a State to the High Court by special leave of the High Court only (s 35). It is difficult to see how there could be any further limitation or restriction on appeals from judgments of the Supreme Court of a State in its original jurisdiction to the High Court in the face of s 73 where the judgment is one from which an appeal lay to the Privy Council in 1900.

In *Collins v Charles Marshall Pty Ltd*, a joint judgment of six judges (including Kitto J) briefly discussed the position that would exist if a federal court had appellate jurisdiction in respect of a State Supreme Court. Their Honours said:

> In the first place a new Federal court of appeal if brought into existence would clearly be a Federal court from which an appeal would lie to the High Court under s 73(ii). It may be assumed that when that provision speaks of a court from which an appeal lies to the Privy Council that means lies as of right. If the court subject to the appeal to the supposed new Federal court of appeal was a Supreme Court of the State or a court whence an appeal lay as of right at the establishment of the Commonwealth, there would be a parallel right of appeal to the High Court. This would be true too if the primary court were exercising Federal jurisdiction. That would mean that alternative rights of appeal would exist from State courts to different Federal courts of appeal, one being subject to appeal in its turn to the other. It is true that the Parliament has a power of making exceptions from the subject matter of the appellate jurisdiction of the High Court, but

---

124 *Parkin v James* (1905) 2 CLR 315.

125 The Court assumed this meant where the appeal lay as of right in *Collins v Charles Marshall Pty Ltd* (1955) 92 CLR 529 at 538, 543-544. Such an appeal lay in the case of judgments involving £500 or more except in Tasmania where the amount was £1000: Quick and Garran, op cit pp 739, 740. This assumption was rejected in *Smith Kline and French Laboratories (Australia) Ltd v Commonwealth* (1991) 173 CLR 194 at 216, where the Court upheld the validity of s 35 of the *Judiciary Act*.

the power is limited in the case of Supreme Courts in the manner already described and moreover after all it is only a power of making exceptions. Such a power is not susceptible of any very precise definition but it would he surprising if it extended to excluding altogether one of the heads specifically mentioned by s 73.[126]

This passage, however, occurred in the course of reasoning that a federal court could not be given jurisdiction over State courts *exercising State jurisdiction* even though the matter on appeal came within s 75 or s 76 of the Constitution. The judges went on to say:

> In the second place it is apparent from s 73(ii) that the principle or policy which it embodies was to place the court that is supreme in the State judicial hierarchy under the appellate jurisdiction of the High Court and no other State courts, unless they were invested under s 77(iii) with Federal jurisdiction.[127]

It would be unfortunate if the Constitution prevented the implementation of the policy reflected in the *Federal Court of Australia Act*, the *Patents Act* 1990 and the *Trade Marks Act* 1995, which is to use the State Supreme Courts as trial courts in relation to some federal matters allowing an appeal to the Federal Court. It is true that in many cases an alternative appeal must lie to the High Court but the fact that that appeal can be had only by special leave ensures that the High Court can have regard to the purpose of the legislation establishing the Federal Court in determining whether to grant leave.

It would seem that there is no authority to support the statement of Kitto J in *R v Spicer* and it is suggested that the Court should not imply this further limitation on Commonwealth power to create federal appellate jurisdiction.

Accrued Jurisdiction

The principle that a party invoking the original jurisdiction of a federal court must show that the subject-matter of his claim is a matter within the original jurisdiction of the court is clear, but particular applications may give rise to difficulty and, on occasion, to sharp division within the High Court.[128] If, however, a matter is raised which brings the case within the original jurisdiction of the court, the fact that that issue is, so to speak, dissolved by a decision on it adverse to the party raising it does not, of itself, strip the court of jurisdiction to dispose of the case. In *R v Carter; ex parte Kisch*,[129] application was made to the High Court for a writ of habeas corpus. The jurisdiction of the High Court was invoked because the applicant based his main claim on the

---

126 (1955) 92 CLR 529 at 543-544.

127 Ibid at 544.

128 See *Hopper v Egg and Egg Pulp Marketing Board* (1939) 61 CLR 665. See p 70 above.

129 (1934) 52 CLR 221.

ground that Commonwealth legislation under which he was detained was invalid. He also argued that the proper steps had not been taken under the Commonwealth *Immigration Act* to declare him a prohibited immigrant. Evatt J rejected the constitutional argument, but upheld the applicant's non-constitutional argument, observing that once the jurisdiction of the High Court was vested it was not lost by the rejection of the constitutional point.[130] This has been affirmed by the High Court on other occasions, and perhaps most picturesquely by Williams J in terms that "whenever there is woven across the warp of the facts constituting a cause of action the woof of a constitutional question, this Court has original jurisdiction to determine the whole of that cause of action".[131] Similarly, when a cause was removed into the High Court as an inter se question under s 40A of the *Judiciary Act,* the Court had authority to determine the entire cause, since it was the cause and not merely the inter se question which was removed.[132]

This is obviously a practical and desirable result since it enables the High Court or another federal court to deal expeditiously with a matter which contains elements which lie partly within and partly outside the original jurisdiction of the court. On the other hand, a statement may allege two or more distinct matters, as was held to be the case in *Carter v Egg and Egg Pulp Marketing Board (Vic).*[133] In that case, the plaintiff brought an action for a declaration in the original jurisdiction of the High Court in which he challenged the validity of the Victorian *Marketing of Primary Products Act* and regulations made thereunder. The High Court unanimously held that this raised a matter involving the interpretation of the Constitution which was within the Court's jurisdiction. The plaintiff also claimed an account on the footing that the State Act and regulations were valid and that the defendant board had not discharged its obligations thereunder. The Court unanimously held that it had no jurisdiction to entertain this matter. The principle was stated in the judgment of Latham CJ:

> There are decisions ... which ... support the view that the Court can adjudicate in a case from which all questions of constitutional significance have been eliminated by the rejection of contentions based upon the Constitution, the whole cause, and not merely the cause so far as its decision depends upon such contentions ... But in each of these cases a single claim or charge or a defence thereto was supported upon several grounds, one or more of which involved the interpretation of the Constitution. None of the cases mentioned presented the feature which is to be found in this case, namely an entirely severable claim having no relation whatever to another

---

130 Ibid at 223-224.

131 *Carter v Egg and Egg Pulp Marketing Board (Vic)* (1942) 66 CLR 557 at 602. See also the judgment of Latham CJ at 580.

132 *O'Neill v O'Connell* (1946) 72 CLR 101 at 116; *Ex parte de Braic* (1971) 124 CLR 162 at 165.

133 (1942) 66 CLR 557.

claim or claims made in the same proceeding which other claim or claims alone involved the interpretation of the Constitution.[134]

This means that if a plaintiff desires to invoke the original jurisdiction of the High Court in such a case as this, he or she must separate the claims, bringing the action in part in the High Court and in part in a State court. If the action is brought wholly in a State court and the High Court exercises its power, under s 40 of the *Judiciary Act*, to remove the cause into the High Court, part of the case (being a separate claim) must remain behind in a State court. This is hardly a convenient or expeditious method of disposing of litigation. Moreover, it is not always clear whether a particular claim is severable. In *Parton v Milk Board (Vic)*,[135] it was argued by the plaintiff that s 30 of the *Milk Board Acts*, and regulations and determinations made thereunder, were invalid since they purported to impose a duty of excise contrary to s 90 of the Constitution. It was also argued that the levy had not been properly made under the authority of the Act since it covered a class of persons excepted under the Act. It was clear that the first contention raised a matter arising under the Constitution or involving its interpretation, but the defendant board argued on the footing of *Carter's Case* that other submissions based upon the construction of the State legislation did not raise a matter within the original jurisdiction of the Court. Three members of the Court dealt with this argument, Latham CJ and Dixon J holding the whole cause was within jurisdiction, McTiernan J contra. Latham CJ pointed to the distinction drawn in *Carter's Case* between a claim completely separate in all its characteristics from the claim raising a constitutional issue, and a single claim which was supported on several grounds, one or more of which involved the interpretation of the Constitution. "The present is a case of the latter description, and in my opinion the Court has jurisdiction to deal with it."[136] McTiernan J disagreed. He observed that the non-constitutional claim involves only the interpretation of the *Milk Board Acts*. Such a question is not within the original jurisdiction of this Court. No declaration should therefore be made as to the validity of the regulations and the determination: *Carter v Egg Board*.[137]

Similarly, in *Airlines of New South Wales Pty Ltd v New South Wales (No 1)*,[138] a matter was referred to the Full Court under s 18 of the *Judiciary Act*. Four questions were put to the Court. Two of them asked whether various provisions of the *State Transport (Co-ordination) Act* 1931 (NSW) were inconsistent with the *Air Navigation Act* 1920 (Cth) and instruments made under that Act. The third question was whether, if the plaintiff complied with the Commonwealth legislation, it was entitled to carry on its business without

---

134 Ibid at 580 per Latham CJ.
135 (1949) 80 CLR 229.
136 Ibid at 249. See also at 257-258 per Dixon J.
137 Ibid at 268.
138 (1964) 113 CLR 1.

being required to be the holder of a licence under the State Act. The fourth question related solely to the construction of the State Act and concerned the power of the Commissioner under that Act to vary licences so as to reallocate routes in the manner in which he had purported to do. The Court answered the first three questions but refused to answer the fourth except to the extent of saying that no provisions of the Constitution or federal law prevented the Commissioner from exercising any power he had under State law to vary the licences in question. Dixon CJ said of the fourth question:[139] "As framed this question may be treated as one directed only to the interpretation of State law without regard to federal law at all." All the other judges except Menzies J agreed with this approach.

The question whether or when a federal court may hear and determine a claim arising under non-federal law when it is joined with a federal claim has in recent times arisen more frequently in relation to the Federal Court. The resolution of that question affects greatly the distribution of judicial power, and its exercise, between the State and federal courts. It became more acute as a result of vesting jurisdiction in the Federal Court in some matters arising under the *Trade Practices Act* 1974. Under s 86 the Court has exclusive jurisdiction in proceedings concerning restrictive trade practices and monopolies, dealt with in Part IV, and had exclusive jurisdiction in proceedings relating to s 52 of the Act, which makes unlawful misleading or deceptive conduct, in certain circumstances, in the course of trade or commerce. The grant of exclusive jurisdiction in the s 52 cases gave rise to a number of difficulties about the relations between federal and State courts, and sharp policy disagreements in the High Court, when State or common law claims were joined with a s 52 claim. In 1987 the Act was amended to invest State courts with concurrent federal jurisdiction with respect to those matters (s 86(2)).

The issue was first examined in relation to the Federal Court in *Philip Morris Inc v Adam P Brown Male Fashions Pty Ltd*,[140] which involved two proceedings in the Federal Court claiming relief in respect of alleged contravention of s 52 of the *Trade Practices Act* and also for relief based on the common law action of passing-off. In one of the proceedings, there were other allegations such as breaches of confidence and of contract, conspiracy and fraud. The defendant argued that the Federal Court did not have jurisdiction in respect of the common law claims.

Five members of the Court (Aickin and Wilson JJ dissenting) upheld the Federal Court's jurisdiction to decide the passing-off claim. Jurisdiction was denied in respect of the other common law claims because they were based on facts different from those pleaded in respect of the s 52 claims.[141] The various

139 Ibid at 30.
140 (1981) 148 CLR 457.
141 In the second proceeding it was held that jurisdiction could extend to a claim based on infringement of copyright on the ground that s 32 of the *Federal Court of Australia Act* conferred jurisdiction in "associated matters". This is discussed below, pp 148-149.

judges differed in their description of the principle they were applying. All agreed that the issue was whether the non-federal claim was part of the "matter" arising under the *Trade Practices Act*. There was also agreement that an important consideration was whether the facts on which the different claims were based were either "identical"[142] or "almost wholly identical".[143]

Section 22 of the *Federal Court of Australia Act* required the Court to grant:

> all remedies to which any of the parties appears to be entitled in respect of a legal or equitable claim properly brought forward by him in the matter, so that, as far as possible, all matters in controversy between the parties may be completely and finally determined and all multiplicity of proceedings concerning any of those matters avoided.

The Court held that that provision did not confer jurisdiction, but empowered the Federal Court to grant appropriate relief in a case which is properly within jurisdiction.

Mason J expressly referred to the underlying conflicting interests in the Australian judicial system and the practical aspects of decision-making in this area. He said:

> Lurking beneath the surface of the arguments presented in this case are competing policy considerations affecting the role and status of the Federal Court and the Supreme Courts of the States. There is on the one hand the desirability of enabling the Federal Court to deal with attached claims so as to resolve the entirety of the parties' controversy. There is on the other hand an apprehension that if it be held that the Federal Court has jurisdiction to deal with attached claims, State courts will lose to the Federal Court a proportion of the important work which they have hitherto discharged, work which the Federal Court has no jurisdiction to determine if it be not attached to a federal claim. Added force is given to this apprehension by the vesting of exclusive federal jurisdiction in the Federal Court, for example, by s 86 of the *Trade Practices Act*.[144]

In weighing these conflicting interests, Mason J considered that the predominant interest was "the speedier determination of entire controversies between parties without undue duplication of proceedings". Wilson J, in dissent, said he was "burdened" by the difficulty of litigants, but referred to s 77(iii) of the Constitution – empowering Parliament to invest any court of a State with federal jurisdiction – as a method of dealing with this difficulty. Such a view would, as a practical matter, restrict the choice that the Constitution gives Parliament to have matters determined by federal or State courts and, in the former case, by exclusive or concurrent jurisdiction. Mason J, in

---

142 (1981) 148 CLR 457 at 499 per Gibbs J.

143 Ibid at 516 per Mason J.

144 Ibid at 513.

effect, made that point. He replied that the Constitution gave these choices and that the Court had to assume that Parliament legislated in the way it did for good reason.

It is clear that Wilson J's main concern was the effect of a broad interpretation of "matter", in respect of s 76(ii), on State courts. He said such an interpretation would "diminish [the Constitution's] effectiveness in maintaining a viable federation". Mason J replied that the consequences for State courts were "secondary to the interests of litigants".[145]

The principles applicable to what has become known as "accrued jurisdiction" were elaborated and, to a degree, clarified in *Fencott v Muller*[146] where a majority (Mason, Murphy, Brennan and Deane JJ) in a joint judgment went beyond *Philip Morris* in broadening the jurisdiction of the Federal Court in respect of non-federal claims. They took the ratio of the earlier case to be that a matter arising under federal law may include another cause of action arising under another law "provided it is attached to and is not severable from the former claim".[147] They regarded the test of "common transactions or facts" as a sound guide for determining whether a cause of action under common law or State law was an inseverable part of the "matter" arising under federal law. They said:

> In identifying a s 76(ii) matter, it would be erroneous to exclude a substantial part of what is in truth a single justiciable controversy and thereby to preclude the exercise of judicial power to determine the whole of that controversy. What is and what is not part of the one controversy depends on what the parties have done, the relationships between or among them and the laws which attach rights or liabilities to their conduct and relationships. The scope of a controversy which constitutes a matter is not ascertained merely by reference to the proceedings which a party may institute, but may be illuminated by the conduct of those proceedings and especially by the pleadings in which the issues in controversy are defined and the claims for relief are set out. But in the end, it is a matter of impression and of practical judgment whether a non-federal claim and a federal claim joined in a proceeding are within the scope of one controversy and thus within the ambit of a matter.[148]

They affirmed the earlier statement of Mason J treating the speedy determination of entire controversies and the avoidance of duplication of proceedings as the predominant object. They went on to say, however, that the federal claim must be a substantial aspect of the controversy for the Court to have the accrued jurisdiction. If it was a trivial or insubstantial aspect of the controversy it would not be "appropriate or convenient" to determine the more

---

145 Ibid at 513-514 (Mason J), 548 (Wilson J).
146 (1983) 152 CLR 570.
147 Ibid at 606.
148 Ibid at 608.

substantial State or common law causes of action. Again, "impression and practical judgment" were given as the means for determining the issue of substantiability.

In *Fencott*, separate claims and applications for different remedies between different parties were held to be part of one matter. In addition to allegations of breach of s 52 of the *Trade Practices Act*, there were allegations of fraud, negligence, misrepresentation and breach of confidence. There were claims by a corporate party against its directors for breach of fiduciary obligations and a claim against another corporation under an indemnity. They were all regarded as part of one matter because they all arose out of "common transactions and facts", namely, "the negotiations for sale, contract of sale and performance of the contract of sale of O'Connor's Wine Bar and Restaurant".[149] The transactions had been complicated by the existence of corporate trustees and indemnities. The Court, however, was prepared to look at the overall commercial realities to determine "common transactions" rather than concentrating on the disparate nature of the several causes of action and remedies.

The dissents of Wilson and Dawson JJ were motivated by concern for other objects and possible consequences. They held that the Federal Court had no jurisdiction over any of the non-federal claims because the facts on which they were based were not identical with those on which the federal claim was based. Furthermore the avoidance of inconvenience to litigants and the object of quelling the entire controversy were for Dawson J "no explanation in legal or constitutional terms".[150] He then pointed out that the majority's approach "is to create problems at the other end". If the whole "matter" before the Court includes claims arising under State law and that Court has exclusive jurisdiction to determine the matter, the jurisdiction in respect of those State claims might be excluded from State court jurisdiction whether or not the jurisdiction of the Federal Court was invoked.[151]

That difficulty arose in *Stack v Coast Securities (No 9) Pty Ltd.*[152] In that case, four separate actions were brought by corporations in the Supreme Court of Queensland for specific performance of a contract for sale of a home unit. The defendants in each State action applied to the Federal Court for an order against the corporations in relation to the same transactions as were before the Supreme Court, alleging breach of s 52 of the *Trade Practices Act*. In three of the Federal Court cases, the corporations in their defences and cross-claims sought a declaration that the contract of sale was valid and a decree of specific performance. As mentioned earlier, the Federal Court's jurisdiction relating to the s 52 claim was exclusive of State courts.

---

149 Ibid at 610.
150 Ibid at 629.
151 Ibid.
152 (1983) 154 CLR 261.

In this case, there was no question concerning the severability or otherwise of federal and non-federal claims. All the judges were of the view that, on the basis of previous decisions, all the claims, defences and counter-claims in these cases were part of a matter arising under the *Trade Practices Act* and, therefore, were within the jurisdiction of the Federal Court. The problem was the extent of the exclusivity of the Court's jurisdiction. It was argued that, as the determination of the application for specific performance was part of the federal "matter", which was exclusive to the Federal Court, the Supreme Court had no jurisdiction in the cases before it. (In two cases orders had been made.) This raised the possibility of bizarre consequences, such as a defendant in the Supreme Court leaving it to the last moment to raise the federal issue and then delaying, or even failing to pursue, the matter in the Federal Court.

It was held that under s 86 of the *Trade Practices Act* the jurisdiction of the Federal Court was not exclusive with respect to the accrued jurisdiction. The Supreme Court, therefore, had jurisdiction with respect to the non-federal claims concurrently with the Federal Court. It was said, therefore, that the Federal Court had a discretion whether to exercise the accrued jurisdiction. As indicated above, there is a principle that the conferral of jurisdiction implies a duty to exercise it when it is invoked.[153] In this case, however, the inconvenience that would result led the High Court to the view that Parliament could hardly have intended that principle to apply[154] or that the accrued jurisdiction should be exclusive to the Federal Court.[155]

Indeed, as Wilson and Dawson JJ pointed out, the principles enunciated in *Fencott v Muller* for determining whether a non-federal claim is "inseverable" are so vague and so dependent on a number of contingencies and discretionary considerations that "it is quite impossible to attach any notion of exclusivity to [such] a jurisdiction".[156] While those judges, for present purposes, applied previous decisions, they added that "until there is an opportunity for reconsideration, the Court may find itself committed to a course of reasoning which involves artificiality and error".[157]

The extension of the concept of accrued jurisdiction had the result that to a considerable degree there was an avoidance of a multiplicity of proceedings. Nevertheless, in many circumstances, jurisdictional conflicts and difficulties remained. There were occasions when federal and non-federal claims were regarded as severable.[158] From 1 July 1988 the concept of accrued jurisdiction

---

153 Pages 77-78 above.
154 (1983) 154 CLR 261 at 282 (Gibbs J), 293-294 (Mason, Brennan and Deane JJ).
155 Ibid at 295-296 per Mason, Brennan and Deane JJ.
156 Ibid at 305.
157 At 302.
158 *Obacelo Pty Ltd v Taveraft Pty Ltd* (1985) 59 ALR 571; Opeskin, "Federal Jurisdiction in Australian Courts: Policies and Prospects" (1995) 46 South Carolina LR 765 at 804-805.

became less significant because of a national scheme for the cross-vesting of jurisdiction among the Supreme Courts of the States and Territories, and the Federal and Family Courts.[159] It is discussed below.[160] As the Federal Court appeared to have conferred on it State jurisdiction as well as federal jurisdiction it was not usually necessary to determine whether a State cause of action was part of the Court's accrued jurisdiction.

In 1999, however, the High Court held a vital aspect of the scheme invalid, namely the purported vesting by the States in the Federal and Family Courts of State jurisdiction, and a Commonwealth legislative provision which authorised those courts to exercise that jurisdiction.[161]

In *Re Wakim*, a creditor of a bankrupt commenced separate proceedings in the Federal Court against the trustee in bankruptcy and the solicitors and counsel advising the trustee. The creditor alleged breach of statutory duty under the *Bankruptcy Act* 1966 by the trustee, and that the solicitors and counsel had been negligent in advising the trustee. As, in that case, the cross-vesting scheme was held invalid, it became necessary to determine whether the negligence actions were part of the same matter as that against the trustee under the *Bankruptcy Act*, in respect of which the Federal Court had jurisdiction. Five members of the High Court answered that question in the affirmative. The judgment of Gummow and Hayne JJ (with which Gleeson CJ and Gaudron J agreed) followed the earlier cases, with some qualifications.

In that case there were three separate proceedings which were not dependent one on another in the sense that success in one depended on success in another. That, however, was not conclusive. It was accepted, as in *Fencott*, that the key to identifying the justiciable controversy was to pay close attention to the pleadings and to the factual basis of each claim. The joint judgment discussed the reference in *Fencott* to the issue being "a matter of impression and practical judgment". It was said that this was not a test but rather a matter of necessity because the question usually arises before evidence is adduced and often before the pleadings are complete. Nevertheless, the judges adopted the test in *Fencott* that the answer depends on a finding of "common transactions or facts" or a "common substratum of facts", even if they do not coincide.

They gave other examples of when a non-federal claim might or might not be severable. A federal and non-federal claim will produce one matter where the determination of one claim is essential to the other (such as third party proceedings). Similarly, if the conclusion is reached that if proceedings were tried in different courts there could be conflicting findings on issues common to both proceedings, that would indicate a single matter. On the other hand, if

---

159 Opeskin, "Cross-vesting of Jurisdiction and the Federal Judicial System" in Opeskin and Wheeler (eds), *The Australian Federal Judicial System*, 2000, ch 10.

160 Pages 152-153 below.

161 *Re Wakim; ex parte McNally* (1999) 198 CLR 511.

several proceedings could not have been joined in one proceeding it is unlikely they could be a single matter.[162]

Gummow and Hayne JJ did not seem to view with favour the principle enunciated in *Fencott* that the exercise of the accrued jurisdiction was discretionary. They said that:

> It may be that the better view is that the references to "discretion" are not intended to convey more than that difficult questions of fact and degree will arise in such issues, questions about which reasonable minds may well differ.

They added that it was not necessary to decide what was meant by "discretion".[163]

While Barwick CJ in *Philip Morris*[164] seemed to regard all the accrued jurisdiction as a matter of discretion, the majority judges in *Stack* concentrated on the application of the particular legislation. While a grant of jurisdiction usually denotes a duty (with some exceptions) to exercise it,[165] the majority in *Stack* found a contrary indication in the consequences that would follow, having regard to the conferral of exclusive jurisdiction on the Federal Court. In that case, Mason, Brennan and Deane JJ[166] were of the view that Barwick CJ in *Philip Morris* had spoken with particular reference to the exercise of (exclusive) jurisdiction conferred by s 86 of the *Trade Practices Act*. They associated the principle that accrued jurisdiction was a matter of impression and practical judgment with the view of Barwick CJ that the exercise of accrued jurisdiction was discretionary. They referred to the Barwick statement as expressing "a similar idea". Gummow and Hayne JJ in *Wakim* appear to have interpreted *Stack* in that way. Also the fact that impression and practical judgment are required in making a determination makes it unlikely, as Gibbs CJ said in *Stack*, that Parliament would intend to grant exclusive jurisdiction.[167]

The nature of the exercise and the imprecision of principle may also justify the view in *Fencott* that the occasions for review of the trial court's determination whether there is accrued jurisdiction should be "restricted to cases where there has been obvious error in holding either that the federal aspect of the matter is substantial or that it is trivial or that the overall area of dispute is susceptible of clear division into component controversies or that it is not".[168] The ordinary principles of review that are relevant where there are

---

162 Ibid at 587-588.

163 Ibid.

164 (1981) 148 CLR 457 at 475.

165 See criticism of the Court, based on this principle, by Aitken, "The Meaning of 'Matter': A Matter of Meaning" (1988) 14 Monash University LR 158 at 183-185.

166 (1983) 154 CLR 261 at 294-295.

167 Ibid at 282. See also 293-294 (Mason, Brennan and Deane JJ), 305 (Wilson and Dawson JJ).

168 (1983) 152 CLR 570 at 610. For a contrary view, see Aitken, op cit p 175.

reasonably clear concepts or rules, express or implied, defining jurisdiction hardly seem applicable to this situation, where they could impair the purpose of conferring federal jurisdiction. It might be objected that this shows the error in choosing such an interpretation of "matter". In the long run, however, that takes us back to deciding which of the policy choices presented by Mason J on the one hand and Wilson J on the other is to be preferred when we contemplate the object of ss 75, 76 and 77 of the Constitution.

Bona Fides and Substantiality

It was pointed out above in relation to the original jurisdiction of the High Court that on occasion the Court has treated as a condition of jurisdiction that a claim apparently involving the Constitution, within s 76(i), be raised bona fide.[169] It seems that such a qualification was found necessary in the light of the principle that the failure of the federal submission does not deprive the Court of jurisdiction to determine other claims that are part of the same matter. *Hopper v Egg and Egg Pulp Marketing Board*[170] is an example of how judges may differ in their views of whether a claim is raised bona fide. Latham CJ could see no reason for saying that the constitutional claim was not bona fide, while Starke J declared that it was "merely colourable".[171] The issue is sometimes put in terms of "fabricated jurisdiction"[172] or "fabricating jurisdiction".[173] It of course is applicable to all heads of federal jurisdiction and to other federal courts.

In relation to applications for certiorari where there is an application under s 75(v) for prohibition or mandamus,[174] the High Court has often insisted that the prohibition or mandamus application is made bona fide and not merely "colourably".[175] Similar comments have been made in respect of other federal claims where it is argued that the Court has jurisdiction to determine different claims as accrued jurisdiction.[176] The same principles have been applied by the Federal Court.[177]

In *Fencott v Muller*,[178] the Court required a federal claim to be "substantial" if it was to attract accrued jurisdiction.[179] Sometimes the courts

169 Pages 70-71.

170 (1939) 61 CLR 665.

171 Ibid at 673-674, 677.

172 Lane, *Lane's Commentary on the Australian Constitution*, 2nd edn, 1997, p 515.

173 *Fitzroy Motors v Hyundai* (1995) 133 ALR 445 at 450; *Burgundy Royale Investments Pty Ltd v Westpac Banking Corp* (1987) 76 ALR 173.

174 See pp 52-54 above.

175 *R v Cook; ex parte Twigg* (1980) 147 CLR 15 at 26.

176 *Re Bowen; ex parte Federated Clerks Union* (1984) 154 CLR 207 at 209.

177 *Westpac Banking Corp v Paterson* (1999) 167 ALR 377 at 381.

178 (1983) 152 CLR 570 at 609.

179 See p 142 above. See *Stack v Coast Securities (No 9) Pty Ltd* (1983) 154 CLR 261 at 298.

combine the need for a federal claim to be bona fide and also substantial before it and other claims can be determined.[180]

Mr Lee Aitken has examined these concepts and has brought to attention a number of unresolved issues.[181] Is "bona fides" concerned with the state of mind of the party and his or her legal advisers or is there an objective standard? What is the relationship between a claim being insubstantial and the question whether the claimant lacks bona fides? Owen Dixon KC in his submissions to the Royal Commission in 1927 said that a claim by a party relating to the Constitution may be "constitutional nonsense, but his case is at once one of Federal jurisdiction".[182] Does this represent the law today in the light of the demand for substantiality and bona fides? If it does, how do you prove that a claim is not substantial or lacks bona fides?

These qualifications on the meaning of "matter" have not had much practical effect. Professor Lane, writing in 1997, said that he knew of only one case where a "s 71 court" had held a claim to be non-genuine.[183] Having regard to experience over several decades it would seem very difficult to have a federal claim rejected on the ground that it was not raised bona fide or that it is not sufficiently substantial to have attached to it any accrued jurisdiction. The main difficulty, as Aitken has emphasised, is to determine what those concepts mean.

Associated Jurisdiction

Section 32 of the *Federal Court of Australia Act* 1976 provides: "To the extent that the Constitution permits, jurisdiction is conferred on the Court in respect of matters not otherwise within its jurisdiction that are associated with matters in which the jurisdiction of the Court is invoked."

Section 33 of the *Family Law Act* 1975 is in similar terms in relation to the jurisdiction of the Family Court. There is also a similar provision in s 18 of the *Federal Magistrates Court Act* 1999.

---

180 *Adamson v West Perth Football Club Inc* (1979) 27 ALR 475 at 499.

181 Aitken, op cit.

182 Dixon, Royal Commission on the Constitution, Minutes of Evidence (1927) p 788: "If a boy is prosecuted before justices of the peace under a municipal by-law for riding a bicycle on the footpath and objects that he did so in the performance of his duties as a messenger of the Post and Telegraph Department and that the by-law cannot affect him, however untenable his objection may be as a defence, yet instantly the justices lose their jurisdiction, because the interpretation of the Constitution is involved ... So, if a tramp about to cross the bridge at Swan Hill is arrested for vagrancy and is intelligent enough to object that he is engaged in interstate commerce and cannot be obstructed, a matter arises under the Constitution. His objection may be constitutional nonsense, but his case is at once one of Federal jurisdiction."

183 Lane, op cit p 517 n 54. The case is *Francis C Mason Pty Ltd v Citicorp Australia Ltd* (1984) 57 ALR 130. The single judge was Northrop J, who had, in an earlier case, held that a claim should be rejected because of lack of bona fides; but he was in a minority: *Westpac Banking Corporation v Eltran Pty Ltd* (1987) 74 ALR 45.

In *Stack v Coast Securities (No 9) Pty Ltd*,[184] Mason, Brennan and Deane JJ, in determining that under s 86 of the *Trade Practices Act* the primary (but not the accrued) jurisdiction was exclusive to the Federal Court, said that the drafter may have intended to achieve that result by a different route, namely by means of s 32 of the *Federal Court of Australia Act*. It was the view of some at the time that actions, now held to be within the accrued jurisdiction because part of the same "matter" as the claims within the primary jurisdiction, would instead be upheld as within s 32.[185]

In *Philip Morris Inc v Adam P Brown Male Fashions Pty Ltd*,[186] the Court, generally, rejected the argument that s 32 empowered the Federal Court to determine non-federal matters if "associated" with the federal matters. It was held that the only power the Commonwealth had to vest jurisdiction was with respect to the matters referred to in ss 75 and 76 of the Constitution. Section 32 did not refer to claims that were part of the same matter as the claim arising under federal law. It purported to confer jurisdiction with respect to a different "matter" from that within the Court's primary jurisdiction. The opening words of the section ensured that it should be so "read down" as to keep its operation within the power of the Parliament. It was, therefore, interpreted to confer on the Federal Court additional jurisdiction "in a federal matter which is associated with another federal matter in which the Federal Court has not otherwise been given jurisdiction".[187] In that case it was held that a claim for breach of copyright was not part of the same matter as a claim under the *Trade Practices Act*, but the Court's jurisdiction extended to the copyright claim, by virtue of s 32, if it was associated with the trade practices matter. No clear principle has emerged as to the meaning of "associated". Gibbs J in *Philip Morris* said that one matter is associated with another if the two matters arose out of substantially the same facts or closely connected facts.[188] This is similar to the view he preferred in respect of accrued jurisdiction. As a majority of judges took a broader view on that issue[189] it is likely that "associated" in s 32 of the *Federal Court Act* will be interpreted no less broadly. Indeed, as the associated matter is required to be one within s 75 or s 76 there is no need for a restrictive approach to the section so far as the Constitution is concerned. There is also no reason why the "matter" within the associated jurisdiction should not include "accrued claims".

---

184 (1983) 154 CLR 261 at 296.

185 See, for example, Gummow, "Pendent Jurisdiction in Australia – Section 32 of the *Federal Court of Australia Act*" (1979) 10 Federal LR 211.

186 (1981) 148 CLR 457.

187 Ibid at 516 per Mason J. See also 494 per Gibbs J, 538 per Aikin J.

188 Ibid at 496.

189 Pages 142-143 above.

Proposals for an "Integrated" Court System

The creation of the Family Court and the Federal Court, and the expansion of the latter's jurisdiction by statute and judicial decision, greatly changed the structure of the Australian court system. Until the 1970s the general picture of the court system, with some exceptions, was of State courts exercising federal and State jurisdictions, with the High Court as a final court of appeal in respect of both State and federal matters. The exceptions included the original jurisdiction of the High Court (constitutional and statutory) and specialised federal courts in areas of bankruptcy and industrial disputes. Today the scene is, in the main, that of a dual system in respect of civil jurisdiction. The Federal Court is very nearly a general federal court possessed of a substantial part of federal jurisdiction, although much of it is exercised concurrently with State courts.

The Commonwealth has therefore rejected the view of Sir Owen Dixon given to the Royal Commission on the Constitution in 1929[190] and in a lecture in 1935.[191] Dixon deplored the distinction made between federal and State jurisdiction. He suggested that Australian superior courts should be independent organs which were neither Commonwealth nor State. Their existence and authority should be derived directly from the Constitution. Their jurisdiction would be to administer the whole law irrespective of its source.

Such a system would, of course, require an alteration of the Constitution. It was considered by the Advisory Committee on the Australian Judicial System in its report to the Constitutional Commission, and by the Commission.[192] A majority of the Committee recommended the retention of State and federal courts. That was also the view of the Commission. They said that a specified parliament and government should be publicly responsible for the establishment, maintenance, organisation and jurisdiction of a court, as well as appointments to it. Any attempt to remove a court from a particular governmental system would mean the creation of an institution which would involve the participation of all Australian governments, with none directly and fully responsible. The Commission said that that "would inevitably fetter boldness and foster conservatism and inertia".[193]

The creation of the two federal courts gave rise to a number of difficulties. One concerned the problem of split proceedings, especially when the federal or State court had exclusive jurisdiction. Until five States referred power in child custody matters to the Commonwealth[194] a dispute, involving children of a family that included children of the marriage and others who were not, would have to be decided in the Family Court in respect of the former and the

---

190 Minutes of Evidence, pp 776ff.
191 "The Law and the Constitution" (1935) 51 Law Quarterly R 590 at 606.
192 *Final Report of the Constitutional Commission*, 1988, vol 1, para 6.16.
193 Ibid.
194 Page 111 above.

State court in respect of the latter.[195] Similar questions arose in the Federal Court where there were claims under the *Trade Practices Act*, for example, and claims at common law or under State law. The development by the High Court of the principle of "accrued jurisdiction"[196] did quite a lot to alleviate that situation. The Federal Court was held to have jurisdiction in respect of the federal and non-federal claims where the latter were attached to, and not severable from, the federal claims.[197] Nevertheless, split jurisdiction remained a problem in a number of cases.[198] Also, in respect of the Family Court, the High Court seemed to adopt a more parsimonious attitude to accrued jurisdiction.[199]

The other problem arose from the success and popularity of the Federal Court. Many believed that, as a result, the status and prestige of the Supreme Courts were declining. Many of the areas of federal jurisdiction relate to fields of business, commerce and finance. If they are made exclusive to federal courts, or if litigants prefer to go to the Federal Court in the case of concurrent jurisdiction, the State courts would suffer what the Constitutional Commission called "a reduction in the richness and variety of much of their work".[200]

As a result of these and other difficulties a number of proposals was put forward to create an "integrated" or "unified" system of courts. One proposal was to give unlimited original jurisdiction over all matters to the Supreme Courts of the States and Territories, with an appeal to an Australian Court of Appeal, below the High Court. The Supreme Courts would remain State and Territory courts and the Court of Appeal would be federal.[201]

Another suggestion was to combine all courts into a Supreme Court of Australia under the High Court. The Supreme Court would have divisions corresponding to the existing Supreme Courts and the Federal and Family Courts, together with an Appeals Division. The judges of the Divisions would be appointed by the corresponding governments; but in the case of the Appeals Division it would consist of the Chief Justices of the other Divisions and other judges that they might consider necessary. All the judges would have full jurisdiction in all State, Territory and federal matters.[202]

The Australian Constitutional Convention in 1983 determined that there should be a unified system of superior courts at trial level and appellate level under the High Court. It referred the proposal to a Committee to recommend a

---

195 Except in Western Australia, where the State Court had sole jurisdiction in both cases.

196 Pages 137-147 above.

197 *Fencott v Muller* (1983) 152 CLR 570.

198 *Obacelo Pty Ltd v Taveraft Pty Ltd* (1985) 59 ALR 571.

199 *Smith v Smith* (1986) 161 CLR 217 at 236-240, 250-251.

200 *Report*, vol 1, para 6.20.

201 Burt, "An Australian Judicature" (1982) 56 ALJ 509.

202 Street, "Towards an Australian Judicial System" (1982) 56 ALJ 515. See also a proposal made before the Federal Court was created: Else-Mitchell, "The Judicial System – The Myth of Perfection and the Need for Unity" (1970) 44 ALJ 516.

model.[203] The Report did not develop the Convention's proposal at trial level, but recommended, instead, that there should be cross-vesting of original jurisdiction among federal courts and State and Territory Supreme Courts, and an Australian Court of Appeal below the High Court. All original federal jurisdiction would be conferred on State Supreme Courts and the States would confer all State original jurisdiction on the federal courts. The Appeal Court would be a federal court with a pool of permanent judges, supplemented by judges of the Federal and Supreme Courts, who would be federally appointed.

The Convention did not accept the recommendation for a Court of Appeal but resolved that there should be cross-vesting at trial level.[204]

The Constitutional Commission, like its Advisory Committee, considered that the conflict of jurisdiction difficulties that could still arise did not in themselves warrant such a great change to the court system that would result from creating an integrated national court system. The Commission was of the view that many of the problems would be relieved by cross-vesting legislation that had recently been enacted. It recommended, however, that the Constitution be amended to ensure the validity of the scheme. It was recognised that the relative status of State Supreme Courts was a more difficult question but, in the light of federal legislation reducing the exclusive jurisdiction of the Federal Court and the cross-vesting legislation, it was considered better to wait until there was more experience. It was noted that senior judges and lawyers on the Advisory Committee and in submissions had made different predictions as to the future of the Supreme Courts.[205] It was thought that the jurisdictional difficulties facing the Family Court were best dealt with by altering the legislative power of the Commonwealth, and the Commission made recommendations in that regard.[206]

Cross-Vesting of Jurisdiction [207]

The cross-vesting scheme was put into effect by the *Jurisdiction of Courts (Cross-vesting) Act* 1987 (Cth) and Acts with the same short titles of the States and Territories. They came into force on 1 July 1988.

The Constitutional Commission, like its Advisory Committee, had recommended that the Constitution be altered to ensure that the States had power to vest State jurisdiction in federal courts with the legislative consent of the Commonwealth. It was decided, however, to proceed with the legislation so that it might be tested in the High Court.

---

203 Australian Constitutional Convention, 1983, vol 1, p 317; ACC Judicature Sub-Committee "Report to Standing Committee on an Integrated System of Courts", 1984.

204 Australian Constitutional Convention, 1985, vol 1, p 422.

205 *Final Report of the Constitutional Commission*, 1988, vol 1, pp 369-371; paras 6.16-6.28.

206 Ibid, vol 2, p 669, para 10.154.

207 See, generally, Opeskin, "Cross-vesting of Jurisdiction and the Federal Judicial System" in Opeskin and Wheeler, *The Australian Federal Judicial System*, ch 10.

The object of the scheme, as stated by the federal Attorney-General, was to ensure that "no action will fail in a court through lack of jurisdiction, and ... no court will have to determine the boundaries between Federal, State and Territory jurisdictions".[208]

The legislation had two aspects: first, vesting jurisdiction in other courts and, secondly, providing for the transfer of proceedings to another court based on stated criteria. Subject to exceptions, the Commonwealth Act vested the civil jurisdiction of the Federal Court and the Family Court in the Supreme Courts of the States and Territories. The State Acts vested jurisdiction in "State matters" in the Federal Court, the Family Court and all the Supreme Courts of the other States and Territories. Subject to exceptions (s 7), appeals were conducted through the appeal system applicable to the trial court. Section 9 of the federal Act provided (1) that there was no intention to override or limit State cross-vesting legislation and (2) that the federal and Territory courts may exercise jurisdiction conferred by State legislation.

It was the purpose of the scheme that the federal and State courts keep within their traditional areas of jurisdiction. The Acts therefore provided for the transfer of proceedings at the discretion of the court to another court which had jurisdiction. Although lower courts were not included in the general cross-vesting scheme, s 8 of each Act gave power to the Supreme Court to remove a lower court proceeding into the Supreme Court, thus allowing that Court to transfer the proceedings. The federal Act, s 6, required courts to transfer proceedings to the Federal Court or the Family Court, as the case may be, where there was involved a "special federal matter", defined to include matters arising under various provisions of the *Trade Practices Act*, the *Family Law Act*, the *Administrative Decisions (Judicial Review) Act*, s 39B of the *Judiciary Act* and statutory appeals from administrative bodies and tribunals.[209]

Despite the existence of the general cross-vesting scheme, specialised schemes were enacted relating to a number of areas including corporations, family law, trade practices and admiralty.[210] The cross-vesting schemes for the twelve years in which they operated appear to have been highly successful. In a judgment, the Chief Justice of the Federal Court said in 1996 that as a result of cross-vesting:

> The problems for litigants arising from the existence of separate systems of federal and State courts, predicted as inevitable in some of the debates about federal courts in the 1970s, simply do not occur ... The history of federal, State and Territory superior courts in Australia over nearly a decade since the general cross-vesting scheme was established shows that

---

208 Commonwealth Parliamentary Debates (H of R), 22 October 1986, p 2556.

209 Industrial relations matters, some *Trade Practices Act* matters and native title matters were excluded from the cross-vesting provisions: s 4(4).

210 Opeskin, "Cross-vesting of Jurisdiction and the Federal Judicial System" in Opeskin and Wheeler (eds), *The Australian Federal Judicial System*, 2000, p 314.

cooperation can avoid jurisdictional conflict and that conflict is not the inevitable consequence of the existence, in a federation, of more than one system of courts.[211]

On the first challenge in the High Court to the validity of cross-vesting, in respect of the *Corporations Law* scheme, it was upheld by an evenly split court, which meant that the decision of the Full Court of the Federal Court (by virtue of s 23(2)(a) of the *Judiciary Act*) was affirmed.[212] As a result of the principle that an evenly divided court does not produce a binding precedent, and changes to the composition of the Court, a further challenge was brought soon after. This time the High Court held six to one (Kirby J in dissent) that federal courts could not be vested with State jurisdiction, despite Commonwealth statutory assent.[213]

The majority took the view that the jurisdiction that could be conferred on a federal court was limited by reference to the matters in s 75 and 76 of the Constitution and no polity other than the Commonwealth could confer jurisdiction. This was said to be the result of Chapter III of the Constitution. As discussed in Chapter 1 of this book, the earlier cases had established that the *Commonwealth* Parliament was limited by ss 75 and 76. But the majority were of the opinion that there was an implication that no other jurisdiction could be given to a federal court by either the Commonwealth or the States. The Commonwealth was also held to have no express or implied power to consent to the court exercising State jurisdiction, despite an earlier case[214] which held that either the Commonwealth or State Parliament could give its authorities or office holders a capacity to receive such powers and functions as may be conferred by another legislature.

Some of the majority were concerned that if the provisions were valid there would be no way to distinguish State provisions which conferred on federal courts (with Commonwealth consent) non-judicial power or jurisdiction to give advisory opinions or which gave additional jurisdiction and functions to the High Court. The judges on the Federal Court and the High Court who had earlier upheld the legislation were of the opinion that there was an implication in Chapter III that that could not be done. The majority, however, were convinced that that chapter required the more sweeping implication on which they founded their decision.

The fact that s 77 of the Constitution authorises the Commonwealth to vest federal jurisdiction in State courts did not imply that the reverse was invalid, because s 77 enables the Commonwealth to use State courts whether or not the States consent and, therefore, cuts across general federal principles.

---

211   *BP v Amann Aviation Pty Ltd* (1996) 137 ALR 447 at 449-450 per Black CJ.

212   *Gould v Brown* (1998) 193 CLR 346.

213   *Re Wakim; ex parte McNally* (1999) 198 CLR 511.

214   *Re Duncan; ex parte Australian Iron and Steel Pty Ltd* (1983) 158 CLR 535.

The judges rejected the view that the conferral of State jurisdiction made the exercise of federal jurisdiction more effective, saying that the most you could say was that it made State jurisdiction more effective. The Court therefore refused to take a practical approach by looking to the general increase in efficiency in the court system leading to a smoother operation, so enhancing the exercise of federal jurisdiction.

It is not proposed to discuss in any further detail the criticisms that have been made of the judgments in this case because they are dealt with fully elsewhere.[215]

The decision in *Re Wakim* has made of more concern issues of accrued and associated jurisdiction and the question of when a claim "arises under" federal law – matters which lay largely dormant during the period of operation of the cross-vesting scheme. Matters arising under State law may, of course, also be determined by a federal court if it is in the course of exercising some other valid head of jurisdiction conferred on the court such as matters arising under the Constitution or involving its interpretation (s 76(i)) or matters in which the Commonwealth is a party (s 75(iii)).[216]

---

215 See Rose, "The Bizarre Destruction of Cross-vesting" and commentary by Opeskin; and Zines, "The Present State of Constitutional Interpretation" in Stone and Williams (eds), *The High Court at the Crossroads*, 2000, chs 6 and 7 respectively; Hill, "The Demise of Cross-Vesting" (1999) 27 Federal LR 547; Hill, "Beyond *Wakim and Hughes*: Unresolved Questions", paper delivered to Constitutional Law Conference, UNSW, 15 February 2002.

216 *Australian Securities and Investments Commission v Edensor Nominees Pty Ltd* (2001) 204 CLR 559.

Chapter 4

The Territorial Courts and Jurisdiction with Respect to the Territories

> It would have been simple enough to follow the words of section 122 and of sections 71, 73 and 76(ii) and to hold that the courts and laws of a Territory were federal courts and laws made by the Parliament. ... But an entirely different interpretation has been adopted, one which brings its own difficulties.[1]

Section 122 of the Commonwealth Constitution provides that "the Parliament may make laws for the government of any territory surrendered by any State to and accepted by the Commonwealth, or of any territory placed by the Queen under the authority of and accepted by the Commonwealth, or otherwise acquired by the Commonwealth, and may allow the representation of such territory in either House of the Parliament to the extent and on the terms which it thinks fit". This is the general legislative power with respect to Commonwealth Territories. In constituting courts for the Territories, it seems clear enough that s 71 of the Constitution could reasonably have been held to support the vesting of the judicial power of the Commonwealth in federal courts created by the Parliament for and within the Territories. Section 77(i) authorises the Parliament with respect to any of the matters mentioned in ss 75 and 76 to make laws defining the jurisdiction of any federal court other than the High Court. Sections 75 and 76[2] mark out the actual and potential original jurisdiction of the High Court. Section 76(ii) authorises the grant of jurisdiction in any matter arising under any laws made by the Parliament and, since s 122 authorises the making of laws by the Parliament, the jurisdiction of Territorial courts could have been simply enough defined under s 77(i). Sections 76(ii) and 122 could have been employed to invest the High Court with original jurisdiction in matters touching the Territories, and appeals from Territorial courts to the High Court would have been authorised by s 73(ii), which confers jurisdiction, subject to parliamentary control, to hear and determine appeals from all judgments, decrees, orders and sentences of *federal*

---

1 *R v Kirby; ex parte Boilermakers' Society of Australia* (1956) 94 CLR 254 at 290 per Dixon CJ, McTiernan, Fullagar and Kitto JJ.
2 See pp 4-5 above.

courts other than the High Court. It is to be noted that, if the Territorial courts had been established as federal courts, they would have had to comply with the requirements of s 72, which, until its amendment in 1977, required life tenure for judges.[3] But, as the High Court observed in the *Boilermakers' Case*, an entirely different course was taken in relation to the Territorial courts.

The Territories and their Judicial Systems

There were three main categories of Commonwealth Territories – internal, external and trust Territories. The trust Territories were New Guinea (which from World War II was administered jointly with Papua as the Territory of Papua and New Guinea under the legislative authority of the *Papua and New Guinea Act* 1949) and Nauru, which Australia administered on behalf of the three trusteeship powers, the United Kingdom, Australia and New Zealand. Nauru became independent in 1968[4] and Papua New Guinea obtained independence in 1975.[5] There are now no trust Territories administered by the Commonwealth.

In 1909, the Federal Capital Territory (now the Australian Capital Territory) was surrendered by New South Wales to the Commonwealth. This was confirmed by the *Seat of Government Surrender Act* 1909 (NSW) and by the *Seat of Government Acceptance Act* 1909 (Cth). In 1915, Jervis Bay was similarly surrendered and s 4(2) of the *Jervis Bay Territory Acceptance Act* 1915 made the laws in force in the Australian Capital Territory applicable to the Jervis Bay Territory. The *Seat of Government Acceptance Act* 1909 declared, until provision was otherwise made, that within the Australian Capital Territory the High Court should have the jurisdiction formerly belonging to the Supreme Court of New South Wales. The *Judiciary Act* 1927 established a registry of the High Court within the Capital Territory and declared that in relation to the Territory the High Court should have the original jurisdiction exercised by the Supreme Court of New South Wales before 1911, together with such original jurisdiction, civil and criminal, as was from time to time conferred on the High Court by ordinance. The *Seat of Government Supreme Court Act* 1933 repealed the *Judiciary Act* 1927. (The title of the Act was altered to the *Australian Capital Territory Supreme Court Act* by the *Statute Law Revision Act* 1950.) The Act created the Supreme Court and provided for appeals and cases stated to the High Court (ss 13, 51, 52).

The Australian Capital Territory was granted self-government in 1989 by the *Australian Capital Territory (Self-Government) Act* 1988. Subject to

---

3   *Waterside Workers' Federation of Australia v JW Alexander Ltd* (1918) 25 CLR 434; *Boilermakers' Case* (1956) 94 CLR 254 at 290.

4   *Nauru Independence Act* 1967.

5   *Papua New Guinea Independence Act* 1975.

exceptions, the Legislative Assembly is given power to make laws for the peace, order and good government of the Territory; however, responsibility for the Supreme Court was not transferred to the Territory until 1992.[6] The *Supreme Court Act* was converted into a Territory enactment and retitled the *Supreme Court Act* 1933 (ACT).[7] It therefore became subject to repeal and amendment by the Legislative Assembly. Certain provisions, however, were entrenched in the federal Act; that is, they were unalterable except by the Commonwealth Parliament. These included provisions for the removal of judges and the general jurisdiction of the Court. Section 48A(1) of the *Self-Government Act* provides:

> The Supreme Court is to have all original and appellate jurisdiction that is necessary for the administration of justice in the Territory.[8]

The Supreme Court at present consists of a Chief Justice, three resident judges, a Master and nine additional judges who are judges of the Federal Court. Acting judges may also be appointed.

The *Federal Court of Australia Act* 1976 provided for appeals from the Supreme Court to the Full Court of the Federal Court (ss 24, 25, 33). Miles CJ has stated that the Supreme Court has appellate jurisdiction concurrent with the Federal Court by virtue of s 48A(1) of the *Self-Government Act* set out above.[9]

The Australian Law Reform Commission recommended that the ACT Legislative Assembly consider establishing an appeal court for the ACT, and that s 24 of the *Federal Court of Australia Act* should then be amended by Parliament to preclude appeals from the Supreme Court to the Federal Court.[10] The Assembly has passed legislation to establish a Court of Appeal.[11] It is expected that the necessary amendment will be made to the Commonwealth legislation.

The *Heard Island and McDonald Islands Act* 1953[12] declares these islands to be a Commonwealth Territory. Section 5 provides that, subject to the Act, the laws in force in the Australian Capital Territory, including the rules of common law and equity, shall be applicable to the Territory and by s 9 the Supreme Court of the Australian Capital Territory is invested with jurisdiction in the Territory, as if it were part of the Australian Capital Territory. Similar provision is made for the Australian Antarctic Territory by the *Australian Antarctic Territory Act* 1954.

---

6   *A.C.T. Supreme Court (Transfer) Act* 1992.

7   See generally Mossop, "The Judicial Power of the Australian Capital Territory" (1999) 27 Federal LR 19; and Miles, "The State of the Judicature in the Australian Capital Territory" (1994) 68 ALJ 14.

8   This provision is substantially repeated in s 20(1)(a) of the *Supreme Court Act* 1933 (ACT).

9   *Kelly v Apps* [2001] ACTSC 27 (4 April).

10   *The Judicial Power of the Commonwealth*, Report 92, 2001, p 670.

11   *Supreme Court (Amendment) Act* 2001 (ACT).

12   See (1953) 1 Sydney LR 374.

The Northern Territory which, at the date of federation, was a Territory of South Australia and was so described in covering clause 6 of the *Commonwealth of Australia Constitution Act*, was acquired by the Commonwealth by the *Northern Territory Acceptance Act* 1910. The Supreme Court of the Northern Territory was established by ordinance in 1911, and was subsequently divided into two courts, the Supreme Court of North Australia and the Supreme Court of Central Australia.[13] In 1931, the Supreme Court of Central Australia was abolished and the Supreme Court of Northern Australia was continued as the Supreme Court of the Northern Territory.[14]

The *Supreme Court Ordinance* 1911 of the Northern Territory and the amendments thereto were repealed by the *Supreme Court Ordinance Repeal Ordinance* 1965.[15] The *Northern Territory Supreme Court Act* 1961 abolished the Supreme Court existing immediately before the commencement of the Act (s 4) and established a superior court of record to be known as the Supreme Court of the Northern Territory of Australia. Appeals were to the High Court (ss 46, 47). The Northern Territory gained self-government under the *Northern Territory (Self-Government) Act* 1978 (Cth). The Legislative Assembly was given plenary legislative power, with some exceptions. On self-government, responsibility for the Supreme Court was transferred to the Territory. Consequently, the federal *Supreme Court Act* was repealed and the Territory legislature enacted the *Supreme Court Act* 1979 (NT).

Unlike the Australian Capital Territory, the general jurisdiction of the Court is not entrenched in the federal *Self-Government Act*. The Court at present consists of a Chief Justice, five judges, two additional judges and a Master. There is provision for acting judges.

Appeals from the Supreme Court were, as mentioned above, to the High Court until the enactment of the *Federal Court of Australia Act* 1976. After self-government the *Supreme Court Act* 1979 (NT) provided for appellate jurisdiction in a Northern Territory Court of Appeal, consisting of three or more Supreme Court Judges. However, it was not until 1985 that these provisions came into operation. Under the *Statute Law (Miscellaneous Provisions) Act (No 1)* 1985 (Cth), s 24 of the *Federal Court of Australia Act* was amended to exclude the Northern Territory from the Federal Court's appellate jurisdiction. The *Judiciary Act* was amended to add s 35AA to provide for appeals to the High Court from the Supreme Court of the Northern Territory, subject to the grant of special leave.

Linked with the Northern Territory are the Ashmore and Cartier Islands. By the *Ashmore and Cartier Islands Acceptance Act* 1933, these small islands

---

13   *Northern Australia Act* 1926, s 40.

14   *Northern Territory (Administration) Act (No 2)* 1931. See *Northern Territory (Administration) Act* 1910 (as amended), s 18. Section 19 made provision for magistrates and justices of the peace. See *Re Ballard; ex parte Wright* (1955) 1 FLR 473 per Kriewaldt J for an account of the history of the court.

15   1965, No 42.

off the north-west coast of Australia became a Commonwealth Territory and s 6 of the Act provides that the Territory shall be deemed to form part of the Northern Territory and that the laws in force in the Northern Territory shall apply.[16]

Norfolk Island was accepted as a Commonwealth Territory by the *Norfolk Island Act* 1913 in anticipation of an Imperial Order-in-Council of 1914 by which it was placed by the King under authority of the Commonwealth. The *Norfolk Island Act* 1957, s 18, provided for the establishment of a Supreme Court to consist of a judge or judges appointed in accordance with the Act. The *Norfolk Island Act* 1979 granted a considerable degree of self-government to the Territory. The Legislative Assembly has power to make laws for the peace, order and good government of the Territory. The Executive is appointed by the Administrator on the advice of the Assembly. The Executive has executive power with respect to prescribed areas and the Commonwealth Government retains power in other areas. The Act repealed the 1957 Act but continued in existence the Supreme Court of Norfolk Island (s 52). The Governor-General is empowered to appoint as a judge a person who is the judge of another court created by Parliament. Other courts may be created by enactment of the Assembly, which also has power to determine the jurisdiction of the Supreme Court (s 59). Appeals from the Supreme Court are to the Federal Court under s 24 of the *Federal Court of Australia Act* 1976.[17] The *Coral Sea Islands Act* 1969 declares those islands to be a Territory by name of Coral Sea Islands Territory. The Territory is subject to the laws of the ACT; but under s 8 the courts of Norfolk Island have jurisdiction in and in relation to the Territory.

The *Cocos (Keeling) Islands Act* 1955 constituted these islands a Commonwealth Territory. The *Supreme Court Ordinance* 1955 established the Supreme Court of the Territory. From 1976 appeals were regulated by the *Federal Court of Australia Act* 1976. The *Christmas Island Act* 1958 declared Christmas Island to be a Territory under the authority of the Commonwealth. Section 11 created the Supreme Court of Christmas Island and provided that it should be constituted by ordinance. Section 16 authorised ordinances to provide for appeals to the High Court but appeals were later regulated by the *Federal Court of Australia Act* 1976.

In 1992, the *Cocos (Keeling) Islands Act* and the *Christmas Island Act* were amended[18] so as to apply the law of Western Australia from 1 July 1992 to the Territories in place of the pre-existing law, subject to specific exceptions. In place of the Supreme Courts, the Courts and Court officers of Western Australia were given jurisdiction (including appellate jurisdiction) in

---

16 See Garran, "The Law of the Territories of the Commonwealth" (1935) 9 *ALJ* (Supplement) 28 at 29.

17 See generally Renfree, *The Federal Judicial System of Australia*, 1984, pp 773-776.

18 *Territories Law Reform Act* 1992.

and in relation to each of the Territories as if it were part of Western Australia.[19]

When federal jurisdiction is vested by Commonwealth Act in State courts it is done pursuant to s 77(iii) of the Constitution, and requires no corresponding State legislative action. The prevailing view in 1992, however, was that jurisdiction vested under s 122 of the Constitution was not federal jurisdiction.[20] Presumably because of doubts as to whether Territorial jurisdiction could be unilaterally imposed on State courts, Western Australia enacted legislation (*Indian Ocean Territories (Administration of Laws) Act* 1992) which, among other things, provided that the State courts and judicial officers may exercise jurisdiction vested under a law of the Commonwealth.[21]

Under the *Federal Court of Australia Act* 1976 provision is made for appeals to the Federal Court of Australia from judgments of the Supreme Court of a Territory other than the Northern Territory (s 24). Appeals to the High Court from Territory Supreme Courts now lie only with special leave given by the High Court (s 24(2)). Under s 26 of the *Federal Court of Australia Act* a Territory Supreme Court may state any case or reserve any question concerning a matter with respect to which an appeal would lie for the consideration of the Federal Court of Australia. Section 33 of the Act provides for appeals to the High Court from judgments of the Federal Court of Australia, by special leave.

Internal and External Territories

The constitutional nature of courts and jurisdiction in relation to the Territories, and whether they are governed by Chapter III, has at times been argued to depend on whether the Territories or any of them are part of the Commonwealth. The argument seems to have been that if a Territory was part of the Commonwealth it could be reasoned that its courts were exercising the judicial power of the Commonwealth; but that would not be so in the case of a Territory not within the Commonwealth. So far as the Australian Capital Territory is concerned, it was once considered that the appropriate constitutional provision for its government was s 52(i) which confers power on the Parliament to make laws for the peace, order and good government *of the Commonwealth* with respect to, inter alia, "The seat of government of the Commonwealth ...".[22] In *Spratt v Hermes*,[23] the High Court unanimously held

---

19   *Cocos (Keeling) Islands Act* 1955, Part IVAA; *Christmas Island Act* 1958, Part IVA.

20   Pages 173, 177 below.

21   See *Kruger v Commonwealth* (1997) 190 CLR 1 at 173-174 per Gummow J.

22   *Federal Capital Commission v Laristan Building and Investment Co Pty Ltd* (1929) 42 CLR 582. See also *Australian National Airways Pty Ltd v Commonwealth* (1945) 71 CLR 29 at 83.

23   (1965) 114 CLR 226.

that s 122 of the Constitution conferred a general power to legislate for the Australian Capital Territory and there was no limitation in s 52(i) upon that power. This was affirmed in *Re Governor, Goulburn Correctional Centre; ex parte Eastman*.[24] While there has been no decision as to where in the Australian Capital Territory the seat of government is or on the ambit of that power,[25] the Court noted that there was a distinction between the seat of government and the Capital Territory and that s 125 referred to the seat of government as being "within territory which shall have been granted to or acquired by the Commonwealth".[26]

A question has arisen whether there is any legally significant distinction between external and internal Territories. In *Mitchell v Barker*,[27] the High Court briefly discussed the question whether a magistrate's court in the Northern Territory was a federal court, so that an appeal lay under s 73(ii) of the Constitution to the High Court. Griffith CJ said:

> In *R v Bernasconi*[28] this Court held that the group of sections comprised in Chapter III of the Constitution do [sic] not apply to a Territory of the Commonwealth. If that is right in its largest sense, the Special Magistrates' Court is not a Federal Court and no appeal lies to this Court. *It may be that a distinction may some day be drawn between Territories which have and those which have not formed part of the Commonwealth.*[29]

In *Waters v Commonwealth*,[30] Fullagar J was called on to decide whether the High Court had original jurisdiction under s 75(iii) of the Constitution in a matter, arising in the Northern Territory, in which the Commonwealth was a party.[31] He said:

> For the purpose of s 122 of the Constitution no distinction can be drawn between Territories surrendered by a State and Territories otherwise acquired by the Commonwealth, but it may be that, for the purposes of s 5 of the *Constitution Act*, a distinction is to be drawn between Territories which are "parts of the Commonwealth" and Territories which are not "parts of the Commonwealth".

Section 5 of the *Constitution Act* (one of the covering clauses) provides that the *Constitution Act* and all laws made by the Commonwealth Parliament under the Constitution shall be binding on the courts, judges and people of

---

24 (1999) 200 CLR 322.

25 This issue was discussed in *Coe v Queensland Mines* (1974) 5 ACTR 53 and *Svikart v Stewart* (1994) 181 CLR 548 at 561.

26 (1965) 114 CLR 226 at 241, 257, 262, 269, 278 and see Ewens, "Where is the Seat of Government?" (1951) 25 ALJ 532.

27 (1918) 24 CLR 365.

28 (1915) 19 CLR 629. This case is discussed at pp 167-170ff below.

29 Italics supplied.

30 (1951) 82 CLR 188 at 192.

31 He held following *R v Bernasconi* that it did not. This decision was overruled in *Spratt v Hermes* (1965) 114 CLR 226.

every State and of every part of the Commonwealth, notwithstanding anything in the laws of any State. These words suggest that the Commonwealth is not coterminous with the area of the States.

The supposed distinction would appear to be based on the fact that, at the time of federation, the Northern Territory was part of South Australia and the area of the Australian Capital Territory was part of New South Wales. In s 6 of the *Constitution Act*, "the States" is defined to include "South Australia, including the northern territory of South Australia". The preamble to the *Constitution Act* states that "the people of" the various colonies "have agreed to unite in one indissoluble Federal Commonwealth".

In *Spratt v Hermes*,[32] the High Court seemed to reject the view that, for constitutional purposes, there is any distinction between internal Territories and external Territories.[33] Barwick CJ, Menzies and Windeyer JJ were of the view that, generally speaking, the Commonwealth included all the Territories of the Commonwealth, although some provisions of the Constitution that refer-red to the Commonwealth were not, because of their nature, applicable to the Territories. This latter question is discussed below. Kitto J was of the contrary view. But none of the judges who discussed the question of the meaning of "the Commonwealth" for this purpose considered that any distinction should be made between internal and external Territories. In *Berwick Ltd v Grey*,[34] Mason J said that the external Territories, except perhaps those held under United Nations Trusteeship, formed part of the Commonwealth of Australia. Barwick CJ, McTiernan, Jacobs and Murphy JJ agreed with Mason J's judgment.

In *Attorney-General (NSW); ex rel McKellar v Commonwealth*,[35] it was held that the phrase "people of the Commonwealth" in s 24 of the Constitution (concerning parliamentary representation) could not include the people of the Territories because of the express provisions of s 122 making Territory representation a matter for the discretion of Parliament. Barwick CJ said:

> In this respect, as indeed in other respects, I am unable to find any relevant distinction between the so-called internal Territories and the external Territories.[36]

That seemed to settle the matter until the case of *Capital Duplicators Pty Ltd v ACT*,[37] where some of the judges said that the internal Territories were part of the Commonwealth, while raising doubts as to the other Territories.

32　(1965) 114 CLR 226. See Zines, "Laws for the Government of any Territory: Section 122 of the Constitution" (1966) 2 Federal LR 72.

33　(1965) 114 CLR 226 at 259. See also *Capital TV and Appliances Pty Ltd v Falconer* (1971) 125 CLR 591 at 625.

34　(1976) 133 CLR 603 at 608.

35　(1977) 139 CLR 527.

36　Ibid at 533.

37　(1992) 177 CLR 248.

In *Berwick v Gray*, referred to above, the purpose of declaring that the external territories were part of the Commonwealth was to reach the conclusion that the power in s 51(ii) of the Constitution to make laws for the peace, order and good government of the Commonwealth with respect to taxation extended to Norfolk Island. The issue of the operation of s 51 in the Territories is dealt with later.[38] In *Capital Duplicators*, however, the issue was different. It was held that an Act of the ACT legislature that levied an excise duty was inconsistent with s 90 of the Constitution, which provides that the Commonwealth Parliament's power to impose duties of customs and excise and to grant bounties on the production or export of goods, is exclusive (Brennan, Deane, Toohey and Gaudron JJ; Mason CJ, Dawson and McHugh JJ dissenting). The majority judges said that s 90 contributed to one of the objectives of federalism, namely the creation of a free trade area embracing the geographical territory of the Commonwealth which comprised the areas of the original States (and any new ones). Those areas included what is now the Australian Capital Territory and the Northern Territory. Those Territories remained part of the Commonwealth and the free trade area; the latter could not be impaired by an independent legislative power (that is, of the Territory Legislatures) to impose excise duties or grant bounties. Brennan, Deane and Toohey JJ said it was unnecessary to consider whether an external Territory could become part of the Commonwealth while it remained a Territory.[39] Similarly, Gaudron J distinguished the internal Territories from others by saying they "are necessarily constituent parts of the Commonwealth of Australia, both geographically and politically".[40] In deference to *Berwick v Gray*, she said that "some territory may be part of the Commonwealth even though it was not in 1901". The issue in *Capital Duplicators* was, therefore, a very specific one related to the free trade area established by the Constitution.

The suggested distinction has not been pursued or developed in later cases. As will be seen, there has been disagreement as to the extent to which various provisions of the Constitution including Chapter III apply in the Territories or limit s 122 of the Constitution.[41] This debate, however, has not involved the making of distinctions between external and internal Territories. It is possible, therefore, that the distinction will be relevant only to the issue of the "free trade" area.

The Commonwealth parliamentary draftsmen, for a number of years, appeared to have proceeded on the assumption that internal Territories were part of the Commonwealth while external Territories were not. In *Waters v Commonwealth*,[42] Fullagar J noted that s 8 of the *Bankruptcy Act*, in its then

38   Pages 172, 173, 176 below.
39   (1992) 177 CLR 248 at 274.
40   Ibid at 285, 289.
41   For example, *Kruger v Commonwealth* (1997) 190 CLR 1.
42   (1951) 82 CLR 188 at 192.

form, contemplated such a distinction. It provided that the Governor-General may by Proclamation declare that the Act shall, with such modifications as are prescribed, extend to any Territory which is not part of the Commonwealth. It was clearly assumed, however, that the Act applied without any such Proclamation to the Australian Capital Territory and the Northern Territory. Section 18, for example, purported to confer what was described as "federal jurisdiction in bankruptcy" on, inter alia, the Supreme Courts of Northern Australia and Central Australia. The Australian Capital Territory was included in "the District of New South Wales and the Australian Capital Territory" under s 12 of the Act.[43] A number of other Acts referred to Territories "not being part of the Commonwealth" or "not forming part of the Commonwealth" in sections that provided for the Acts' extension to such Territories.[44]

The *Statute Law Revision Act* 1973 amended these provisions by omitting phrases such as "Territories not forming part of the Commonwealth" and inserting "external Territories". The *Acts Interpretation Act* was amended to define "Australia" and the "Commonwealth", when used in a geographical sense, to include the Territories of Christmas Island and Cocos (Keeling) Islands, not any other external Territory (s 17(a)). "External Territory" means "a Territory, not being an internal Territory, for the government of which as a Territory provision is made by any Act" (s 17(pd)). "Internal Territory" means "the Australian Capital Territory, the Jervis Bay Territory or the Northern Territory" (s 17(pe)).

Territorial Courts in the United States

In the United States, a distinction has been drawn between constitutional courts, established under Art III of the Constitution, and legislative courts whose constitutional basis is found elsewhere in the Constitution.[45] The Supreme Court of the United States held in *American Insurance Co v Canter*[46] that the courts of the Territories were legislative courts organised outside the framework of Art III, and therefore not capable of receiving an investment of jurisdiction under that Article. The constitution and jurisdiction of these courts depended upon "the general right of sovereignty which exists in the government, or in virtue of that clause which enables Congress to make all needful

---

43 Commonwealth Gazettes, 1928, p 2199; 1938, p 2533.

44 For example, *Life Insurance Act* 1945, s 6; *National Service Act* 1951, s 5; *Consular Privileges and Immunities Act* 1972, s 4; *Copyright Act* 1968, s 4; and *Defence Act* 1903, s 5A.

45 See Katz, "Federal Legislative Courts" (1930) 43 Harvard LR 894; Note, "The Restrictive Effect of Article III on the Organisation of the Federal Courts" (1934) 34 Columbia LR 344; "The Judicial Power of Federal Tribunals not Organised under Article Three" (1934) 34 Columbia LR 746; *Hart and Wechsler's The Federal Courts and the Federal System*, 4th edn, 1996, pp 399-416; Wright, *Law of Federal Courts*, 5th edn, 1994, pp 47-60.

46 1 Pet 511 (1828).

rules and regulations respecting the territory belonging to the United States". From this it was said to follow that the jurisdiction of the Territorial courts could be extended beyond the cases and controversies enumerated in Art III and that the tenure of judges of these courts was not controlled by that Article. It is to be noted that the Territorial courts are not the only tribunals within the category of legislative courts.[47]

Although the Territorial courts are classified as legislative courts, it is long settled, notwithstanding a strong dissent by Taney CJ,[48] that they are subject to the appellate jurisdiction of the Supreme Court of the United States. There is no elaborate exposition in the cases of the basis on which this appellate jurisdiction depends, and the fullest statement is to the effect that the United States exercises plenary authority over the Territories, that this includes ultimate legislative, executive and judicial power, from which it is said to follow that the Supreme Court has appellate jurisdiction over the courts established by Congress in the Territories.[49] This appellate jurisdiction does not depend upon the character of the court from which the appeal is taken, but on the nature of the proceeding in the lower court. It is only from *judicial* and not from *administrative* determinations of Territorial courts that an appeal lies to the Supreme Court.[50] This is a rather odd chapter of the law. Though the legislative courts can exercise no part of the judicial power of the United States, and the Supreme Court can exercise only that power, the latter nonetheless can review judgments of the former.[51]

Special considerations arise with respect to the courts of the District of Columbia. The District of Columbia, under Art I, s 8, of the United States Constitution, is the Seat of Government of the United States. It is to be noted that in Australia the Seat of Government is within, but is not coterminous

---

47 See *Northern Pipeline Construction Co v Marathon Pipe Line Co* 458 US 50 (1982).

48 *Gordon v United States* 2 Wall 561 (1865). This was posthumously printed 20 years after it was prepared. See the *Boilermakers' Case* (1956) 94 CLR 254 at 291.

49 *Freeborn v Smith* 2 Wall 160 at 173 (1864); *United States v Coe* 155 US 76 at 86 (1894). See Katz, op cit pp 899, 903.

50 Katz, op cit p 903. See *National Mutual Insurance Co v Tidewater Transfer Co Inc* 337 US 582 (1949). There was some difference of view in this case on the question whether the appellate jurisdiction of the Supreme Court depended on the matter being enumerated in the cases and controversies in Art III, s 2. The majority (followed by Katz, op cit p 902) said that the jurisdiction was not limited in this way, but Vinson CJ and Douglas J dissented. "The appellate jurisdiction of this court is, in fact, dependent upon the fact that the case reviewed is of a kind within the Art III enumeration. That Article, after setting out the cases of which inferior courts may take cognisance and the original jurisdiction of this Court, extends the appellate jurisdiction of the Supreme Court only as far as all other cases before mentioned ... We can no more review a legislative court's decision of a case which is not among those enumerated in Art III than we can hear a case from a state court involving purely state law questions." *Hart and Wechsler*, op cit pp 441-444.

51 There is a short discussion of the American law on this subject in the majority judgment in the *Boilermakers' Case* (1956) 94 CLR 254 at 290-292.

with, the Australian Capital Territory.[52] Through a long course of decisions, the courts of the District of Columbia were regarded as legislative courts[53] but, in 1933 in *O'Donoghue v United States*,[54] the Supreme Court of the United States held that for purposes of tenure and the compensation of judges the courts of the District were constitutional courts within Art III. It was said that in establishing courts for the District of Columbia Congress was exercising dual powers: under Art III Congress had exercised the power to constitute courts inferior to the Supreme Court, and under Art I, s 8 (the power to legislate for the District of Columbia), it had invested the District of Columbia courts with non-judicial as well as judicial functions.[55]

In 1970, the judicial system of the District of Columbia was reorganised so that the United States District Court for the District of Columbia and the United States Court of Appeal for the District of Columbia Circuit has the jurisdiction of other federal courts. Local jurisdiction was transferred to a local trial court and appeal court whose judges have a term of office of 15 years. The result is that the DC courts, which under the *O'Donoghue* principle were "hybrid" courts, are now divided into courts which are created under Art III and local courts which are legislative courts created under Art I.[56]

At no stage does there appear to have been any consideration of the possibility of conferring original jurisdiction on the Supreme Court of the United States in cases or controversies in or affecting the Territories.

The Territories Power in Australia : The Early Cases

The law relating to the Commonwealth Territorial courts and to jurisdiction in the Territories has been profoundly affected by the "extraordinary" decision[57] in *R v Bernasconi*.[58] That case was foreshadowed by *Buchanan v Commonwealth*,[59] where the High Court unanimously held that in legislating for the Northern Territory under s 122 it was not necessary to comply with s 55 of the Constitution, which provides that laws imposing taxation shall deal only with the imposition of taxation and that laws imposing taxation, subject to defined

---

52   See Ewens, "Where is the Seat of Government?" (1951) 25 ALJ 532 at 533; *Re Governor, Goulburn Correctional Centre; ex parte Eastman* (1999) 200 CLR 322.

53   They were expressly described as such by the Supreme Court of the United States in *Ex parte Bakelite Corporation* 279 US 438 (1929).

54   289 US 516 (1933).

55   See the discussion in *National Mutual Insurance Co v Tidewater Transfer Co* 337 US 582 (1949).

56   The DC court system and its constitutional position is discussed in *Palmore v US* 411 US 389 (1973).

57   Sawer, "Judicial Power under the Constitution" in Else-Mitchell (ed), *Essays on the Australian Constitution*, 2nd edn, 1961, p 77.

58   (1915) 19 CLR 629.

59   (1913) 16 CLR 315.

exceptions, shall deal only with one subject of taxation. This prohibition of tacking was inserted to safeguard the position of the Senate. Barton ACJ dwelt on the inconvenience which would follow a restriction of the power to legislate for the Territories under s 122 by reference to s 55. The core of the argument was that the Senate was protected as a *States'* House; that s 55 was linked to s 51(ii), which confers power on the Parliament to legislate, subject to the Constitution, with respect to taxation but so as not to discriminate between States or parts of States, and that s 55 was not therefore to affect the plenary powers of the Parliament in legislating for the Territories under s 122. In the words of Isaacs J, the Northern Territory

> is a territory of the Commonwealth ... (but) ... is not fused with it, and the provisions of ss 53 and 55 of the Constitution intended to guard the Senate and the States have no application to the Northern Territory. The taxation involved in the Northern Territory Acts is quite outside the "taxation" referred to in s 55 of the Constitution.[60]

The argument is not entirely convincing. It is true and notorious that the Senate was fashioned as a States' House, but it is a House of the *Parliament*, which is invested with authority to legislate for the Territories under s 122. Section 122 provides that Parliament "may allow the representation of such territory in either House of the Parliament to the extent and on the terms which it thinks fit".[61] Sections 55 and 53, it may reasonably be argued, were written into the Constitution to regulate the relations of the two Houses not only when the Parliament was legislating for the area comprised within the States but whenever the Parliament was exercising its powers as such.

In *R v Bernasconi*, it was held that the exercise of Commonwealth legislative power under s 122, whether exercised directly by Parliament or through a subordinate agency, was not restricted by s 80 of the Constitution, which provides that:

> [T]he trial on indictment of any offence against any law of the Commonwealth shall be by jury, and every such trial shall be held in the State where the offence was committed, and if the offence was not committed within any State the trial shall be held at such place or places as the Parliament prescribes.

As interpreted, s 80, which was designed to safeguard the right to trial by jury in serious criminal cases, is a very frail reed. It does not operate if the

---

60 Ibid at 335.
61 In *Western Australia v Commonwealth* (1975) 134 CLR 201, the High Court by a majority upheld the validity of the *Senate (Representation of Territories) Act* 1973 providing for the representation of the people of the Australian Capital Territory and the Northern Territory in the Senate. This decision was affirmed in *Queensland v Commonwealth* (1977) 139 CLR 585.

procedure of indictment is not adopted.[62] But the final words of the section suggest the possibility of a trial at a place outside the area of a State.

Nevertheless, in *R v Bernasconi*, it was held that the trial in a Territory of a person on indictment for an offence against a law of the Commonwealth need not be by jury. The offence in that case was constituted by an ordinance of the Territory of Papua which excluded trial by jury and it was argued that a law passed by the legislature of a Territory under the authority of an Act of the Commonwealth Parliament could not properly be regarded as a law of the Commonwealth, but was more properly described as a "law of the territory concerned" and therefore not within the ambit of s 80. Griffith CJ, in whose judgment Rich and Gavan Duffy JJ concurred, declined to decide the case on this narrow ground,[63] while Isaacs J was of opinion that a Territorial ordinance was a law of the Commonwealth "because its present force subsists by virtue of the declared will of the Commonwealth Parliament".[64]

In the view of Griffith CJ, s 80 was enacted to parallel in the case of indictable offences under Commonwealth laws those provisions in State laws which provided for trial by jury on indictment. From this he drew the broad conclusion that "Chapter III is limited in its application to the exercise of the judicial power of the Commonwealth in respect of those functions of government as to which it stands in the place of the States, and has no application to territories".[65] It is to be noted that Griffith CJ's judgment extended to the whole of Chapter III of the Constitution, that is to the Judicature chapter. The Chief Justice's reasoning does not demonstrate very clearly why the operation of s 80 should be *geographically* limited to the area of the States, particularly in view of the fact that the words of s 80 contemplate the commission of an indictable offence outside that area. Isaacs J advanced additional arguments of policy to support the conclusion that s 80 did not extend to the Territories. He observed that s 122 was an unqualified grant of power, complete in itself, which implied that a Territory was

> not yet in a condition to enter into the full participation of Commonwealth constitutional rights and powers. It is in a state of dependency or tutelage, and the special regulations proper for its government until, if ever, it shall be admitted as a member of the family of States, are left to the discretion of the Commonwealth Parliament ... Parliament's sense of justice and fair dealing is sufficient to protect them, without fencing them round with what

---

62   See per Isaacs J in *R v Bernasconi* (1915) 19 CLR 629 at 637; *R v Archdall and Roskruge* (1928) 41 CLR 128; *R v Federal Court of Bankruptcy; ex parte Lowenstein* (1938) 59 CLR 556; *Boilermakers' Case* (1956) 94 CLR 254 at 290: "As s 80 has been interpreted there is no difficulty in avoiding trial by jury where it does apply"; *Kingswell v R* (1985) 159 CLR 264. On the operation of s 80, in other respects, see also *Brown v R* (1986) 160 CLR 171 and *Cheatle v R* (1993) 177 CLR 541.

63   (1915) 19 CLR 629 at 634.

64   Ibid at 637.

65   Ibid at 635.

would be in the vast majority of instances an entirely inappropriate requirement of the British jury system.[66]

It is fair comment that this was a sound policy reason for excluding the
operation of jury trial in some of the Territories – though it made no sense at
all, for example, in the case of the Australian Capital Territory – but it is also
fair comment to point out that such considerations should have been more
appropriately addressed to those who were responsible for drafting the Constitution.[67] There is no warrant, however, in the actual terms of the Constitution
for excluding the Territories from the operation of s 80, or for that matter from
the operation of Chapter III as a whole.

The tendency was to regard a Territory as being outside or subordinate to
the Commonwealth proper and to give the Commonwealth unfettered power
in the Territory; but, also, to support this view by an appeal to policy considerations relating to the particular provisions involved.

In *Porter v The King; ex parte Yee*,[68] s 21 of the *Supreme Court
Ordinance* 1911-1922 of the Northern Territory made under s 13 of the
Northern Territory (Administration) Act 1910 provided for an appeal to the
High Court from the Supreme Court of the Northern Territory. It was argued
that the provision was void, first, because Chapter III of the Constitution did
not apply to the Territories; a court of a Territory was, therefore, not a federal
court within the meaning of s 73, which is included in Chapter III and which
provides for an appeal to the High Court from judgments of, inter alia, a
federal court. Secondly, Parliament could not confer appellate jurisdiction on
the High Court under s 122 because it had been held in *In re Judiciary and
Navigation Acts*[69] that the jurisdiction of the High Court was confined to such
jurisdiction as was conferred or authorised by Chapter III.

The High Court (Isaacs, Higgins, Rich and Starke JJ; Knox CJ and Gavan
Duffy J dissenting) rejected these submissions and upheld its jurisdiction to
hear the appeal on the ground that the exclusive and exhaustive nature of
Chapter III, providing for the judicature and its functions, referred only to the
federal system. Knox CJ and Gavan Duffy J dissented on the grounds that *In
re Judiciary and Navigation Acts* established that the whole of the original and
appellate jurisdiction of the High Court was to be found within Chapter III and
that laws for the government of the Territory did not include a power to
impose duties on persons or organisations (such as the High Court) not within
the Territory.

The judgment of Higgins J, one of the majority in *Porter's Case*, was
to cause difficulty later. Higgins J had dissented in *In re Judiciary and
Navigation Acts* on the grounds that the jurisdiction Parliament purported to

---

66   Ibid at 637-638.
67   Sawer, op cit p 77.
68   (1926) 37 CLR 432.
69   (1921) 29 CLR 257.

confer in that case (the giving of advisory opinions) was within Chapter III and that, even if it did not come within those provisions, Chapter III did not exhaustively describe the jurisdiction that could be vested in the Court. In *Porter's Case*, Higgins J did not distinguish *In re Judiciary and Navigation Acts* on the same basis as the other majority judges. Instead, he seemed to accept that decision as applicable to the High Court in relation to the Territories but declared that it was binding only in respect of the conferring of original, and not appellate, jurisdiction on the High Court.[70]

Putting aside the views of Higgins J, the opinions of the majority and minority judges in *Porter's Case* both involved the notion of the Territories power being in some sense separated from the rest of the Constitution. The Court considered that *R v Bernasconi* established that Chapter III did not extend to the Territories, which were governed under s 122 alone.

A More Integrated View of the Territories Power

A case which had great effect on the development of the law relating to jurisdiction in the Territories is *Lamshed v Lake*,[71] where the High Court considered the operation of s 10 of the *Northern Territory (Administration) Act* 1910, which provided that trade, commerce and intercourse between the Northern Territory and the States, whether by means of internal carriage or ocean navigation, shall be absolutely free. The High Court held that that section validly operated in the States so as to override any inconsistent State law. As a result, it was held that a South Australian Act which prohibited carriers from using certain roads without a licence did not apply to a carrier in the course of a journey from Adelaide to Alice Springs because of the application of s 109 of the Constitution.

The State of South Australia had argued that under s 122 the Commonwealth Parliament was in the position of a local legislature in and for the Territory with its power limited to the area of the Territory. Dixon CJ replied:

> To my mind s 122 is a power given to the national Parliament of Australia as such to make laws "for", that is to say "with respect to", the government of the Territory. The words "the government of any territory" of course describe the subject matter of the power. But once the law is shown to be relevant to that subject matter it operates as a binding law of the Commonwealth wherever territorially the authority of the Commonwealth runs.[72]

---

70   In *Federal Capital Commission v Laristan Building and Investment Co Pty Ltd* (1929) 42 CLR 582 at 585, Dixon J said: "It thus appears that three of the six members of the Court who took part in the decision of *Porter v The King; ex parte Yee* treated s 122 as insufficient to empower the Legislature to invest the High Court with original jurisdiction in respect of a Territory."

71   (1958) 99 CLR 132.

72   (1958) 99 CLR 132 at 141. This case was followed in *Attorney-General (WA) v Australian National Airlines Commission* (1976) 138 CLR 492.

The Chief Justice pointed out that, on any view, it was necessary in applying s 122 to refer to some other parts of the Constitution. The reference to "The Parliament" in s 122, for example, necessarily referred to Parts I, II, III and IV of Chapter I. Section 122 deals with Territories accepted by and placed under the authority of the "Commonwealth", which word must refer to the executive government described in Chapter II.

His Honour saw no reason why, for example, s 116 (the religion clause) should not apply to laws made under s 122 and why s 120 (dealing with the custody of offenders against the laws of the Commonwealth) should not include offences created under s 122. Dixon CJ even considered that there were a number of powers in s 51 that were applicable to the Northern Territory: for example, the powers with respect to "postal, telegraphic, telephonic, and other like services", "the naval and military defence of the Commonwealth", "fisheries in Australian waters beyond territorial limits", "banking, other than State banking; also State banking extending beyond the limits of the State concerned", "naturalisation and aliens" and the incidental power.

Similarly, it was thought that a law operating in the Northern Territory which interfered with the freedom of interstate trade, for example, the carriage of goods between Queensland and Western Australia, might be obnoxious to s 92. On this reasoning, s 10 of the Commonwealth Act was held to operate validly in South Australia and to be a "law of the Commonwealth" within the meaning of s 109.

Where did this decision leave the earlier cases? Were they to be explained merely in the inappropriateness to the Territories of the particular constitutional provisions involved? Dixon CJ did not expressly approve of *R v Bernasconi* or the view that Chapter III was inapplicable to the Territories. However, he said:

> [S]ince Chapter III has been considered to be concerned with jurisdiction in relation to that division of powers [between a central and local State legislature] it may be treated as inapplicable so that laws made mediately or immediately under s 122 are primarily not within the operation of the Chapter.[73]

Territorial Courts and Section 72

Section 71 of the Constitution vests the judicial power of the Commonwealth in the High Court and in "such other federal courts as the Parliament creates and in such other courts as it invests with federal jurisdiction". Section 72 requires justices of the High Court and "other courts created by the Parliament" to be appointed by the Governor-General in Council, provides for their term of office and contains provisions relating to removal from office and remuneration.

---

73   Ibid at 142.

JURISDICTION IN THE TERRITORIES

In *Spratt v Hermes*,[74] it was held unanimously that s 72 of the Constitution did not apply to a magistrate sitting as a Court of Petty Sessions in
the Australian Capital Territory to hear a charge alleging an offence under the
Post and Telegraph Act 1901. All the judges followed *R v Bernasconi* to the
extent that they considered that the magistrate was not exercising the judicial
power of the Commonwealth within the meaning of s 71 of the Constitution.
While all the judges professed to follow the earlier cases in reaching their
decision, their judgments varied considerably. Barwick CJ and Windeyer J
emphasised their view that the Territories were all part of the Commonwealth
and that any general limitation on Commonwealth power applied in respect of
s 122 unless it was shown that the limitation concerned was intended only to
deal with "federal" powers, that is, those in ss 51 and 52 of the Constitution
which operated in the States. Section 71 was in the latter category and the
reference there to "federal courts" made this clear. The reference in s 72 to
"other courts created by the Parliament" was interpreted as referring to
"federal courts" in s 71. Menzies J went further. He regarded the Territories
not only as parts of the Commonwealth but also as within "the federal
system". No distinction, he thought, could be made between the Commonwealth in its federal and non-federal aspects. Generally, there was no reason
for regarding any provision as inapplicable to the Territories; however, he felt
constrained by prior decisions to hold that courts created under s 122 need not
comply with the provisions of s 72.

None of these three judges was, however, prepared to accept in its entirety
the broad statement in *R v Bernasconi* that the whole of Chapter III was inapplicable to the Territories. The Chief Justice pointed to the fact that an inter se
question under s 74 could, for example, arise out of the exercise of power
under s 122 because such a law was a "law of the Commonwealth" within
s 109, as had been held in *Lamshed v Lake*. On the other hand, Kitto and
Taylor JJ appeared to accept the broad statement in *R v Bernasconi* and Kitto J
in particular considered that "the Commonwealth" had a prima facie meaning
of "federated States". The emphasis in his judgment was on the unlimited
power given by s 122 and the inapplicability of most of the provisions in the
Constitution to the exercise of power under that section. In this respect, he had
completely changed his position since *Lamshed v Lake*.

The conclusion of all judges of the Court that a Territorial court was not a
"federal court" was affirmed in *Capital TV and Appliances Pty Ltd v
Falconer*.[75] In that case, it was held that s 73(ii) of the Constitution, providing
for appeals to the High Court from, inter alia, any "federal court or court exercising federal jurisdiction", did not apply to judgments of the Supreme Court
of the ACT. While in later cases a number of judges disagreed with that case so
far as the exercise of federal jurisdiction is concerned, the Court has reaffirmed

---

74   (1965) 114 CLR 226. See Zines, "'Laws for the Government of any Territory': Section 122
     of the Constitution" (1966) 2 Federal LR 72.

75   (1971) 125 CLR 591.

the earlier decisions that s 72 of the Constitution is inapplicable to Territorial courts.

In *Re Governor, Goulburn Correctional Centre; ex parte Eastman*,[76] a person was appointed by the ACT Government as a judge of the ACT Supreme Court for a limited term for the purpose of conducting a trial for murder. If s 72 was applicable it was breached in two respects: (a) the appointment was not made by the Governor-General in Council, and (b) the term of office did not comply with the section. Six judges (Kirby J dissenting) followed *Spratt v Hermes*. Gleeson CJ, Gaudron, McHugh and Callinan JJ held that s 72 was inapplicable to any court established under s 122. In a joint judgment, Gleeson CJ, McHugh and Callinan JJ declined to discuss generally the relationship between Chapter III and s 122 but considered that the earlier decisions holding that Territorial courts were not within the expression "the other courts created by Parliament" in s 72 "produces a sensible result, which pays due regard to the practical considerations arising from the varied nature and circumstances of Territories".[77] Gaudron J was of the view that as a matter of ordinary language s 72 was apt to include a Territorial court. However, she said that the reference to "federal courts" in s 71 comprised only courts upon which Parliament could confer jurisdiction to be exercised throughout the Commonwealth, and therefore did not include a court created under s 122. In view of past decisions and the fact that Parliament had acted on those decisions, she was prepared to read the phrase "other courts created by the Parliament" in s 72 as referring to "federal courts" in s 71, as Barwick CJ had done in *Spratt v Hermes*. She was also assisted in that conclusion by her view that federal jurisdiction could be conferred on Territorial courts, which would put them within the phrase "such other courts as it invests with federal jurisdiction" in s 71. This is discussed below.

Gummow and Hayne JJ decided the case on the ground that the Supreme Court was to be treated as a court created by the Legislative Assembly of the ACT, and therefore was not one of "the other courts created by the Parliament"[78] within s 72. That was because although the Court had been established by Commonwealth Act it was transferred to the authority of the Australian Capital Territory by being converted into an ACT enactment and had been amended by the Legislative Assembly. Nevertheless, they accepted the view of the other four majority judges that even if the Court was created by Parliament it was not governed by s 72.

Had the Court decided to overrule *Spratt v Hermes* it would have had serious consequences in respect of convictions and other judgments delivered by Territorial courts over many decades, based on decisions going back to *Bernasconi*.

---

76 (1999) 200 CLR 322.

77 Ibid at 332.

78 This distinction is discussed below.

"Separation" v "Integration"

Despite the six to one decision in *Eastman*, members of the High Court have in recent years taken differing views on the place of s 122 in the Constitution and the relationship of the Territories to the Commonwealth as a whole. Some have tended to support the principle in *Bernasconi*, while others have preferred the approach in *Lamshed v Lake*. For the former judges, restrictions on federal legislative power such as Chapter III, s 51(xxxi) (acquisition on just terms) or s 116 (religion) are inapplicable to the legislative power granted by s 122, which is described as "plenary". For the other judges s 122 should be treated like all other legislative powers of the Commonwealth.

While a number of these cases did not specifically involve courts or jurisdiction in the Territories, the different approaches to the general issue also affected answers to questions whether a federal court could be given (and if so to what extent) jurisdiction in respect of matters arising in the Territories and whether a Territorial court could ever exercise (or was always exercising) federal jurisdiction so as to provide a constitutional right of appeal under s 73 of the Constitution to the High Court.

In *Kruger v Commonwealth*,[79] a number of Aborigines sued the Commonwealth on the ground that, as children, they had been unlawfully removed from their parents and detained in institutions or reserves in the Northern Territory by the Chief Protector of Aboriginals. Among other grounds it was argued that the removal and detention was in breach of Chapter III because the actions amounted to an exercise of the judicial power of the Commonwealth which that chapter vested exclusively in courts referred to in s 71. The Court held there was no breach of the separation of judicial power required by Chapter III. Brennan CJ, Dawson and McHugh JJ held that the judicial power in the Territories was not the judicial power of the Commonwealth and therefore was not subject to Chapter III. In any case, the actions complained of were not regarded as having a judicial character. Toohey, Gaudron and Gummow JJ also agreed that, even if s 122 was subject to Chapter III, the relevant law did not purport to confer judicial power. The latter three judges, however, indicated that they were dissatisfied with the earlier cases holding that s 122 was separated from Chapter III and other provisions of the Constitution which restrict Commonwealth power. Toohey J referred to the argument that Chapter III extended to the Territories as "very persuasive".[80] Gummow J was concerned that the earlier cases meant that (apart, perhaps, from s 75(v)) there was "no constitutionally entrenched avenue for access to the High Court" in matters which are within the original jurisdiction of the High Court and entrusted to Territorial courts such as constitutional matters. This principle was inconsistent with other principles established in more recent times,

---

79   (1997) 190 CLR 1.
80   Ibid at 84.

namely that the Constitution creates an integrated system of law and that s 73 (High Court appeals) ensures that the High Court is guardian of the Constitution and ultimate interpreter of the common law of Australia.[81] Gaudron J pointed out that *Bernasconi* and *Spratt* required reading limitations into provisions which their terms did not require. Also she found no convincing reason for treating the words "The judicial power of the Commonwealth" in s 71 as not extending to disputes regarding laws enacted by Parliament under s 122. She put to one side, however, laws enacted by the legislature of a self-governing Territory.[82] All these remarks of Toohey, Gaudron and Gummow JJ were obiter dicta, but they were straws in the wind, and were opposed to the "separation" approach of the other three judges.

This dichotomy of "integration" and "separation" continued in other cases. In *Teori Tau v Commonwealth*,[83] it had been held that, in making laws under s 122 for the acquisition of property in the Territories, the Commonwealth was not bound by the provisions of s 51(xxxi), which confers power in respect of "the acquisition of property on just terms from any State or person for any purpose in respect of which the Parliament has power to make laws". This power has been held to restrict the other powers in s 51 so that the requirement of "just terms" is respected. In the case of s 122, the power was held to be plenary and unqualified.

That case was re-examined in *Newcrest Mining (WA) Ltd v Commonwealth*.[84] The Commonwealth had acquired property in the Northern Territory under an Act which had the purpose of the performance of Australia's international obligations. That purpose was held to come within the external affairs power (s 51(xxix)). Accordingly, it was held that legislative power was fettered by s 51(xxxi) in fulfilling that purpose (Toohey, Gaudron, Gummow and Kirby JJ; Brennan CJ, Dawson and McHugh JJ dissenting). This decision accepted the view in *Lamshed v Lake* and *Berwick Ltd v Gray* that s 51 could operate in the Territories. Three of the four majority judges (Gaudron, Gummow and Kirby JJ) went further and held that the acquisition for a purpose within s 122, and not within s 51, was included within the words "any purpose in respect of which Parliament has power to make laws" in s 51(xxxi). The other majority judge, Toohey J, was not prepared to override *Teori Tau*, but distinguished it on the basis that in *Newcrest* the law gave effect to a treaty and came within the external affairs power. To that extent it came within s 51(xxxi), even though it was also a law within s 122.

The dissenting judges, Brennan CJ, Dawson and McHugh JJ, followed their previously expressed "separation" view and held that *Teori Tau* should not be overruled. Dawson J said that laws operating throughout the

---

81   Ibid at 174-175.
82   Ibid at 108-109.
83   (1969) 119 CLR 564.
84   (1997) 190 CLR 513.

Commonwealth operated in the Territories under s 122. He disapproved of *Lamshed v Lake*.[85] The dissenting judges also rejected the view that s 122 could operate to authorise an acquisition of property in a State, despite the reasoning in *Lamshed v Lake*.

Gummow J, with whose judgment Gaudron J agreed, took the opportunity to expound a broad "integration" view of the Territories power. Kirby J's judgment was to similar effect.

Territorial Matters and Federal Jurisdiction

Despite the decision in the *Capital TV Case* to the contrary, a number of judges have suggested in recent times that, even though Territorial courts are not federal courts within s 71 of the Constitution, they can be invested by Parliament with federal jurisdiction. As mentioned earlier, s 71 vests the judicial power of the Commonwealth in the High Court, such other federal courts as the Parliament creates, and in such other courts as it invests with federal jurisdiction. Section 73(ii) provides for appeals to the High Court from, among others, the judgments of courts exercising federal jurisdiction. Neither provision explicitly states that the sole repositories of vested federal jurisdiction are *State* courts. Section 77(iii) provides that, with respect to any of the matters mentioned in ss 75 and 76, Parliament may make laws investing *State* courts with federal jurisdiction. If Parliament can vest a Territorial court with federal jurisdiction within the meaning of ss 71 and 73, the power must lie in s 122. If such a court can be given federal jurisdiction, its exercise is subject to appeal to the High Court under s 73. As mentioned earlier, this issue is connected to the broader question of the extent to which the Territories power is separated from or integrated with the rest of the Constitution.

In *Northern Territory v GPAO*,[86] the *Family Law Act* conferred jurisdiction on the Family Court in respect of parenting orders. A Northern Territory Act provided that a welfare officer was not obliged to disclose certain documents. One issue was whether the Northern Territory provision was binding on the Family Court under s 79 of the *Judiciary Act*. That in turn depended on whether the Court was exercising "federal jurisdiction". The matter before the Court concerned ex-nuptial children, so it did not involve the marriage power (s 51(xxi)) and could arise only under s 122. A majority of the High Court held that the Family Court was exercising federal jurisdiction (Gleeson CJ, Gaudron, Gummow and Hayne JJ; McHugh and Callinan JJ dissenting). In so deciding, it was made clear that matters arising under a Commonwealth Act made pursuant to s 122 came within s 76(ii) of the Constitution: "matters arising under any laws made by the Parliament". It

---

85   Ibid at 551-558.
86   (1999) 196 CLR 553.

followed that s 77(i) allowed that jurisdiction to be vested in a federal court.[87] The majority therefore followed the view of Menzies J in *Spratt v Hermes*.[88] The judgment of Gleeson CJ and Gummow J confined the decision to laws made by the Parliament and to jurisdiction conferred on a federal court. The issue of whether Territorial courts could be invested with federal jurisdiction was left open.

The decision in *GPAO* was followed in *Spinks v Prentice*[89] where it was held by the whole court that the *Corporations Act* 1989 (Cth) validly conferred jurisdiction on the Federal Court with respect to civil matters arising under the *Corporations Law* (ACT), which was an enactment of the Commonwealth Parliament.

In *Re Governor, Goulburn Correctional Centre; ex parte Eastman*,[90] there was no decision whether (contrary to *Capital TV and Appliances Pty Ltd v Falconer*) a Territorial court could be invested with federal jurisdiction. However, Gaudron J expressed the opinion that a court created under s 122 could be invested with such jurisdiction to the extent that the matter arises under or involves the application of a Commonwealth law in its operation in a Territory.[91] As a matter arising under a s 122 law was within s 76(ii), it came within federal jurisdiction and that jurisdiction could be conferred on a Territorial court. In those circumstances, there was an appeal to the High Court by virtue of s 73(ii) of the Constitution in so far as it refers to judgments of any "court exercising federal jurisdiction". Gummow and Hayne JJ also gave as their preferred construction that a court created by Parliament for a Territory, while not a federal court under ss 71 and 72, might be invested with federal jurisdiction so as to bring it within the operation of the phrase "such other courts as it [the Parliament] invests with federal jurisdiction" in s 71. It would be then exercising the judicial power of the Commonwealth pursuant to that section and judgments made within that jurisdiction would be within the appellate jurisdiction of the High Court under s 73.

Gleeson CJ, McHugh and Callinan JJ did not express any view on this issue. Kirby J dissented in the case by holding that the ACT Supreme Court was a federal court and therefore governed by the appointment and tenure

---

87 Ibid at 589-592 per Gleeson CJ and Gummow J, 604-605 per Gaudron J, 650-651 per Hayne J.

88 McHugh and Callinan JJ at 617-618 agreed that ss 76(ii) and 77(i) were wide enough to confer original jurisdiction in respect of a law under s 122 on the High Court and original or appellate jurisdiction on a federal court. They did not accept, however, that it was "federal jurisdiction" within the meaning of s 71. They regarded federal jurisdiction as concerned only with the determination of matters involving laws made under ss 51 and 52 of the Constitution. This view differs from that which has been generally accepted, namely, that federal jurisdiction includes matters under all the heads of jurisdiction in ss 75 and 76. See s 39 of the *Judiciary Act* and Chapter 5 below.

89 Under name *Re Wakim; ex parte McNally* (1999) 198 CLR 511.

90 (1999) 200 CLR 322.

91 Ibid at 339.

provisions of s 72. As one of his concerns was to ensure that there was a con-stitutional right of appeal to the High Court,[92] it is clear that he would prefer the views of Gaudron, Gummow and Hayne JJ to the decision of *Capital TV and Appliances* in respect of federal jurisdiction of Territorial courts.

In respect of matters arising under laws made by Parliament pursuant to s 122, therefore, it is likely to be held, with the present composition of the Court, that a Territorial court is exercising federal jurisdiction and, therefore, the judicial power of the Commonwealth. Any other view would be difficult to reconcile with the decision in *GPAO* that a federal court, in determining a matter arising under a s 122 law, was exercising jurisdiction referable to s 76(ii). The same is no doubt true in respect of matters arising under ordi-nances or other forms of delegated legislation. In *Federal Capital Commission v Laristan Building and Investment Co Pty Ltd*,[93] Dixon J said:

> But it is at least clear that a claim of right conferred by or under ordinances made by the Governor-General in Council under s 12 of the *Seat of Government (Administration) Act* is a matter arising under an enactment of the Parliament.[94]

There is more doubt, however, regarding laws made by the legislatures of the self-governing Territories, which at present comprise the Australian Capital Territory, the Northern Territory and Norfolk Island.

Self-Governing Territories

In *Capital Duplicators Pty Ltd v Australian Capital Territory (No 1)*,[95] it was held by Brennan, Deane, Toohey and Gaudron JJ (Mason CJ, Dawson and McHugh JJ dissenting), that the Australian Capital Territory's legislature could not levy an excise duty because s 90 renders the power to levy such duties exclusive to the Parliament of the Commonwealth. While Parliament could delegate its power, the Legislative Assembly of the ACT is not a dele-gate. It is a separate legislative body with independent general legislative authority. Brennan, Deane and Toohey JJ held that the Assembly was, in relation to the Commonwealth Parliament, in a similar position to colonial Parliaments, which had been declared by the Privy Council not to be delegates of the Imperial Parliament, but intended to have powers as plenary and ample and of the same nature as the Imperial Parliament itself.[96] This reasoning

---

92 Ibid at 375-376.

93 (1929) 42 CLR 582 at 585-586.

94 Compare *Anderson v Eric Anderson Radio and TV Pty Ltd* (1965) 114 CLR 20 at 35-37 per Taylor J. See *Northern Territory v GPAO* (1999) 196 CLR 553 at 590 per Gleeson CJ and Gummow J.

95 (1992) 177 CLR 248.

96 At 281, referring to *Powell v Apollo Candle Co* (1885) 10 App Cas 282 and *Union Steamship Co of Australia Pty Ltd v King* (1988) 166 CLR 1.

could lead to the conclusion that laws made by the legislature of a self-governing Territory are not "made by the Parliament" within s 76(ii), and so matters arising under them cannot be the subject of federal jurisdiction.

The decision in *Capital Duplicators*, however, was based on the proposition that to treat laws of the ACT Legislative Assembly, for purposes of that case, as an exercise of federal legislative power would destroy a central objective of the federal compact, namely the creation of a free trade area throughout the geographical territory of the original States. The express requirement of uniformity of the bounties referred to in s 51(iii) of the Constitution and made exclusive by s 90 would, they said, also be defeated.[97]

Where that consequence has not been in issue the Court has not regarded the independent nature of Territorial legislatures as significant in respect of other exclusive powers. In *Svikart v Stewart*,[98] for example, it was held (Mason CJ, Brennan, Deane and McHugh JJ; Toohey and Gaudron JJ dissenting) that s 52(i) of the Constitution, conferring exclusive power on Parliament to make laws with respect to, among other things, "all places acquired by the Commonwealth for public purposes", did not apply to places in the Northern Territory. The word "exclusive" was taken in that context to mean exclusive of State Parliaments. *Capital Duplicators* was distinguished on the basis of the circumscribed nature of the taxation and bounties power and the object of creating a free trade area.

In *Kruger v Commonwealth*,[99] Gaudron J, after discussing why she considered that the "judicial power of the Commonwealth" in s 71 extended to the determination of disputes involving Commonwealth laws made under s 122, added that "it may be that different considerations apply to laws enacted by the legislature of a self-governing Territory". On the other hand, in his dissenting judgment in *Newcrest*,[100] McHugh J gave as one of his reasons for holding that s 122 was not subject to s 51(xxxi) that otherwise self-governing Territories would "be in an inferior position to the States", which are not restricted by any "just terms" requirement.[101] He did not think any distinction could be made between dependent and self-governing Territories.[102]

As earlier mentioned, in *Eastman* Gleeson CJ, McHugh and Callinan JJ rejected the submission that the phrase "the other courts created by the Parliament" in s 72 applied to courts created under s 122. They said that their interpretation had regard to the practical considerations arising from the varied nature and circumstances of the Territories. They went on to say that:

97   (1992) 177 CLR 248 at 279.

98   (1994) 181 CLR 548.

99   (1997) 190 CLR 1 at 109.

100 (1997)190 CLR 513.

101 As held in *Durham Holdings Pty Ltd v NSW* (2001) 205 CLR 399.

102 (1997)190 CLR 513 at 574.

> Even if the applicant's argument were correct, whether a court in a self-governing territory satisfied the description of a court created by the Federal Parliament might depend upon whether the territory legislature had legislated concerning the territory's courts, and upon the form of such legislation.[103]

As indicated above, Gummow and Hayne JJ in that case held that even if it were otherwise applicable s 72 would not apply to a court created by the legislature of a self-governing Territory. They relied on *Capital Duplicators*.

Although McHugh and Callinan JJ joined with Gleeson CJ in *Eastman* they expressed the opinion in *GPAO* that if Chapter III restricted Commonwealth power in s 122 such restriction would apply equally to the power of the legislature of a self-governing Territory.[104] This is consistent with the remarks of McHugh J in *Newcrest* referred to above regarding the application of the acquisition power in s 51(xxxi) to the Territories power. It seems, therefore, that the statement of Gleeson CJ, McHugh and Callinan JJ is merely referring to a *possibility* that Gummow and Hayne JJ's approach could be followed if their reasoning was rejected.

In *Eastman*, Kirby J, in his dissenting judgment, considered that the legislature of a self-governing Territory was subject to any restrictions binding the Commonwealth acting under s 122. He said:

> Moreover, because the grant of legislative power to the Territory Assembly is made under s 122 of the Constitution, it cannot enlarge the power which it is within the province of the Federal Parliament to grant. Thus it cannot override the requirements of Chapter III.[105]

So far as the Court as a whole is concerned, therefore, there is no decision as to whether, for purposes of Chapter III generally and other restrictions on Commonwealth power, a differentiation between dependent Territories and self-governing Territories should be made.

The issue is only of importance if one accepts an interpretation of s 122 that requires Commonwealth laws made under that provision to be subject to constitutional restrictions such as those derived from s 116, s 51(xxxi) and s 80 (requiring the overruling of *Bernasconi*) and other provisions of Chapter III. Is there then a case for holding that references to the "Commonwealth" or "the Parliament" in such provisions do not include a self-governing Territory or its legislature? The reasoning of *Capital Duplicators* provides a means of making the differentiation. On the other hand, the special circumstances associated with the "free trade area" in that case and the decision in *Svikart v Stewart* lead to the conclusion that a differentiation for present purposes is not compelling.

---

103 (1999) 200 CLR 322 at 332-333.
104 (1999) 196 CLR 553 at 617.
105 (1999) 200 CLR 322 at 379.

If it is thought that s 122 should be interpreted so as to enable the Parliament to create a polity that is in a similar position to a State, that can be achieved to an extent by holding that restrictions on Commonwealth legislative power are not applicable to power conferred on the legislature of a self-governing Territory. The States are not subject to the restrictions in ss 51(xxxi), 80 or 116 or, to a substantial degree, Chapter III.

Whatever might be said about that, however, there is no way that a Supreme Court of a self-governing Territory can be put constitutionally in the same position as the Supreme Court of a State in relation to High Court appeals. If matters arising under an enactment of a Territorial legislature do not come within s 76(ii) because they do not arise under laws made by the Parliament, those matters are not, as such, determined in federal jurisdiction and, therefore, s 73 does not guarantee an appeal. On the other hand, s 73 expressly provides for appeals from all judgments of the Supreme Courts of the States.

In the judgments, referred to above, that concluded that a Territorial court can have federal jurisdiction and that a matter arising under a Commonwealth law made pursuant to s 122 is a matter of federal jurisdiction,[106] concern was shown with ensuring that there was a guarantee of an appeal to the High Court under the Constitution. That is because s 73 of the Constitution provides the unifying element of our judicial system. To distinguish an enactment of a Territory legislature from that of the Commonwealth Parliament would defeat much of that object.

As Gummow J put it in *Kruger v Commonwealth*:[107]

> [I]t is fundamental that the Constitution creates an "integrated system of law" and a "single system of jurisprudence". The entrusting by Ch III, in particular by s 73, to this Court of the superintendence of the whole of the Australian judicial structure, its position as ultimate interpreter of the common law of Australia and as guardian of the Constitution, are undermined, if not contradicted, by acceptance, as mandated by the Constitution, of the proposition that it is wholly within the power of the Parliament to grant or withhold any right of appeal from a territorial court to this Court.[108]

This object will not be achieved unless matters arising under laws of a Territory legislature are regarded as also arising under the Commonwealth law that confers the power on the legislature, so as to be included in s 76(ii) of the Constitution.

---

106 Pages 177-179 above.

107 (1997) 190 CLR 1 at 175.

108 Citations omitted.

Common Law Matters in the Territories

The next question is whether a matter arising under the common law in a Territory is within federal jurisdiction. If the Commonwealth, on accepting a Territory, did not legislate in respect of the law that was immediately to apply to the new Territory, it may be that the common law would operate to apply so much of the law existing before acceptance as was applicable to the new situation, by analogy to the rules relating to the cession of territory. Litigation relating to rights arising under that law could not be said to be matters "arising under any laws made by the Parliament" for the purposes of s 76(ii). They would arise under the common law. But in fact the Commonwealth Parliament has always legislated in the case of each Territory to make statutory provision to apply the law of a State or other Territory or the law previously operating at a particular date, subject to future alteration by legislation. In the case of the Australian Capital Territory, for example, s 6(1) of the *Seat of Government Acceptance Act* 1909 provides:

> (1) Subject to this Act, all laws in force in the Territory immediately before the proclaimed day shall, so far as applicable, continue in force until other provision is made.

Section 4 of the *Seat of Government (Administration) Act* 1910 provides that where a law is continued in force by the above section it shall "have effect in the Territory as if it were a law of the Territory".

In *Federal Capital Commission v Laristan Building and Investment Co Pty Ltd*,[109] Dixon J said in respect of the Australian Capital Territory:

> It may well be that all claims of right arising under the law in force in the Territory come within this description [ie within s 76(ii)] because they arise indirectly as the result of the *Seat of Government Acceptance Act* 1909 (see s 6), and the *Seat of Government (Administration) Act* 1910 (see ss 4 to 7 and s 12).[110]

If Dixon J's reasoning is accepted it is difficult to conceive of any matter that may be tried in a Territorial court, in pursuance of jurisdiction of the sort conferred on Supreme Courts of the Territories, which does not arise under an Act of Parliament. All the common law (including private international law) operating in a Territory has a statutory basis.

In *Kruger v Commonwealth*,[111] Gummow J referred to the quoted passage from *Laristan* and the conclusion stated above, appearing in the second edition of this work, that all the common law in the Territory has a statutory basis. In *Eastman v R*,[112] McHugh J, on the other hand, said that "difficult questions

---

109 (1929) 42 CLR 582.
110 Ibid at 585. This argument was put in *Anderson v Eric Anderson Radio and TV Pty Ltd* (1965) 114 CLR 20. See Kitto J at 29.
111 (1997) 190 CLR 1 at 169.
112 (2000) 172 ALR 39 at 74 n141.

arise as to the nature of an appeal from a Territory court [to the Federal Court] … where the subject matter of the appeal arises under the common law". It was held by Finn J in the Federal Court that a common law defamation action in the Australian Capital Territory arose under a law made by Parliament within the meaning of s 76(ii) of the Constitution and therefore was within the Federal Court's jurisdiction under s 39B of the *Judiciary Act*. He relied on the reasoning of Dixon J in *Laristan* and the remarks of Gummow J in *Kruger* and in the earlier edition of this work.[113]

It might be argued that such a conclusion is inconsistent with the decision in *Western Australia v Commonwealth* (*Native Title Act Case*),[114] where the Court held invalid s 12 of the *Native Title Act* 1993, which provided that:

> Subject to this Act, the common law of Australia in respect of native title has, after 30 June 1993, the force of a law of the Commonwealth.

The reasoning in the case is rather difficult, but s 12 seems to have been held invalid because of the following:

(a) It did not come within the race power in s 51(xxvi) or the external affairs power in s 51(xxix).

(b) It attempted to confer legislative power on the courts, in so far as the common law is understood as the body of law which the courts create and define.

(c) The provision constituted an attempt to convert a judicial function into a legislative function and to do that simply in order to use s 109 of the Constitution to make the common law immune from the operation of a valid State law.

(d) The legislative power of the State, confirmed by s 107 of the Constitution, is necessarily a power to override the common law. If s 12 were valid it would diminish that power.

These arguments are inapplicable to those provisions which apply (or continue) the law of a particular jurisdiction in a Territory, as in the case of the ACT provisions discussed above. The power in s 122 to "make laws for the government of any territory" clearly includes the power to create institutions for its government and to make provision for a legal system, including a body of law. The purpose of such provisions is not to attempt to deprive a State of any of its power referred to in s 107 or to have s 109 apply to that end. Neither the purpose nor effect of such legislation is to convert the power of the judiciary to develop the common law into delegated legislative power, but rather to establish both legislative and judicial power to make and develop law in a manner similar to that which exists in other Australian jurisdictions.

---

113 *O'Neil v Mann* (2000) 175 ALR 742 at 748-749.

114 (1995) 183 CLR 373 at 484-488.

There is, therefore, nothing in the *Native Title Case* which would preclude the conclusion that a matter arising under the common law operating in a Territory also "arises under" the provision made by Parliament to establish a body of law in the Territory.[115]

Gaudron J has provided an alternative ground for the conclusion that all matters for determination by a Territorial court come within s 76(ii) and are, therefore, matters of federal jurisdiction. In *Northern Territory v GPAO*,[116] she referred to a principle formulated by Latham CJ as to when a matter "arises under" a Commonwealth law. He said it does so "if the right or duty in question in the matter owes its existence to Federal law or depends upon Federal law for its enforcement".[117] Gaudron J said that any right or duty in question in a Territorial court must "ultimately depend for its enforcement on the [Commonwealth] law creating that court".

In *Re Governor, Goulburn Correctional Centre; ex parte Eastman*,[118] Gaudron J said that in *GPAO* she had assumed that the Territorial court was created by Parliament. If that was wrong and the court should be regarded as created by the legislature of the ACT (as Gummow and Hayne JJ held) its existence was, nevertheless, ultimately sustained by a law authorised by s 122 of the Constitution. Therefore, the rights and duties at issue in matters before it must ultimately depend for enforcement on the law by which that court was sustained.

If it should be concluded that s 76(ii) cannot sustain jurisdiction in respect of matters arising in a Territory under the common law (or arising under legislation of a self-governing Territory), appeals to the High Court or to another federal court will not be supported by s 73. Such appeals would require legislation under s 122 supported by the decision in *Porter v The King; ex parte Yee*.[119] It is recognised by a number of judges that that case is inconsistent with the principle that Chapter III is exhaustive of the jurisdiction that can be possessed by the High Court or other federal courts.[120] It would be necessary to qualify that general proposition by adding that it applies only to "the federal system", that is the area of the States. That would be inconsistent with the "integration" approach of judges such as Gaudron, Gummow, Hayne and Kirby JJ.

---

115 In *Australian Competition and Consumer Commission v CG Berbatist Holdings Pty Ltd* (2000) 169 ALR 324, French J held valid s 51AA of the *Trade Practices Act* 1974, which prohibited "conduct that is unconscionable within the meaning of the unwritten law, from time to time, of the States and Territories".

116 (1999) 196 CLR 553 at 605.

117 *R v Commonwealth Court of Conciliation and Arbitration; ex parte Barrett* (1945) 70 CLR 141 at 154. See p 66 above.

118 (1999) 200 CLR 322 at 341.

119 (1926) 37 CLR 432; see pp 170-171 above.

120 For example, *Gould v Brown* (1998) 193 CLR 346 at 426 per McHugh J; *Northern Territory v GPAO* (1999) 196 CLR 553.

Nevertheless, if the Court should hold that matters arising under common law in the Territories do not come within Chapter III it is desirable that the Court follow *Porter* to that extent despite the incoherence of principle that results. Otherwise, a broader principle will be permanently impaired, namely, the existence of a common law of Australia under the national superintendence of the High Court.[121] That same principle, however, provides one of the reasons for interpreting such matters in the Territories as "arising under any laws made by the Parliament" in s 76(ii) of the Constitution.[122]

Summary

(1) A court created under s 122 of the Constitution is not governed by s 72. The judges, therefore, do not have to be appointed by the Governor-General nor do the tenure provisions apply to them.[123]

(2) A matter arising under a law made by Parliament in pursuance of s 122 is a matter "arising under any law made by the Parliament" within the meaning of s 76(ii) and jurisdiction may be conferred on a federal court.[124]

(3) It is likely that the jurisdiction possessed by a Territorial court in respect of matters arising under Commonwealth laws authorised by s 122 is federal jurisdiction within the meaning of ss 71 and 73 of the Constitution. The appellate jurisdiction of the High Court under s 73 is, therefore, applicable.[125]

(4) It is uncertain whether (a) matters arising under laws made by the legislature of a self-governing Territory and (b) matters arising under the common law in any Territory come within the scope of s 76(ii). The policy arguments used to support (3), above, namely the unified nature of the legal and judicial system and the establishment of a national common law under the High Court, would require affirmative answers to both these questions.[126]

(5) If it should be concluded by the Court that s 76(ii) of the Constitution cannot sustain, in the Territories, matters arising under common law or the Acts of self-governing Territories, *Porter's Case* should be followed, allowing Parliament under s 122 to authorise an appeal to the High Court or to another federal court.[127]

---

121 *Lange v Australian Broadcasting Corporation* (1997) 189 CLR 520 at 563; *Lipohar v The Queen* (1999) 200 CLR 485 at 505-510; Zines, *The Common Law in Australia; Its Nature and Constitutional Significance*, 1999.

122 *Kruger v Commonwealth* (1997) 190 CLR 1 at 175 per Gummow J.

123 Pages 172-174 above.

124 Pages 177-178 above.

125 Pages 178-179 above.

126 Pages 179-185 above.

127 Pages 185-186 above.

Federal Courts and Original Jurisdiction Not Within Section 76(ii)

On the assumption that some matters in relation to the Territories, such as those arising under the common law, are not included in s 76(ii) of the Constitution, it is necessary to consider whether original jurisdiction in respect of such matters can be given to a federal court (including the High Court) under s 122. In *Porter v The King; ex parte Yee*,[128] the Court was evenly divided on this question.[129]

This was brought about by the fact that Higgins J disagreed with the rest of the majority judges as to the effect of *In re Judiciary and Navigation Acts*.[130] Whereas the other majority judges based their judgments on the ground that Chapter III was not applicable to the Territories, Higgins J distinguished *In re Judiciary and Navigation Acts* by declaring that it was binding only in respect of the original, and not the appellate, jurisdiction of the High Court. He observed that ss 75 and 76 were so drafted as to carry the implication that the matters therein specified were the only matters in which original jurisdiction was or could be conferred on the High Court. Section 73 was differently drafted and simply declared that the Court should have jurisdiction to hear appeals from specified courts. "The form of expression used is 'the High Court shall have jurisdiction' etc, just as if it were 'the High Court shall have a marshall'; this would not forbid other officers appointed under some other power."[131] It was likewise competent to Parliament under s 122 to provide for the grant of additional appellate jurisdiction to the High Court from Territorial courts.

In *Spratt v Hermes*, all the judges agreed that s 13 of the *Australian Capital Territory Supreme Court Act*, providing for a case stated to the High Court, could be read down to refer only to matters within ss 75 and 76 of the Constitution. That was sufficient for the instant case, as it arose under the Constitution. Nevertheless, the judges (assuming that s 13 conferred jurisdiction that went beyond those provisions) expressed their views whether original jurisdiction could be conferred on the High Court under s 122. Barwick CJ, Kitto and Menzies JJ considered such jurisdiction could be conferred. Taylor, Windeyer and Owen JJ took the opposite view. The Court was again evenly divided. In the *Capital TV Case*, Menzies J reiterated his earlier view and Walsh and Gibbs JJ both stated that it might be possible under s 122 to confer original jurisdiction on the High Court or another federal court.

It is difficult to understand why appellate and original jurisdiction should be treated differently. The reasoning of Higgins J in *Porter v The King* is, with

---

128 (1926) 37 CLR 432.

129 Pages 170-171 above.

130 (1921) 29 CLR 257.

131 (1926) 37 CLR 432 at 446.

respect, not very persuasive. It seems that the maxim expressio unius exclusio alterius should apply, if at all, to cases of original jurisdiction and appellate jurisdiction. It might be thought that the clear implication in s 73 is that it exhaustively marks out the appellate jurisdiction of the High Court. Windeyer J, in *Spratt v Hermes*, expressed this view in the following terms:

> The distinction between appellate and original jurisdiction may seem slender if it is based on nothing more than the difference in the language between s 73 and ss 75 and 76; for in each case the language of the grant of jurisdiction in the cases mentioned may seem to carry a negative implication.[132]

(However, he did go on to rely partly on the difference in language, "slight though it is".) The reasoning that was used to support appellate jurisdiction in the High Court was that Chapter III did not apply to the Territories and that the source of constitutional authority was to be discovered in s 122. As a matter of principle, it is difficult to see why that reasoning does not apply equally to original jurisdiction. This was in fact accepted by Barwick CJ, Kitto and Menzies JJ in *Spratt v Hermes*. The reasons given by Taylor, Windeyer and Owen JJ for the opposite view varied. Taylor J relied on "the balance of authority"[133] and thought that view should be accepted. Owen J considered that the justification for the distinction was to be found in Higgins J's judgment in *Porter's Case*.[134] Windeyer J supported the appellate jurisdiction on the basis that "[t]he special position and function of this Court under the Constitution require that it should be able to declare the law for all courts that are within the governance of Australia".[135] However, he did not think that the same considerations applied in the case of original jurisdiction. He referred to the distinction as a "workable anomaly".

If, as suggested above, all matters that come before a Territorial court are within s 76(ii) of the Constitution, the issue of whether additional original jurisdiction may be conferred on the High Court or another federal court is, as Comans says, "largely academic".[136] If, however, the contrary view is taken, the reasoning of Barwick CJ, Kitto and Menzies JJ is more convincing.

The Limits of Jurisdiction of Territorial Courts

If, as suggested above, the High Court should accept that all the jurisdiction which a Territorial court possesses is federal jurisdiction, the only reason why it is necessary to determine whether a court created by a Commonwealth Act is a federal or Territorial court relates to s 72 of the Constitution. If judges of a

---

132 (1965) 114 CLR 226 at 277.
133 Ibid at 265.
134 Ibid at 279.
135 Ibid at 277.
136 "Federal and Territorial Courts" (1974) 4 Federal LR 218 at 226.

court are not appointed in accordance with s 72 they cannot have any juris-diction that does not relate to a Territory.[137]

Although Gaudron J has referred to the limits of jurisdiction under s 122 as being matters "within" a Territory,[138] the more common reference is to occur-rences "in or concerning a Territory".[139] The latter formulation is probably more consistent with *Lamshed v Lake*,[140] which held that a law made under s 122 may validly operate outside the Territory if it has a relevant connection with it. That view was followed in *Attorney-General (WA); ex rel Ansett Transport Industries (Operations) Pty Ltd v Australian National Airlines Commission*.[141]

In a number of Acts operating throughout the Commonwealth, the juris-diction of Territorial courts is limited so as to provide an adequate nexus with the Territory. In the *Patents Act* 1990, s 155, and the *Trade Marks Act* 1995, s 192, for example, jurisdiction is conferred on the Supreme Courts of specified Territories in respect of certain proceedings "to the extent that the Constitution permits". In other cases, the jurisdiction is limited to proceedings initiated by a natural person resident in the Territory or a corporation that has its principal place of business there. Similarly, under the *Admiralty Act* 1988, where a Territorial court has jurisdiction conferred on it, the jurisdiction, in the case of an action in rem, is "only so far as the Constitution permits and within the limits of the jurisdiction of that court as to the amount claimed as to *locality* and as to remedies but not otherwise".[142] This is in contrast with the jurisdiction vested in a State court where the reference to locality is omitted. The power in s 77(iii) enables Parliament to vest jurisdiction in State courts without regard to State jurisdictional limitations. In the case of Territorial courts, however, the provision conferring jurisdiction must be one "for the government of a Territory" within the meaning of s 122.

By contrast with these provisions the *Judiciary Act*, s 68(5), confers juris-diction on a court of a State or Territory in relation to summary proceedings "notwithstanding any limits as to locality of the jurisdiction of the courts under the law of that State or Territory". Subsection (5C) confers jurisdiction on those courts in respect of committal, trial and conviction on indictment, where the offences are committed outside the State or Territory (including in over or under any area of the seas). This jurisdiction is conferred notwith-standing any limits as to locality of the courts' jurisdiction under State or Territory law.

---

137 *Re Governor, Goulburn Corrective Centre; ex parte Eastman* (1999) 200 CLR 322 at 338-339 per Gaudron J.
138 Ibid.
139 For example, *Spratt v Hermes* (1965) 114 CLR 226 at 242 per Barwick J; *Eastman* (1999) 200 CLR 322 at 349 per Gummow and Hayne JJ.
140 (1958) 99 CLR 132.
141 (1976) 138 CLR 492.
142 See s 39(1).

Unless provisions such as these can be "read down" under s 15A or
s 15C(c) of the *Acts Interpretation Act* they do not seem to be sufficiently
related to the government of the Territory. As a variety of connections with
the Territory would probably satisfy s 122 of the Constitution it is not clear
how such provisions should be read down.[143] In any case the express language
of s 68(5) seems to preclude it so far as locality is concerned.

Jurisdiction Relating to Service of Process

Under general law, the jurisdiction of a court in relation to actions in personam does not depend on the subject-matter but upon the amenability of the
defendant to the writ of the court. Under common law, the writ does not run
beyond the limits of the territorial jurisdiction of the court.[144] The jurisdiction
of the Supreme Court of a State, therefore, extends to all cases (unless
excepted by the Constitution or a valid Commonwealth or State Act) where a
defendant is present in the State, whatever the subject-matter of the suit. In the
light of *Spratt v Hermes* and the *Capital TV Case*, there is, subject to one
qualification mentioned below, little doubt that a similar jurisdiction conferred
on a Territorial court in relation to a Territory is within power conferred by
s 122 of the Constitution. Section 11(a) of the *Australian Capital Territory
Supreme Court Act* 1933 conferred on that Court in relation to the Australian
Capital Territory "the same original jurisdiction ... as the Supreme Court of
the State of New South Wales had in relation to that State immediately before
the first of January 1911". In the *Capital TV Case*, all the judges considered
that this conferral of jurisdiction was valid under s 122.

In principle, there is no justification for treating the jurisdiction of Territorial courts in this respect in a manner different from State courts. If laws
providing for the jurisdiction of State courts are for "the peace, order and good
government" of the State, a law providing for a similar jurisdiction in relation
to a Territory must be for "the government of the Territory". Difficult issues,
however, arise because, while the authority of a State only operates throughout the area of the State, it is the Commonwealth that is the "sovereign" in
relation to a Territory and a law for the government of a Territory "operates as
a binding law of the Commonwealth wherever territorially the authority of the
Commonwealth runs".[145]

In *Cotter v Workman*,[146] Fox J, in the Supreme Court of the Australian
Capital Territory, considered the validity and effect of a rule of court which
provided that writs issued out of the Court might be served anywhere in the
Commonwealth without leave. It had been previously held by Gibbs J in *Cope*

143 Compare *Pidoto v Victoria* (1943) 68 CLR 87.
144 *Laurie v Carroll* (1958) 98 CLR 310.
145 *Lamshed v Lake* (1958) 99 CLR 132 at 141.
146 (1972) 20 FLR 318.

Allman (Australia) Ltd v Celermajer[147] that, as a result of these provisions, the Court had jurisdiction if the writ had been served on the defendant anywhere in the Commonwealth, even though the only connection with the Australian Capital Territory in that case was that a deed, out of which an action arose, was executed in Canberra. His Honour did not regard even that slight connection with the Territory as material. Fox J held that the extension of the jurisdiction of the Court which followed from the provision for service was invalid as not authorised by s 122 as it purported to give jurisdiction where there was not a sufficient connection with s 122.

Mr Comans has suggested[148] that the provisions for service outside the Territory without any other connection with the Territory might be valid if the court's order was not enforceable outside the Territory. It is in this way that State provisions for service outside the jurisdiction are upheld. The jurisdiction is referred to as "assumed jurisdiction" and the orders given under that jurisdiction are not enforceable outside the State. It was similarly argued in *Cotter v Workman* that the rules for service throughout the Commonwealth were valid, but the order was enforceable only in the Australian Capital Territory. Fox J held that, in the light of the *State and Territorial Laws and Records Recognition Act* 1901 and Part IV of the *Service and Execution of Process Act* 1901, it was unlikely that any such result was intended. He went further, however, and said that in any case "a legislative power which is limited by reference to territorial considerations cannot be the source of an assumed jurisdiction which does not satisfy those territorial limitations". It is suggested that the considerations involved in the case of a State and a Territory are in this respect identical. In each case, there must be a sufficient connection with the State or Territory concerned. If the "assumed jurisdiction" is valid in the case of a State court – and it would appear that it is[149] – then it is valid in the case of a Territorial court. As Barwick CJ said in *Attorney-General (WA) v Australian National Airlines Commission*, "the test of the validity of such a law [that is, one made under s 122] must be whether the law is a law for the peace, order and good government of the Territory – treating the word 'for' in s 122 as implying the concepts expressed in that traditional formula".[150]

Problems have arisen regarding the "personal" or "service" jurisdiction of the Territorial courts, in the light of the *Service and Execution of Process Act* 1992. That Act provides for the service of the process of a court of a State or Territory upon a person in another State or Territory. The service of the process has the same effect as if it had been served at the place of issue (s 12). The effect of the Act, therefore, is to extend the territorial jurisdiction of each

147 (1968) 11 FLR 488.

148 Comans, "Federal and Territorial Courts" (1971) 4 Federal LR 218 at 228-229.

149 *Ashbury v Ellis* [1893] AC 339.

150 (1976) 138 CLR 492 at 500.

court into every other State or Territory.[151] Provision is made for the enforcement of the orders of the court made pursuant to the Act throughout the
Commonwealth. The judgments can be enforced notwithstanding any rules of
private international law.

In respect of the process and judgments of State courts, the provisions of
the Act are authorised by s 51(xxiv) of the Constitution: "The service and
execution throughout the Commonwealth of the civil and criminal process and
the judgments of the courts of the States." However, the provisions in respect
of Territorial process and judgments must depend upon s 122 of the Constitution. While *Lamshed v Lake* established that a law made under the power
may operate in the States, it is, of course, essential that it can be characterised
as a law "for the government of a territory". The only connection that the
relevant provisions of the Act have with a Territory is that it is the place of
issue of a writ, summons or other legal process. This renders the validity of
those provisions doubtful. The Law Reform Commission, which made recommendations relating to service and execution of process, recognised this
problem and had proposed that there be a provision to the effect that the
jurisdiction conferred on a Territory court, by virtue of service of process
under the Act, is to be no greater than could be validly conferred under the
Constitution.[152] The draftsman may have been relying on s 15C(c) of the *Acts
Interpretation Act* which limits the jurisdiction of a Territorial court in that
manner where an Act authorises a proceeding to be instituted in a "particular
court". Query whether it is applicable to an Act which deals with all courts.

Conclusion

In 1978 in the second edition of this book, it was said that the baroque
complexities and many uncertainties associated with courts and jurisdiction in
the Territories have come about partly as a result of conflicting theories and
partly by a desire of the judges not to disturb earlier decisions. The general
approach in *R v Bernasconi*, with its emphasis on the separation of the Territories from the Commonwealth and of s 122 from the rest of the Constitution,
is fundamentally opposed to the approach of *Lamshed v Lake*, which attacked
this theory and underlined the fact that there is but one Commonwealth and
that s 122 was meaningless unless read with other provisions of the Constitution. These propositions were quoted by Gummow and Hayne JJ in *Re
Wakim; ex parte McNally*[153] with approval and as reflecting the continuing
situation in 1999.

---

151 The Act has no effect on jurisdiction that is limited by subject-matter or amount. For an
analysis of these different forms of jurisdiction, see *David Syme v Grey* (1992) 115 ALR
247 at 256ff.

152 Australian Law Reform Commission, Report no 40, *Service and Execution of Process*,
1987, pp 95-96, para 197.

153 (1999) 198 CLR 511 at 594-595.

In the past few years, judges have adopted opposing positions based on these different approaches, as High Court judges had done for decades. All the present Court, with the exception of Kirby J, have followed *Bernasconi* to the extent that it has been firmly decided that Territorial courts are not federal courts within s 71 and that s 72, relating to appointment and tenure, is not applicable to the judges of those courts. Otherwise, however, there is a tendency by most of the present Court to construe s 122 in the context of the Constitution as a whole, including Chapter III, rather than as a disparate power. The emphasis given in *Kable v Director of Public Prosecutions (NSW)*[154] to an "integrated" system of courts, and in that and other cases to a national common law, support that approach. Whether those ends can be achieved in respect of the Territories depends on whether all the jurisdiction of Territorial courts can be regarded as coming within s 76(ii) of the Constitution. It has been argued that that is the preferable interpretation.

---

154 (1996) 189 CLR 51.

Chapter 5

The Autochthonous Expedient:

The Investment of State Courts with Federal Jurisdiction

Section 77(iii) of the Constitution

Section 71 of the Constitution vests the judicial power of the Commonwealth in the High Court, in such other federal courts as the Parliament creates, and in such other courts as it invests with federal jurisdiction. Although the section does not specifically name State courts as repositories of federal jurisdiction, the orthodox view was that the only alternatives open to the Parliament were to create federal courts or to invest State courts with federal jurisdiction. Griffiths CJ said in the *Inter-State Commission Case*,[1] "the provisions of s 71 are complete and exclusive and there cannot be a third class of courts which are neither Federal courts nor State courts invested with Federal jurisdiction". (As discussed in Chapter 4, however, a number of judges now take the view that federal jurisdiction may also be vested in Territorial courts under s 122.[2]) Section 77, as we have seen, in para (i) authorises the legislative definition of the jurisdiction of any federal court other than the High Court. Section 77(ii) provides for the definition of the extent to which the jurisdiction of any federal court shall be exclusive of that which belongs to or is invested in State courts, while s 77(iii) authorises the investment of any court of a State with federal jurisdiction.

The use of State courts as repositories of federal jurisdiction was described by the High Court as an "autochthonous expedient",[3] as indigenous or native to the soil. It has no counterpart in the American Constitution.

In the United States, Congress has on many occasions vested concurrently the enforcement of federal rights in State and federal courts. The Supreme Court of the United States has upheld the obligation of the State courts to enforce those rights where they are courts of general jurisdiction or their

---

1   *New South Wales v Commonwealth* (1915) 20 CLR 54 at 62.
2   Pages 177-186 above.
3   *Boilermakers' Case* (1956) 94 CLR 254 at 268.

jurisdiction is otherwise adequate under State law.[4] That does not mean, however, that the State courts exercise federal jurisdiction in the sense that that expression is used in s 77(iii) of the Commonwealth Constitution nor does it enable Congress to legislate in the manner that the Commonwealth Parliament has done in, for example, s 39 of the *Judiciary Act*.[5]

We have seen[6] that in the American Constitutional Convention arguments were advanced in favour of employing State courts as courts of *general* original jurisdiction, so as to avoid any necessity for the creation of inferior federal courts, but that these arguments failed to carry.

That a different view should have prevailed in Australia is not surprising. There was no comparable apprehension of the dangers that lurked in a federal court structure and the most ardent Australian admirers of the American judicature accepted a modification of that system whereby the High Court was fashioned as a general court of appeal. The device of investing State courts with federal jurisdiction was economical; as Bailey observed, "the burden which such a system (that is, the creation of a hierarchy of federal tribunals) would have imposed on the small population of Australia gave rise to the expedient adopted in s 77(iii), of authorising the Commonwealth Parliament to make use for federal purposes of the existing judicial organisation of the States, just as the Imperial Parliament made use of it for Admiralty purposes".[7] Economy alone does not explain the departure from American precedent, for the United States was small in population and resources in 1787; but the desire for economy linked to a more willing acceptance of a unified judicial system furnishes an adequate explanation. This is underlined by the comments of Quick and Garran in 1901.[8] The large original and potentially original jurisdiction of the High Court, marked out in ss 75 and 76 of the Constitution, can most sensibly be explained on the assumption that the founding fathers believed that the High Court would in all probability be the only general federal court. It is difficult otherwise to account for the translation of what in the American Constitution are matters of federal jurisdiction, though not for the most part matters within the original jurisdiction of the Supreme Court of the United States, into matters of original jurisdiction, actual or potential, of the High Court of Australia.[9]

---

4   Small and Jayson (eds), *Constitution of the United States of America: Analysis and Interpretation*, 1964, pp 725-727; Fallon, Meltzer and Shapiro, *Hart and Wechsler's The Federal Courts and the Federal System*, 4th edn, 1996, pp 469-491.

5   *Felton v Mulligan* (1971) 124 CLR 367 at 393-394.

6   See p 107 above.

7   "The Federal Jurisdiction of State Courts" (1940) 2 Res Judicatae 109. See also *Commonwealth v Limerick Steamship Co Ltd, Commonwealth v Kidman* (1924) 35 CLR 69 at 90 per Isaacs and Rich JJ where the power conferred by s 77(iii) is said to be "obviously a very convenient means of avoiding the multiplicity and expense of legal tribunals".

8   *The Annotated Constitution of the Australian Commonwealth*, 1901, p 804.

9   See p 3 above.

There is a change of language from s 77(i) to s 77(iii) of the Constitution. The Parliament may *define* the jurisdiction of federal courts, while it may *invest* State courts with federal jurisdiction. There is a possible argument that "definition" has a broader sweep than "investment", in the sense that the exercise of the power to define carries with it power to regulate the structure of appeals, whereas investment suggests rather that the State courts must be taken as they are found, leaving the system of appeals to be regulated by State law. This is a matter of practical importance, because s 39 of the *Judiciary Act*, which is the most general exercise of the powers conferred by s 77(iii), purports to regulate the system of appeals from State courts invested with federal jurisdiction. This, and other problems arising from s 39 of the *Judiciary Act*, will be considered more fully later, but it is clear on the authorities that there is no significance in the change of language from s 77(i) to s 77(iii).[10] The federal jurisdiction which may be conferred on federal courts and on State courts also includes original and appellate jurisdiction, even though the subject-matters of such a grant must be within the nine matters of original or potential original jurisdiction of the High Court.[11]

Non-Federal Jurisdiction in respect of Matters in Sections 75 and 76

Apart from any investment of State courts with federal jurisdiction, it is clear that the State courts already possessed jurisdiction in respect of a number of matters within ss 75 and 76. For example, the State courts had jurisdiction in matters between residents of different States; if the rules of service were satisfied, it was within the normal competence of a State court to try a case involving a Victorian plaintiff and a New South Wales defendant. The operation of the Commonwealth Constitution intruded a new element, and s 5 of the *Constitution Act* provided that the Constitution and all laws made by the Parliament under the Constitution should be binding on the courts, judges and people of every State and every part of the Commonwealth notwith-standing anything in the laws of any State. This meant that, apart from any special enactment, a State court would have jurisdiction in a matter arising under the Constitution or involving its interpretation, in matters arising under laws made by the Parliament, and that the Commonwealth might come into the State courts as a plaintiff – all without any necessity for a grant of federal jurisdiction. The fact that a State court assumes jurisdiction on service under the *Service and Execution of Process Act* 1992, a Commonwealth statute,

---

10   *Lorenzo v Carey* (1921) 29 CLR 243; *Commonwealth v Limerick Steamship Co Ltd* (1924) 35 CLR 69 at 89-93, 115-116; *Commonwealth v Bardsley* (1926) 37 CLR 393 at 407-409. See Bailey, op cit p 184.

11   *Ah Yick v Lehmert* (1905) 2 CLR 593. See pp 130-131 above.

does not mean that it is therefore exercising *federal* jurisdiction[12] and it is a misunderstanding of the notion of federal jurisdiction to describe the process by which a State court gives effect to rights arising under federal statutes in terms that "when such rights are adjudicated upon, it is, in a sense, Federal jurisdiction which is being exercised".[13] The confusion arises from an identification of federal jurisdiction with the application of federal law; it is clear that what determines whether there is an exercise of federal jurisdiction by a State court is the source of the *grant* of jurisdiction, not the source of the *law* being applied. "To confer federal jurisdiction in a class of matters upon a State court is therefore not, if no more be added, to change the law which the court is to enforce in adjudicating upon such matters; it is merely to provide a different basis of authority to enforce the same law."[14]

It was held, however, that there were matters, attendant upon the establishment of the Commonwealth, which State courts were not competent to entertain in the absence of an express grant of jurisdiction. In its State jurisdiction, a State court could not assume jurisdiction in a matter in which the Commonwealth was a defendant[15] and in *Ex parte Goldring*[16] it was held that the State court had no power to issue mandamus or other order to command or prohibit a federal officer in the absence of any affirmative grant of jurisdiction by the Commonwealth Parliament. Within the framework of the Commonwealth Constitution, this means that any such grant must depend on an investment of federal jurisdiction pursuant to s 77(iii). There is a qualified investment of federal jurisdiction in State courts in matters in which the Commonwealth is a defendant, by ss 39 and 56 of the *Judiciary Act*, and these provisions are the federal source of the jurisdiction of State courts in such matters.

Section 38 of the *Judiciary Act* defines the jurisdiction of the High Court to issue prohibition and mandamus against an officer of the Commonwealth as exclusive of that of the State courts. While s 44(2) authorises the High Court to remit most matters in s 38 to State courts and sub-s (3) confers jurisdiction in respect of remitted matters, that does not include s 38(e), namely matters in which a writ of mandamus or prohibition is sought against an officer of the Commonwealth or a federal court. Section 9(1) of the *Administrative Decisions (Judicial Review) Act* 1977 provides:

---

12 See *A Patkin and Co Pty Ltd v Censor and Hyman* [1949] ALR 557; *Alba Petroleum Co of Australia Pty Ltd v Griffiths* [1951] VLR 185; *Flaherty v Girgis* (1987) 162 CLR 574 at 597-598.

13 *Ex parte Australian Timber Workers' Union; Veneer Co Ltd* (1937) 37 SR (NSW) 52 per Jordan CJ.

14 *Anderson v Eric Anderson Radio & TV Pty Ltd* (1965) 114 CLR 20 at 30.

15 *Commonwealth v Limerick Steamship Co Ltd* (1924) 35 CLR 69; *Commonwealth v Bardsley* (1926) 37 CLR 393 at 405; Moore, *Commonwealth of Australia*, 2nd edn, 1910, pp 212-213; Bailey, op cit p 111.

16 (1903) 3 SR (NSW) 260.

9(1) Notwithstanding anything contained in any Act other than this Act, a court of a State does not have jurisdiction to review:

    (a) a decision to which this section applies that is made after the commencement of this Act;

    (b) conduct that has been, is being, or is proposed to be, engaged in for the purpose of making a decision to which this section applies; or

    (c) a failure to make a decision to which this section applies; or

    (d) any other decision given, or any order made, by an officer of the Commonwealth or any other conduct that has been, is being, or is proposed to be, engaged in by an officer of the Commonwealth, including a decision, order or conduct given, made or engaged in, as the case may be, in the exercise of judicial power.

Subsection (2) defines "review" to mean review by way of (a) the grant of an injunction; (b) the grant of a prerogative or statutory writ (other than a writ of habeas corpus) or the making of orders of the same nature or effect; or (c) the making of a declaratory order.

With one exception it seems that, apart from habeas corpus, State courts have no jurisdiction to issue any of the remedies mentioned in relation to administrative or judicial action by Commonwealth officers or judges. The exception is by virtue of an amendment made to s 39B of the *Judiciary Act* in 2000, by adding sub-ss (1B) to (1E) and (3). These provisions give jurisdiction to the Supreme Court of the States and Territories in respect of mandamus, prohibition and injunction against officers of the Commonwealth in respect of decisions relating to the prosecution of offences and matters related thereto such as committal, the issue of warrants, investigation, summoning witnesses and so on.[17]

State Courts and "The Federal Judicature"

A question arises as to the "character" of State courts invested with federal jurisdiction. Sections 71 and 77 draw a definite distinction between federal courts and courts invested with federal jurisdiction. It is clear, therefore, that federally invested State courts cannot properly be described as federal courts within the Australian constitutional framework. The answer to the further question whether State courts invested with federal jurisdiction are to be regarded as part of the "Federal Judicature" is less certain. As Wynes pointed out,[18] the answer is of more than academic interest, as it may affect the exercise of Commonwealth legislative power under s 51(xxxix), which authorises the making of laws with respect to matters incidental to the execution of any power vested by the Constitution in the Parliament, the executive government

---

17   The operation of these provisions is examined in *Phong v Attorney-General (Cth)* (2001) 185 ALR 753. The Supreme Courts of the States also have jurisdiction in chambers in any matter pending in the Federal Court: s 32A of the *Federal Court of Australia Act* 1976.

18   *Legislative, Executive and Judicial Powers in Australia*, 5th edn, 1976, pp 495-497.

or *in the Federal Judicature* or in any department or officer of the Common-wealth. A conclusion that State courts invested with federal jurisdiction are not part of the federal judicature does not altogether deny the operation of s 51(xxxix), for that power may and, as the cases establish, does operate upon the exercise of the legislative power which s 77(iii) itself confers. The cases yield no clear indication of the character of State courts invested with federal jurisdiction.

In *R v Murray and Cormie*,[19] Isaacs J observed that the Constitution draws the clearest distinction between federal and State courts and that, while it enables the Parliament to utilise the judicial services of State courts, it recognises in "the most pronounced and unequivocal way that they remain State courts". But in *Le Mesurier v Connor*,[20] Isaacs J, dissenting, spoke of State courts invested with federal jurisdiction as "pro hac vice, a component part of the Federal Judicature". In that case, the majority, Knox CJ, Rich and Dixon JJ, appeared to prefer the earlier view expressed by Isaacs J in *R v Murray and Cormie*. In *Lorenzo v Carey*,[21] the High Court described a court exercising federal jurisdiction as "the judicial agent of the Common-wealth", while Starke J in *Commonwealth v Limerick Steamship Co Ltd*[22] spoke of State courts invested with federal jurisdiction as "substitute tribunals". Of the writers, Wynes argued that the language of Chapter III and the general scheme of the Constitution supported the view that such courts remained State courts and should not be regarded as part of the federal judicature.[23] Bailey, to the contrary, was of opinion that the Constitution "appears to treat a State court exercising federal jurisdiction as part of the federal judicature",[24] though he did not specifically relate the discussion to s 51(xxxix). Lane's view is that "Federal Judicature" in s 51(xxxix) probably relates to "the Judicature" for which provision is made in Chapter III, including s 77(iii) State courts.[25]

Apart from s 51(xxxix), the matter is of little importance, for the term "Federal Judicature" appears only in that paragraph and is not mentioned in Chapter III, which is headed "The Judicature". It is believed that the better view is that State courts invested with federal jurisdiction are to be regarded as part of the federal judicature for the purposes of s 51(xxxix). There is no clear warrant for regarding the federal courts and the federal judicature as coterminous; it would seem to be a better reading of the Constitution to regard all repositories of the judicial power of the Commonwealth as part of the

---

19   (1916) 22 CLR 437 at 452.

20   (1929) 42 CLR 481 at 514.

21   (1921) 29 CLR 243 at 252.

22   (1924) 35 CLR 69 at 116.

23   Op cit pp 496-497.

24   Op cit pp 101-110.

25   *Lane's Commentary on the Australian Constitution*, 2nd edn, 1997, p 373.

system of federal judicature,[26] and there is no necessary inconsistency between the views expressed by Isaacs J in *R v Murray and Cormie* and in *Le Mesurier v Connor*. State courts invested with federal jurisdiction remain State courts, but, while acting in this capacity, are properly regarded as a component part of the federal judicature. This conclusion is confirmed by the reasoning of a number of judges in *Kable v Director of Public Prosecutions (NSW)*[27] that all the courts referred to in s 71 of the Constitution, in which is vested the judicial power of the Commonwealth, including State courts invested with federal jurisdiction, are parts of an integrated judicial system.[28]

Limits on Investing Power

The limits of the power to invest State courts with federal jurisdiction are pre-scribed by s 77, so that a grant will be invalid unless it is with respect to a matter enumerated in ss 75 and 76. In *Hooper v Hooper*,[29] a question arose whether the investment of State Supreme Courts with jurisdiction in matri-monial causes by the *Matrimonial Causes Act* 1945 was within power and it was argued that this was a bare grant of jurisdiction not referable to any of the heads of ss 75 and 76. The High Court rejected the argument and pointed out that the grant of jurisdiction had to be read together with the choice of law rule in that statute directing the application of the lex domicilii; that the Act was to be construed as giving the force of federal law to the State laws, so that Parliament had effectively exercised its powers under ss 51(xxii) and 77(iii) and that the grant of jurisdiction was, therefore, referable to s 76(ii) of the Constitution.

There is a further broad constitutional restraint on the exercise of Com-monwealth legislative power with respect to State courts. As Latham CJ observed in *Federal Council of British Medical Association in Australia v Commonwealth*,[30] it is only by virtue of ss 71 and 77(iii) that the Common-wealth Parliament can invest a State court with jurisdiction so that the court becomes bound to exercise it. There is no constitutional provision under which the Parliament may require State courts to exercise any form of non-judicial power. So, in *Queen Victoria Memorial Hospital v Thornton*,[31] it was held that the provisions of the *Re-establishment and Employment Act* 1945, which purported to invest State courts with a very broad discretionary jurisdiction to determine questions of preference as between candidates for

---

26 *Commonwealth v Limerick Steamship Co Ltd* (1924) 35 CLR 69 at 105 per Isaacs and Rich JJ.

27 (1996) 189 CLR 51.

28 See pp 244-246 below.

29 (1955) 91 CLR 529.

30 (1949) 79 CLR 201 at 236.

31 (1953) 87 CLR 144.

employment, were unconstitutional, since they purported to invest State courts with non-judicial power. It was observed:

> It would be strange indeed if the Constitution contained a grant of legislative power which would enable the Parliament to require or to authorise State courts as such to exercise duties, functions or powers which were not judicial.[32]

The only source of legislative power to affect State courts outside Chapter III is s 51(xxxix) which apparently confers legislative power in respect of matters incidental to the exercise of jurisdiction invested in State courts. It appears, therefore, that no power other than judicial power, and authority strictly incidental thereto, may be lawfully conferred by the Parliament on State courts.[33] Any attempt to authorise State courts to exercise non-judicial functions or duties (at any rate in the absence of the legislative consent of the State) would in any case be contrary to implied restrictions on Commonwealth power based on the federal nature of the Constitution,[34] as either discriminating against the States or their institutions or interfering with the State's capacity to function as an independent unit of the federation.[35] The express provision of s 77(iii) overcomes this implication in respect of the investment of federal judicial power (but not non-judicial power) in State courts.

Delegation of Investing Power

As s 77(iii) is the exclusive source of power to invest State courts with federal jurisdiction, it must be clear that any investment derives from that source. In *Peacock v Newtown, Marrickville and General Co-operative Building Society No 4 Ltd*,[36] the purported investment of federal jurisdiction in State courts under the *National Security (Contracts Adjustment) Regulations* was held bad on the ground that the regulation-making power under the *National Security Act*, which in very broad terms authorised the making of regulations for defence purposes, did not expressly authorise the making of regulations for the purpose of investing State courts with federal jurisdiction. As it then stood, the *National Security Act* rested on s 51 and it may be on s 122 of the Constitution, and it could not, therefore, be regarded as authorising the making of regulations for the investment of State courts with federal jurisdiction, which must depend on Chapter Ill.

---

32 Ibid at 152.
33 *Insurance Commissioner v Associated Dominions Assurance Society Pty Ltd* (1953) 89 CLR 78 at 85 per Fullagar J.
34 *Queensland Electricity Commission v Commonwealth* (1985) 159 CLR 192; *Re Education Union; ex parte Victoria* (1995) 184 CLR 188.
35 Zines, *The High Court and the Constitution*, 4th edn, 1997, pp 328-336.
36 (1943) 67 CLR 25.

The *National Security Act* was consequently amended in 1943 specifically to authorise the investment of judicial power by regulation. This raised the further question whether the power conferred by s 77(iii) may be exercised in this way. The validity of the 1943 amendment was not judicially tested,[37] but there have been conflicting expressions of opinion in the High Court on the matter. In *Le Mesurier v Connor*,[38] the High Court discussed the question whether s 18(1)(b) of the *Bankruptcy Act* 1924, which provided that the courts having jurisdiction in bankruptcy should be such State courts as were specially authorised by the Governor-General by proclamation to exercise that jurisdiction, was a law investing State courts with federal jurisdiction within s 77(iii). The majority, Knox CJ, Rich and Dixon JJ, after observing that it was not necessary for the purposes of the case to decide the question, expressed the view that the power conferred by s 77(iii) "requires that the law made by the Parliament should not only define the jurisdiction to be invested but also identify the State Court in which the jurisdiction is thereby invested. The power is to make laws 'investing', not, as in s 51, 'with respect to' a subject-matter".[39] For this reason it was not a case in which the Parliament, which was constituted to exercise plenary legislative power, could, under the doctrine of such cases as *Hodge v The Queen*,[40] *R v Burah*[41] and *Powell v Apollo Candle Co*,[42] delegate its powers in this way. Isaacs and Starke JJ dissented on the broad ground that it was settled practice that the legislature could delegate its authority; as Starke J said: "The jurisdiction in the State Court is invested by the authority of the Act under which the proclamation was issued. Since the decision of the Judicial Committee in *Powell v Apollo Candle Co*, the position seems to me clear and beyond doubt."[43]

In *Peacock's Case*,[44] three members of the High Court made a further offering of dicta on the subject. Latham CJ said that the view of the majority in *Le Mesurier v Connor*, if valid, applied only to an executive act, such as a proclamation, but would not apply to a regulation, legislative in character. Starke J reaffirmed his position in *Le Mesurier v Connor* and said that a denial of power to invest by regulation was "plainly contrary"[45] to authority.

---

37 It was raised in argument in *R v Ray; ex parte Smith* [1948] SASR 216, but the Court did not expressly deal with it. The regulation was, however, held valid. It was also referred to in *Ex parte Coorey* (1945) 45 SR (NSW) 287 at 302, where Jordan CJ expressed his pleasure in not having to decide the point. See also Sawer, *Australian Constitutional Cases*, 3rd edn, 1964, p 658.

38 (1929) 42 CLR 481.

39 Ibid at 500.

40 (1883) 9 App Cas 117.

41 (1878) 3 App Cas 889.

42 (1885) 10 App Cas 282.

43 (1929) 42 CLR 481 at 521.

44 (1943) 67 CLR 25.

45 Ibid at 44.

Williams J did not express a definite opinion, but said that he might feel obliged on grounds of principle and authority to follow the majority in *Le Mesurier v Connor*. He doubted the validity of the distinction between "executive" and "legislative" regulations which, he said, was "a fine one"[46] and suggested difficulties which might arise if the power of investment of State courts with federal jurisdiction and, by parity of reasoning, the power to define the jurisdiction of federal courts, were exercisable by delegated authority.

Certainly no clear statement of the law emerges from these dicta. In *Ex parte Coorey*,[47] Jordan CJ referred to the division in the High Court and declined to make any further contribution. It is perhaps surprising that the validity of the *National Security Act* amendment of 1943 was not directly challenged in the High Court though the argument was put to the Supreme Court of South Australia in *R v Ray; ex parte Smith*,[48] where it was virtually ignored by the Court, which upheld the validity of the investment of the local court under the *National Security (Landlord and Tenant) Regulations*.

In *Willocks v Anderson*,[49] the High Court was faced with regulations made under the *Apple and Pear Organisation Act* 1948, which purported to confer jurisdiction on the High Court. Although the constitutional provision involved was s 76(ii), the cases referred to above were discussed and a joint judgment of six members of the Court appeared to regard the question whether Parliament could delegate under ss 76 and 77 as involving the same issue. They expressly did not decide the question as they held that the Act did not authorise the making of the regulations conferring jurisdiction on the Court.

The question turns on the significance of the change of language from laws "with respect to" in s 51, to laws "investing" in s 77(iii). Distinctions drawn between regulations of "executive" and of "legislative" character are not persuasive, and raise some doubtful questions of law, and the practical arguments in favour of direct legislative investment by Williams J in *Peacock's Case*,[50] while perhaps stronger, are not compelling. On a strictly grammatical reading, it is not easy to construe a law as *investing* jurisdiction unless a court can immediately be identified as the repository of the jurisdiction, but the broader arguments in favour of construing the grant of power

---

46 Ibid at 51.
47 (1945) 45 SR (NSW) 287 at 302.
48 [1948] SASR 216.
49 (1971) 124 CLR 293.
50 (1943) 67 CLR 25 at 51. Williams J said that, if federal jurisdiction could be invested in State courts by regulation, the definition of federal jurisdiction under s 77(i) could, by parity of reasoning, be effected by regulation. Such regulations are subject to disallowance by either House of Parliament under s 48 of the *Acts Interpretation Act*. This would mean that a federal court with judges appointed for life might be created by regulation, that could be subsequently disallowed with unfortunate practical consequences.

so as to permit Parliament to provide for the investment of State courts by regulation are practical and strong. As Sir Owen Dixon has written in the context of the *general* power of Parliament to delegate: "it seemed unbelievable that the executive should be forbidden to carry on the practice of legislation by regulation – the most conspicuous legal activity of a modern government"[51] and it was on this broad basis that Isaacs and Starke JJ strongly and dogmatically supported the view that Parliament might delegate its power under s 77(iii). It is submitted that this is the preferable view.

In any case, it has never been suggested that Parliament could not delegate its power in s 96 of the Constitution to "grant financial assistance to any State on such terms and conditions as the Parliament thinks fit", despite the absence in that provision of the phrase "with respect to". The Court has upheld legislation authorising a Minister to fix the terms and conditions.[52]

The Organisation of Courts : Court Officers

Leaving aside issues related to Territorial courts, we have seen that the Constitution provides for the vesting of the judicial power of the Commonwealth exclusively in federal courts and in State courts invested with federal jurisdiction. The Parliament may not avoid compliance with the constitutional requirements for the establishment of federal courts, prescribed by s 72, by remaking or reconstituting a State court whose judges, under State law, need not necessarily have the tenure prescribed by s 72 of the Constitution.[53] Section 79 of the Constitution authorises a specific measure of interference with State courts by providing that the federal jurisdiction of any court may be exercised by such numbers of judges as the Parliament prescribes.[54] Beyond this, the limits of permissible interference with State courts exercising federal jurisdiction are spelled out in the cases. It was stated early in the High Court that "when the Federal Parliament confers a new jurisdiction upon an existing State Court it takes the Court as it finds it, with all its limitations as to jurisdiction unless otherwise expressly declared".[55] There are also repeated

---

51 "The Law and The Constitution" (1935) 51 Law Quarterly R at 606. It may well be that this comment was directed only to powers to legislate "with respect to" a particular matter and was not intended to apply beyond that.

52 *Deputy Federal Commissioner of Taxation (NSW) v WR Moran Pty Ltd* (1939) 61 CLR 735 at 763. See Lane, *Lane's Commentary on the Australian Constitution*, 2nd edn, 1997, pp 634-635, and the delegation in the legislation considered in *Attorney-General (Vic); ex rel Black v Commonwealth* (1981) 146 CLR 559, which is set out at 636-643. The question of delegation was not argued.

53 *Adams v Chas S Watson Pty Ltd* (1938) 60 CLR 545 at 554-555; *Peacock's Case* (1943) 67 CLR 25 at 37.

54 An unresolved question is whether Parliament can prescribe a number *above* that prescribed by State law. See *Harris v Caladine* (1991) 172 CLR 84 at 93-94, 121.

55 *Federated Sawmill etc Association (Adelaide Branch) v Alexander* (1912) 15 CLR 308 at 313 per Griffith CJ.

statements in the cases that the Parliament in the exercise of its powers under ss 77(iii) and 51(xxxix) may not affect or alter the constitution of a State court or the organisation through which its jurisdiction and powers are organised. In *Le Mesurier v Connor*,[56] it was held, accordingly, that the provisions of the *Bankruptcy Act* 1924, which purported to make registrars, acting as Commonwealth officers, part of the organisation of State courts and which authorised them to exercise powers and functions as officers of the courts in the administration of their jurisdiction, were invalid. This was said to be an attempt to alter the constitution and structure of State courts, forbidden by the Constitution. The Constitution, it was held, envisaged the selection by Parliament of existing judicial organisations which depended alike for their structure and being on State law, and the investment of federal jurisdiction in such courts.

The principle stated in *Le Mesurier v Connor* has been reaffirmed by the High Court and State courts on many occasions[57] and the limits of its operation have also been considered. In *Bond v George A Bond and Co Ltd and Bond's Industries Ltd*,[58] the High Court upheld the validity of the *Bankruptcy Act* 1929, passed in consequence of the decision in *Le Mesurier v Connor*, which made registrars and deputy registrars independent of the State courts, required them to perform "administrative" duties as directed by the State courts, and by s 24 gave registrars independent functions, including the power to hear debtors' petitions and to make sequestration orders. It was held that these amendments overcame the objections to the sections in the earlier Act. Section 77(iii), considered with s 51(xvii), authorised the grant by Parliament to State courts of all powers appropriate to the exercise of bankruptcy jurisdiction, and all authority incidental to the exercise of such powers, including the grant of authority to enable such courts to direct the performance of ministerial acts. The Court was prepared if necessary to read the authority to perform "administrative" acts conferred by the amending Act as meaning "ministerial" acts. Doubts were expressed as to the validity of s 24, on the ground that it conferred judicial power on the registrars, but it was held that the section was in any event severable.

Although the above cases establish that the Commonwealth in exercising power under s 77(iii) cannot alter the structure or organisation of a State court, it was also held that it could not make use of the existing organisation of such a court in certain circumstances.

---

56   (1929) 42 CLR 481.

57   See eg *Bond v George A Bond and Co Ltd and Bond's Industries Ltd* (1930) 44 CLR 11; *Adams v Chas S Watson Pty Ltd* (1938) 60 CLR 545; *Silk Bros Pty Ltd v State Electricity Commission of Victoria* (1943) 67 CLR 1; *Aston v Irvine* (1955) 92 CLR 353. See also *Ex parte Australian Timber Workers' Union; Veneer Co Ltd* (1937) 37 SR (NSW) 52; *Ex parte Coorey* (1945) 45 SR (NSW) 287; *R v Ray; ex parte Smith* [1948] SASR 216; *Russell v Russell* (1976) 134 CLR 495.

58   (1930) 44 CLR 11.

In *R v Davison*,[59] Dixon CJ and McTiernan J pointed out that, although a court is composed of judges which form it, courts are provided with officers and, under a unitary system of government, it is not uncommon to find that certain duties falling to a court are executed, subject to judicial confirmation or review, by an officer of the court. They added that: "There is no distinct decision of this Court that under Chapter III no authority can be made by statute for the discharge in this way of the duties of a Federal court, although there are dicta to that effect." The dicta referred to included that of Isaacs J in *Le Mesurier v Connor*,[60] who distinguished judges comprising a court and the officers of the court. His Honour said that only the former constituted the court and, therefore, the judicial power of the Commonwealth, which, by s 71, is vested in courts, could not be exercised by the latter.

The High Court later considered the purported exercise of judicial power by an officer of a State court exercising federal jurisdiction. In *Kotsis v Kotsis*,[61] it was held (Gibbs J dissenting) that a deputy registrar of the Supreme Court of New South Wales did not have power to make an order in matrimonial causes under the *Matrimonial Causes Act* 1959 (Cth) directing the payment by the husband of the wife's interim costs in that cause. The main reason for the decision was that the deputy registrar, although an officer of the Supreme Court, was not part of that Court. This conclusion was arrived at by all the judges from an examination of the legislation relating to the constitution and organisation of that Court. However, State legislation gave power to the judges by Rules to delegate certain authority and jurisdiction to the registrar (which included the deputy registrar), including jurisdiction to make an order of the sort made. When acting under this delegation, the registrar was "deemed to be exercising the jurisdiction and powers of the Supreme Court".

The majority were of the view that, as s 77(iii) authorised the investiture of jurisdiction only in a "court of a State", a person who was a delegate of the court but not part of it could not exercise the jurisdiction. Gibbs J, however, was prepared to give the word "court" under s 77(iii) a wider and less technical meaning as including the organisation of the court "and particularly the officers of the court by which it exercises its functions under State law in analogous cases".[62] The case of *Le Mesurier v Connor* was relied on by both the majority and the minority, particularly the statement in that case that State law "determines the constitution of the court itself and the organisation through which its powers and jurisdiction are exercised".[63]

---

59   (1954) 90 CLR 353 at 365.

60   (1929) 42 CLR 481 at 511, 512, 522-525.

61   (1970) 122 CLR 69.

62   Ibid at 104.

63   (1929) 42 CLR 481 at 495.

The majority pointed to the clear distinction made between the "constitution of the court" and "the organisation through which its powers and jurisdiction are exercised" for coming to the conclusion that the "court" did not include the "organisation". Gibbs J, on the other hand, reasoned that, as the Commonwealth could not alter either of these elements as laid down by State law, that must be because the "court", upon which s 77(iii) authorised the investiture of jurisdiction, included both. The decision of *Kotsis v Kotsis* was unfortunate from a practical point of view. Additional burdens were placed on the judges and an incongruous situation arose as a result of a State court being prevented from using, in the case of federal jurisdiction, the services of court officers who were available when State jurisdiction was involved. These practical consequences were adverted to by Gibbs J. He said:

> The exercise of federal jurisdiction is not necessarily any more difficult, complicated or important than the exercise of State jurisdiction, and in fact, of course, some matters which formerly fell within State jurisdiction are now within federal jurisdiction; matrimonial causes and bankruptcy are obvious examples. The nature of federal jurisdiction did not require any different kind of organization, and there was no less need for courts exercising federal jurisdiction to be organized so that their officers, acting subject to confirmation or review by the judges, might perform on behalf of the court judicial functions which were of a routine or comparatively minor character or which could for other reasons be safely entrusted to them. There is no reason of which I am aware why the exercise of federal jurisdiction should necessarily be less flexible and more costly than the exercise of State jurisdiction.[64]

In *Knight v Knight*,[65] the Court applied the reasoning in *Kotsis v Kotsis* in invalidating an order for maintenance pending a divorce suit made by the Master of the Supreme Court of South Australia.

These cases were overruled in *Commonwealth v Hospital Contribution Fund of Australia*,[66] which upheld the power of a master of the Supreme Court of New South Wales to hear and determine a claim to privilege by the Commonwealth. As the Commonwealth was a party (s 75(iii) of the Constitution), the matter was one of federal jurisdiction under s 39(2) of the *Judiciary Act*.

The Court examined the *Supreme Court Act* 1970 (NSW) and concluded that a master was not part of that Court. Section 25, for example, provided that the Court "shall be composed of" specified judges. Other sections provided for the master to exercise certain powers of the Court and a master's judgment or order had the effect, subject to judicial review, of a judgment or order of the Court. If *Kotsis* were followed, the conclusion would be that as a

---

64   (1970) 122 CLR 69 at 110.

65   (1971) 122 CLR 114.

66   (1982) 150 CLR 49.

master was not a member of the Court he or she could not be invested with federal jurisdiction under s 77(iii) of the Constitution. Gibbs CJ pointed out, however, that the position could have been different in some other States where the legislation (following *Kotsis*) provided that the Supreme Court should consist of not only judges, but also masters.[67] Most of the judges in *Kotsis* had concentrated on the State legislation to determine the issue; but Barwick CJ stated that, for purposes of s 73 (appeals to the High Court) and s 77(iii), a State tribunal would not constitute a "court" if its membership included court officers who were not judges.

In *Hospital Contribution Fund*, the Court (Brennan J dissenting) rejected the reasoning in *Kotsis* and held that "court" (in s 77(iii)) and "courts" (in s 39(2) of the *Judiciary Act*) of a State meant the court as an institution, and not the persons of which it was composed. Mason J emphasised the power of a State to alter the structure and organisation of its courts. As federal jurisdiction could at any point intrude into the exercise of non-federal jurisdiction (perhaps without the court or the parties being aware of it), *Kotsis* could affect the State's control of its courts for non-federal purposes. The majority, generally, followed the reasoning of Gibbs J in *Kotsis*.

Neither *Kotsis* nor *Hospital Contribution Fund* dealt with the issue whether a *federal* court might be empowered to delegate jurisdiction to an officer of the court. While that issue belongs strictly in Chapter 1 (High Court) or Chapter 3 (Federal Courts) of this book, it is discussed here because the decision of *Hospital Contribution Fund* was influential in determining the matter. Three judges took the view that in the light of that case it "makes little sense", or it is "incongruous", to require federal courts to operate differently.[68]

In *Harris v Caladine*,[69] the *Family Law Act* 1975 empowered the judges of the Court to make rules delegating to registrars the powers of the Court, with some exceptions. Orders of a registrar were reviewable by the Court. Subject to that, an order of a registrar was deemed to be made by the Court. The rules provided that a review by the Court should be a de novo hearing, but regard should be had to the proceedings, including the evidence, before the registrar. The High Court (Mason CJ, Deane, Dawson, Gaudron and McHugh JJ; Brennan and Toohey JJ dissenting) held that the provisions were valid and did not breach Chapter III of the Constitution. Mason CJ and Deane J said that the *Hospital Contribution Fund Case* was inconsistent with the notion that the exercise of jurisdiction by judges to the exclusion of registrars was an essential characteristic of a Chapter III court. It would, they said, be

---

67 *Constitution Act* 1975 (Vic), s 75; *Supreme Court Act* 1935 (WA), s 7; *Supreme Court Act* 1935 (SA), s 7.
68 *Harris v Caladine* (1991) 172 CLR 84 at 93 per Mason CJ and Deane J, 145 per Gaudron J.
69 Ibid.

"somewhat surprising" if the word "court" in s 77(iii) had a meaning different from that in s 71 and s 77(i) and (ii). As it had been decided that the federal jurisdiction of a State court could be exercised by registrars it was difficult to argue that the jurisdiction of federal courts required a different result.

It was recognised, however, there were other limitations on Parliament's power in respect of federal courts which did not apply in the case of State courts. Chapter III requires a federal court's jurisdiction to be exercised by a court whose members are judges appointed under s 72 of the Constitution. This requirement means that any judicial power exercisable by a registrar of a federal court must be appropriately controlled, supervised and capable of review by the judges. The members of the High Court in *Harris v Caladine* varied in their description of this limitation. Mason CJ and Deane JJ required that the judges bear the major responsibility at least in respect of the more important aspects of contested matters and that the Court also have power to review a registrar's order in respect of both facts and law.[70] McHugh J declared that it was not enough that the court could exercise appellate review; there must be (as there was in that case) a complete rehearing of the facts and the law as they exist when the judge reviews the registrar's order.[71]

The overruling of *Kotsis* has removed impediments to Commonwealth use of State courts for federal jurisdiction and to the effective power of the States in respect of the structure and organisation of their courts. *Harris v Caladine* ensures that federal courts (including the High Court) may, subject to the limitations mentioned, have the advantage of using court officials in a manner that has been available to other courts both in Australia and elsewhere.

Prescribing the Number and Character of Judicial Officers

Section 79 of the Constitution authorises parliamentary control of the number of judges who may exercise the federal jurisdiction of a State court. But before any question of the operation of s 79 arises, there is a question whether there has been an investment of a State court under s 77(iii), and the choice of designated *persons* who may be qualified to constitute State courts is not a valid investment under this power. So, in *Silk Bros Pty Ltd v State Electricity Commission of Victoria*,[72] regulations constituting Fair Rents Boards provided that they might be constituted by police magistrates and, if the Governor in Council deemed fit, by two other persons. It was not specifically required that such other persons should be justices of the peace, so that it was possible to appoint a Fair Rents Board which could not constitute a Court of Petty

---

70   Ibid at 121-122.

71   Ibid at 164.

72   (1943) 67 CLR 1.

Sessions. The Governor in Council appointed police magistrates for the time being assigned to adjudicate at Courts of Petty Sessions to constitute Fair Rents Boards, and in the metropolitan area specified police magistrates were appointed as Fair Rents Boards. It was held that the investment was bad on the ground that there was no investment of State Courts of Petty Sessions as such, but an appointment of particular persons, described as police magistrates, to be Fair Rents Boards at places at which Courts of Petty Sessions were held.

In *Ex parte Coorey*,[73] Jordan CJ said that s 79 did not authorise the Parliament to select one among several judges, each of whom was capable of constituting a State court, and to provide that he alone should constitute the court when exercising federal jurisdiction. If this means that Parliament may not direct that the federal jurisdiction of a State court of summary jurisdiction shall be exercised by members of that court possessing specified qualifications, as, for example, a stipendiary magistrate, it is contrary to the clearly expressed view of the High Court. If it means that Parliament may not declare that the federal jurisdiction of a State court shall be exercised by a *named* judge of that court, it is not easy to see how this case can be distinguished from the one immediately preceding. It has been held that, if federal jurisdiction is conferred in terms on a justice of a Supreme Court, and not upon a Supreme Court, eo nomine, it will be a valid exercise of power if the true construction of the grant is that the jurisdiction is conferred on the judge *as a member of the Supreme Court,* and if he, as a single judge, is capable of constituting the court. In such a case, the designation of the single judge is an exercise of power under s 79.[74]

Various Commonwealth statutes purport to invest State courts with federal jurisdiction and to prescribe that that jurisdiction shall be exercised by judges described by a particular qualification. The most obvious example is s 39 of the *Judiciary Act,* which provides in sub-s (2)(d) that:

> The Federal jurisdiction of a court of summary jurisdiction of a State shall not be judicially exercised except by a Stipendiary or Police or Special Magistrate, or some Magistrate of the State who is specially authorized by the Governor-General to exercise such jurisdiction ...[75]

Similar provision is made by s 68(3) of the *Judiciary Act.*

On their face such provisions do not appear to be exercises of power under s 79, which authorises prescription of the *number,* not of the *qualification,* of judges who may exercise the federal jurisdiction of State

---

73   (1945) 45 SR (NSW) 287 at 304-305.

74   *Aston v Irvine* (1955) 92 CLR 353.

75   The Australian Law Reform Commission has recommended that this provision be altered to provide that the jurisdiction may be exercised by a State magistrate only if the magistrate is qualified for admission as a legal practitioner in the Supreme Court of that State: *Judicial Power of the Commonwealth*, Report 92, 2001, p 174.

courts. In *Ex parte Coorey*,[76] Jordan CJ said that "so far as s 39(2)(d) and s 68(3) [of the *Judiciary Act*] purport to enable the Governor-General to select a particular magistrate of the State and specifically authorise him to exercise Federal jurisdiction as a State court, I am of opinion that they are ultra vires the Constitution as interpreted by the High Court". The difficulty in this view, as a matter of authority, is that in such cases as *Baxter v Commissioner of Taxation, New South Wales*,[77] *Lorenzo v Carey*,[78] and *Commonwealth v Limerick Steamship Co Ltd*,[79] the High Court discussed s 39 of the *Judiciary Act* in terms which, though not specifically directed to s 39(2)(d), assumed its validity. In *Queen Victoria Memorial Hospital v Thornton*,[80] where jurisdiction was conferred on police, stipendiary or special magistrates under the *Re-establishment and Employment Act* 1945, the High Court, while holding the investment bad on other grounds,[81] stated in the clearest terms, and by reference to the authorities cited above, that s 39(2)(d) was valid. "Whether the power to enact s 39(2)(d) of the *Judiciary Act* arises under s 51(xxxix) of the Constitution or under s 79 need not be considered, for the validity of the provision has been upheld."[82]

The matter was also considered by the Full Supreme Court of South Australia in *R v Ray; ex parte Smith*.[83] In an action brought under the *National Security (Landlord and Tenant) Regulations* in a local court, the court rejected the argument that there was any right to a trial of the issue by a court constituted by a special magistrate and two justices of the peace in accordance with the terms of the State *Local Courts Act* because the *National Security (Landlord and Tenant) Regulations* specifically provided that such jurisdiction should be exercised by a special magistrate sitting alone. Napier CJ said:

> It was contended that the Commonwealth, when it invests the court of a State with Federal jurisdiction, must take the court as it finds it, but that does not compel the Commonwealth to adopt rules of procedure which it regards as inapplicable or inappropriate. If the State Court is so organised as to function in different ways for different purposes, I think that the Commonwealth must have the power to commit Federal jurisdiction to the State court functioning in the manner that is, or is considered to be, best suited to its purpose (*Troy v Wigglesworth; Lorenzo v Carey*). Once the jurisdiction becomes Federal, the Commonwealth can at will regulate the procedure and control the method of the relief.[84]

---

76   (1945) 45 SR (NSW) 287 at 305.

77   (1907) 4 CLR 1087.

78   (1921) 29 CLR 243.

79   (1924) 35 CLR 69.

80   (1953) 87 CLR 144.

81   See pp 200-201 above.

82   (1953) 87 CLR 144 at 152.

83   [1948] SASR 216.

84   Ibid at 223.

The Court did not specify the constitutional authority to prescribe the composition of State courts invested with federal jurisdiction, but the language of Napier CJ's judgment suggests that it is to be discovered in s 51(xxxix), rather than in s 79. It appears to have been the Court's view that the regulation of the composition of State courts is a matter of procedure, and that it is open to the Federal Parliament to control the procedure to be adopted by a State court invested with federal jurisdiction. The breadth of the proposition stated by Napier CJ suggests that it also is open to Parliament, contrary to Jordan CJ in *Ex parte Coorey*, to designate a particular judge (or judges) to exercise the federal jurisdiction of a State court, and it is not easy to distinguish that case from such legislation as s 39(2)(d), which the High Court has expressly declared to be valid. In *Kotsis v Kotsis*,[85] Gibbs J, referring to s 39(2)(d), said that "[a]lthough the grounds on which that provision was treated as valid were not made altogether clear I see no reason to doubt the correctness of the opinion expressed by seven members of the Court" (in *Queen Victoria Memorial Hospital v Thornton*).

There is much to be said for the practical outcome which upholds the Commonwealth legislative policy that matters arising in the exercise of federal jurisdiction by a State court of summary jurisdiction should be entrusted to specially qualified magistrates rather than to lay justices of the peace. There is some difficulty, however, in locating the constitutional authority to control State courts in this way and the High Court in *Queen Victoria Memorial Hospital v Thornton* pointed to the alternative sources of ss 51(xxxix) and 79, but was content to rest on authority which itself does not carry the matter forward. It strains the language of s 79 to make "number" include "qualification" of judges. This suggests recourse to s 51(xxxix), but the constitutional scheme generally, and notably the express terms of s 79, suggest a very limited power of recourse to the incidental power to authorise interference with the composition of State courts exercising federal jurisdiction. The law on this matter is apparently settled, though the source of constitutional power remains obscure.

Other difficulties arise from the holding that the Parliament may validly prescribe the qualification of judges of State courts invested with federal jurisdiction. It may be that a State court of summary jurisdiction will exercise federal jurisdiction without knowing it and, indeed, without any reasonable opportunity of finding out.[86] A further question arises as to the consequences of a failure by a State court of summary jurisdiction to constitute itself in accordance with s 39(2)(d) of the *Judiciary Act* when it exercises federal jurisdiction. Does such an omission constitute a failure to exercise federal jurisdiction altogether; or is there an exercise of federal jurisdiction, albeit an unlawful one, so that an appeal lies as prescribed by s 73 of the Constitution

---

85   (1970) 122 CLR 69 at 111. See also *Brown v The Queen* (1986) 160 CLR 171 at 200.
86   See p 90 above.

and the *Judiciary Act* as from a State court exercising federal jurisdiction? In *Troy v Wigglesworth*,[87] a majority in the High Court held that this was not the usurpation of a non-existent federal jurisdiction, but was a wrongful exercise of an existing jurisdiction. Whatever the analytical difficulties, this may now be regarded as settled law.[88]

Jurisdictional Limits

While Parliament may not reshape State courts which it invests with federal jurisdiction and must, subject to the qualifications already noted, respect their constitutions and organisations as prescribed by State law, it may fix and control the *jurisdiction* of those courts in investing them with federal jurisdiction. Unless there is an express declaration to the contrary, the limitations of jurisdiction prescribed by State law will be respected,[89] but by such express declaration "the Federal Parliament may in conferring jurisdiction in respect of Federal subject matter, extend or limit the jurisdiction of a State Court in respect of persons, locality, amount or otherwise, as it may think proper".[90] Thus, in *Peacock's Case*,[91] regulations under the *National Security Act*, which increased the amount recoverable in a New South Wales district court invested with federal jurisdiction beyond the limits prescribed by State law, were held not to be invalid on this ground. In *Adams v Chas S Watson Pty Ltd*,[92] it was held that federal law could prescribe limitation periods which a State court invested with federal jurisdiction must recognise in disregard of limitation periods imposed by State law. Other Acts confer jurisdiction on State courts of summary jurisdiction to try offences against the Act committed outside Australia.[93] Those provisions would appear to have extended the locality of the jurisdiction of such courts although in all other respects the Acts expressly confine the jurisdiction within the limits prescribed by State law.[94] Under s 68(5) and (5C) of the *Judiciary Act* 1903, the jurisdiction

---

87 (1919) 26 CLR 305.

88 See *Keetley v Bowie* (1951) 83 CLR 516 at 520; *Cocchiaro v Pearce* (1977) 14 ALR 338 at 364.

89 *Federated Sawmill etc Association (Adelaide Branch) v Alexander* (1912) 15 CLR 308 at 313.

90 *Peacock's Case* (1943) 67 CLR 25 at 39 per Latham CJ.

91 Ibid.

92 (1938) 60 CLR 545.

93 See Renfree, *The Federal Judicial System of Australia*, 1984, pp 649-668.

94 In *R v Bull* (1974) 131 CLR 203, the High Court considered the jurisdiction of the Supreme Court of South Australia in 1911 in respect of offences committed at sea for the purposes of determining the jurisdiction of the Supreme Court of the Northern Territory. While the particular exercise of jurisdiction was upheld in that case (a customs matter) the reasons of the judges varied greatly: McTiernan, Menzies and Gibbs JJ considered that the Supreme Court of South Australia had in 1911 jurisdiction in respect of all offences against local laws committed at sea. Stephen and Mason JJ confined their reasoning to customs laws and Barwick CJ dissented.

vested in State or Territorial courts with respect to offences against the laws of the Commonwealth is expressly declared to be conferred "notwithstanding any limits as to locality of the jurisdiction of the court under the law of the State or Territory".

Procedure

The Court has drawn a distinction between an attempted alteration of the constitution of a State court or the organisation through which its jurisdiction and powers are exercised (which, as we have seen, is outside the limits of Commonwealth power) and legislating to make the investiture of federal jurisdiction effective (which is within Commonwealth power).

In *Lorenzo v Carey*,[95] a judgment of five members of the Court approved a statement by Isaacs J in *Baxter v Commissioner of Taxation*[96] that: "Once the jurisdiction became federal the Commonwealth Parliament could at will regulate the procedure and control the method and extent of relief." As in the case of s 39(2)(d) of the *Judiciary Act* there has been no general agreement among the judges as to the source of this power. Isaacs and Rich JJ in *Commonwealth v Limerick Steamship Co Ltd*[97] considered the power was derived from s 51(xxxix) because of their view that the State courts exercising federal jurisdiction were part of the "Federal Judicature" within the meaning of that provision. On the other hand, in *Bond v George A Bond and Co Ltd*,[98] Rich and Dixon JJ considered that s 77(iii) together with the particular substantive head of power in s 51 provided the constitutional authority. They said: "Section 77(iii) considered with s 51(xvii) confers ample power upon the Parliament to bestow upon State Courts all powers appropriate to bankruptcy jurisdiction and all authority incidental to the exercise of such powers." Menzies J in *Kotsis v Kotsis*[99] seemed to agree with this view when he said that a provision of the *Matrimonial Causes Act* which authorised the Governor-General to make rules relating to the practice and procedure of courts with jurisdiction under the Act was an exercise of power under s 51(xxii). In *Russell v Russell*,[100] Gibbs J left the source of authority to deal with procedure undecided;[101] Stephen J appeared to regard it as within the incidental area of power granted by s 77(iii); on the other hand, Mason and Jacobs JJ[102] preferred to rely on the particular subject in s 51 under which the substantive rules were made. Mason J said:

95 (1921) 29 CLR 243.
96 (1907) 4 CLR 1087 at 1145.
97 (1924) 35 CLR 69.
98 (1930) 44 CLR 11 at 22.
99 (1970) 122 CLR 69 at 89.
100 (1976) 134 CLR 495.
101 Ibid at 518-519.
102 Ibid at 533-534 and 554-555 respectively.

For my part, I should be inclined to think that the general powers to legislate in s 51 confer authority to enact procedural as well as substantive rules of law upon the topics there enumerated and that a vesting under s 77(iii) in a State court of federal jurisdiction in matters arising under a Commonwealth statute gives that court authority and imposes upon it a duty to hear and determine those matters according to the substantive and procedural rules thereby enacted without the need for co-operative assistance from s 51(xxxix). However, this is a matter which need not be explored, for the existence of the legislative power to regulate the procedure to be followed in the exercise of federal jurisdiction by State courts has been frequently and authoritatively asserted in the past.[103]

It is suggested that (contrary to the view expressed by Stephen J) rules of procedure for a court invested with federal jurisdiction cannot easily be described as incidental to the act of investing the court with jurisdiction and are more appropriately seen as incidental to the actual exercise of judicial power granted by s 71 of the Constitution and, therefore, "incidental to the execution of any power vested by this Constitution in ... the Federal judicature ..." within the meaning of s 51(xxxix) if, as has been suggested, State courts exercising federal jurisdiction are within the concept of the "Federal Judicature".[104] Alternatively, or perhaps additionally, the subject-matters mentioned in the various paragraphs in s 51 would, for the reasons stated by Mason J, provide a source of power.

The distinction between laying down rules of procedure and attempting to interfere with the structure of the court or the organisation through which it operates is not always a clear one. In the *Family Law Act* 1975, s 97(1) provided that, with certain exceptions, all proceedings in the Family Court or in another court, when exercising jurisdiction under the Act, should be heard in a closed court. Section 97(4) provided that neither the judge nor counsel in respect of proceedings under the Act should robe. In *Russell v Russell*,[105] the Court held that, in relation to State courts exercising jurisdiction under the Act, s 97(1) was invalid (Barwick CJ, Gibbs and Stephen JJ; Mason and Jacobs JJ dissenting) and s 97(4) was valid (Stephen, Mason and Jacobs JJ; Barwick CJ, and Gibbs J dissenting).

Barwick CJ and Gibbs J considered that both provisions went beyond mere practice and procedure and interfered with the nature and organisation of the Court. Mason and Jacobs JJ were equally clear that both those provisions were procedural rules which had nothing to do with the constitution or organisational structure of State courts. Stephen J was of the view that the provision regarding the non-wearing of robes was procedural but that relating to the closure of courts intruded into the constitution and organisation of the

---

103 Ibid at 536.
104 Pages 199-200 above.
105 (1976) 134 CLR 495.

court. It is difficult to see why the issue of the judges' robes has much to do with the organisation of a court. The conflicting interests involved, namely the dignity of the court as against the advantage of informality for the litigants, are suitable for resolution by a legislature having legislative power with respect to the subject-matter of the litigation. It requires no rearrangement of the court's structure or organisation.

The question of whether an open or closed court is a purely procedural issue is more controversial. Courts open to the public have been traditional in our legal system and the reason for open courts has always been regarded as important, as Stephen J's judgment indicates. All the majority judges said that in their view the issue went to the nature of the court.

In recent times, it has been suggested that the doctrine of the separation of judicial power derived from Chapter III prevents Parliament from legislating to authorise courts to exercise judicial power in a manner inconsistent with "the essential character of a court or with the nature of judicial power".[106] Some have suggested that open justice is essential to that principle. In *Re Nolan; ex parte Young*,[107] Gaudron J emphasised that the judicial process included "open and public inquiry (subject to limited exceptions)"; McHugh J has also said that "[o]pen justice is the hallmark of the common law system of justice and is an essential characteristic of the exercise of federal judicial power".[108]

Of course, even if an open court is regarded as an essential feature of the exercise of the judicial power of the Commonwealth, it is subject to counter-vailing factors, as Gaudron J's statement indicates, but it is doubtful whether *all* family law matters would be regarded as justifying closed proceedings. This principle would prevent the Commonwealth from requiring a closed court in proceedings before State courts exercising federal jurisdiction, apart from the principle applied in *Russell v Russell*. It is clear, however, that if an open court is seen as essential to federal judicial power it could also be reasonably regarded as going to the nature and organisation of the State court.

Assuming the views of Gaudron and McHugh JJ are followed, an attempt by a State to provide for the wholesale closure of courts would probably be inconsistent with their exercise of federal jurisdiction in accordance with the principle in *Kable v Director of Public Prosecutions (NSW)*,[109] which is discussed below.[110]

---

106 *Chu Kheng Lim v Minister for Immigration* (1992) 176 CLR 1 at 27 per Brennan, Deane and Dawson JJ.

107 (1990) 172 CLR 460 at 496.

108 *Grollo v Palmer* (1995) 184 CLR 348 at 379.

109 (1996) 189 CLR 51.

110 Pages 242-246.

Section 39 of the *Judiciary Act*

Some of the more difficult problems affecting the investment of State courts with federal jurisdiction arise from s 39 of the *Judiciary Act*, which may conveniently be set out in full:

> 39. (1) The jurisdiction of the High Court, so far as it is not exclusive of the jurisdiction of any Court of a State by virtue of section 38, shall be exclusive of the jurisdiction of the several Courts of the States except as provided in this section.
>
> (2) The several Courts of the States shall within the limits of their several jurisdictions, whether such limits are as to locality, subject-matter, or otherwise, be invested with federal jurisdiction, in all matters in which the High Court has original jurisdiction or in which original jurisdiction can be conferred upon it, except as provided in section 38, and subject to the following conditions and restrictions:
>
> (a) A decision of a Court of a State, whether in original or in appellate jurisdiction, shall not be subject to appeal to Her Majesty in Council, whether by special leave or otherwise.[111]
>
> (b) ...[112]
>
> (c) The High Court may grant special leave to appeal to the High Court from any decision of any Court or Judge of a State notwithstanding that the law of the State may prohibit any appeal from such Court or Judge.
>
> (d) The federal jurisdiction of a Court of summary jurisdiction of a State shall not be judicially exercised except by a Stipendiary or Police or Special Magistrate, or some Magistrate of the State who is specially authorized by the Governor-General to exercise such jurisdiction, or an arbitrator on whom the jurisdiction, or part of the jurisdiction, of that Court is conferred by a prescribed law of the State, within the limits of the jurisdiction so conferred.

Section 39(1) purports to be an exercise of power under s 77(ii) of the Constitution, while s 39(2) rests on s 77(iii). In *Lorenzo v Carey*,[113] Higgins J observed that only para (d) of s 39(2) was aptly described as a condition of the exercise of the jurisdiction invested by that subsection; while s 39(2)(a) and (c) and former para (b) were more appropriately described as substantive enactments relating to appeals from State courts *after* they had exercised federal jurisdiction. A contrary view was expressed by Isaacs and Rich JJ in

---

111 Before its amendment by Act No 134 of 1968, para (a) provided: "Every decision of the Supreme Court of a State, or any other Court of a State from which at the establishment of the Commonwealth an appeal lay to the Queen in Council, shall be final and conclusive except so far as an appeal may be brought to the High Court."

112 Before its omission by Act No 164 of 1976, para (b) provided: "Wherever an appeal lies from a decision of any Court or judge of a State to the Supreme Court of the State, an appeal from the decision may be brought to the High Court."

113 (1921) 29 CLR 243 at 255.

Commonwealth v Limerick Steamship Co Ltd.[114] They held that these paragraphs were a valid exercise of power under s 77(iii), in so far as regulation of the right to appeal from any State court invested with federal jurisdiction was appropriately construed as a limitation on that court's jurisdiction, and that s 77(iii) therefore authorised the investment of such courts with federal jurisdiction, subject to defined and limited rights of appeal. It is to be noted, however, that s 39(2)(c) does not, of itself, *confer* rights of appeal to the High Court. Section 73(ii) of the Constitution allows a right of appeal to the High Court from State courts invested with federal jurisdiction and s 39(2)(c) is properly construed as a "regulation" of that appeal within s 73 requiring special leave to appeal.[115]

It is difficult to see, in the light of s 73 of the Constitution, relating to appeals from State courts exercising federal jurisdiction to the High Court, how a State could prohibit such an appeal in the manner contemplated by para (c). Because of that, the Australian Law Reform Commission recommended that that paragraph be repealed. They also recommended, however, that s 35 of the *Judiciary Act*, which now directly conditions appeals from the State Supreme Courts and State courts exercising federal jurisdiction on the obtaining of special leave, should be amended to provide that any State law that purports to restrict or limit an appeal from a State court to the High Court shall not apply. No satisfactory explanation is given as to why such a provision is necessary in view of s 73 of the Constitution.[116]

The legislative policy which s 39 of the *Judiciary Act* was designed to accomplish has been discussed many times and, in *Minister of State for the Army v Parbury Henty and Co Pty Ltd*,[117] it was described by Dixon J in the following terms:

> The provision was meant to cover the whole field of Federal jurisdiction so that the conditions embodied in the four paragraphs of sub-s 2 should govern its exercise whether the cause of action, the procedure and the liability to suit arose under existing or future legislation. To that end it invested State courts with the full content of the original jurisdiction falling within the judicial power of the Commonwealth and, as it has been held, some of the appellate jurisdiction. The limits of jurisdiction of any courts so invested found their source in State law, and, I presume, any change made by the State in those limits would, under the terms of s 39(2) ipso facto make an identical change in its Federal jurisdiction. An acknowledged purpose was to exclude appeals as of right to the Privy Council, and it was intended to exclude them over the whole field of Federal jurisdiction. That jurisdiction was, therefore, conferred in its entirety, leaving it to future legislation to bring into being new subject matters and deal with procedure and liability to suit.

114 (1924) 35 CLR 69.
115 *Wishart v Fraser* (1941) 64 CLR 470 at 480 per Dixon J.
116 *Report on The Judicial Power of the Commonwealth*, Report 92, 2001, p 174.
117 (1945) 70 CLR 459 at 505.

So far as this passage suggests that every investment of a State court with federal jurisdiction falls within the ambit of s 39, and is subject to the control of that section, its correctness is open to question. In the *Parbury Henty Case*, three members of the Court were of opinion that the State courts were invested with federal jurisdiction in that case by the *National Security (General) Regulation* in question and not by s 39. But discussion of this question may be postponed for the present. Subject to this qualification, s 39 has a very broad operation. Isaacs J in *Le Mesurier v Connor*[118] spoke of it as "a standing provision constantly speaking in the present", and in a later case the High Court characterised the section as a law operating upon the courts of the States as those courts exist from time to time and said that its operation was to invest those courts with federal jurisdiction.[119] The section has an ambulatory operation and in the *Parbury Henty Case* Dixon J expressed this in terms that any change made by State law in the limits of the jurisdiction of the State courts would ipso facto make an identical change in the federal jurisdiction of those courts.[120] In *Commonwealth v District Court of the Metropolitan District*,[121] it was unsuccessfully argued that the federal jurisdiction of the New South Wales district courts conferred by s 39 was fixed as at the date of the *Judiciary Act* 1903, so that the Commonwealth could not sue to recover an amount which was not recoverable in that State jurisdiction in 1903, although the jurisdictional amount had been substantially raised by subsequent law.

The section is also ambulatory in the sense that it applies to a State court which has come into existence since the date of the *Judiciary Act*,[122] but this does not mean that s 39(2) operates as a delegation of power to the States to invest a court with federal jurisdiction, so that it does not raise afresh the issues debated in the High Court in *Le Mesurier v Connor*[123] and in *Peacock's Case*[124] touching the power of Parliament to delegate its power to invest under s 77(iii). As was pointed out in *Commonwealth v District Court of the Metropolitan District*,[125] s 39(2) does not delegate any power to the States to invest courts with federal jurisdiction; for the transformation into federal jurisdiction is effected directly by the section. Notwithstanding Isaacs J's arguments by analogy to s 39(2) in dissent in *Le Mesurier v Connor*,[126] the cases are different; the law in question in *Le Mesurier v Connor* purported to

---

118 (1929) 42 CLR 481 at 503.
119 *Commonwealth v District Court of the Metropolitan District* (1954) 90 CLR 13 at 22.
120 (1945) 70 CLR 459 at 505.
121 (1954) 90 CLR 13.
122 *Collins v Charles Marshall Pty Ltd* (1955) 92 CLR 529 at 536.
123 (1929) 42 CLR 481.
124 (1943) 67 CLR 25.
125 (1954) 90 CLR 13 at 22.
126 (1929) 42 CLR 481 at 504-505.

empower the Governor-General to select any court of a State and, by naming it, to effect an investment of federal jurisdiction. Whatever the validity of such an exercise of power, it is plainly distinguishable from a law which, according to its terms, operates to confer federal jurisdiction on State courts of a given description as they are brought into existence, and as the limits of their respective jurisdictions are defined and redefined.

The operation of s 39 on the jurisdiction of State courts calls for closer examination. Section 38 of the *Judiciary Act*, an exercise of power under s 77(ii), declares certain matters within the jurisdiction of the High Court to be exclusive of State courts subject to the High Court's power to remit matters to those courts under s 44 of the *Judiciary Act*. Section 39(1), also an exercise of power under s 77(ii), then declares the jurisdiction of the High Court to be exclusive of that of State courts, so far as it has not already been rendered exclusive by s 38. Section 39(2), pursuant to s 77(iii), invests State courts with federal jurisdiction in all matters enumerated in ss 75 and 76, except as provided in s 38. It appears, therefore, that there is not a perfect correspondence between the *divesting* operation of s 39(1) and the *vesting* operation of s 39(2). Section 77(ii) can only operate to declare the jurisdiction of the High Court exclusive of that of State courts in respect of those matters in s 76 in which the Parliament has conferred original jurisdiction on the High Court. Under s 77(iii), at least on the face of the section, Parliament could invest State courts with federal jurisdiction in respect of all matters within ss 75 and 76, whether or not original jurisdiction had been conferred on the High Court by legislation under s 76. Section 39(2) purports to invest State courts with jurisdiction in respect of all such matters, so that it appears, for example, that in respect of s 76(ii) (matters arising under laws made by the Parliament) where original jurisdiction has not been generally conferred on the High Court, State courts are invested with federal jurisdiction, without any divestment of their State jurisdiction to try such matters by reason of the obligation imposed upon them by s 5 of the *Commonwealth of Australia Constitution Act*.[127]

The question arose early whether s 39(2) could have this operation; that is to say, could confer federal jurisdiction on State courts in respect of all matters in ss 75 and 76. In *In re Income Tax Acts, Outtrim's Case*,[128] the question was whether the salary of a Commonwealth officer was liable to State income tax, a matter which raised issues arising under the Constitution or involving its interpretation, in respect of which original jurisdiction had

---

127 "This Act, and all laws made by the Parliament of the Commonwealth under the Constitution, shall be binding on the courts, judges, and people of every State and of every part of the Commonwealth, notwithstanding anything in the laws of any State; and the laws of the Commonwealth shall be in force on all British ships, the Queen's ships of war excepted, whose first port of clearance and whose port of destination are in the Commonwealth."

128 [1905] VLR 463.

been conferred on the High Court by s 30 of the *Judiciary Act* under authority of s 76(i) of the Constitution. Hodges J, in the Supreme Court of Victoria, upheld the defendant's claim to immunity, but granted leave to appeal to the Privy Council. This was a case in which, in the absence of s 39 of the *Judiciary Act*, the Supreme Court would have had jurisdiction without any investment of federal jurisdiction. Section 39 would have operated in this case to withdraw State jurisdiction and to invest the Supreme Court with federal jurisdiction only, subject to the condition imposed by s 39(2)(a), shutting out any appeal as of right to the Privy Council. Hodges J, in granting leave to appeal, offered what he described as "a few crude observations"[129] on the constitutional issues. We are not concerned here with those aspects of his observations which bear on the power of the Commonwealth Parliament to qualify, alter or in part repeal any Imperial Order-in-Council authorising appeals from the Supreme Court to the Privy Council. Hodges J directed attention to the divesting and the investing provisions of s 39, and observed that it was not open to the Commonwealth Parliament under s 77 to take away jurisdiction which "belonged to" a State court, and then to return it in the form of federal jurisdiction with conditions attached. The investing clauses "repeal the provision which takes the jurisdiction away, and it is back, belonging, as it originally belonged, to the State Courts".[130] On this view of s 77(iii), Parliament could only invest State courts with federal jurisdiction in respect of those matters which, apart from such a grant, were not within their jurisdiction.

In *Webb v Outtrim*,[131] the Privy Council allowed the appeal on the merits, but expressly adopted the reasoning of Hodges J in granting leave to appeal, and amplified those reasons very little. In *Baxter v Commissioner of Taxation (NSW)*,[132] the High Court treated *Webb v Outtrim* as a decision not on the vesting provisions of s 39(2), but on the condition imposed by s 39(2)(a). Conceding, without deciding, the invalidity of s 39(2)(a), the Court offered an alternative construction of the vesting provisions of s 39, which was subsequently adopted and amplified by the High Court in *Lorenzo v Carey*.[133] That case and *Baxter's Case* raised questions touching the right of appeal from State courts to the High Court under s 39(2). In *Lorenzo v Carey*, Mr Dixon, for the State of Victoria intervening, unsuccessfully argued[134] that s 39 was invalid in whole for the reason stated by Hodges J in *Outtrim's Case*. The High Court upheld the general validity of the section, expressing no opinion

---

129 Ibid at 465.
130 Ibid at 468.
131 [1907] AC 81 at 91-92.
132 (1907) 4 CLR 1087 esp at 1141ff.
133 (1921) 29 CLR 243.
134 Ibid at 245-246. He argued further that the decision in *Webb v Outtrim* that s 39(2)(a) was invalid involved the whole section in invalidity, on the ground that s 39(2)(a) was not severable.

as to s 39(2)(a), which was said to be severable in any event. The Court's favourable view of s 39 called for a definition of federal jurisdiction:

> The phrase "Federal jurisdiction" as used in ss 71, 73 and 77 of the Constitution means jurisdiction derived from the Federal Commonwealth. It does not denote a power to adjudicate in certain matters, though it may connote such a power; it denotes the power to act as the judicial agent of the Commonwealth, which must act through agents if it acts at all. An agent may have a valid authority from a number of independent principals to do the same act. A State Court must recognize the laws of the Commonwealth and be guided by them in exercising its State jurisdiction, and precisely the same duty or a diverse duty may fall upon it by virtue of a grant of Federal jurisdiction under s 77(iii). But even if the duty to be performed under the two jurisdictions be identical, the two jurisdictions are not identical: they are not one but several. When Federal jurisdiction is given to a State Court and the jurisdiction which belongs to it is not taken away, we see no difficulty in that Court exercising either jurisdiction at the instance of a litigant. The position of such Courts is no more anomalous than that of the Courts of Australia and other parts of the British Empire which have administered law and equity in distinct proceedings before the same tribunal.[135]

On this view, there is no analytical difficulty in the concurrent possession of State and federal jurisdiction by a State court in respect of a particular matter, nor in the withdrawal of State jurisdiction and the investment of federal jurisdiction in respect of the same matter. Federal jurisdiction is properly viewed from the standpoint of the *source* of authority to adjudicate, not from the standpoint of the *subject-matter* of adjudication. Moreover, the language of s 77(iii) supports this view of federal jurisdiction; it authorises the investment of State courts with federal jurisdiction with respect to *any* of the matters mentioned in ss 75 and 76.[136] It is clear that State courts possessed State jurisdiction in respect of some of these matters; but the grant of power authorises the investment of State courts without distinguishing between such matters and those which specifically required a grant of jurisdiction to State courts.

There may be good practical sense in the conclusion reached by Hodges J and unsuccessfully argued by Mr Dixon in *Lorenzo v Carey*. It is absurd that a State court should possess two separate jurisdictions, with differing incidents, in respect of the same matter. It is a safe guess that the founding fathers did not foresee these complications when they drew s 77(iii). While it makes sense to authorise the definition of jurisdiction in s 77(i) and (ii) by reference

---

135 Ibid at 251-252. See also *Commonwealth v Limerick Steamship Co Ltd* and *Commonwealth v Kidman* (1924) 35 CLR 69; *Commonwealth v Kreglinger and Fernau Ltd* and *Commonwealth v Bardsley* (1926) 37 CLR 393.

136 Hodges J in *Outtrim's Case* did not consider this problem. See Bailey, "The Federal Jurisdiction of State Courts" (1940-41) 2 Res Judicatae 109 at 116.

to *any* of the matters mentioned in ss 75 and 76, there was no call for a grant of power to invest State courts with federal jurisdiction – assuming any need to introduce a concept of *federal* jurisdiction here at all – except in respect of those matters which lay outside the ordinary jurisdiction of State courts, such as matters in which the Commonwealth was a defendant, or where some order was sought against a Commonwealth officer, in which latter case, anyway, the jurisdiction of the High Court was defined as exclusive by s 38 of the *Judiciary Act*. The power to invest State courts with federal jurisdiction should have been separated from the other two paragraphs of s 77, and should have been more narrowly drawn to ensure that State courts should have been competent to exercise jurisdiction in matters enumerated in ss 75 and 76, otherwise outside their competence, which might be the subject of a *supplementary* grant of jurisdiction by Parliament. It is beyond belief that there was an intention to give State courts the same subject-matter jurisdiction twice over. This, however, beats the air; power was conferred in terms of s 77(iii) and, as a construction of constitutional language, it is not easy to fault the reasoning in *Lorenzo v Carey*.

In *Northern Territory v GPAO*,[137] McHugh and Callinan JJ denied that the term "federal jurisdiction" in Chapter III of the Constitution and s 79 of the *Judiciary Act* included all the matters mentioned in ss 75 and 76. In their view, the only jurisdiction that could be vested as federal jurisdiction under s 77(iii) was jurisdiction relating to matters arising under laws made under ss 51 or 52 of the Constitution, that is, which came within s 76(ii). On that view, it would seem to follow that s 39(2) of the *Judiciary Act* is invalid in so far as it purports to confer federal jurisdiction in all matters in which the High Court has original jurisdiction or in which such jurisdiction can be conferred on it.[138]

In relation to s 77(iii), the suggestion that the word "federal" reduces the operation of the phrase "with respect to any of the matters mentioned in the last two sections" (that is ss 75 and 76) to only one of the nine heads of jurisdiction referred to in those sections is unconvincing. This interpretation has not been followed by any other judge and, it seems, is not now accepted by McHugh J. In *Austral Pacific Group Ltd (in liq) v Airservices Australia*,[139]

---

137 (1999) 196 CLR 553.

138 Ibid at 621-623. McHugh and Callinan JJ purported to follow a statement of Barwick CJ in *Capital TV and Appliances Pty Ltd v Falconer* (1971) 125 CLR 591 that a Territorial court did not exercise federal jurisdiction because federal jurisdiction arose from the exercise of powers conferred by ss 51 and 52. The issue, however, was the distinction between federal and Territorial courts and jurisdiction, and the matter of immediate concern was a provision made by or under a Commonwealth Act. The Chief Justice was emphasising that federal jurisdiction extended to matters arising under laws made under ss 51 and 52, while Territorial jurisdiction was concerned with laws made under s 122. That matter is dealt with above in Chapter 4. Admittedly his language was somewhat loose and might be given the meaning attributed to him by McHugh and Callinan JJ if unrestrained by the context of the case.

139 (2000) 203 CLR 136 at 154.

he said: "In proceedings between a State and a resident of a different State (a
s 75(iv) matter), for example, a State court will be exercising federal jurisdiction by virtue of s 39(2)."[140]

In *Baxter v Commissioner of Taxation (NSW)*,[141] the High Court did not
consider s 39(2)(a) and, in *Lorenzo v Carey*, the Court referred to *Webb v
Outtrim* as deciding that s 39(2)(a) was invalid so far as it purported to take
away the right to appeal to the Privy Council. Until 1968, s 39(2)(a) provided:

> Every decision of the Supreme Court of a State, or any other Court of a
> State from which at the establishment of the Commonwealth an appeal lay
> to the Queen in Council shall be final and conclusive except so far as an
> appeal may be brought to the High Court.

In *Baxter's Case* and in *Lorenzo v Carey*, the discussion of s 39 proceeded on the basis that s 39(2)(a) was, in any event, severable. By the 1940s,
at any rate, it was accepted that s 39(2)(a) was valid. As Dixon J said in
McIlwraith McEacharn Ltd v Shell Co of Australia Ltd,[142] "in this Court,
which considered that by reason of s 74 of the Constitution it was not a matter
for the Privy Council to decide, the provision has been treated as valid". This
conclusion was accepted in *Commonwealth v Queensland*.[143] Indeed, several
of the High Court cases which were concerned with whether a State judgment
had been delivered in respect of a matter in federal or State jurisdiction were
in relation to whether s 39(2)(a) operated to preclude an appeal from the State
court to the Privy Council.[144] As appeals from all judgments of State courts to
the Privy Council were abolished as a result of the *Australia Act* 1986 (Cth)
and (UK) it is unnecessary to repeat here the analysis that was made, in the
previous editions of this work, of how the High Court dealt with the issues
concerning Commonwealth power to prevent appeals as of right and (from
1968 as a result of the amendment of s 39(2)(a)) prerogative appeals by
special leave of the Privy Council, in respect of matters of federal jurisdiction.[145]

Federal Criminal Jurisdiction

Further problems arise in connection with the investment of State courts with
federal *criminal* jurisdiction. Section 39 of the *Judiciary Act* is expressed in
general terms, and, on its face, applies equally to civil and criminal jurisdiction. There are, however, specific statutory provisions with respect to

140 See also *Kable v Director of Public Prosecutions* (1996) 189 CLR 51 at 115.
141 (1907) 4 CLR 1087.
142 (1945) 70 CLR 175 at 209.
143 (1975) 134 CLR 298.
144 For example, *Felton v Mulligan* (1971) 124 CLR 367.
145 See 2nd edn, pp 206-213.

criminal jurisdiction, notably s 68 of the *Judiciary Act*. The historical background is of some interest. The *Punishment of Offenders Act* 1901 was a temporary measure which was to cease to have effect when the High Court was established. It provided that the laws in each State respecting the arrest and custody of offenders, and the procedure for their summary conviction or for their examination and commitment for trial on indictment or information, or for the grant of bail, should apply so far as applicable to persons charged with offences against the laws of the Commonwealth committed within the State. The courts and magistrates of each State exercising jurisdiction in these matters were given the like jurisdiction with respect to persons charged with offences against the laws of the Commonwealth, subject to the proviso that jurisdiction should only be exercised with respect to summary conviction, or examination and commitment for trial, by stipendiary, police or special magistrates or by a State magistrate specially authorised by the Governor-General. The Act then gave appellate jurisdiction "to the Court and in the manner provided by the law of that State for appeal from the like convictions, judgments, sentences or orders in respect of persons charged with offences against the laws of the State".

It was necessary to make some temporary provision until the establishment of the High Court. Section 73(ii) of the Constitution allowed an appeal to the High Court from State courts invested with federal jurisdiction, but that depended upon the establishment of the High Court. The appeals section of the *Punishment of Offenders Act* bridged the gap,[146] but on the inauguration of the High Court the force of the Act was spent. The *Judiciary Act* 1903, however, included not only s 39, but also s 68, which substantially reproduced the provisions of the *Punishment of Offenders Act*, except that the appeal section was not re-enacted. Following the decision of *Seaegg v The King*,[147] s 68 was amended in 1932. It was further amended in 1976 and in later years and now reads as follows:

> 68. (1) The laws of a State or Territory respecting the arrest and custody of offenders or persons charged with offences, and the procedure for:
> (a) their summary conviction; and
> (b) their examination and commitment for trial on indictment; and
> (c) their trial and conviction on indictment; and
> (d) the hearing and determination of appeals arising out of any such trial or conviction or out of any proceedings connected therewith;
> and for holding accused persons to bail, shall, subject to this section, apply and be applied so far as they are applicable to persons who are charged with offences against the laws of the Commonwealth in respect of whom jurisdiction is conferred on the several courts of that State or Territory by this section.

146 *Ah Yick v Lehmert* (1905) 2 CLR 593 at 606-607.
147 (1932) 48 CLR 251.

(2) The several courts of a State or Territory exercising jurisdiction with respect to:
(a) the summary conviction; or
(b) the examination and commitment for trial on indictment; or
(c) the trial and conviction on indictment;
of offenders or persons charged with offences against the laws of the State or Territory, and with respect to the hearing and determination of appeals arising out of any such trial or conviction or out of any proceedings connected therewith, shall, subject to this section and to section 80 of the Constitution, have the like jurisdiction with respect to persons who are charged with offences against the laws of the Commonwealth.

(3) Provided that such jurisdiction shall not be judicially exercised with respect to the summary conviction or examination and commitment for trial of any person except by a Judge, a Stipendiary or Police or Special Magistrate, or some Magistrate of the State or Territory who is specially authorised by the Governor-General to exercise such jurisdiction.

(4) The several Courts of a State or Territory exercising the jurisdiction conferred upon them by this section shall, upon application being made in that behalf, have power to order, upon such terms as they think fit, that any information laid before them in respect of an offence against the laws of the Commonwealth shall be amended so as to remove any defect either in form or substance contained in that information.

(5) Subject to subsection (5A):
(a) the jurisdiction conferred on a court of a State or Territory by subsection (2) in relation to the summary conviction of persons charged with offences against the laws of the Commonwealth; and
(b) the jurisdiction conferred on a court of a State or Territory by virtue of subsection (7) in relation to the conviction and sentencing of persons charged with offences against the laws of the Commonwealth in accordance with a provision of the law of that State or Territory of the kind referred to in subsection (7);
is conferred notwithstanding any limits as to locality of the jurisdiction of that court under the law of that State or Territory.

(5A) A court of a State on which jurisdiction in relation to the summary conviction of persons charged with offences against the laws of the Commonwealth is conferred by subsection (2) may, where it is satisfied that it is appropriate to do so, having regard to all the circumstances, including the public interest, decline to exercise that jurisdiction in relation to an offence against a law of the Commonwealth committed in another State.

(5B) In subsection (5A), "State" includes Territory.

(5C) The jurisdiction conferred on a court of a State or Territory by subsection (2) in relation to:
(a) the examination and commitment for trial on indictment; and
(b) the trial and conviction on indictment;
of persons charged with offences against the laws of the Commonwealth, being offences committed elsewhere than in a State or Territory (including offences in, over or under any area of the seas that is not part of a State or Territory), is conferred notwithstanding any limits as to locality of the jurisdiction of that court under the law of that State or Territory.

(6) Where a person who has committed, or is suspected of having committed, an offence against a law of the Commonwealth, whether in a State or Territory or elsewhere, is found within an area of waters in respect of which sovereignty is vested in the Crown in right of the Commonwealth, he or she may be arrested in respect of the offence in accordance with the provisions of the law of any State or Territory that would be applicable to the arrest of the offender in that State or Territory in respect of such an offence committed in that State or Territory, and may be brought in custody into any State or Territory and there dealt with in like manner as if he or she had been arrested in that State or Territory.

(7) The procedure referred to in subsection (1) and the jurisdiction referred to in subsection (2) shall be deemed to include procedure and jurisdiction in accordance with provisions of a law of a State or Territory under which a person who, in proceedings before a court of summary jurisdiction, pleads guilty to a charge for which he or she could be prosecuted on indictment may be committed to a court having jurisdiction to try offences on indictment to be sentenced or otherwise dealt with without being tried in that court, and the reference to subsections (1) and (2) to "any such trial or conviction" shall be read as including any conviction or sentencing in accordance with any such provisions.

(8) Except as otherwise specifically provided by an Act passed after the commencement of this subsection, a person may be dealt with in accordance with provisions of the kind referred to in subsection (7) notwithstanding that, apart from this section, the offence would be required to be prosecuted on indictment, or would be required to be prosecuted either summarily or on indictment.

(9) Where a law of a State or Territory of the kind referred to in subsection (7) refers to indictable offences, that reference shall, for the purposes of the application of the provisions of the law in accordance with that subsection, be read as including a reference to an offence against a law of the Commonwealth that may be prosecuted on indictment.

(10) Where, in accordance with a procedure of the kind referred to in subsection (7), a person is to be sentenced by a court having jurisdiction to try offences on indictment, that person shall, for the purpose of ascertaining the sentence that may be imposed, be deemed to have been prosecuted and convicted on indictment in that court.

(11) Nothing in this section excludes or limits any power of arrest conferred by, or any jurisdiction vested or conferred by, any other law, including an Act passed before the commencement of this subsection.

The 1932 amendments affected sub-ss (1) and (2), and conferred *appellate* jurisdiction on State courts in respect of offences against the laws of the Commonwealth. This raises questions as to the relationship between ss 39 and 68 of the *Judiciary Act* and the general question of the extent to which s 39 applies to criminal matters. In *Ah Yick v Lehmert*,[148] the issue was whether a Victorian Court of General Sessions was competent to entertain an

---

148 (1905) 2 CLR 593.

appeal from a conviction by a police magistrate under the Commonwealth *Immigration Restriction Act* 1901. The High Court held that the appeal lay, that it was authorised by s 39 of the *Judiciary Act*, that under s 77(iii) federal appellate jurisdiction could validly be conferred on the court,[149] and that s 68, which at that time made no investment of appellate criminal jurisdiction, should not be construed as a limitation on the scope and operation of s 39. Griffith CJ said:

> Now, if ss 68 and 39 of the *Judiciary Act* 1903 covered precisely the same ground, there might be some force in that argument,[150] though it would still be contrary to the accepted canons of construction to hold that, where there are two affirmative enactments in the same Act each dealing with the same matter, one is to be taken as negativing the other. But on examination it will be seen that ss 68 and 39 probably do not cover the same ground. Section 39 applies only to the nine classes of cases enumerated in ss 75 and 76 of the Constitution. Section 68 applies to all persons charged with offences against the laws of the Commonwealth. Now, unless it can be asserted that there can be no offence against the laws of the Common-wealth which does not fall within one of the nine classes of cases enumerated in ss 75 and 76 of the Constitution, s 68 of the *Judiciary Act* 1903 was necessary. I should be very sorry to affirm that ss 75 and 76 of the Constitution do cover every possible case of offences against the laws of the Commonwealth. They cover every offence against the statutes of the Commonwealth as they at present exist, so far as I know, but I apprehend that many cases may arise in which it will be at least doubtful whether those sections cover them.[151]

Barton J expressed agreement with this view. The meaning of the passage is not altogether clear and Griffith CJ did not find it necessary to develop the argument. The limits of the power to invest State courts with federal jurisdiction are expressly defined by reference to the nine matters enumerated in ss 75 and 76, and it follows, therefore, that any such investment whether by ss 39 or 68 of the *Judiciary Act* may not transcend these limits. It does not follow, of course, that jurisdiction with respect to offences against the laws of the Commonwealth will necessarily be referable to s 76(ii) – matters arising under laws made by the Parliament; jurisdiction in respect of offences against the common law applicable to the Commonwealth may properly be referable to s 75(iii) – matters in which the Commonwealth is a party.[152]

While an investment of State courts with federal jurisdiction may not extend beyond the limits fixed by ss 75 and 76, it is clear that ss 39 and 68 of the *Judiciary Act* do not cover precisely similar ground. In *Seaegg v The*

---

149 See p 130 above.

150 That is, that no appeal lay under s 39.

151 (1905) 2 CLR 593 at 607-608.

152 *R v Kidman* (1915) 20 CLR 425. See pp 6-8 above.

King,[153] it was held that the vesting provisions of s 39 of the *Judiciary Act* did not convert a right of appeal conferred by State law to a State court in respect of offences under *State* law into a right of appeal to that court in respect of an offence under *federal* law. The question was whether a person convicted of an offence against a law of the Commonwealth by a New South Wales Court of Quarter Sessions could appeal to the Supreme Court of New South Wales as a Court of Criminal Appeal under the provisions of the *Criminal Appeal Act* 1912. The High Court held that, on its proper construction, the statutory right of appeal was confined to convictions on indictment preferred according to State law. The Court held further that s 68 of the *Judiciary Act*, as then enacted, did not confer a right of appeal in such a case.

This decision led to the amendment of s 68 in 1932. The amendments, as Dixon J pointed out in *Williams v The King (No 2)*,[154] were "intended to confer upon the Courts of Criminal Appeal of the States a jurisdiction to hear and determine appeals in the case of Federal offences such as existed in the case of State offences". It is clear that in its amended form s 68 confers a more extensive jurisdiction on State courts than do the vesting provisions of s 39. The scope of the amended s 68 was considered by the High Court. In *Williams v The King (No 1)*,[155] the Court unanimously held, reversing the New South Wales Court of Criminal Appeal, that s 68 did not entitle the Attorney-General of the *State*, who, under the terms of the *Criminal Appeal Act*, was authorised to appeal to the Court of Criminal Appeal against any sentence pronounced by the Supreme Court or any Court of Quarter Sessions, to appeal against a sentence imposed for an offence against *federal* law. Thereupon the Attorney-General for the *Commonwealth* appealed to the Court of Criminal Appeal against the sentence imposed on the prisoner, and the court increased the sentence.

On an application to the High Court for special leave to appeal, the Court in *Williams v The King (No 2)*[156] was equally divided so that leave to appeal was refused. Rich, Starke and Dixon JJ held that the amendments to s 68 of the *Judiciary Act* operated on the New South Wales statute which conferred power on the State Attorney-General to appeal against sentence imposed on convictions under State law, to permit the Attorney-General for the Commonwealth to bring the like appeal to the State court against sentence imposed on a conviction for a federal offence. As Dixon J said:

> When s 68(2) speaks of the "like jurisdiction with respect to persons who are charged with offences against the laws of the Commonwealth", it recognises that the adoption of State law must proceed by analogy. The proper officer of the Crown in right of the Commonwealth for representing

---

153 (1932) 48 CLR 251.
154 (1934) 50 CLR 551 at 559.
155 (1934) 50 CLR 536.
156 (1934) 50 CLR 551.

it in the Courts is the Federal Attorney-General. I do not feel any difficulty in deciding that, under the word "like" in the expression "like jurisdiction", the functions under s 5D of the State Attorney-General in the case of State offenders fall to the Federal Attorney-General in the case of offenders against the laws of the Commonwealth.[157]

Gavan Duffy CJ, Evatt and McTiernan JJ rested the contrary argument partly on the construction of the words of s 68, but mainly on the view that the grant of any right of appeal to the Crown against sentence should be discovered only on a clear and unequivocal expression of intention in s 68. The matter was raised again in *Peel v The Queen*[158] and this time there was a majority of four to three in favour of the view of Rich, Starke and Dixon JJ. Menzies, Windeyer, Owen and Gibbs JJ (Barwick CJ, McTiernan and Walsh JJ dissenting) held that s 68(2) of the *Judiciary Act* operated upon s 5D of the *Criminal Appeal Act* (NSW) so as to enable the Commonwealth Attorney-General to appeal to the Court of Criminal Appeal against a sentence pronounced by the Supreme Court or a Court of Quarter Sessions upon conviction of a party charged with an offence against Commonwealth law.

The matter is, of course, one of statutory interpretation rather than constitutional power. While the language of s 68 is obscure, it is suggested that the majority view is preferable. That interpretation, as Dixon J pointed out, ensures that federal criminal law is administered in each State upon the same footing as State law and avoids the establishment of two independent systems of criminal justice.[159]

This view was expounded by Mason J in *R v Loewenthal; ex parte Blacklock*[160] as follows:

> Although the distinction between federal and State jurisdiction has created problems, they were largely foreseen by the authors of the *Judiciary Act*. Part X of the Act provided a solution to the difficulties arising from a duality of jurisdiction by applying to criminal cases heard by State courts in federal jurisdiction the laws and procedure applicable in the State (s 68). The purpose of the section was, so far as possible, to enable State courts in the exercise of federal jurisdiction to apply federal laws according to a common procedure in one judicial system.

Peel was followed by the whole Court in *Rohde v Director of Public Prosecutions*.[161]

Section 68(2)(b) of the *Judiciary Act* purports to confer on the courts of a State exercising jurisdiction with respect to the examination and commitment for trial on indictment of persons charged with offences against the laws of

---

157 Ibid at 561-562.

158 (1971) 125 CLR 447.

159 *Williams v The King (No 2)* (1934) 50 CLR 551 at 560.

160 (1974) 131 CLR 338 at 345.

161 (1986) 161 CLR 119.

the State "the like jurisdiction with respect to persons who are charged with offences against the laws of the Commonwealth". It is clearly established that the act of an examining magistrate in determining whether an accused should be discharged or committed to prison or admitted to bail to await trial is purely an executive act.[162] It might be argued, therefore, that the provision is invalid in attempting to invest a State court with non-judicial power. In *Pearce v Cocchiaro*,[163] the Court was concerned with s 273(2) of the *Bankruptcy Act* 1966, which provides that, where proceedings for certain offences under the Act are brought in a court of summary jurisdiction, the court may either determine the proceedings or commit the defendant for trial. Gibbs J (with whom Stephen, Jacobs and Aickin JJ agreed) stated that, in so far as the power which a special magistrate was invested is judicial power, it is validly enacted under s 77(iii) of the Constitution. In so far as it confers power of a non-judicial kind (being the same sort of power that the magistrate already exercises in relation to offences against State law), it is a valid law with respect to those matters in relation to which the Parliament created the criminal offences. In that case, the relevant power was s 51(xvii). It was made clear in that case that a magistrate exercising either power was properly described as a court. This reasoning would also apply to s 68(2) of the *Judiciary Act* and, on that basis, para (b) of that subsection is valid. Section 68(3), however, provides that the jurisdiction referred to in sub-s (2) shall not be "judicially exercised" with respect to the summary conviction or examination and commitment for trial of any person except by a magistrate of the type set out in that provision. In *Pearce v Cocchiaro*, Gibbs J said as to that provision:

> There can be no doubt that a special magistrate conducting an examination for the purpose of deciding whether an alleged offender should be committed for trial would come within the description of a court within s 68(2) and it appears that the Parliament, in enacting s 68(3), proceeded on the assumption that a magistrate exercising such a function would be exercising the jurisdiction judicially. It is immaterial whether this assumption was right or wrong, for the only substantive requirement of s 68(3) is that a person charged with an offence against a law of the Commonwealth shall not be summarily convicted, or examined and committed for trial, except by a magistrate of one of the kinds described. The intention was to preclude the exercise of this jurisdiction by justices of the peace who are not such magistrates.[164]

It would seem to follow on this reasoning that para (b) of s 68(2) is valid. There is a question, however, whether the Commonwealth can impose

---

162 *Amman v Wegener* (1972) 129 CLR 415 and cases cited therein by Gibbs J at 435.
163 (1977) 137 CLR 600. Referred to with approval in *R v Murphy* (1985) 158 CLR 596 at 618.
164 Ibid at 608-609.

functions, including duties, on a State officer, at any rate in the absence of State legislation consenting to it. Such a provision could be regarded as either discriminating against the States or an interference with the organisation of State government, contrary to implications that have been made as a result of the federal nature of the Constitution.[165]

The issue was raised in *R v Murphy*,[166] where it was held that s 68(2) of the *Judiciary Act* was a valid law under ss 76(ii) and 77(iii) of the Constitution. The Court avoided having to deal with the issue of federal implications by characterising the committal process as incidental to the judicial power vested under s 77(iii), in relation to the trial for the offence.

It had previously been accepted that powers incidental to judicial functions can be conferred on State courts invested with federal jurisdiction and on federal courts. This is based on the general constitutional principle that the ambit of a power extends to what is incidental to the subject-matter.[167] What was unusual about s 68(2)(b), however, was that the "incidental" function was vested in a State court which did not have the jurisdiction to exercise the core judicial power, namely, the trial. So, if one concentrates only on the courts referred to in s 68(2)(b), the function could be perceived as merely administrative, because not performed by that court in association with a judicial function. The High Court said, however, that the hearing of the committal proceeding is a function that is sui generis. It consists of curial proceedings that have "the closest, if not an essential, connection with an actual exercise of judicial power".[168]

Section 39(2)(b) of the *Judiciary Act* operated to authorise an appeal to the High Court from a conviction by a State court invested with federal jurisdiction for an offence against federal law until the provision was repealed by the *Judiciary Amendment Act* 1976. In *Lorenzo v Carey*,[169] it was held by the High Court that such an appeal lay by way of case stated from a dismissal by a magistrate of an information charging an offence against the Commonwealth *Crimes Act*. The case was argued as a challenge to the validity of s 39 and, so far as appears from the report, there was no discussion of the relationship of that section to s 68. In *Adams v Cleeve*,[170] the respondent was charged in a Victorian Court of Petty Sessions with an offence under the *Sales Tax Assessment Act* (Cth). The information was dismissed and the informant appealed by way of order to review to the High Court under s 39(2)(b) of the *Judiciary Act*. It was argued that the appeal was incompetent, on the ground

---

165 *Queensland Electricity Commission v Commonwealth* (1985) 159 CLR 192; *Re Australian Education Union; ex parte Victoria* (1995) 184 CLR 188.

166 (1985) 158 CLR 596.

167 Ibid at 614.

168 Ibid at 616.

169 (1921) 29 CLR 243.

170 (1935) 53 CLR 185.

that s 58 of the *Sales Tax Assessment Act* made specific provision for appeals by declaring that the provisions of law in force in the State relating to summary proceedings before justices should apply and that an appeal should lie in the manner and to the court provided by State law for appeals from convictions or orders of dismissal. It was said that this excluded s 39 of the *Judiciary Act*, and that federal jurisdiction in respect of such offences depended on the *Sales Tax Assessment Act* and not on the general vesting provisions of s 39. It was also argued that the appeal provisions in s 68(2) of the *Judiciary Act* excluded the appeal to the High Court under s 39. These arguments were unanimously rejected by the Court. In a joint judgment, Rich, Dixon and Evatt JJ said:

> Neither the provisions of s 58 of the *Sales Tax Assessment Act (No 1)* nor those of s 68 of the *Judiciary Act* appear to indicate any intention of excluding the operation of s 39 of the *Judiciary Act*. Among the purposes of s 39 are the exclusion of State jurisdiction and the substitution of Federal jurisdiction, subject to provisions relating to appeals from the Courts of the States to the Privy Council and to this Court and in the case of summary jurisdiction relating to the constitution of the Court. Section 39 is expressed in terms of perfectly general application, and such an application accords with the principles upon which the enactment proceeds. To exclude its operation upon any part of Federal jurisdiction, more is required than a special provision conferring part of the jurisdiction, either original or appellate, which s 39 also confers. If the special provision conferred a different authority, or imposed conditions or restrictions or otherwise disclosed an intention at variance with the full operation of s 39, an intention to exclude it might be inferred.[171]

In *R v Bull*,[172] the judges referred to *Adams v Cleeve* and to the relationship of ss 39 and 68 of the *Judiciary Act*, but there was no extensive discussion. The case concerned the position in 1911. This matter has been clarified by the enactment of s 39A of the *Judiciary Act* in 1968 which, inter alia, subjects the federal jurisdiction invested by a provision of the *Judiciary Act* other than s 39 to the conditions and restrictions in paras (a) to (d) of s 39(2). In *Brown v The Queen*,[173] Brennan J described the relationship between s 39(2) and s 68(2) as follows: "Jurisdiction to try persons charged on indictment with federal offences is conferred on State courts by s 68(2) of the *Judiciary Act* and s 39(2) of that Act so far as the general provisions of s 39(2) are not inconsistent with the more particular provisions of s 68(2)."

---

171 Ibid at 190-191.
172 (1974) 131 CLR 203.
173 (1986) 160 CLR 171 at 197.

Investment of Jurisdiction under Other Provisions

In *Adams v Cleeve*, reference was made to the possibility of an investment of State courts with federal jurisdiction which did not depend on s 39 of the *Judiciary Act.* As a general provision with respect to the exercise of federal jurisdiction by State courts s 39 was taken, prima facie, to apply to all exercises of such jurisdiction,[174] and it was clear that the section was meant to cover the general field of federal jurisdiction. So, in *Adams v Cleeve*, it was held that the specific provisions of the *Sales Tax Assessment Act* (Cth) did not exclude the operation of s 39. But it was said that, if a particular Act conferred a different authority on State courts to exercise federal jurisdiction or imposed conditions or restrictions at variance with the full operation of s 39, an intention to exclude it might be inferred.[175]

In the first edition of this book[176] the question was discussed whether the conditions and restrictions set out in the paragraphs of s 39(2) of the *Judiciary Act* should apply generally to an exercise of federal jurisdiction by State courts where it appeared that the investiture was made by another Act. This matter has now been expressly dealt with by s 39A of the *Judiciary Act*, which was enacted in 1968 and is as follows:

> 39A. (1) The federal jurisdiction with which a Court of a State is invested by or under any Act, whether the investing occurred or occurs before or after the commencement of this section, including federal jurisdiction invested by a provision of this Act other than the last preceding section:
>
> (a) shall be taken to be invested subject to the provisions of paragraph (a) of subsection (2) of the last preceding section; and
>
> (b) shall be taken to be invested subject to the provisions of paragraphs (b), (c) and (d) of that subsection (whether or not it is expressed to be invested subject to both or either of those provisions), so far as they are capable of application and are not inconsistent with a provision made by or under the Act by or under which the jurisdiction is invested;
>
> in addition to any other conditions or restrictions subject to which the jurisdiction is expressed to be invested.
>
> (2) Nothing in this section or the last preceding section, or in any Act passed before the commencement of this section, shall be taken to prejudice the application of any of sections 72 to 77 (inclusive) of this Act in relation to jurisdiction in respect of indictable offences.

---

174 *Minister of State for the Army v Parbury Henty and Co Pty Ltd* (1945) 70 CLR 459 at 476 per Latham CJ.

175 *Adams v Cleve* (1935) 53 CLR 185 at 190-191; see also *Ffrost v Stevenson* (1937) 58 CLR 528 at 571; *Goward v Commonwealth* (1957) 97 CLR 355.

176 Pages 187-193.

A special statutory provision may, of course, exclude the operation of s 39A but, in the light of the wording of that section, the court would probably insist on a clear expression by Parliament of an intention to do so.[177]

Federal and State Jurisdiction Regarding the Same Matter

An "unnecessary piece of mystification"[178] remains to be clarified. In *Lorenzo v Carey*,[179] the High Court said that it could see no difficulty in a State court exercising either State or federal jurisdiction at the instance of a litigant. This involved the rejection of earlier views that it was only possible under s 77(iii) to invest State courts with federal jurisdiction in respect of matters which, apart from any such investment, lay outside their competence, and the acceptance of a definition of jurisdiction in this context as a source of authority, so that a State court might at any one time be seised concurrently of State and federal jurisdiction in respect of such a matter.

Such was the problem which confronted the Supreme Court of Victoria in *Booth v Shelmerdine*.[180] This case involved the validity of a judgment of a Victorian Court of Petty Sessions which was exercising jurisdiction in respect of a matter arising under a law made by the Commonwealth Parliament. The court was constituted by a magistrate and honorary justices, and if it was exercising federal jurisdiction it was not constituted in accordance with s 39(2)(d) of the *Judiciary Act*. On the authority of *Lorenzo v Carey* this was a matter in which s 39(2) conferred federal jurisdiction on the State court, but in which s 39(1) did not deprive it of the jurisdiction which belonged to it, because the matter was not one in which original jurisdiction had been conferred on the High Court under s 76(ii). McArthur J experienced rather more difficulty in reaching a conclusion than the High Court had apparently thought possible in *Lorenzo v Carey,* but concluded that the State court was not exercising federal jurisdiction. The result was reached by an examination of the intention of the parties and the court. The search after intent does not carry conviction; and a better resolution of the difficulty might have been achieved by resort to a presumption in favour of validity: s 39(2)(d) not being satisfied, it should be presumed that the court was exercising its State jurisdiction.[181]

The surprising thing is that this problem did not arise more frequently in the reported cases.[182] It is obvious that the possession of concurrent jurisdiction could have raised other difficulties posed by the provisions of

---

177 See, for example, *R v Ward* (1978) 140 CLR 584.
178 Sawer in Else-Mitchell (ed), *Essays on the Australian Constitution*, 2nd edn, 1961, p 86.
179 (1921) 29 CLR 243 at 253.
180 [1924] VLR 276.
181 Sawer, op cit p 85.
182 Ibid.

s 39(2)(a) and (c) in relation to appeals to the Privy Council and the High Court, where it might not have been enough to rely on presumptions of validity.

Dixon J in *Ffrost v Stevenson*[183] suggested that a solution to these problems, or at least some of them, might be found in s 109 of the Constitution. He said:

> It has always appeared to me that, once the conclusion was reached that Federal jurisdiction was validly conferred, then under s 109 it was impossible to hold valid a State law conferring jurisdiction to do the same thing, whether subject to no appeal or subject to appeal in a different manner or to a different tribunal or tribunals or otherwise producing different consequences.

In the *Parbury Henty Case*,[184] Latham CJ referred to these observations and added that, in such cases when one law permits an appeal and another prohibits an appeal in the same proceedings, there is a stronger case for holding that the laws are inconsistent than when each of two laws permits different appeals in a proceeding.

In *Felton v Mulligan*,[185] a widow sought a declaration in the Supreme Court of New South Wales that she was entitled to payments from her deceased husband's executors under a deed entered into by her and her deceased husband for payment of maintenance to her. The executors argued that the deed was void on the ground that it attempted to oust the jurisdiction of the court to determine by order a proper sum for maintenance under the *Matrimonial Causes Act* 1959 (Cth). The Court upheld the executors' contention and the widow applied for leave to appeal to the Privy Council. If the Supreme Court was exercising federal jurisdiction, there could be no appeal to the Privy Council because of the provisions of s 39(2)(a) of the *Judiciary Act*. Upon the matter being removed into the High Court pursuant to s 40 of the *Judiciary Act*, the Court held (Barwick CJ, McTiernan, Windeyer and Walsh JJ; Menzies, Owen and Gibbs JJ dissenting) that the matter was one arising under the *Matrimonial Causes Act*. Under the view adopted in *Lorenzo v Carey* it would have been necessary to determine whether the Court was exercising State or federal jurisdiction. As it was a matter in respect of which jurisdiction had not been conferred on the High Court, the State jurisdiction had not, therefore, been removed under s 39(1) of the *Judiciary Act*, although federal jurisdiction had been conferred under s 39(2). Barwick CJ, Windeyer and Walsh JJ adopted the argument of Dixon J in *Ffrost v Stevenson* and held that, where s 39(2) invests a State court with federal jurisdiction in respect of a matter, any concurrent State jurisdiction is

---

183 (1937) 58 CLR 528 at 573.

184 (1945) 70 CLR 459 at 483.

185 (1971) 124 CLR 367.

excluded by virtue of s 109 of the Constitution. McTiernan J did not deal with this question but he held that the Supreme Court had been exercising federal jurisdiction and said that, as a result, the restriction in s 39(2)(a) was applicable. As he did not discuss any choice of jurisdiction made by the litigants, it seems likely that he agreed with the view of the other three majority judges that there was no room for the exercise of State jurisdiction. The minority judges did not express any view on this question as they held that the matter did not arise under federal law and, therefore, the only jurisdiction the Court could have been exercising was State jurisdiction.

The most detailed examination of the question was made by Walsh J (with whom Barwick CJ agreed on this issue). He pointed to the unsatisfactory nature of the solution proffered in *Lorenzo v Carey*. There would, he said, be no acceptable way of determining what jurisdiction the Court had exercised if that case were followed. If it was said that a litigant could elect, there was no reason why the right of election should reside in one litigant to the exclusion of the other and it was impossible to suppose that it resided in both of them. His Honour concluded that "the problem must be resolved by treating the Commonwealth law as paramount and as excluding, in relation to the matters to which that law applies, the operation of the laws under which the State jurisdiction of the court would be exercised".[186]

Walsh J referred to the doubts expressed in the first edition of this book[187] and by Professor Sawer[188] as to whether s 109 could be applied in this type of case. These doubts arose from the fact that s 39 of the *Judiciary Act* discloses no intention to cover the field. Indeed, s 39(1) supports a contrary view. It is expressly restricted to removing jurisdiction from State courts only in matters in which the High Court has jurisdiction. If s 109 operates as suggested in *Ffrost v Stevenson* and *Felton v Mulligan*, any legislative action designed directly to deprive State courts of jurisdiction would have been otiose: the object would have been achieved by the vesting provisions of s 39(2) which, by investing State courts with federal jurisdiction (subject to the exceptions in s 38) in all nine matters mentioned in ss 75 and 76 of the Constitution, would have invalidated any exercise of State jurisdiction in respect of those matters.

Walsh J said that "in spite of difficulties created by the manner in which s 39 has been framed", it should be held "that Parliament intended that in the federal matters to which the section relates the only jurisdiction to be exercised by the State courts was to be federal jurisdiction".[189]

The issue, however, is not merely one of parliamentary intention to cover the field but is one of constitutional power. There is no express power in the Commonwealth to deprive State courts of the jurisdiction that belongs to them

---

186 *Felton v Mulligan* (1971) 124 CLR 367 at 412.
187 Page 195.
188 Op cit p 86.
189 (1971) 124 CLR 367 at 412-413.

other than that which is consequential on the power under s 77(ii) of the Constitution to define the extent to which the jurisdiction of a federal court should be exclusive of that which belongs to the courts of the States. Taylor and Menzies JJ in *Williams v Hursey*[190] pointed out that there could be no deprivation of State jurisdiction except in relation to matters within the jurisdiction of a federal court.

The majority judges in *Felton v Mulligan* did not consider this question of power, as distinct from the operation of s 109. However, while the reasoning is unsatisfactory, the result is certainly desirable. The basic difficulty, as mentioned above, is the distinction made between federal and State jurisdictions to deal with the same matter. Once that distinction is accepted, and s 39(2) of the *Judiciary Act* is regarded as valid, the attempted solution provided by *Lorenzo v Carey* is, for the reasons stated by Walsh J, obviously impractical or, if one litigant could determine the jurisdiction to be exercised, unjust. No other solution can be readily envisaged short of the legislative solution of giving concurrent jurisdiction to the High Court or the Federal Court of Australia. The solution put forward by at least three judges in *Felton v Mulligan*, although intellectually unsatisfying, has the merit of removing an absurd situation.[191]

Admiralty and Maritime Jurisdiction

This area of jurisdiction of State courts was for many years considered obscure until the enactment of the *Admiralty Act* 1988. It was explained in Chapter 1[192] that from 1939 the High Court had no jurisdiction conferred under s 75(iii) – matters of "Admiralty and maritime jurisdiction". It exercised Admiralty jurisdiction under the *Colonial Courts of Admiralty Act* 1890.[193] In addition, it was held that from 1939 the State Supreme Courts were also Colonial Courts of Admiralty under that Act.[194]

To the extent that matters within the jurisdiction conferred by the 1890 Act were included in the meaning of s 76(iii) of the Constitution, they would on a literal reading be covered by the federal jurisdiction vested in State courts by s 39(2) of the *Judiciary Act* 1903. Section 6 of the 1890 Act provided for a right of appeal to the Privy Council, while s 39(2)(a) of the *Judiciary Act*, in effect, prohibited such an appeal. In *McIlwraith McEacharn*

190 (1959) 103 CLR 30 at 89 and 113.
191 *Moorgate Tobacco Co Ltd v Philip Morris Ltd* (1980) 145 CLR 457 at 471, 476. Since the enactment of the *Australia Act* 1986 the precise issue in *Felton v Mulligan* cannot arise as appeals to the Privy Council have been abolished, and s 39(2)(a) is otiose.
192 At pp 71-77.
193 Jurisdiction was also conferred under the *Merchant Shipping Act* 1894 (UK). See Zelling, "Constitutional Problems of the Admiralty Jurisdiction" (1984) 58 ALJ 8.
194 *McIlwraith McEacharn Ltd v Shell Co of Australia Ltd* (1945) 70 CLR 175; *Lewmarine Pty Ltd v The Ship "Kaptayanni"* [1974] VR 465.

Ltd v Shell Co of Australia Ltd, Dixon J construed s 39 so as not to vest jurisdiction in relation to matters that would otherwise belong to the State courts as Colonial Courts of Admiralty.[195] He pointed out that s 39 was passed before the *Statute of Westminster* 1931 and if it included matters in s 76(iii) it could be repugnant to the Imperial Act. Such repugnancy or inconsistency would follow from the reasoning of Dixon J in *Ffrost v Stevenson*[196] to the effect that two provisions, each giving an authority or jurisdiction in the same matter and involving varying courses of appeal or review, amount to repugnancy. This view was followed in respect of the application of s 109 of the Constitution to State and federal jurisdiction in *Felton v Mulligan*.[197] That raised the question whether (assuming that s 39(2) did include the jurisdiction in s 76(iii)) the *Colonial Laws Validity Act* had the effect of invalidating s 39(2) to the extent of the repugnancy. One possible answer was that the Constitution was an Imperial statute enacted after the *Colonial Courts of Admiralty Act* 1890 and therefore it prevails over earlier Acts. *Commonwealth v Kreglinger and Fernau Ltd*,[198] which held that s 39(2)(a) of the *Judiciary Act* was not invalid for repugnancy to the *Judicial Committee Act* 1844 (UK), supports that view. On the other hand, *Union Steamship Co of New Zealand v Commonwealth*,[199] which held some provisions of the *Navigation Act* invalid for repugnancy to the *Merchant Shipping Act* 1894 (UK), could lead to a different result. The issue was not resolved, although, as stated earlier, a number of cases affirmed the existence in State courts of jurisdiction under the *Colonial Courts of Admiralty Act*. Those cases did not address this particular issue, apart from Dixon J's judgment in *McIlwraith McEacharn*, which tried to avoid it.

With the enactment of the *Australia Act* 1986 the issue of Privy Council appeals ceased to be a problem, but the question whether a State court had federal jurisdiction in Admiralty arose earlier in a different context in *China Ocean Shipping Co v South Australia*.[200] In that case, South Australia brought an action against the owner, agent and master of a ship in respect of damage to a wharf. The defendants sought to limit their liability under provisions of the *Merchant Shipping Act*. It was held that those provisions applied in South Australia and the decision was largely based on their construction. It was argued that s 64 of the *Judiciary Act* 1903 applied. That section provides, among other things, that in a suit in which a State is a party the rights of the parties shall as nearly as possible be the same as in a suit between subject and subject. It is accepted that the provision can apply only where federal

---

195 (1945) 70 CLR 175 at 210.
196 (1937) 58 CLR 528 at 572-573.
197 (1971) 124 CLR 367. See pp 236-237 above.
198 (1926) 37 CLR 393.
199 (1925) 36 CLR 130.
200 (1979) 145 CLR 172.

jurisdiction is exercised. Only three judges found it necessary to consider that question. They held that s 64 did not apply. Gibbs CJ said that the State was not a party within the meaning of the section and whether s 39 on its proper construction included Admiralty jurisdiction was a question that for him was "completely open".[201] Stephen and Aickin JJ agreed with Dixon J's view in *McIlwraith McEacharn*. Stephen J concluded that s 39 was as inapplicable to a State's jurisdiction under the *Merchant Shipping Act* as it was to its jurisdiction under the *Colonial Courts of Admiralty Act*.[202] The issue was not resolved before the passing of the *Admiralty Act* 1988.[203] It should be noted, however, that whatever the appropriate solution to the problem where a matter came within the jurisdiction conferred by the Imperial legislation, s 39 of the *Judiciary Act* clearly vested federal jurisdiction in respect of all matters within s 76(iii) which were not covered by the Imperial legislation.

The *Admiralty Act* 1988 vests jurisdiction in respect of actions in personam in all State and Territorial courts and in the Federal Court (s 9). Jurisdiction regarding actions in rem is vested in the Federal Court and all Supreme Courts of the States and Territories, as well as other courts declared by the Governor-General (ss 10, 11). Section 13 restricts the jurisdiction conferred by the Act to matters of a kind mentioned in s 76(ii) and (iii) of the Constitution. As discussed in Chapter 1, the High Court has given a broad interpretation to the phrase "Admiralty and maritime jurisdiction" in s 76(iii).[204] It seems clear that the jurisdiction vested in State courts by this Act overrides any Admiralty and maritime jurisdiction otherwise vested in them by s 39 of the *Judiciary Act*.

Section 44 repeals the *Colonial Courts of Admiralty Act* in so far as it is part of the law of the Commonwealth or an external Territory. There is a question as to the validity of this provision in relation to jurisdiction conferred on State courts by the Imperial Act. A similar question arises in respect of the repeal of other Imperial legislation by s 45 of the *Admiralty Act*. As discussed earlier,[205] the Commonwealth has no power directly to deprive State courts of State jurisdiction, except by the exercise of s 77(ii) of the Constitution, which gives power to define the extent to which the jurisdiction of any federal court shall be exclusive of that which belongs to or is invested in the courts of the States. The *Admiralty Act* does not confer exclusive jurisdiction on the Federal Court; it is concurrent with that of State courts. *Felton v Mulligan*[206] held that s 39(2) of the *Judiciary Act* made inoperative any State jurisdiction

---

201 Ibid at 204.

202 Ibid at 229-230.

203 See Australian Law Reform Commission Report no 33, *Civil Admiralty Jurisdiction*, pp 23-25.

204 *Owners of the Ship "Shin Kobe Maru" v Empire Shipping Co Inc* (1994) 181 CLR 404. See pp 76-77 above.

205 Pages 237-238 above.

206 (1971) 124 CLR 367.

in respect of the matters included in federal jurisdiction; but that was not because of any repeal of State jurisdiction by the Commonwealth, but by operation of s 109 of the Constitution relating to inconsistent Commonwealth and State legislation.[207]

The repeal of Imperial provisions in so far as they operated in areas otherwise within State legislative power was upheld in *Kirmani v Captain Cook Cruises Pty Ltd*.[208] What was involved in that case was a Commonwealth Act purporting to repeal a provision of the *Merchant Shipping Act* limiting the liability of shipowners "in so far as it was part of the law of the Commonwealth". It was held that the latter phrase applied to shipping operations not within the legislative power of the Commonwealth. (The same phrase appears in ss 44 and 45 of the *Admiralty Act*.) The provision was held valid by Mason, Murphy, Brennan and Deane JJ; Gibbs CJ, Wilson and Dawson JJ dissenting. Mason, Murphy and Deane JJ considered that the provision was valid under the external affairs power (s 51(xxix)), because it brought to an end the operation in Australia of a law enacted for Australia by the legislature of the United Kingdom. Therefore, the law clearly involved relations with another country.[209] The other member of the majority, Brennan J, however, did not rely on the external affairs power and expressed no view on it. He upheld the legislation under s 2 of the *Statute of Westminster*, which grants to the parliament of a dominion power to repeal or amend any United Kingdom Act "in so far as the same is part of the law of the dominion". This power is restricted by s 9(1), which provides that nothing in the Statute shall be deemed to authorise the Commonwealth to make laws on any matter that is, in effect, within the exclusive power of the States. The matter was not within State power, according to Brennan J, because the Imperial Act prevented the exercise of that power. Clearly, since the *Australia Act*, which gives the States power to repeal or amend Imperial Acts (s 3), Brennan J's reasoning is no longer available. It would be within State power to repeal any jurisdiction conferred on its courts by the *Colonial Courts of Admiralty Act* or the *Merchant Shipping Act*.

There is also some doubt whether, assuming the views of Mason, Murphy and Deane JJ to be correct, their reasoning is now applicable to the repeal of Imperial Acts operating in State areas of power. Such Acts now have the same status as inherited English law. They are simply part of the general corpus of State law, all of which is, subject to the Commonwealth Constitution and the *Australia Act*, within State legislative power to repeal or amend. It is possible, therefore, that the repeal of such legislation could not be described as a law with respect to "external affairs". Mason J emphasised that in *Kirmani* what was involved was a Commonwealth law which opened the way to State

---

207 Pages 236-237 above.

208 (1985) 159 CLR 351.

209 Ibid at 381.

legislation "free from the fetters created by the repealed law". Otherwise the repeal could be achieved only by a law of the United Kingdom. That indicated its nature as a matter of external affairs.[210] That reasoning does not apply to s 44 of the *Admiralty Act.*

Even if the Commonwealth repeal of Imperial legislation in relation to the jurisdiction of State courts is invalid, there is no doubt that only federal jurisdiction is operative in respect of any matter that comes within the jurisdiction conferred by the *Admiralty Act.* That follows from the reasoning in *Felton v Mulligan.*[211]

Chapter III Restrictions on State Legislative Power

As mentioned above, it has frequently been said that, in vesting federal jurisdiction in a State court, the Commonwealth must take the State court as it finds it. Parliament cannot alter the constitution of the court or the organisation through which its jurisdiction and powers are exercised.[212] If, for example, a State abolished trial by jury for criminal offences, the Commonwealth could not provide for such a trial in that State's courts.[213]

In *Commonwealth v Hospital Contribution Fund*,[214] Mason J said that Chapter III of the Constitution contains no provision which restricted the legislative competence of the States to alter the composition, structure or organisation of the State courts. He went on to say: "Nor does it make any discernible attempt to regulate the composition, structure or organisation of the Supreme Courts as appropriate vehicles for the exercise of invested federal jurisdiction." Chapter III, for example, does not provide for a separation of judicial power in respect of State courts, nor provide for the tenure of their judges. In the *Hospital Contribution Fund Case*, Mason J pointed out that, if the Commonwealth did not approve of the structure or organisation of State courts as determined by State law, it had the choice of establishing and conferring jurisdiction on federal courts.

In *Kotsis v Kotsis*,[215] Barwick CJ said that, if State law were to change the composition of its Supreme Court "in a radical way", what the State called "the Supreme Court" would not come within those terms as used in s 73 of the Constitution. While Barwick CJ took the now rejected view that a State court could be composed only of judges for purposes of ss 73 and 77, the point for present purposes is that he was not suggesting that the "radical" changes

---

210 Ibid at 381-382.
211 On the *Admiralty Act*, generally, see Butler and Duncan, *Maritime Law in Australia*, 1992; White (ed), *Australian Maritime Law*, 2nd edn, 2000.
212 Pages 204-205 above.
213 *Brown v The Queen* (1986) 160 CLR 171 at 199, 218-219.
214 (1982) 150 CLR 49 at 61.
215 (1970) 122 CLR 69 at 77.

would be invalid, but merely that there could be no appeal to the High Court from such a body, nor could it be vested with federal jurisdiction.

This long-standing view of the largely unrestricted power of State Parliaments in relation to their courts was greatly changed by the decision in *Kable v Director of Public Prosecutions (NSW)*.[216] A New South Wales Act applied to, and only to, a named person, Gregory Wayne Kable, who had been convicted of the manslaughter of his wife. The Act was passed, shortly before he was due to be released from prison, as a result of his having sent letters to several persons threatening to kill them when he was released.

The Act declared that its object was to protect the community by providing for Kable's preventive detention. The Supreme Court was empowered to make an order for detention if satisfied on reasonable grounds that he was more likely than not to commit a serious act of violence and that it was appropriate for the protection of the community that he be held in custody. In construing the Act, the need to protect the community was to be given paramount consideration. The standard of proof was the balance of probabilities and the court could have regard to specified material which would otherwise have been inadmissible.

It was held by a majority that the Act was invalid because it was inconsistent with Chapter III of the Constitution (Toohey, Gaudron, McHugh and Gummow JJ; Brennan CJ and Dawson J dissenting). All the judges accepted that Chapter III did not impose on the States the principle of the separation of judicial power; so there was nothing which, as a general rule, denied a State Parliament power to confer non-judicial functions on a State court. The principle of the case is that a State cannot confer on a court which exercises federal jurisdiction powers or functions that are "incompatible with" or "repugnant to" the exercise of that jurisdiction. The powers vested in the court by the Act were held to be of that nature.[217]

According to the majority, the flaw in the Act was that it undermined public confidence in the integrity of the Court in its exercise of the judicial power of the Commonwealth. The incompatible functions were that the Court was required to participate in a preventive detention order, where there was no trial for an offence or finding of guilt.[218] There was no rule of general application,[219] and the statutory rules which bound the court could lead a person to believe that the court was "an instrument of executive government policy".[220]

The majority in this regard applied the same principle of incompatibility that had in earlier cases been used to determine whether functions conferred

---

216 (1996) 189 CLR 51.
217 See Hardcastle, "A Chapter III Implication for State Courts" (1998) 3 Newcastle LR 13.
218 (1996) 189 CLR 51 at 98 per Toohey J, 106-107 per Gaudron J.
219 Ibid at 107 per Gaudron J.
220 Ibid at 124 per McHugh J. See also at 134 per Gummow J.

on a federal judge, not as a member of a court but as persona designata, were invalid because of the separation of judicial power. The incompatibility in both cases arises where the judges are prevented from acting in accordance with the judicial process or the provision diminishes public confidence in the integrity of the court in exercising federal jurisdiction.[221]

Gaudron, McHugh and Gummow JJ referred to all the courts specified in s 71 of the Constitution, and therefore exercising the judicial power of the Commonwealth, as an "integrated" system,[222] and they said that the Constitution did not provide for two different grades of federal justice or judicial power.[223] One aspect of the integrated system was related directly to the object of s 77(iii) as the majority saw it. They said that the Constitution implies and requires that the States have courts in which the Commonwealth may vest jurisdiction under s 77(iii). Gaudron J said:[224]

> Were [the States] free to abolish their courts, the autochthonous expedient, more precisely the provisions of Chapter III which postulate an integrated judicial system, would be frustrated in their entirety. To this extent, at least, the States are not free to legislate as they please.[225]

It followed also that State law could not require or authorise a court to exercise functions or processes that were incompatible with the exercise of the judicial power of the Commonwealth.

On one important issue, however, the majority judges were not unanimous. Toohey J, unlike the others, confined the principle he applied to incompatible aspects operating while the State court was exercising federal jurisdiction. The other three judges regarded the issue as arising at all times because the exercise of any power or jurisdiction by the court can affect public confidence in the integrity of a court in which federal jurisdiction is vested. Toohey J did not express disagreement with the latter view; he simply indicated that he had no need to consider it.[226]

The purpose of the Act was not to interfere with federal jurisdiction.[227] It dealt with a purely State matter which, no doubt, seemed at the commencement of the proceedings not to attract any of the nine heads of federal jurisdiction. What changed the character of the matter was that Kable pleaded that the Act was unconstitutional. It thus became a matter "arising under the Constitution or involving its interpretation" within the meaning of s 76(i) of

---

221   *Grollo v Palmer* (1995) 184 CLR 348; *Wilson v Minister for Aboriginal and Torres Strait Islander Affairs* (1996) 189 CLR 1.

222   (1996) 189 CLR 51 at 102-103 per Gaudron J, 112, 114-115 per McHugh J, 137-139 per Gummow J.

223   Ibid at 103, 115, 127.

224   Ibid at 103.

225   See also ibid at 111 per McHugh J, 140 per Gummow J.

226   Ibid at 99.

227   See McHugh J at 116.

the Constitution and thereby falling within s 39(2) of the *Judiciary Act*, vesting federal jurisdiction in the court.

The fact that a matter may be converted to one of federal jurisdiction, by the defendant bona fide[228] pleading the principle in *Kable*, makes the approach of Toohey J less desirable; it depends too much on particular circumstances and what the defendant chooses to plead. In so far as the decision is based on the public perception of the court which exercises federal jurisdiction, it is clear that that perception can be affected by its exercise of other powers and jurisdiction. As McHugh J said,[229] it remains the same court consisting of the same judges. As federal jurisdiction can be exercised by State courts in a wide variety of situations (including some where the court may not be aware of it), it would be impossible for the State Parliament effectively to provide for a dual set of powers and procedures, even if Toohey J's judgment were followed.

There is considerable uncertainty as to what powers, functions and procedures are to be regarded as incompatible with the exercise of federal jurisdiction both in relation to a State court and a federal judge acting as persona designata.[230] The issue of public perception can be a particularly controversial one. It is presented as an empirical question, but no empirical evidence was examined.

It is clear that *Kable* would restrict State legislative power to control the judicial process so as to impair the principles of natural justice and due process. In that respect, Chapter III results in both the Commonwealth and State Parliaments being under the same limitations. It can be said that the "autochthonous expedient" and the concept of federal jurisdiction have resulted in a partial separation of powers applicable to State courts.

Another strand of the "integration" argument emphasised by McHugh and Gummow JJ relates to the effect of s 73 (appeals to the High Court). It is less directly concerned with the subject-matter of this chapter, namely the federal jurisdiction of State courts, but is an essential aspect of the integration theory of the two judges and so cannot sensibly be omitted from any discussion of the effect of *Kable*.

To a considerable extent McHugh and Gummow JJ saw the key to the integration of the court system as the provision in s 73 for appeals to the High Court from the judgments of courts exercising federal jurisdiction and of the Supreme Courts of the States. The only judgments of a State court exercising State jurisdiction from which an appeal lies to the High Court are those of the Supreme Courts. McHugh and Gummow JJ deduced from those provisions that it is an object of the Constitution to ensure the unity of the common law

---

228 See pp 147-148 above.

229 (1996) 189 CLR 51 at 114.

230 Walker, "Persona Designata, Incompatibility and the Separation of Powers" (1997) 8 Public LR 153.

as a national system. It followed that the States could not abolish their Supreme Courts, because it would undermine that constitutional purpose.[231] McHugh J also pointed out that the integrated system of courts could also be impaired by preventing appeals to, or review by, the Supreme Court in relation to the decisions of the lower courts. If a matter of State jurisdiction could not get to the Supreme Court, there could be no High Court appeal. These remarks were obiter dicta but were given in reply to the argument that the court systems of the States stood outside, and had no constitutional relationship with, the federal judicature.

There is much to be said for these views. It is undoubtedly the case that the framers intended that the High Court (together with the Privy Council) be an ultimate court of appeal in relation to all matters, whether federal or State. The *Australia Act* 1986 (Cth) and (UK) finally disposed of the Privy Council as far as Australia was concerned. Chapter III not only assumes the existence of the Supreme Courts at the head of the State systems, under the High Court; they seem to be an essential feature of the constitutional scheme. That aspect of s 73 was, moreover, a deliberate departure from the United States model. It was described by Quick and Garran[232] as making "the High Court not merely a federal court of appeal but a national court of appeal of general and unlimited jurisdiction". This function of the Court is described as "constitutionally secured". It is a reasonable implication from that constitutional purpose that a State cannot impair it.

---

231 (1996) 189 CLR 51 at 109-110, 137-139.
232 Op cit p 747.

Index